Sport and Society

Series Editors
Benjamin G. Rader
Randy Roberts

Books in the Series *Sport and Society*

A Sporting Time: New York City and the Rise
of Modern Athletics, 1820–70
Melvin L. Adelman

Sandlot Seasons: Sport in Black Pittsburgh
Rob Ruck

West Ham United: The Making of a Football Club
Charles Korr

Beyond the Ring: The Role of Boxing in American Society
Jeffrey T. Sammons

John L. Sullivan and His America
Michael T. Isenberg

Television and National Sport: The United States and Britain
Joan M. Chandler

The Creation of American Team Sports:
Baseball and Cricket, 1838–72
George B. Kirsch

City Games: The Evolution of American Urban Society
and the Rise of Sports
Steven A. Riess

The Brawn Drain: Foreign Student-Athletes
in American Universities
John Bale

The Business of Professional Sports
Edited by Paul D. Staudohar and James A. Mangan

Reprint Editions

The Nazi Olympics
Richard D. Mandell

Sports in the Western World, Second Edition
William J. Baker

The Business of Professional Sports

THE
BUSINESS OF
PROFESSIONAL
SPORTS

Edited by

Paul D. Staudohar and James A. Mangan

With a Foreword by Leonard Koppett

UNIVERSITY OF ILLINOIS PRESS

Urbana and Chicago

Portions of Chapter 4 earlier appeared in Kahn and Sherer, "Racial Differences in Professional Basketball Players' Compensation," *Journal of Labor Economics* 6 (January 1988): 40–59, © by the University of Chicago Press. Used by permission.

Illini Books edition, 1991

This book is printed on acid-free paper.

Library of Congress Cataloging-in-Publication Data

The Business of professional sports / edited by Paul D. Staudohar and
    James A. Mangan : with a foreword by Leonard Koppett.
        p.   cm. — (Sport and society)
    Includes index.
        ISBN 0–252–01767–6 (cloth : alk. paper). — ISBN 0–252–06161–6 (paper :
    alk. paper)
        1. Professional sports—Economic aspects—United States.
    2. Professional sports—Economic aspects—Canada.   3. Professional
    sports—Social aspects—United States.   4. Professional sports—
    Social aspects—Canada.   5. Professional sports—Law and
    legislation—United States.   6. Professional sports—Law and
    legislation—Canada.   7. Collective bargaining—Sports—United
    States.   8. Collective bargaining—Sports—Canada.   I. Staudohar,
    Paul D.   II. Mangan, J. A.   III. Series.
    GV716.B87   1991
    338.4'7796'0973—dc20   90–45150
                                                                          CIP

Contents

Foreword

Leonard Koppett

As a working sportswriter most of my life I acquired a natural prejudice against academics and theoreticians. Newspapermen (we didn't call ourselves "journalists" when I broke in almost fifty years ago, and we weren't concerned with gender-neutral titles) saw themselves as dealing with day-to-day reality in a disorderly world, trying to get a few immediate facts straight without regard for their larger meanings or logical connections. The "thinkers," in books and studies, were doing something quite different. And while I could appreciate and accept the validity and value of their deeper analysis in such far-reaching subjects as politics, history, and science and other traditional academic concerns, I rejected out of hand the possibility that they could understand—let alone explain—the mundane activities of commercialized spectator sports.

After all, the sports events that comprised this "toy department of the newspaper" were the ultimate in practicality: hit the ball, knock someone down, sell a ticket, collect prize money, stimulate recreational argument, master mechanical techniques. How could anyone immersed in secondary sources (documents, statistics, misleading quotes, sketchy and therefore unrealistic descriptions, and collations of isolated incidents), not to mention personal prejudices, know anything about what was "really" going on?

Today I have a different view. I think the academicians who have been working with sports material, especially the historians, have been providing entirely realistic and enormously enlightening insights. In fact, their work, taken as a whole, is turning out to be more tough-minded, reality-based, and perceptive than that of the professionals in what we now call "the media."

It would be nice to say that I have this new perspective because I have matured, gained respect for those who have degrees, and now understand the world better than I used to. But I don't think that's true. I think my original prejudice was thoroughly justified and objectively correct. What has changed is the external world.

During the 1970s I began to have more contact with sports academics. Increasingly since then, I have found them—and their work product—to be not only more in touch with my own impressions of sports reality than I expected, but more in touch with that reality than most of my journalistic colleagues care to admit. I have found my press box buddies, and people in the sports business as well, to be more susceptible to myth and cliché than the ivory-tower minds. Sports promotion (which is all we're really talking about—a direct descendant of Barnum's principles) remains a hands-on, ultra-expedient, entirely practical, nontheoretical enterprise with no significant academic base (despite graduate degree programs in sports management). But understanding sports promotion, as distinct from practicing it, has turned out to be the proper province of the academically trained.

I think there are several reasons for this. One is the evolution of the sports business itself. Until television became widespread, it was essentially an office-in-your-hat activity of individual entrepreneurs. As it has moved more into the corporate universe, it has taken on characteristics and methods more common to the general business and accounting world, and these are more suited to established forms of analysis.

Another is the abundance of subject material. Until a generation ago, the paper trail was thin, and it was closely held in private hands. Now lawsuits, legislative hearings, archival research, labor negotiations—and enterprising journalists—have generated an immense amount of data that can be studied in ways that were not possible in the past.

Another is the increasing sophistication of the sports audience, including sports academics. As an occasional guest speaker to Stanford Law School students on sports law, I always begin my addresses by saying: "Stop thinking as a fan. If you want to be a fan, enjoying vicariously some team's fortunes, identifying with personalities, and feeling involved with game details and memories, fine. But if you intend to understand how this business works, disconnect yourself from those lifelong attitudes. They will distort what you're trying to grasp."

The sports historians, economists, and other analysts I have come across in the last ten years or so have been doing exactly that. Better than I would ever have expected, they have focused on actualities and not on simply satisfying an urge to somehow be associated with the sports scene that attracts them. This improvement has come about because, I suspect, contemporary television and print media deliver far more inside information than what used to be available, enabling academics to seek more knowledge from a sounder base—including, of course, the academics represented in this book.

I certainly cannot say I agree with the interpretations or conclusions of every discussion in this volume. (If I did, it would mean that they were not only worthless to me but undoubtedly flawed and of questionable use to others). But I am impressed with the force, honesty, and thoroughness of the arguments the contributors have made. This is a valuable collection, not because it supplies some kind of final answer or evaluation, but because it is such an authentic stimulus to continuing investigation.

And this is another reason the field I used to doubt has flourished in recent times. Today's analysts are able to build upon the groundwork of pioneers, while the pioneers had to start from scratch. In any academic sphere, I suppose, there is such a thing as critical mass, a certain minimal amount of accumulated material needed to ignite a self-sustaining chain reaction. In the serious study of American sports phenomena, which have such great cultural and societal ramifications, that critical mass was attained some ten or twenty years ago, and this book is just one product of the ongoing chain reaction. It is an important link that will enable others to keep the reaction going.

Acknowledgments

We would like to thank several people who contributed to the genesis of this book. Clark Kerr deserves special thanks for making the book possible by introducing the coeditors and for being an academic role model greatly admired by us. Nanette Sand and Clara Stern, librarians at the Institute of Industrial Relations, University of California, Berkeley, were always helpful. We are grateful to Roger Siebert of the library at California State University, Hayward, who did outstanding work on a computer search of the literature. Several of the contributors made constructive suggestions on the nature of the book and the structure of the contents, and particular thanks are due in this regard to Professors Roger G. Noll of Stanford University, James B. Dworkin of Purdue University, Stephen F. Ross of the University of Illinois at Urbana-Champaign, and Charles P. Korr of the University of Missouri, St. Louis. Series editors Benjamin G. Rader and Randy Roberts deserve our plaudits. We also appreciate the efforts of Doris Mangan and Lynn Crawford as well as those of the great staff at the University of Illinois Press, including Richard L. Wentworth, Karen Hewitt, Beth Bower, Harriet P. Stockanes, and former staff member Lawrence J. Malley. Leonard Koppett, former leading sportswriter for the *New York Times* and author of several books, including *Sports Illusion, Sports Reality,* was kind enough to lend his talent to the book's Foreword.

Introduction

Paul D. Staudohar and James A. Mangan

This book draws its authors from a wide range of academic disciplines, including history, sociology, economics, and law. Its multidisciplinary approach provides a unique opportunity to consider one of the most significant cultural aspects of modern North American society from various important and related angles. Professional team sports is a topic that has considerable potential for scholarly development as well as widespread popular interest. Arguably no single subject binds together more people in such animated interest, regardless of their race, sex, age, education, or income.

The heavy insularity of sports studies and models that has characterized sports academics for so long is lamentable. We wanted to adopt a more comprehensive approach that contains historical, social scientific, economic, and legal analysis—a multidisciplinary approach that recognizes the dynamic nature and diverse parameters of the sports industry and focuses on the participants both individually and as they interact in a system. The contributions comprising this book provide a model that complements existing ones, and we hope this book's approach will stimulate a more eclectic view of sports.

Professional team sports as packaged events provide considerable entertainment and pleasure for spectators. Even interruptions such as the player strikes of the 1980s have seemed to do little to dampen enthusiasm. And fans are interested in the foibles as well as the heroics of modern players and owners, in the struggles of labor and capital as well as the actual games.

Another side of the sports business concerns those who are part of delivering sports entertainment to the fans: labor, management, and government. Labor includes the players and their unions; management is comprised of the owners and leagues; and the government, mostly at the federal level, determines public policy and operates primarily as a regulator of the actions of labor and management. Significant though it is, the sports business as yet is relatively small. It is considered an industry here because of its service boundaries, distinct identity, and unique relationship to the media.

The scope of this book is limited to professional team sports—baseball, football, basketball, and hockey—because these sports dominate fan attendance and media exposure in North America. These sports also have significant commonalities: individually owned franchises that are organized together in leagues; unions that represent players in collective bargaining; agents that negotiate individual players' salaries; regulation under national labor and antitrust laws; and significant revenues from television contracts. Although individual teams in these sports are not themselves big businesses, the league that holds the clubs together and the satellite industries that derive all or part of their revenues from sports add up to a large and growing part of the U.S. and Canadian economies.

Labor, management, and government, the three principals in the sports industry, interact in a dynamic system. According to this model, power is not equalized among them, although a general balancing of power over time may be desirable for the long-term prosperity of the system. Power and how it is used are important issues because the goals of the participants sometimes conflict. The players, for instance, want a bigger share of gate receipts and television revenues; the owners want to retain as much income as possible. The model's dynamics thus stem in major part from the contest for power between labor and management.

Today professional athletes perceive themselves as human resources to be developed, packaged, advertised, and sold for as much money and for as long a time as possible. The total number of players in baseball, football, basketball, and hockey is approximately three thousand. Virtually all these players are members of separate unions for each sport. These unions negotiate contracts with the leagues that cover a variety of issues that are of interest to players collectively. In addition, nearly all players are also represented by agents who handle the individual negotiation of players' salaries. It is through these business dealings that players seek to maximize their economic return over relatively short and hazardous careers.

Modern sports owners experience satisfaction and challenge from the operation of their teams, but they must also keep a close watch on bottom-line profits. Prospects for growth in the sports industry have never been better. Owners are mastering the use of marketing techniques to make their teams more attractive to spectators. New, larger, more luxurious stadiums have elevated gate receipts, while revenues from network and cable televison contracts have risen rapidly. Given their domestic success, owners are beginning to turn an eye toward international expansion through setting up exhibition games abroad, establishing foreign franchises, and selling television rights to games originating in the United States.

It is the government's role to ensure that the entertainment side of sports—the relationship of the fans to their games—is preserved and protected. The government is also charged with the responsibility of ensuring that the sports business is conducted in accordance with the law. Although it has been more watchful during the present era of rapid growth in the industry, it has yet to take an active regulatory role. Most of the government's involvement has been through litigation; only a few legislative measures aimed specifically at sports have been passed. The government thus applies existing law and seeks to achieve a balance between the legitimate interests of labor and management.

Owners versus Players

The relationship between owners and players centers on four areas: (1) allocating revenues from the sports industry, (2) cooperating to achieve mutual gain, (3) establishing a behavioral environment conducive to reaching contract agreements, and (4) reconciling the interests of diverse elements within the structure of ownership and within the organization of players. These elements stand out in the sports industry because it is characterized by league structures, on the one hand, and the organization of players into unions for collective action on the other.

Collective bargaining in sports takes place primarily over economic issues on which the parties perceive themselves as adversaries in a win-lose game, with each side trying to maximize its share at the expense of the other. This struggle for power has been especially prominent in baseball and football, where the militancy of owners and players has led to numerous work stoppages that have closed down operations. Most of the strikes or lockouts have disrupted preseason training rather than the official schedule of games. But in 1981, 1985, and 1990 in baseball, and 1982 and 1987 in football, the renegotiation of collective bargaining agreements resulted in interruption of the regular season.

Although individual player salaries are negotiated between the club and the player, the latter usually represented by an agent, disputes over many important issues are resolved through the process of collective bargaining. For example, arguments about minimum pay, pensions, insurance, artificial turf, free agency, and methods for handling grievances are all decided at the bargaining table. Negotiations are usually confrontational, with each side reluctant to compromise. The principal criteria for determining economic issues in sports are ability to pay and relative power of the participants. The greater the revenues generated by a sport, the higher will be the salaries.

But no perfect correlation exists between these elements since ability to pay does not necessarily translate into willingness to pay. In 1987, for instance, owners in football had a substantial ability to pay, but because they were unwilling to share more revenues with the players, a 24-day strike occurred. Since the owners were more powerful than the players, they could not be forced to share the disputed income with the players.

As illustrated by relations between owners and players in basketball and hockey, however, it is not necessary that adversarial thinking dominate discussions. It is possible for the parties to work toward joint solutions to common problems that benefit both sides. Instead of choosing confrontation at the bargaining table, negotiators in basketball and hockey have emphasized reasoned agreements that seek to reflect the interests of both sides and that also attach significance to the growth of the industry.

The drug control program worked out between the owners and players in basketball, for example, is beneficial to the image of the game because it provides treatment to players who come forward for help and at the same time lets the public know that continued or undisclosed drug abuse will not be tolerated. Similarly, rather than engaging in a test of economic strength, basketball negotiators have cooperated to work out a revenue-sharing arrangement (at least 53 percent to the players) that promotes an equitable distribution of income.

The negotiators in hockey have also been cooperative, perhaps because they are mindful of the sport's comparatively limited revenues. They seem to realize the futility of continual conflict and have instead devised innovative arrangements to increase revenue; for example, the agreements reached between the league, the players' association, and international hockey federations for playing games, such as the Canada Cup, with teams from Europe and the Soviet Union. If the parties had viewed themselves as adversaries rather than partners, they could not have begun to work out such arrangements.

Both the equitable distribution of income and the production of greater revenues in the sports industry are facilitated by an atmosphere promoting understanding. If negotiators engage in personal vendettas full of inflammatory rhetoric and recrimination, as has often occurred in baseball and football, it is very difficult to reach agreement. On the other hand, not only agreement, but equitable and wise agreement, can be stimulated by creating an environment that promotes trust, mutual respect, face saving, and accommodation.

Establishing this environment is, of course, not as easy to accomplish as it might seem. Sports owners are wealthy, tough-minded men who are not accustomed to sharing authority with underlings. And something about the "fishbowl" environment in professional sports turns even normally placid people into fiery competitors, as the glare of the media intensifies the pressures of negotiations. As incidents in basketball and hockey have demonstrated, however, showing the other side trust and respect is contagious. People who give respect are apt to receive it; negotiators should recognize this truth and seek to cultivate mutual respect.

Much of the negotiation in the sports business is done behind the scenes, within the organizations involved. The owners meet regularly on a formal basis in league meetings to discuss the position they want to take as a group on important issues such as television agreements, franchise movement, and international expansion, as well as the multitude of issues the owners negotiate with players' unions. Some of the most lively disagreements occur in these meetings, but once a consensus is reached, the dissidents try hard to cement the common foundation that is necessary for organizational unity.

The players, too, strive for consensus and solidarity, although they have not been as successful as the owners in maintaining their unity when a crisis arises. The players' association in football, for example, has seen its solidarity crumble during strikes as players cross picket lines to return to work. It takes exceptionally strong, capable leadership to satisfy and hold together the diverse elements within a sports union. Marvin Miller's special success as the executive director of the baseball players' association was because of his shrewdness and toughness in the face of adversity combined with his extraordinary ability to communicate what was best for the union to the players.

Areas of Inquiry

Despite the proliferation of studies dealing with the history of sport throughout the world in the last decade, little has been written on the commercial history of sport. It is, in fact, a fascinating area of inquiry in its own right. Pioneering sports entrepreneurs, for example, were captains of industry who brought major league sports to the cities of the United States and Canada and enriched the lives of millions of urbanites. Early leaders of sports unions, many of whom were prominent players, fought hard to improve working conditions and increase wages in the face of stiff resistance from owners. They played their part in transforming the image of both sport and player. Both groups deserve their recorders and commentators; both have contributed to the making of modern North America.

The sports industry has produced some exceptional innovators who have not only shaped the industry but indirectly influenced wider society as well—Bowie Kuhn, Marvin Miller, Walter O'Malley, and Peter Ueberroth in baseball; Pete Rozelle, George Halas, Vince Lombardi, and Ed Garvey in football; Larry O'Brien, Larry Fleisher, Red Auerbach, and David Stern in basketball; and Clarence Campbell, Conn Smythe, Alan Eagleson, and John Ziegler in hockey. At the same time, changes in the wider environment of sports—in laws, in television, in the formation of rival leagues—have moved sports in new directions. The dynamic interaction between influential leaders and environmental change makes sports a fascinating historical study. The truth of the matter is that modern entrepreneurs and union leaders, together with the business arrangements of sports, are all—at least in part—a product of the past. Continuity and discontinuity require investigation if the full canvas, offering the complete picture of professional team games in North American life, past and present, is to be properly covered.

The academic study of the sports business is heavily influenced by economics. The success of professional sports ventures is based on the extent to which they can deliver games to large numbers of people who are willing to pay for this entertainment. With widespread markets in large cities and through television, professional sports have become a golden goose that provides riches for owners and players. Cities take substantial pride in their teams. The symbiotic interaction between sports, television, and advertising exerts a powerful effect on the pocketbooks of consumers.

As noted above, the sports business is characterized by team franchises owned by wealthy entrepreneurs or corporations, which are joined together in leagues. These leagues operate as a cartel to limit competition. Providing major league entertainment is the exclusive province of these cartels, which limit their growth to maintain exclusivity and avoid overexposure. The player draft, itself an uncompetitive business practice, seeks to achieve some balance among teams in the league. Amateur players are chosen by teams according to the inverse order of the teams' won-loss records in the previous season. Allowing the worst teams the highest draft choices helps these teams improve. Nevertheless, although the draft promotes balance among teams, it stifles competition in the labor market for players because they can sell their services to only one team. In all sports, however, it is possible for players to become free agents after a certain period of service, and they are then allowed to contract with other clubs in the league. Free agency has caused competitive bidding among owners that drives salaries upward, in effect defeating the purpose of the league cartel. Much of the conflict in the sports business has occurred over control of the labor market.

Teams derive their revenues mainly from ticket sales, the sale of television rights, parking fees, and sales of concessions. Their major expense is salaries for players, scouts, and front-office staff, but most teams also incur significant expenses from stadium rentals and from marketing games locally. Although some teams may show operating losses (i.e., expenses exceed revenues), tax advantages help to make the ownership of franchises a lucrative business in nearly all cases.

The present and future of the sports business is tied closely to television. Although revenues are increased by raising ticket prices, building luxury boxes, and league expansion, television has become the dominant part of the sports success story. There is no more efficient way to deliver sports to consumers than by television. The multimillion dollar contracts signed by players in baseball, football, and basketball are directly made possible by large payments to teams from television networks. It is not surprising that hockey salaries are by far the lowest in professional team sports, because the National Hockey League does not have any contracts with U.S. television networks. Yet as important as the role of network television is, a growing share of the future market will be taken over by cable and pay-per-view television, which give sports fans more direct access to a larger number of specialized sporting events.

A key feature of the sports business is its extensive unionization. Although players' associations had a difficult time in gaining a foothold in sports, today nearly all the players in each of the four major team sports belong to a union. These unions have been highly successful in altering the balance of power between owners and players. Although many of the rules governing labor relations in sports have been set through collective bargaining, some of the most significant ones are the result of legal victories won by the unions. The U.S. judiciary has on numerous occasions applied federal antitrust laws to sports in such a way as to reduce the power of the owners to operate as a cartel. Economics and law are closely linked in sports, with each area very much influencing the other, as the discussion of the legal side of professional sports in this book illustrates.

The two principal statutes that have been applied to the sports business are the National Labor Relations Act and the Sherman Antitrust Act. The NLRA gives employees in private industry the right to join unions, engage in collective bargaining, and use pressure tactics such as strikes. These rights, which form the core of U.S. labor policy, have been put to good use by players and their unions in the major team sports. The Sherman Act prohibits the use of monopoly power to restrain trade or commerce and assesses treble damages on violators. Because sports leagues operate as cartels, many of the practices they engage in have come under judicial scrutiny on antitrust grounds.

Although the NLRA was passed in 1935, it was not until the 1960s that professional athletes began to use this law effectively to seek economic gain. The first sport union to make substantial use of the NLRA was the Major League Baseball Players Association, which was formed in 1952. It was not until 1966, however, when Marvin Miller was hired as its executive director, that the union broke away from domination by the owners. Miller, a former official of the United Steelworkers of America, realized that the law and collective bargaining could be used as powerful weapons to break the grip that the owners had on salary determination and the freedom of players to move from one team to another. The pioneering developments in baseball have had a substantial influence on the evolution of business practice in other sports.

Antitrust suits have been brought by players on a variety of issues, including the draft, free agency, league age rules concerning the signing of players, and the system of waiver by which players are released by one team for possible signing by another. Franchise movement is another important issue. All four major team sports have experienced litigation concerning attempts by franchise owners to move their teams to other cities. Antitrust issues are raised when a league tries to block an attempted move—its action may be a restraint of trade. In the past several years bills have been introduced in Congress that would regulate franchise movement, although none of them has yet come close to passage.

In sum, history, economics, and law combine to affect the business of sport, including management, finance, marketing, and collective bargaining. The business of sport is what transforms the games into organized entertainment for viewing by a large segment of the population. These games provide recreation and diversion but at the same time have a significant impact on the socioculture.

The Literature

We do not attempt in this book to survey the entire scope of the sports business. Many important issues are addressed only briefly; others not at all. Indeed, no single encyclopedic source of information covers all facets of the sports business. The scholar who wants to acquire a breadth of knowledge on the subject must consult a variety of sources. To provide some assistance in this regard, we offer a concise review of the literature. We are mindful that the academic literature on the sports business is large and growing rapidly. Our recommendations for additional reading are limited to selected references that appear to have exceptional merit.

A useful starting point for the serious scholar is a 1974 book entitled *Government and the Sports Business* (Washington, D.C.: The Brookings Institution), edited by Roger G. Noll. This is a seminal book that has had particular influence on scholars in economics, law, and business administration. Although some of the material has been outdated by new court decisions on antitrust issues, changes in tax law, and the salary explosion for professional athletes, the sophisticated level of analysis and writing sets a standard that should attract the contemporary reader. For a good discussion of the unique characteristics of baseball as a business enterprise, a valuable source is Jesse W. Markham and Paul V. Teplitz, *Baseball Economics and Public Policy* (Lexington, Mass.: Lexington Books, 1981). From another vantage point, one of America's preeminent sports writers, Leonard Koppett, offers his view of sports, journalism, and society in *Sports Illusion, Sports Reality* (Boston: Houghton Mifflin, 1981).

Scholars wishing to pursue a social science perspective of professional and amateur sports should consult the *Handbook of Social Science of Sport,* edited by Günther Lüschen and George Sage (Champaign, Ill.: Stipes Publishing, 1981). Many top scholars contributed to this collection, including Stanley Eitzen, Michael Ellis, Gladys Lang, Roger G. Noll, Eldon Snyder, and Brian Sutton-Smith. This book incorporates strictly sociological interpretations as well as approaches from cultural anthropology, history, psychology, and social philosophy in the analysis of sport and games. It also contains an extensive international bibliography. A similarly diverse collection can be found in *Sport and the Sociocultural Process,* third edition, edited by Marie Hart and Susan Birrell (Dubuque, Iowa: Wm. C. Brown, 1981).

The importance of labor-management relations to the sports business has generated several volumes that explore the subject from different perspectives. In James B. Dworkin's *Owners versus Players: Baseball and Collective Bargaining* (Boston: Auburn House, 1981), the emphasis is on baseball, but attention is given to football, basketball, and hockey as well. Robert C. Berry, William B. Gould, and Paul D. Staudohar's book, *Labor Relations in Professional Sports* (Dover, Mass.: Auburn House, 1986), emphasizes labor-management relations primarily in a legal context, focusing on antitrust law, National Labor Relations Board decisions, and the web of rules governing the operation of leagues, teams, and unions. A legal approach is also found in Robert C. Berry and Glenn M. Wong's *Law and Business of the Sports Industries* (Dover, Mass.: Auburn House, 1986), volume 1, *Professional Sports Leagues.* Staudohar's book, *The Sports Industry and Collective Bargaining,* second edition (Ithaca, N.Y.: ILR Press, Cornell University, 1989), provides an overview of critical employment issues such as free agency, strikes, drug abuse, and violence.

Another book that discusses labor issues, as well as business and public policy on amateur and professional sports, is *Government and Sport: The Public Policy Issues,* edited by Arthur T. Johnson and James H. Frey (Totowa, N.J.: Rowman and Allanheld, 1985). Among the topics covered are substance abuse, free agency, and franchise movement. The issues of media impact, fan alienation, and the role of the sports commissioner may be found in Benjamin G. Rader, *In Its Own Image: How Television Has Trans-*

formed Professional Sports (New York: Free Press, 1984); John Underwood, *Spoiled Sport: A Fan's Notes on the Troubles of Spectator Sports* (Boston: Little, Brown, 1984); and Bowie Kuhn, *Hardball: The Education of a Baseball Commissioner* (New York: Times Books, 1987).

Besides the publishers mentioned above, several major university presses are bringing out scholarly works, often in special series on sports, that include the business side. One is the University of Illinois Press, which has published works by several of the contributors to this book, including Charles P. Korr, Joan M. Chandler, and Steven A. Riess. Oxford University Press in New York is publishing a new series on Sports History and Society, devoted to the historical, economic, and cultural aspects of sports in the United States and abroad. The first volume to appear in this series is Ronald Smith's *Sports and Freedom.* The University of North Carolina Press has produced two recent noteworthy books: Allen Guttmann's *A Whole New Ball Game: An Interpretation of American Sports* (1988), which shows what America's fascination with sports reveals about our culture, and James Edward Miller's *The Baseball Business: Pursuing Pennants and Profits in Baltimore* (1990), a case study that analyzes the changing relationship between the major and minor leagues, marketing, television, and racial discrimination. Other significant books are coming from Manchester University Press in Great Britain under its sports series, International Studies in the History of Sport, edited by James A. Mangan. A recent book from the University of Chicago Press, Gerald W. Scully's *The Business of Professional Baseball* (1989), uses sophisticated models of economic analysis.

Masters theses and Ph.D. dissertations were researched by the editors for the years 1980–87, using a computerized listing of theses abstracts. We found a growing interest in the business side of sports, especially among students of physical education, business administration, economics, history, and sociology. A sampling of these works includes Linda Rae Stanley, "Essays in Applied Economics: Evidence of Non–Profit-Maximizing Firm Owners and Bargaining within the Shadow of the Law" (Ph.D. diss., University of Wyoming, 1985, University Microfilms Order No. AD685-29745); Gerald F. Middlemiss, "Occupational Attainment of Former Professional Football Players" (Ed.D. diss., Rutgers University, 1984, University Microfilms Order No. AD685-09406); Christopher James Stoy, "Elitism and Professional Team Sports: An Ownership Profile" (Ph.D. diss., University of Southern California, 1983); and Robert Louis Gaillard, "The Effects of the Salary Arbitration Process on Performance," which discusses salary arbitration in baseball (Ed.D. diss., University of San Francisco, 1985, University Microfilms Order No. AD685-18651). The most common topic, selected in several theses, was how professional athletes adjust their lives after their playing careers are over.

Another valuable source of information for scholars is the journal literature. Although no journal is devoted exclusively to the sports business, many have published information on the subject. Among these are the *Industrial and Labor Relations Review, Industrial Relations, Labor Law Journal, American Economic Review, Canadian Journal of Economics, Compensation Review, Personnel, Arbitration Journal, Personnel Journal, Journal of Sport History, International Journal of the History of Sport, Quarterly Review of Economics and Business, Contemporary Sociology, Law and Society Review, Law and Contemporary Problems, Work and Occupations, Sporting Traditions, The Annals of the American Academy of Political Science, Journal of Labor Research, Journal of Labor Economics, Atlanta Economic Journal, Review of Business and Economic Research, Editorial Research Reports, Journal of Business and Economics, American Economist, Journal of Human Resources, Journal of Sport Sociology, The Sociological Quarterly,* and *Monthly Labor Review.* In addition to these sources, many law reviews published by university law schools have contributed worthwhile studies of the sports business, ranging across a variety of issues such as antitrust law, violence, television rights, and labor relations.

Overview of the Book

Both the sports business and sports games involve conflict over goals and challenge to human ability. Rules dictate how the contests are waged. Winners and losers are sorted out. Sports administrators and players alike are financially rewarded, at least in part, on the basis of performance. But although the games have a stability marked by tradition, the business side of sports is more subject to constant change. Old strategies are discarded and new ones emerge in response to pressures from the outside economic and political environment. The relative power of labor, management, and government shifts over time. Technological changes like cable television spawn new relationships in the industry. Rival leagues form. Problems like drug use by players necessitate revised rules.

This book reflects the dynamics of the sports business and how it influences, and is influenced by, the larger society. Several of the contributors also recommend changes in the sports industry based on their analysis. It is an objective of this book to promote thinking about change among scholars and practitioners and perhaps even bring improvements to the operation of the industry.

Of the scholars who have directed their attention to professional sports, none has made a greater contribution than Roger G. Noll. *Government and the Sports Business* (1974), which he edited and contributed to, was the first comprehensive examination of the business of professional sports. It is thus fitting that this book's opening chapter, entitled "Professional Basketball: Economic and Business Perspectives," should be from his pen. It is an analysis of virtually all aspects of basketball's business operation. Although Noll concentrates on basketball, he brings out many economic, financial, and management developments that are applicable to all professional team sports. He takes the reader from the origins of professional basketball through the formation of the National Basketball Association (NBA) to the rivalry of the American Basketball Association (ABA) and the eventual merger between the two leagues. Detailed financial analysis is made of individual teams as well as the teams in the league as a whole. Attendance, comparative records of teams in big and small cities, compensation, free agency, collective bargaining, and the future of the industry are additional concerns.

In "Sport as TV Product: A Case Study of 'Monday Night Football,' " Joan M. Chandler analyzes a television show whose duration and high ratings make it one of the most popular shows ever presented. This weekly National Football League (NFL) game has made celebrities of its announcers and brought significant attention to the cities in which it is played, and it has had a host of other influences on U.S. sociocultural life. Chandler analyzes "Monday Night Football" in terms of how it got started, why it has been successful, and what its future may be. The show's level of popularity each NFL season has become a yardstick by which the health of the football business is measured. An interesting issue addressed by Chandler is whether the show is on the wane, given its weaker ratings in recent years. She also inquires into the technical presentation of the broadcasts, the reasons for the popularity of professional football, and the ways in which the game is perceived by broadcasters. In short, she offers an assessment that covers both the vices and virtues of this media event.

In "Player Compensation in the National Football League," Dennis A. Ahlburg and James B. Dworkin use a novel statistical model to determine the factors that are most influential in determining comparative salaries of players. It is well known that the absolute level of salaries varies among sports based on factors such as the number of players per team, size of arenas, number of playing dates, attendance, and relative size of television contracts. Less is known, however, about why salaries vary within a sport. Ahlburg and Dworkin explore the differences between relative salaries among football players. What impact does seniority have on a player's salary? The draft round is obviously significant, but how important is it compared to other variables? What weight is given in the salary determination process to position played? The answers to these questions are not only interesting in their own right but should provide information valuable for collective bargaining. In recent years both the NFL and the players' association have made proposals at the bargaining table to tie salaries to a formula that takes into account the same factors as those discussed in this chapter. Thus the kind of statistical analysis used by the authors has not only academic value but also practical application.

In "Racial Discrimination in the National Basketball Association," Lawrence M. Kahn and Peter D. Sherer employ a sophisticated quantitative model to analyze differences in the salaries of white and black basketball players. Complementing Ahlburg and Dworkin's chapter, Kahn and Sherer's looks at the relative differences between players' salaries. Basketball provides an excellent opportunity to analyze discrimination in sports because a large majority of the players are black, but salary levels in basketball are the highest of any in the team sports. Discrimination is difficult to measure quantitatively, hence the elaborate statistical framework devised by the authors to isolate key elements to explain differentials. The question the authors ask, to which they provide carefully researched answers, are ones that need to be resolved. How is discrimination measured? Does it exist in the NBA, and if so, by how much? What factors cause discrimination? Is a conclusion that discrimination exists in the NBA consistent with findings from other studies?

In "Serfs versus Magnates: A Century of Labor Strife in Major League Baseball," David Q. Voigt presents a compendium of the events and personalities in early professional baseball in the United States and discusses their significance. As the first sport to be developed at the major league level, baseball established precedents that were later followed by other sports. Unions evolved in baseball long before they did in other sports. Although we often associate the beginnings of sports unions with the names of Marvin Miller, Ed Garvey, and others who took the helm of fledgling players' associations in the modern era, in fact baseball features a rich history of labor-management relations dating as far back as the late nineteenth century. Tightfisted entrepreneurs like Albert G. Spalding and John T. Brush skirmished with players like John Montgomery Ward and Nap Lajoie over salaries and working conditions. Voigt covers these battles and other developments as well—lawsuits, new leagues, team mergers, and even a one-day strike by Ty Cobb and his teammates. The colorful characters in baseball and their struggles described by Voigt have a special place in the history of U.S. sport.

Charles P. Korr's chapter, "Marvin Miller and the New Unionism in Baseball," starts where David Voigt's chapter leaves off, with an analysis of the beginnings of the modern era of labor-management relations in professional sports. Of all the labor leaders in sports, none has accomplished more than Marvin Miller. Korr demonstrates that Miller was the right man at the right time for the Major League Baseball Players Association, revealing both his bulldog tenacity and communication skills. Korr also examines the circumstances under which Miller came to the union, the owners' resistance to him, and the ways in which he consolidated his power. He describes how the first few years were crucial to the later success of Miller and the union and explains how Miller transformed the union from one dominated by the owners to one that fought hard for the players. The players' solidarity under Miller's leadership led to important achievements in collective bargaining. Korr also discusses the role of players like Bob Friend and Jim Bunning in the transformation of the association. But the part played by Miller receives, and deserves, the most attention.

Gary R. Roberts presents an excellent analysis of "Professional Sports and the Antitrust Laws." Probably no area of law has had a greater impact on professional sports over the past twenty years. Roberts argues that antitrust law should not be used to challenge the decisions of sports leagues, at least not nearly so much as it has been in the past. He presents an exercise in logic and precedent firmly grounded in the principles of law and economics that covers all professional sports. His analysis deals with the essence of business monopoly, how antitrust law has dealt with it in the past, and how it should deal with it in the future. Legal specialists will especially appreciate Roberts's ground-breaking perspectives, but they are quite accessible to nonlegal analysts as well with Roberts's step-by-step progression of facts and argument.

In the next chapter, "Break Up the Sports League Monopolies," Stephen F. Ross presents a thoughtful analysis that challenges the status quo of sports leagues. The structure of professional sports is dominated by leagues that exercise tight control over new franchises, player allocation, television broadcasts, and other important aspects of the business. This control raises questions of monopoly and antitrust regulation. Legal scholars, such as Gary Roberts, may question particular aspects of the leagues' operation, but they accept the leagues' existing monopoly structures as appropriate. In contrast, Ross rejects the status quo and does not assume that the leagues should continue in their present form. Instead, he proposes that monopoly leagues be dissolved and be replaced by competitive leagues. Concentrating on major league baseball and football, Ross addresses many controversial issues. What is wrong with the operation of current sports leagues? Why should they be broken up? How would such a breakup occur? What would be the result of increased competition between sports leagues? Ross answers these and other key questions in a logical fashion and gives impressive evidence to support his views.

In "The Blue Line and the Bottom Line: Entrepreneurs and the Business of Hockey in Canada, 1927–90," David Mills examines two of the most prominent owners in the National Hockey League (NHL)—Conn Smythe and Peter Pocklington. Smythe was influential in the early development of the NHL. His involvement in the operation of the Toronto Maple Leafs and Maple Leaf Gardens from 1927 to 1961 provides ample illustration of the pioneering hockey entrepreneur. Pocklington, owner of the Edmonton Oilers since 1977, is a good example of the contemporary hockey owner. Mills gives the reader a carefully drawn profile of these two prototype entrepreneurs, looking at how they raised capital in outside business ventures that allowed them to purchase their NHL teams and how their approach to the business of hockey is both similar and different. Although corporations have increasingly made their way into professional sports ownership, the entrepreneurial function usually remains in the hands of a single individual who dominates decision making. The examples of Smythe and Pocklington, both highly successful, provide insight into sports personalities, management behavior, and financial operations.

In the next chapter, "The Impact of Corporate Ownership on Labor-Management Relations in Hockey," Rob B. Beamish looks at ownership in the NHL from a different perspective. Beamish's focus is more on the owners as managers, and he examines the diverse business interests of the individuals and corporations that own Canadian franchises in the NHL. He analyzes ownership in terms of control by individuals or groups, by families, and by conglomerate corporations. Regardless of the form of control, NHL team owners can influence substantial amounts of capital. How do these capital resources affect labor-management relations? Beamish assesses the power relationship between hockey owners and the NHL players' union, and he comes up with interesting conclusions that appear to be applicable to all professional team sports.

Steven A. Riess's chapter, "A Social Profile of the Professional Football Player, 1920–82," combines sociology and history to compare the players of the past with those of the present. Who are these players, and where do they come from? How long do they play, and what happens to them after their playing careers are over? In answering these and other questions through the use of research data, Riess provides a contrasting portrayal of typical players who performed in the NFL during several eras. Among the comparisons he makes are how the socioeconomic backgrounds of players have changed over the years and how their ethnic and racial backgrounds have varied. He also discusses why players view the game differently today—as a career with significant income potential rather than a pastime with little financial reward. The role of college in the life of professional players is explored, too. Riess provides an analysis of what colleges players have attended, their graduation rates, and the impact that college has had on their post-football careers. The sharp distinction between contemporary college-educated players and those from other eras makes this study an interesting one.

In "The Role of Sports Agents," Leigh Steinberg examines the reasons why agents have come to represent athletes and the impact they have had on professional sports. As the representatives of players in individual salary negotiations and on other business matters, agents provide services that are vital to the players' economic prosperity and security during their short risky careers. The astronomical salaries of players are a highly visible testimonial to the success agents have had in extracting for their clients a larger share of the growing revenues from team operations. But agentry also has a seamy side, which Steinberg describes in detail as to its effects on athletes, sports, and society. He is concerned especially with early signings of college players by agents (with accompanying payoffs) and the eligibility requirements for playing college football as compared with those for other sports and careers. Steinberg's most important contribution may be his thoughtful recommendations for changing the rules that govern amateur and professional sports. These recommendations are based on his experience as a leading sports and entertainment agent who has placed particular emphasis on high ethical standards for both himself and his clients and on generous community support, thus setting standards by which other agents should be judged.

The book concludes appropriately with John J. MacAloon's chapter, "Are Olympic Athletes Professionals? Cultural Categories and Social Control in U.S. Sport." MacAloon puts sport into perspective by examining its amateur and professional elements, whose definitions have become increasingly blurred and complex. MacAloon shows that the Olympic games are a source of public pride, but also of controversy over their commercialization, the exploitation of athletes, and athletes' drug use. MacAloon also provides an international perspective by noting the similarities and dissimilarities in the relationships between athletes and the governing sports bureaucracies in Western nations and Eastern-bloc nations. Now that U.S. professional sports leagues are establishing or seeking to establish relationships with international sports organizations, the author's comments on this issue are especially timely. MacAloon explores numerous other interesting questions as well. Are the concepts of amateurism and professionalism converging? What are the connections between the Olympics and the "corporate-sport-media" complex? How does the U.S. public view the financing of amateur athletes by the government? Taking an intellectually challenging yet practical approach, MacAloon uses concepts from sociology, history, and economics to form provocative conclusions about the impact of sports on U.S. culture.

As we have already remarked, the academic community has belatedly awoken to the relevance of sport in the modern world. For this reason the editors have been able to draw on a distinguished vanguard of contributors who have made a close study of professional team games of baseball, football, basketball, and hockey and their relationship to society. But who is the book written for? In the first instance, we have responded to the increasing number of academics from a wide range of disciplines who are demanding and seeking multidisciplinary studies of modern sports for their students. Undergraduate and graduate students in economics, history, law, and sociology will also find the book valuable. In addition, it will be of help to students of business administration who want to know more about the sports industry and students of sports administration who aspire to hold executive posts in major sports industries. Finally, the many sports fans who appreciate the extent to which events off the field determine the development of their sports will find much to interest them here. The book was written in such a manner, we hope, that it will appeal not only to the academic community but to all involved, in one way or another, in the mass entertainment industry that modern sports have become—to general managers, coaches, magazine editors and writers, broadcasters, agents, players, and the enthusiastic fan who wants the whole picture, not just the play.

Professional Basketball: Economic and Business Perspectives

1

Roger G. Noll

Like baseball and football, professional basketball in the United States has experienced a boom that began in the 1960s and, with few interruptions, has continued through the 1980s. Indeed, basketball's performance has been, in many ways, the most remarkable. From the brink of financial disaster and possible dissolution in the early 1950s, the National Basketball Association has grown more rapidly in both revenues and teams than either baseball or football. Moreover, prospects for further growth are good, for the revenue potential of televised sports events on national off-air and cable networks and local pay-TV only began to be tapped in the 1980s.

Each sport has its unique features, and in basketball these are its underlying cost structure and the relative placidity of its labor-management relations. Promoters in the entertainment industry (including sports) refer to the minimum cost of staging an event as the "nut," and in basketball the nut is far smaller than in any other team sport. Basketball teams have few players and minimal needs in terms of equipment and facilities. As a result, both low-income areas, such as big-city ghettos, and sparsely populated communities, such as midwestern farming towns and western mining camps, are hotbeds of interest in the sport and produce a disproportionate share of its players.

The relative placidity of basketball's labor relations is easy to discern but difficult to explain. Basketball players receive higher salaries and more freedom to choose for whom they will work than athletes in baseball or football, and they have achieved these gains without launching disruptive strikes. The collective bargaining history of the three top sports during the mid-1980s illustrates the point. Strikes occurred in both baseball (1985) and football (1987), but in basketball (following a year of negotiation after the previous agreement had expired) a settlement was reached (1988) that further reduced the restrictions on competition among teams for players. Although the negotiations were tense, and even punctuated by litigation on antitrust and labor issues, the settlement came without even a threat of a strike.

Historical Background

The professional basketball leagues of the present differ in many ways from the leagues that emerged after World War II. Although the game itself is basically unchanged, it is played substantially more skillfully than before, and its players have different origins. Instead of rural whites, they are blacks from large cities, and they have far different socioeconomic backgrounds than the crowds that cheer them on. The fans are different, too. Today the image of the basketball fan is an upscale yuppie, an impression that is sharpened by television closeups of actors and rock stars in attendance at games played in the nation's media centers. It was not always so.

The birth of basketball was distinctly middle class. Dr. James A. Naismith organized the first game on January 20, 1892, at the International YMCA College in Springfield, Massachusetts. The game was quickly adopted by other universities, becoming an intercollegiate sport before the turn of the century.[1] This beginning makes basketball unique. It is the sole popular and financially significant sport that is truly modern in origin.

Only two decades after its invention, the sport was professionalized. The first truly successful professional team was probably the New York Celtics (later the Original Celtics), and it was organized in the winter of 1914. The early professional teams sometimes formed leagues, but they were primarily barnstormers. They played exhibition games against each other on an intermittent basis and against amateur teams from the areas where games were staged. Thus the early history of professional basketball parallels the history of baseball from the 1850s until the formation of the National Association of Professional Baseball Players in 1871, the first professional sports league of the form we know today.

As in other sports, the key event that set the stage for basketball as a big business was the formation of the first stable league, the National Basketball League (NBL), in 1937. The change from barnstorming to stable league play is important because of the effect it had on both demand for sports entertainment and the management strategy of teams. Barnstorming teams play schedules of varying lengths and difficulty, and the product they market is a single game against a particular team. The formation of leagues brings parity in schedules, a firm basis for comparing the qualities of teams and players, unification of rules, and an eventual champion, so that teams can market the quest for a championship as well as a particular game.

Leagues also produce a different style of play. In a league a team's financial performance depends upon its success over an entire season against teams of comparable quality. By contrast, barnstorming professionals pile up numerous wins against local amateurs or weaker professional teams. They give greater emphasis to entertainment and the demonstration of unique individual skills, in part to divert the attention of paying customers from the fact that, in most cases, the game is a gross mismatch. In the league format teams place more emphasis on strategy and team play, and they generally take the game more seriously. These differences are apparent from a comparison of a typical NBA game and a match between the Harlem Globetrotters and their perennial patsies, the Washington Generals.

Of course, both forms of the game are entertainment, and both feature players who are excellent at what they do, so that an argument over their intrinsic relative merits is pointless. The important observation is that the history of professional sports makes clear that consumers prefer, and are willing to pay more for, organized championships featuring serious, intense play. Because the NBL was the first league to provide reasonably balanced competition and stability, its formation in 1937 began the transformation of professional basketball from casual entertainment to a major factor in U.S. sports.

After an interruption owing to World War II, professional basketball boomed in the mid-1940s. Three leagues began operation in 1945 or 1946: a revived NBL, which contained teams primarily in small midwestern cities; the American Basketball League (ABL), which had an eastern small-city focus; and the Basketball Association of America (BAA), which located its teams in large eastern and midwestern cities. The strategy of the NBL and ABL of placing teams in small towns reflected the origin of most players and the sport's primary base of popularity at amateur levels. Unfortunately this strategy proved to be misdirected and overly ambitious, for most of the small-town teams failed, and the three leagues collapsed to one, today's NBA, by the beginning of the 1949–50 season. Because most of the surviving teams came from the BAA, the start of the NBA typically is traced to the BAA's first season, 1946–47, rather than either 1937 (when the NBL was formed) or 1949 (the year of the merger).

The membership of the BAA/NBA during the 1940s reveals the business plan of basketball's early entrepreneurs. In its first season, 1946–47, the BAA featured eleven teams. Except for a team in Providence, all were located in the major population centers of the Northeast (see Table 1.1). Four teams folded before the next season, and another—Baltimore—was added from the ABL when that league disbanded. In 1948–49 the BAA expanded to four smaller cities: Fort Wayne, Indianapolis, Minneapolis, and Rochester. The next year the NBA was formed by merging teams from six small cities from the NBL into the BAA. Meanwhile the Providence team folded, leaving a seventeen-team league. Of these teams, only six were located in the ten most populous U.S. metropolitan areas. Two were in the second ten,

Table 1.1 BAA/NBA Membership, 1946–47 Season to 1963–64 Season

1946–47	1947–48	1948–49
Boston	Baltimore	Baltimore
Chicago	Boston	Boston
Cleveland	Chicago	Chicago
Detroit	New York	Fort Wayne
New York	Philadelphia	Indianapolis
Philadelphia	Providence	Minneapolis
Pittsburgh	St. Louis	New York
Providence	Washington, D.C.	Philadelphia
St. Louis		Providence
Toronto		Rochester
Washington, D.C.		St. Louis
		Washington, D.C.

1949–50	1954–55	1963–64
Anderson	Boston	Baltimore
Baltimore	Fort Wayne	Boston
Boston	Milwaukee	Cincinnati
Chicago	Minneapolis	Detroit
Denver	New York	Los Angeles
Fort Wayne	Philadelphia	New York
Indianapolis	Rochester	Philadelphia
Minneapolis	Syracuse	St. Louis
New York		San Francisco
Philadelphia		
Rochester		
St. Louis		
Sheboygan		
Syracuse		
Tri-Cities		
Washington, D.C.		
Waterloo		

and the remaining nine were in metropolitan areas ranking below twenty-fifth. Some, like Waterloo and Sheboygan, were located in areas one would hardly regard as fertile territory for major league sports.

The new NBA began to shrink immediately. By 1954–55 it was down to eight teams, only three of which were located in large cities (New York, Philadelphia, and Boston). A fourth team, Minneapolis, was among the twenty largest metropolitan areas, and a fifth team, the Tri-Cities (Moline, Davenport, and Rock Island) had sought greener pastures by moving to Milwaukee, also a top-twenty area. The remaining three stayed in cities that have never since had a major league franchise in the four leading professional sports: Fort Wayne, Rochester, and Syracuse.

A year later the migration of teams to more lucrative markets continued with the move of the Milwaukee team to St. Louis. Another year later the Fort Wayne and Rochester teams moved to Detroit and Cincinnati. In the early 1960s Minneapolis and Syracuse were replaced by Los Angeles and San Francisco, and Chicago and Baltimore/Washington, D.C., were added through expansion. In approximately ten years the NBA had been transformed from a league comprised primarily of teams from smaller cities to one in which all ten teams were located in the dozen most populous metropolitan areas.

The reasons for the changes in the composition of the NBA were complex, but two factors were especially important. One was the growth of the popularity of basketball in the largest cities. Integration of the sport at all levels opened the game to blacks from large cities, who quickly came to dominate the game. In addition, much of the growth of large cities was due to migration from the areas where basketball had been so popular—the smaller cities of the Midwest. A second factor was television. Until the mid-1950s, broadcasting was not an important source of revenue for professional basketball teams. Basketball is not a game that is particularly amenable to radio, for the action is too quick and too continuous. Indeed, very few sportscasters are capable of coming close to describing the action, a notable exception being Chick Hearn. On television, where announcers are required more to comment on the action than to describe it, basketball is far more interesting, and so revenues from broadcasting finally began to emerge only when television became important in the early 1950s.

By this time the NBA had scaled back and was stuck in several small media markets. It had managed to swim against two strong economic tides: while Americans were migrating to industrial metropolises, it had put its teams in smaller cities, and despite the fact that television was on the rise, it had oriented itself exclusively to gate receipts. The NBA's relocations and expansions between the mid-1950s and the late 1960s rectified this situation by strategically placing the NBA in all of the largest media centers, increasing the value of its product both at the gate and over the air.

But the relocation and expansion were not fast enough to leave all of the choice larger markets occupied, and these attracted competitors. In 1961 Abe Saperstein, the founder and owner of the Harlem Globetrotters, formed the American Basketball League. Saperstein had good market sense, placing teams in then-unoccupied large cities such as Chicago, Pittsburgh, and Washington, D.C., but his organizational sense was not as impressive. He made himself the commissioner of basketball, the sole owner of one franchise (Chicago), and the partial owner of some others. The conflict of interest became apparent on the first day of the first season, when owner Saperstein's Chicago team lost a one-point game to Washington and immediately protested the outcome to Commissioner Saperstein.

A key element in the success of league sports is integrity. If the league members are going to succeed in selling the championship season, rather than games as exhibitions, fans must have faith in the integrity of the outcome. At some point in history all sports have toyed with, and been burned by, syndication of a league—that is, an arrangement in which all or most teams have a single owner or management structure. In every case syndication has been disastrous. Perhaps Saperstein did not fully appreciate the difference between marketing his highly successful Globetrotters and a new professional basketball league, but whatever the reason, the league folded on December 30, 1962, in the middle of its second season.

The next attempt at entry into urban markets was more successful, although its origins were just as unusual. Two Orange County, California, lawyers, Gary Davidson and Don Regan, who played pick-up basketball together, decided to live out their fantasies by forming a new league, and in 1967 the American Basketball Association began play. Its membership seemed to be borrowed from the NBA of the 1940s. Although it placed a few teams in large media markets (New York, Los Angeles, Dallas–Fort Worth, Washington, Pittsburgh), a majority of its teams were in smaller cities. It also had a distinctly southern flavor, with teams in Greensboro-Charlotte, Louisville, Memphis, Miami, and San Antonio, as well as Dallas.[2]

Among the more interesting innovations of the ABA league, along with the three-point shot and the red-white-and-blue basketball, was the concept of the regional franchise. All sports teams have occasionally played home games in secondary cities, such as the Green Bay Packers playing in Milwaukee or the old Brooklyn Dodgers playing in Jersey City. The practice was quite common in basketball; indeed, Wilt Chamberlain's awesome 100-point game was played in Hershey, Pennsylvania, not Philadelphia, the home of his team, the Warriors. But the ABA made what was an occasional practice a policy, for it had several teams with no distinct home base.[3] The idea seemed sound enough—to combine basketball's popularity in smaller cities with the advantage of having a large population base, especially to increase the league's television audience but also to sell more tickets. Unfortunately, this strategy did not work. By the time the ABA merged with the NBA in 1976, its remaining six teams had a fixed home base (New York, Denver, Indianapolis, San Antonio, Louisville, and Salt Lake City).

The ABA was not a financial success, but it was not the disaster the ABL had been a few years before. In the ABA's early years its teams suffered average cash-flow losses of a few hundred thousand dollars a year, and even these were buffered by the favorable tax treatment of sports franchises at the time.[4] The resulting losses were only a little larger than the amounts reported by the NBA expansion franchises of the era—except, of course, for Milwaukee, which drafted Kareem Abdul-Jabbar in its second season in 1969–70 and promptly became a financial success.

The ABA teams, viewed as substitutes for expansion franchises, were relatively good investments. In fact, the objective of any new league usually is to force a merger with the established league. Even the ABL, led by a meteoric Cleveland owner named George Steinbrenner, almost succeeded in getting a few of its teams into the NBA after its first year. Steinbrenner tried to force the issue by signing the outstanding college player of 1962, Jerry Lucas, to play for his Cleveland ABL team, but merger negotiations eventually broke down, and shortly before the ABL's second season Steinbrenner folded his club, much to everyone's surprise and the NBA's delight.

The ABA came far closer to pulling off the merger strategy early in its existence, for at the end of the 1969–70 season—the ABA's third—the two leagues announced a merger agreement that would have preserved all teams in both leagues. Unfortunately for the owners, the players in the two leagues realized that they were benefitting from interleague competition, and their union filed an antitrust suit to block the merger. Facing years of litigation with a doubtful outcome, the leagues immediately petitioned Congress for the same antitrust exemption for a merger that baseball had enjoyed since 1922 and that football had acquired only a few years earlier to permit the merger between the NFL and the American Football League (AFL).

But then the ABA owners received their second bad break. The chairman of the Senate Subcommittee on Antitrust and Monopoly, Phil Hart of Michigan, had to excuse himself from participation in the legislative process. Through marriage he was connected to the owner of the Detroit Tigers, and he regarded himself as facing a conflict of interest. This handed the gavel to Senator Sam Ervin of North Carolina, who was unsympathetic to almost any antitrust exemption (except, of course, in the case of marketing orders for tobacco) and to the way sports entrepreneurs treated players. The result was that the ABA and the NBA were not permitted to merge until they obtained the acquiescence of the players, an event that was not to happen for another six years.

Had the ABA achieved merger in 1970 when the deal was cut, or in 1971 after passage of a congressional antitrust exemption, it would have reaped a significant financial benefit. The teams that had been formed in the ABA's first year had paid a $25,000 entry fee and had suffered annual cash losses of about $300,000 thereafter. To merge with the NBA all ABA teams would have been required to pay an entry fee with a present value of perhaps

$100,000.[5] For this price, each of the original owners would have acquired NBA franchises that were stronger than the NBA expansion teams of the early 1970s. These expansion teams were priced by the NBA at $1.8 million and faced projected annual losses of about $500,000 for about two years until they could gain respectable playing strength. Thus the cost of a healthy expansion franchise in the NBA in 1970 or 1971 was close to $3 million, but the ABA teams could have joined for about $1 million.

When the merger did take place, in 1976, the four teams that joined the NBA each paid $3.2 million to the league and equal shares of $1.5 million to the other two ABA teams, which were not permitted to join. By this time NBA franchises were more valuable than they had been in 1970. Even at this higher entry cost, though, the ABA teams entered the NBA at roughly the same cost as the going price for established teams.

The blocking of the merger by the players was doubly costly to the owners of the ABA. The six-year delay tripled the number of years of financial losses a team had to sustain before it could gain NBA membership. Moreover, it preserved competition, which meant higher player salaries than would have been the case had a merger been consummated earlier. Obviously, events proved that entry was not a bonanza for the ABA. Nonetheless, even after losing several million dollars each season for nine seasons and paying several million more to merge, a decade after the merger the four former ABA franchises were worth upwards of $50 million—a sum that no doubt exceeded the initial expectations of the two pick-up basketball players who had organized the league in 1967.

Financial Performance

In any given season NBA teams divide into three categories. At the bottom are the teams that do not make the playoffs, usually do poorly at the gate, and roughly break even or experience small losses. Eight teams have mediocre records and make the playoffs but lose in the first or second round. These teams make a small profit. The remaining eight teams are the elite. They draw well during the regular season, appear frequently on television, and benefit from several home playoff games. These teams are quite profitable, some of them highly so.

Within the upper echelon of NBA teams is the legendary Boston Celtics. This team's financial performance during the 1980s demonstrates that the Celtics are a highly profitable organization (see Table 1.2). Their operating income (revenues less direct costs, not including interest and amortization) grew rapidly, averaging over $5 million per year during the 1980s. The Celtics' revenue approximately doubled in six years (1981–87). Because the Celtics sell out virtually every game, this growth came primarily from in-

Table 1.2 Summary of Financial Statements of the Boston Celtics, 1981–87
(Figures in Millions of Dollars)

Item	1981–82	1982–83	1983–84	1984–85	1985–86	1986–87
Revenues						
Regular season	8.6	10.7	12.5	14.9	18.6	16.3
Playoffs (net)	.7	.6	1.7	1.8	1.8	2.8
Expenses						
Direct cost	6.7	7.8	9.7	11.1	11.9	10.7
Amortization	.4	.4	3.0	3.0	3.1	2.0
Interest	1.5	1.0	1.0	.8	.5	.0
Pretax profits	.9	2.2	.6	1.7	4.8	6.5
Operating income	2.8	3.6	4.6	5.5	8.4	8.5
Finish	lost C.C.[a]	lost 2nd Rd	L.C.[b]	C.C.	L.C.	C.C.

Sources: Prospectus of Boston Celtics Limited Partnership, 1986, and Boston Celtics, *Annual Report,* 1987.
Note: Playoff revenues are net of player shares.
[a]Conference championship/conference champion.
[b]League champion.

creases in ticket prices and rapid growth in revenues from broadcasting. Although player costs, which constitute most of the team's direct costs, have also increased rapidly, they have not kept pace with income. Additionally, amortization of player contracts, which accounts for nearly all of the amortization expense, shelters a significant amount of the Celtics' profits from taxation. During 1981–87 the value of the tax savings from amortization was more than half the total amount taken for amortization (considering both federal and state taxes); after 1987, however, these tax savings fell to slightly less than half that amount. When the Celtics were reorganized in 1983–84, the amortization amount increased substantially; the change in ownership structure enabled the team to revalue its investment in players and to begin anew the amortization of player contracts.

The financial statements of the Celtics are not typical for the entire league, but neither are they unmatched. The handful of teams that in any given year are a serious threat to win the league championship would most likely show a similar performance. Indeed, the Celtics are probably not the most successful franchise in the league; that honor probably belongs to the Los Angeles Lakers, although that team's financial performance is not known because its records are not public.

More detailed estimates of the 1987–88 financial performance of NBA teams in each of the three categories described earlier show, on average, an approximate positive cash flow of a few million dollars (see Table 1.3). The teams also benefit from what remains of the sports tax loophole. The dif-

Table 1.3 Estimated Financial Performance of NBA Teams, 1987–88 (Millions of Dollars)

	Type of Team		
Item	Weak	Average	Strong
Revenues			
Regular season games	4.8	8.3	13.0
Playoff games	.0	1.5	3.0
Broadcasting	2.6	3.2	7.0
Other	.2	.3	.5
Total	7.6	13.3	23.5
Expenses			
Team	3.7	5.5	8.5
Game	1.1	1.3	1.8
Rent	.6	1.5	2.4
Sales	.2	.3	.5
Playoffs	.0	.7	1.5
Gen. & adm.	.9	1.4	2.8
Total	6.5	10.7	17.5
Operating profit	1.1	2.8	6.0
Player amortization	2.0	2.5	4.0
Interest	.3	.5	1.0
Book profit	-1.2	-0.2	1.0

Note: A weak team has an average attendance of 400,000; an average team, an attendance of 600,000 (including playoffs); a strong team, an attendance of 750,000 (including playoffs). Average ticket prices range from $12 to $20 for the regular season, and average playoff prices are $30 per ticket. Team expenses include salaries of players and coaches; game expenses include travel to away games. Rent is assumed to be 15 percent of the gate, even if the team owns its arena, for comparison purposes. General and administrative includes legal costs and salaries of front-office personnel, including the salaries of owners as corporate officers and those of other officers. Player amortization assumes that the team was sold within the past few years for between $20 and $40 million, that half of this amount was allocated to player contracts, and that these contracts were amortized over five years. In fact, some teams have been sold for much more. The perpetually strong teams, such as the Lakers and the Celtics, are worth closer to $100 million. Interest expense arises from the owners' practice of using loans rather than equities to invest in a team and of using a team as collateral for other investments. Actual amounts vary greatly but are generally larger for more successful teams because they are better collateral.

ferences in revenues among teams are greater than the variance in their attendance records would suggest. Most successful teams are likely to find attendance constrained by arena capacity and to charge substantially higher prices in response. In addition, most teams have flexible local broadcasting arrangements under which more games are likely to appear on television, free or pay, if the team is a winner. The only revenue source that is equal across teams is fees for national television broadcasts. In the late 1980s teams received about $2.5 million each from this source.

On the expenditure side, teams typically pay about 15 percent of their revenues in arena rentals, assuming the normal case, in which the team does not own its home court. Team costs refer to salaries and benefits for players and coaches, including the current payments for deferred compensation and to injured or retired players to whom the team still has a contractual obligation. Game costs include all other expenditures on the game, including travel. The principal cost associated with the playoffs, aside from rent, is the share of playoff revenues that goes to players, which is a little less than half.

General and administrative (G&A) costs refer to the front-office staff, legal costs, and other expenditures unrelated to staging games. This item includes the salaries of owners who also hold managerial positions, such as Arnold "Red" Auerbach of the Celtics, a part-owner who is also paid $250,000 per year as its president (and who will receive approximately $120,000 a year after his retirement in 1992 until his death or the death of his wife, whichever occurs later). In general, G&A expenses vary greatly among teams according to their financial success. Owners of the more successful teams tend to pay themselves substantially higher executive salaries than owners of struggling franchises; hence the distinction between administrative costs and profits is blurry.

As with the Celtics, the entire league has experienced rapid growth in revenues during the 1980s. Initially the major factor in the growth of gate receipts was increasing attendance. In 1970 NBA teams averaged about 8,000 fans per game; a decade later average attendance was up 50 percent. In the 1980s, however, the primary source of growth in gate receipts was rising ticket prices. As more teams reach the point of selling all or most of their good seats on a season-ticket basis, they are in a stronger position to increase ticket prices.

In addition, television broadcasting revenues are growing rapidly. Under the leaguewide contracts in force in the late 1980s, the twenty-three established NBA teams shared revenues from national broadcasts. Revenues from CBS totaled $39 million in 1986–87 and $47.5 million in 1989–90, and revenues from the Turner Broadcasting Company averaged $12.5 million per year for 1986–87 and 1987–88. Local off-air and pay-cable revenues, which are not shared across teams, are growing even more rapidly. Teams with aggressive local marketing, such as the Celtics, Lakers, and Knicks, have seen these revenues increase by several hundred percent in the 1980s. The Celtics, for example, received approximately $5.7 million from local radio, television, and cable contracts in 1986–87, about five times as much as they received in 1980–81.

Players have generally shared in basketball's revenue bonanza. In 1987–88 the average player salary was over $400,000, and the best players earned over $2 million. The median salary was around $250,000, and the minimum was $75,000. For the 1989–90 season the minimum was $160,000 for players chosen in the first draft round and $110,000 for all others. In the mid-1980s player salaries grew much more slowly than revenues and in 1986–87 accounted for only 51 percent of revenues. Not only was this figure the lowest in two decades, it was actually lower than the minimum required by the collective bargaining agreement with the players' union. An issue in the 1987–88 negotiations was the exact magnitude of the shortfall and the appropriate means for increasing player compensation.

Nonetheless, basketball players remain the best-paid team athletes. Even after the merger of the NBA and ABA reduced competition, the average player salary continued to grow rapidly, tripling in the first ten years after the merger. No doubt owing to the small number of people involved in a basketball franchise, the sport has managed to make all of its principals wealthy: owners, players, and coaches.

Basketball Product Markets

Professional basketball has two primary product markets: ticket sales for games and the sale of broadcasting rights. In addition, it operates in a few other, less important, product markets such as parking, concessions, programs, and endorsements and other uses of team logos, as well as various media productions such as season highlight films and team guides. Media productions will be largely ignored here, primarily because they are affected by essentially the same factors as those affecting the market for gate attendance. The league also operates in a third important market: the sale of franchises to play in the league.

A basketball team participates in both local and national product markets. At home, it tries to sell tickets to its games and broadcast rights to local radio, television, and pay-cable outlets. Naturally, it plays games in all the other cities in the league (and perhaps a few others) and participates in the sale of television rights to off-air and cable networks.

Like all other sports leagues, the NBA sells a leaguewide package of national broadcasting rights and divides the revenues equally among all teams. The sale of local broadcasting rights to games not shown on national television and the promotion of local games are the exclusive responsibility of the home team. In return, it keeps all of the revenues; the NBA does not practice revenue sharing except with regard to national broadcasting. One consequence is that the teams within the league exhibit wide variability in total revenues; the two or three strongest teams receive about five times as much revenue as the two or three weakest. This difference is far greater than the one in football, and considerably greater than the one in baseball. It also creates important incentives for owners. Because a team in a smaller market derives no benefit from its sold-out games in Los Angeles, Detroit, Boston, or Chicago, it must work especially hard on developing its home market. The importance of home gate receits explains why basketball franchises are substantially more prone than teams in other sports to move from city to city and why owners compete intensively for the best free-agent players.

The success of teams in a league depends on two categories of factors: those that affect the league in general, and those that affect an individual team. (These do, of course, overlap somewhat, but this separation is analytically useful.) The most important factors for a league are its absolute quality, its competitive balance, its reputation for integrity of play, and the match of its fans, in numbers and demographics, to the audience that advertisers most want to reach through national television. For a team, absolute and relative quality of play are also important, as is the size of the market (in terms of active basketball fans) in which it plays its home games.

The absolute quality of play refers to the overall quality of a team and to the presence of superstars in the league—the great players of an era whose athletic abilities attract fans beyond their contributions to the outcome of games. In order for a league to have "major league" status, its fans must believe that the quality of play in the league is roughly equal to, or exceeds, the quality of play in any other league. Similarly, a single team cannot confer major league status on itself; it must be a member of a group of teams with that status.

The importance of absolute quality is best illustrated by the differences in attendance records and TV audience ratings for major and minor league teams in otherwise similar market circumstances. Typically when a large-city team in a particular sport moves from minor to major status by relocation or expansion, attendance at professional games in that sport increases by approximately a factor of ten. For example, a good minor league baseball team will draw 200,000 to 300,000 fans, but when a major league team moves in, it will draw two million. Of course, basketball has few minor league teams, but some Continental Basketball Association (CBA) teams play in cities that used to have NBA franchises, cities that are candidates for a future expansion franchise, or cities that are comparable in size to the smaller cities in the league. Yet crowds of a few hundred to a few thousand are the standard pattern for the CBA, compared to average crowds of about 13,000 in the NBA during 1987–88.

Historically, convincing fans that a new league has major league status has proven to be very difficult. Typically actual parity in play occurs several years before parity is acknowledged by fans. Consider the case of the American Basketball Association. The public widely regarded the ABA as considerably weaker than the NBA until its demise through merger, and its teams consistently did much more poorly financially than NBA teams, especially in terms of broadcasting contracts, but also at the gate.[6] Yet the four ABA teams that merged with the NBA in 1976 did quite well as a group (see Table 1.4).

The Denver Nuggets'1976–77 record was tied with Philadelphia's for the second best in the NBA, and San Antonio's record was the same as that of the fabled Boston Celtics. Two additional ABA teams were excluded from the NBA, the Utah Rockies and the Kentucky Colonels. Both were weaker than the other four but featured several players who later went on to become stars in the NBA, such as Artis Gilmore, Maurice Lucas, and Moses Malone. Thus events after the merger indicate that the six ABA franchises still operating in 1975–76 were within the range of quality of their NBA competitors. Indeed, a Denver–San Antonio contest in 1975 was probably roughly comparable to, say, a Philadelphia-Washington game, matching the quality of the second-place finishers in the Atlantic and Central divisions; however, the ABA game would have garnered only a fraction of the revenue earned from the NBA game, and the latter would have been far more likely to receive exposure on national television.[7]

The relative quality of teams is also important in determining team and league financial success. In general, the size of the crowd in attendance at a game and the size of a game's television audience are governed by two somewhat conflicting factors: the closeness of the match between the teams and the likelihood that the ultimate victor will be the team that most fans support. For a team that derives nearly all its revenues from home gate receipts and local broadcasts, these factors create an incentive to have a club that is slightly better than the opposition. For a league, the incentives are more complex: to ensure that the teams do not differ too much in quality, but also to ensure that, over the long run, teams with a larger number of fans (e.g., those in larger cities) will tend to have better teams.

Table 1.4 Records of ABA Teams after Merger, 1976–77

Team	Won-Lost Record	Finish
Denver Nuggets	50–32 (.610)	1st, Midwest Division
San Antonio Spurs	44–38 (.537)	3rd, Central Division
Indiana Pacers	36–46 (.439)	5th, Midwest Division
New York Nets	22–60 (.268)	5th, Atlantic Division
All four teams (total)	152–176 (.463)	—

The relationship between team quality and attendance is illustrated by the following comparison of attendance and won-lost records for the 1987–88 NBA season. Of the ten top teams in terms of attendance, eight won more than 60 percent of their games, and only one, the Knicks, won fewer than half. Of the ten teams ranking at the bottom in attendance, only two won more than half of their games, Seattle and Milwaukee. The bottom three had an aggregate won-lost percentage of .293, whereas the top three had a won-lost percentage of .675.

Teams in larger cities tend to draw more fans.[8] This tendency is most clearly revealed by comparing the attendance data for teams with essentially the same won-lost records who played in cities of different sizes. Table 1.5 compares the won-lost records of NBA teams for the 1987-88 season, showing all circumstances in which two teams from areas with very different population sizes finished with essentially the same record (that is, their won-lost records differed by less than .03). Indiana did very well, given its population base, and Detroit drew far better than one would predict. Indiana's good showing probably reflects the high interest of the state's public in basketball; Detroit's is due to the fact that the Pistons played in the cavernous Silverdome, where they sold a very large number of bad seats at low prices. But overall, all else equal, the data indicate that playing in one of the larger markets gives a team an attendance boost of between 25 and 35 percent over a team in one of the small markets.

Of course, the effects of population and relative team quality are confounded in the attendance data because the better teams tend to be located in the larger cities. Of the ten leading NBA teams in terms of won-lost percentage in 1987–88, six were located in the ten largest metropolitan areas. Of the remaining thirteen teams in the NBA, six were in the ten largest areas, two of which were second teams in New York and Los Angeles. Hence, in six of the ten largest cities with NBA teams, a home team was a

Table 1.5 Attendance Differences by City Size, 1987–88

Team in Larger City	Team in Smaller City	Won-Lost Records	Attendance Difference
Detroit	Denver	.659	+545,524
Chicago	Atlanta	.610	+145,440
Dallas	Portland	.646	+175,286
Houston	Utah	.56/7	+177,082
New York	Indiana	.463	+84,433
New York	Washington, D.C.	.463	+153,376
Washington, D.C.	Indiana	.463	−68,943
Philadelphia	Indiana	.44/6	+10,794
Dallas	Denver	.65/6	+174,711

serious contender for the NBA championship (the worst of the ten best teams were Utah and Houston). In the remaining eleven cities with NBA teams, four teams were serious contenders (the best of the bottom thirteen teams were Seattle, Cleveland, and Milwaukee). Thus fans in the largest cities were about twice as likely to have a home team in contention for the championship than fans in smaller cities.[9]

The patterns evident from the 1987–88 standings data are by no means atypical of the history of basketball.[10] Of the 43 NBA championships from 1947 through 1989, 31 have been won by teams in the top ten metropolitan areas. Only five cities have been home to teams that won more than a single championship: Boston (16), Los Angeles (6), Minneapolis (5), Philadelphia (4), and New York (2). Four of these are among the nation's largest urban areas. The fifth, Minneapolis, was abandoned by its team, the Lakers, for more populous Los Angeles. The major anomaly is Chicago, a large city where teams have failed financially twice, and which has been host to precisely one conference champion in the twenty-seven years it has had a team.[11] Only a little less unusual is Detroit, whose team did not win a conference championship until 1988 and an NBA title until 1989. The NBA team in Dallas, a top-ten metropolitan area, has never won a conference championship, but it has only been in the NBA since 1980–81. Except for Dallas, all top ten cities have seen their teams win at least one conference championship and, except for Chicago and Houston, a league championship.

Why do big cities have better teams? One reason is the attendance effect, which causes better entrepreneurs to move to larger cities where their talents will be more highly rewarded. The historical pattern of team movement in the NBA bears out this tendency: the Atlanta Hawks were originally in the Tri-Cities, with intermittent stops in Milwaukee and St. Louis; the 76ers were originally in Syracuse; the Pistons began in Fort Wayne.[12] San Diego has lost two teams, one to Houston and the other to Los Angeles.

The second reason for big-city dominance is the incentive created by national broadcasting. Since teams in big cities have more fans who will watch their games on television, the audience for national telecasts is maximized if big cities have strong teams. Consequently, when leagues contemplate policies that affect the location and strength of teams, they will tend to favor big cities. For example, leagues could ensure approximate competitive balance by prohibiting trades and sales of player contracts or by enforcing exactly the same salary cap on every team. In practice they do not because to do so would be economically irrational for all owners, not just those in the best markets.

The importance of this point is widely misunderstood and deserves emphasis because of the lip service paid by the press and sports management to "parity" in a league. In reality, parity is unlikely, for it is not in the financial interest of a league. Instead, leagues want sufficient uncertainty of outcomes to keep all fans interested—a far cry from having every team have an equal chance of winning a league championship. A good team will do better financially and contribute more to the value of a league's national broadcast package if it is in a big city. Even in the absence of explicit sharing of local revenues, as is the case in the NBA, teams in smaller markets will derive financial benefits from the success of teams in the big markets by sharing in fatter national broadcast packages and being able to make lucrative player contract sales. The teams in the big markets periodically buy contracts for established players in order to retain their competitive edge; the revenues from these sales constitute an indirect form of revenue sharing for the selling teams.

Of course, even taking into account these benefits, it is still more profitable to be a big-city team. The NBA's avoidance of sharing local revenues heightens the desirability of a big-city location. It is no surprise that a team in San Diego violated league rules by relocating in Los Angeles, thereby invading the home territory of the Lakers.

League practices regarding franchise locations remain in something of a legal limbo. As in other leagues, an NBA team must win the approval of an overwhelming majority of league members to move, and if a team moves to a city already occupied by another league member, it must indemnify the incumbent for diluting the market. For example, when the ABA and NBA merged, the Nets were required to indemnify the Knicks for playing in the New York metropolitan area.

The legality of these rules is in doubt and remains unclear. In litigation involving the unauthorized moves of the San Diego Clippers to Los Angeles in 1984 and the Oakland/Los Angeles Raiders to Los Angeles in 1982, the courts ruled that franchise relocation policies must be governed by a "rule of reason." This ruling is based upon the obvious conflicting values behind these policies. On the one hand, all members of a league have a legitimate interest in the location of other members. The league's structure determines its value to national broadcasters, and the financial security of each team is important to ensure that competition will be relatively even and that teams will not disrupt the league by folding in the middle of the season.[13] On the other hand, requiring the payment of indemnities for established teams is blatantly anticompetitive, as is giving one team a say in a vote as to whether another team will be permitted to become its competitor.

As yet, no clear legal signals have come from the courts on where the boundary stands between legitimate protection of leaguewide interests and anticompetitive restrictions. Meanwhile, after winning a lower-court decision, the Los Angeles, né San Diego, Clippers settled their litigation with the NBA. They sacrificed their share of the entry-fee revenues from the

NBA's 1988 expansion (about $3 million), but the league permitted them to stay in Los Angeles.

The NBA expansion of 1988–89 suggests that the league believes it has solved the problem of unauthorized relocations. Presumably if it did not, it would have been reluctant to let in four new teams, all in relatively small cities, for the reason that established franchises would be in danger of their future unauthorized relocation. A few years down the road, an athletically successful but financially troubled expansion team might copy the San Diego precedent and move in on an established team—especially a weaker team in a good market. For example, during most of the 1980s the New York Knicks were weak or mediocre, owing in part to a string of devastating injuries. In such a circumstance, a strong but poorly drawing team in Miami or Minneapolis might go head to head against the Knicks in New York. (Why only the San Diego Clippers have tried this tactic, and why, when they did, they picked as their new competitor the Los Angeles Lakers, the most successful franchise of the 1980s, remains a mystery.)

The future for NBA expansion is uncertain. The remaining potential franchise sites are in either small cities or large metropolises that already have one or two teams. In either case, the financial risks of expansion are high. The success of the new expansion teams will no doubt have a major effect on the league's assessment of the viability of further expansion. Moreover, NBA owners are likely to face a declining incentive to expand if national broadcasting revenues continue to climb. Each expansion team has a claim to the common pool of national broadcast revenues. After the 1988 and 1989 expansions twenty-seven teams divided approximately $60 million from national broadcasts. Adding a new team, therefore, would cost teams over $2 million annually in revenues. If broadcast revenues in basketball approach those for baseball (which would mean a fivefold increase per team), the revenue sacrifice for old teams from further expansion would be about $10 million per year.[14]

To see how this potential for lost revenues affects the ardor of existing teams for further NBA expansion, we need to compare the feasible level of expansion fees with the capitalized value of the revenues these teams would lose from further dividing national broadcast revenues. The 1988–89 expansion teams each paid approximately $36 million for an NBA franchise. Suppose that basketball teams expect that, correcting for inflation, one share of national broadcasting is likely to rise to $5 million in the early 1990s and thereafter increase only at the rate of inflation. Assuming that basketball owners use a 10-percent real rate of discount, the lost revenues from a twenty-eighth expansion franchise would have a present value at the time of expansion of $50 million. Obviously the existing owners would not be willing to expand at $36 million per team at the cost of a $50-million revenue sacrifice. Perhaps an expansion team will sell for as much as $50 million in the early 1990s, but obviously, as the importance of shared broadcasting revenue increases, the likelihood of further expansion is reduced.

The Market for Players

The most important input to professional basketball is, of course, its players. In the 1970s basketball teams paid more than 70 percent of their revenues in salaries and benefits to players. Arena rental accounted for a little more than 10 percent, and all other costs totaled about 15 percent. In the 1980s the players' share of revenues fell to a little more than half, but it was still the highest of the major-league sports.

Since the 1880s, all sports have adopted rules to limit competition among teams for the services of players. Basketball is no exception. Until the mid-1970s the NBA relied on a system of perpetual draft rights for rookies and an option/compensation system for veterans. In the first system, each rookie entering the sport who has any serious chance of making a team, let alone becoming a star, is assigned to a single team. The method of assignment is a draft in which each team, usually in inverse order of quality based on the previous season record, selects a player from the remaining pool of those eligible for the draft. The player must then sign his first contract with the team that selected him (or a team designated by the selecting team).

In the option/compensation system, a team can unilaterally renew a player's expired contract for one year, usually at the same salary that the player earned the previous year (although the details have differed through the years). After the so-called option year, a player is free to negotiate with another team, but if he signs with another team, his original club is entitled to compensation in the form of cash, draft rights, and other players, to be determined by the commissioner of basketball. Before the mid-1970s compensation awards were high in the NBA, so that teams did not bid aggressively for available players and normally would not sign a player unless a compensation arrangement had already been worked out with the player's former team.

The effect of these practices is to give each team a monopsony in its share of players in the league. This system depresses player salaries because it forces players either to accept one team's take-it-or-leave-it offer or else retire from the game. Because basketball players typically have no alternative occupations that are nearly as rewarding as professional basketball, they have no real choice other than to accept the team's offer. The monopsony system also prevents players from having much of a say about where they play. A player who does not like the city in which his team plays or the coaching staff there simply must endure. He does not have the choice to move elsewhere, even at a cut in pay.

Prior to the mid-1970s the only check on a team's monopsony power was competition from other basketball leagues. Brief interleague competition in the mid 1940s and early 1960s and durable competition with the ABA from 1967 to 1976 gave players an alternative to accepting their NBA offers. Although all the competing leagues used a rookie draft, the veterans in the NBA were generally fair game for any team in the fledgling league and vice versa.

The case of ABA competition is especially instructive. The league was durable and well managed, and ABA-NBA competition took place when basketball was growing rapidly in popularity. When the ABA was formed in 1966, the median salary in the NBA was approximately $20,000. Five years later, in 1971, it was $90,000, and five years after that, as the leagues merged in 1976, it was $140,000. The share of revenues going to players nearly doubled during this period.

As mentioned earlier, the two leagues were allowed to merge only after settling an antitrust suit brought against them by the National Basketball Players Association. The settlement softened the NBA rules against inter-team competition for veteran players without eliminating the monopsony power of teams. The rookie draft was retained, but players were permitted to become free agents, available to be signed by any team, if they did not sign with the drafting team within two years. The option clause for veteran players was removed immediately, but the compensation clause was only eliminated in 1980, when it was replaced by a ''right of first refusal'' provision.[15] This provision allows a player's old team to retain his services by matching the offer the player accepted from another team.

In 1983 the NBA adopted the salary cap. In general, this cap provides both a minimum and maximum amount each team is allowed to pay in total salaries. The minimum guarantees that 53 percent of all league revenues (with some minor corrections) will be paid in player salaries. The maximum for a team is also 53 percent of average team revenues, but it is subject to numerous exceptions that push it higher.[16] In addition, a team can always retain a veteran player by matching a salary offered by another team, and it can always replace a retired or injured veteran by hiring a replacement. If a player retires, is released, or is injured, a team can pay his replacement 50 percent of his salary regardless of the cap. If a player is lost through trade or free agency, the team can pay 100 percent of his salary to his replacement.

The 1988 agreement between the owners and players changed the system once again. The salary cap was retained, but it was agreed that the right of first refusal will be phased out. In addition, the rookie draft was reduced to three rounds in 1988 and to two rounds thereafter.

The salary cap is an especially complicated means for controlling player salaries because of the subtle incentives it creates. Most obviously, a team whose total salary amount is at or above the cap cannot compete for high-quality players unless it first releases an expensive veteran. Even then, under the rules, releasing a player is worth only fifty cents on the dollar in terms of making funds available to bid for a replacement. For these reasons, only teams with relatively low salaries are likely to compete for most free agents. Presumably these teams are also weaker; hence it would appear that weaker teams have a good shot at strengthening themselves in the free-agent market. In practice, this possibility is vitiated by two facts: a player's current team is permitted to match any external salary offer, and most players would rather stay with a good team than switch to a weak one. Thus the salary cap serves more to prevent the wealthy teams from competing for each other's players—and thereby to suppress salaries—than to help out the weak teams in the league.

The more subtle aspect of the salary cap is its effect on bidding strategy. If a team has a total salary amount below the cap, another team can force it to reach or go above the cap by offering a pay increase to a star player who is certain to have the offer matched by his current team. This maneuver diminishes the ability of the team retaining the player to operate in the free-agent market or to sign a rookie draft pick, for once total salaries exceed the cap, a team cannot offer a rookie or a veteran free agent more than the minimum salary or half of the salary of the player released to make room for the new player on the roster, whichever is larger. Thus an effective means to prevent a competitor from improving its quality is to bid up the price of its veterans until the cap is reached.

The most important change in 1988 was the agreement to phase out the right of first refusal, which had enabled teams to keep players who would have preferred to accept pay cuts to change teams.[17] Most obviously, eliminating this clause enables a player to live where he wants or to play for a team that he especially likes. More subtly, it places constraints on the treatment of players by a team. A team with an especially obnoxious owner or coach, or a team that provides poor medical attention for injured players, can now lose its players regardless of the money it offers. Finally, elimination of the right of first refusal should make teams more willing to bid for free agents. Since their probability of success will be higher, they will be more willing to negotiate.

Nonetheless, the retention of the rookie draft system and the salary cap clause will depress player salaries below the levels that would develop in a free market. The interesting question that arises from this fact is why the players agree to such provisions. In the NBA, as in other sports, the courts handed the players the right to complete free agency in the mid-1970s. The *Robertson* case held that the player draft, uniform contract, and reserve clause were in violation of federal antitrust law. Had no collective bargaining agreement been signed, the players could have had a complete free market: no salary cap, no rookie draft, no compensation system, no right of first refusal. But the players have not pushed for complete free agency.

The standard explanation for why players would be willing to limit their rights is that restrictions on competition among teams for players benefit the players by improving the competitive balance among teams in a league. The essence of the argument is that with the completely free movement of players, all the stars would play for a few teams in the best markets (or for owners willing to spend the most). The rest of the teams would be perpetual doormats, paying low salaries and perhaps even failing. By agreeing to restrictions on the competition for players, goes the argument, players are advancing their own interests by improving fan interest in the game and preserving well-paid jobs for all.

The preceding argument is both wrong as a matter of economic theory and disproved by the history of competition in basketball. Restrictions on competition for players lower player salaries, but they do not prevent the movement of players among teams through trades, sales of player contracts, and the trade or sale of draft choices. If one team values a player more than his current team, it will acquire him by offering a higher salary if the player market is competitive or by striking a deal with the player's current team if the market is not.

To test whether the extent of competitive balance in a sports league is affected by the degree of competition in the player market, competitive balance must first be measured. One test is the extent to which the same teams persist in winning. In the NBA it is apparent that the Celtics and the Lakers have managed to be the strongest teams, decade after decade, regardless of the state of the player market. These two teams have won two-thirds of the league's championships during its forty-year history; they have won multiple championships in every decade since the 1950s. Obviously their ability to dominate the league was unaffected by whether the NBA's teams were safe, secure monopsonies (as was the case from about 1950 until the mid-1960s) or whether they were involved in some form of competition for players, either within the league or with teams from another league.

If anything, these teams were less dominant during the period of the NBA's competition with the ABA than they were before or after. From the 1948–49 season, when Minneapolis entered the league, until the 1966–67 season, when the ABA commenced play, either the Celtics or the Lakers won the NBA championship in fourteen of this period's nineteen seasons, or more than 70 percent of the time. Between the 1967–68 and 1975–76 seasons they won five of nine championships. In the 1980s, when the salary cap rules and right of first refusal were in force, the Celtics and the Lakers won all but two championships.

A second measure of competitive balance is the difference between the records of the best and worst teams, calculated as the difference in their won-lost percentage. An analysis of player-market competition and the won-lost spread throughout the history of the NBA shows that the league has never departed for long from a won-lost spread of between .4 and .6, regardless of the state of competition among teams (see Figure 1.1). The most balanced period was in the early 1950s, when the league was a monopoly; however, the primary cause of this balance was the league's contraction. The NBA shrank from seventeen to eight members by shedding its weak teams; those that remained were the best among the original group, and so for a few years the league remained relatively well balanced. By 1957, though, the historical dominance of a few teams and the competitive imbalance within the league—in which the best team wins about 75 percent of the time while the worst team wins about 25 percent—had reestablished themselves despite the fact that the league remained a monopoly. In addition, the average spread for each period of changing market competition demonstrates the absence of any relationship between competitive balance and player-market competition (see Table 1.6). Again, with the exception of the 1950s, there is no discernible difference between the periods.[18]

Still another test of competitive balance is the extent to which any team remains a doormat for a long period. One version of this test is to examine the difference between the number of teams that never win a championship and the theoretical number that would not win if the NBA were evenly balanced. This test is more complicated than the previous two. It involves calculating the probability that a team never wins, which in turn depends strongly on the number of teams in the league (see Table 1.7). In an eight-team league few teams will go winless in a decade, but in the present NBA of 27 teams, most will not be able to win a championship even once per decade.

Two periods of player-market competition are relevant in applying this test. In the first period, 1951–67, the NBA was relatively stable in size (8 to 11 teams), and the player markets were relatively monopsonized.[19] In the 1967–89 period the league averaged about 20 teams, and these teams either faced competition or limited free agency within the league. A comparison of the test results for each period shows that the more monopsonized period was freer of perpetual losers than the more competitive period (see Table 1.7); however, the difference is accounted for by the difference in the size of the league. In both periods, about twice as many teams are perpetual doormats as would be expected in a balanced league.

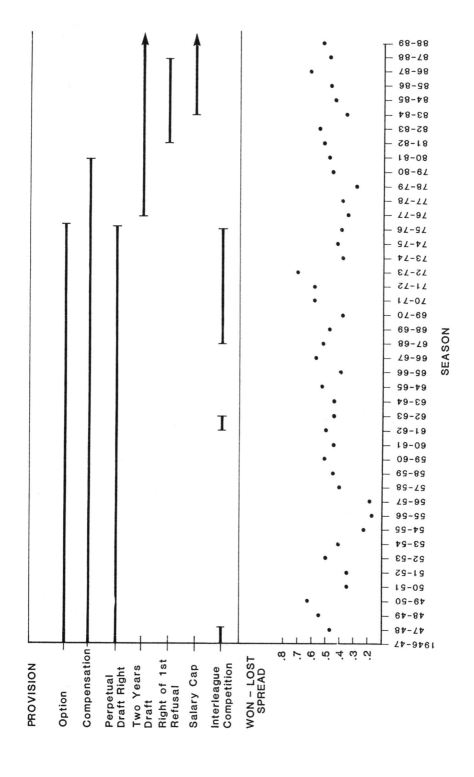

Table 1.6 The Relation between Won-Lost Spread and Player-Market Competition

Period	Years	Average Won-Lost Percentage		
		Best	Worst	Spread
Unstable competition	1946–47 to 49–50	74	19	55
Small monopsony	1950–51 to 60–61	67	29	38
Growth and monopsony	1961–62 to 66–67	76	25	51
ABA competition	1967–68 to 75–76	76	23	53
Merger, modest free agency	1976–77 to 82–83	73	23	50
Salary cap, right of first refusal	1983–84 to 88–89	78	24	54

The leaders of the NBA players' union are aware of the absence of any relation between monopsony in the player market and competitive balance in the league. Indeed, they have argued before Congress and in court that no significant connection exists between the two. Hence the traditional defense of player reservation systems cannot explain why, since winning the *Robertson* case, the union has been willing to allow restrictions on competition for players.

A more likely explanation is that the players and their union believe that they are able to obtain compensating benefits that outweigh the suppression of salaries arising from restrictions on competition for players. The union is a democratic organization in which the typical member is a veteran player who is not a star; stars are few, so they are outvoted, and rookies who will play in the future are unrepresented. Hence one would expect the union to acquiesce to policies that suppress salaries for rookies and stars if they are accompanied by benefits for journeymen ballplayers. Policies such as the rookie draft and restrictions on competition for dominant players are likely

Table 1.7 Actual Frequency and Theoretical Probability of a Team Failing to Win an NBA Championship, 1951–88

Period	Years	Actual Frequency[a]	Theoretical Chance[b]	Difference
More monopsonized	1951–67	.375	.168	.207
More competitive	1967–89	.550	.309	.241

[a]Calculated by first taking the difference between the average number of teams in the league during the period and the number of teams that had won at least one championship, and then dividing by the average number of teams during the period.

[b]Defined as the probability that a team in an equally balanced league of the average size of the NBA during the period could be without a championship for the entire period.

to be tolerated as long as a minimum salary is in force, for example, or financial benefits are equal for all players, regardless of their ability, such as fringe benefits and the players' share of playoff revenues.

Of course, the average players are limited in the extent to which they can use the union to produce a redistribution of income in their favor. If salaries of rookies and stars are depressed too much, a financial incentive is created for a new league to be formed that will bid away these players. Competitive entry is probably easier in basketball than in the other sports because it requires so little investment in fixed costs and because basketball arenas of reasonable size are available throughout the United States. Consequently, at least since the late 1960s, the status quo has been that the NBA cannot expect to persist in paying any group of players substantially less than their market values, whether by monopsonizing the player market generally or by agreeing to a contract with the union that redistributes a substantial fraction of the league's wage bill.

The relative ease of entry in basketball, therefore, provides an explanation for why labor relations in basketball have been more placid than in baseball or football: less is at stake in the negotiations, both between labor and management and within the union, than in the other two sports. For this reason, both sides have a lower expected payoff from trying to punish the other side through a strike or a lockout. Hence labor strife should be less frequent and less intense.

Conclusions

Most likely the 1990s will be the golden age of professional basketball. A long-term contract between the players and the owners ensures continuing stability in labor relations, and the growth in revenues from gate receipts and television contracts shows no signs of abating. Average revenues per team are quite likely to hit $20 million in the early 1990s. Moreover, because so few people are involved in staging basketball games, the average income per participant will be even more impressive than it has been so far.

The future structure of basketball has one major source of uncertainty: the number of NBA-calibre teams that will be playing at the turn of the century. The NBA is not likely to expand much beyond the additions of 1988 and 1989. As the league approaches thirty teams, the price of an expansion club is unlikely to compensate the existing owners for the resulting loss in their shares of national television revenues. Moreover, the current size of the NBA is large enough to necessitate the existence of a relatively permanent cohort of also-rans. On average, a team can expect to win an NBA championship three or four times per century, but for most teams the prospects are far worse if the Celtics and the Lakers continue to soak up more than half the championships. Can a league remain financially healthy if most teams will win zero or, at most, one championship in the entire lifetime of a fan? Or will long-suffering fans in Sacramento, New Jersey, Atlanta, and so on, lack the tenacity of Chicago Cubs fans and eventually lose interest?

If the NBA decides to stop at roughly its current size for either of the above reasons, one might expect a new league to form sometime during the next decade. To an outsider, NBA membership, forced by merger, is likely to remain attractive even after the existing teams have no financial incentive to accept further expansion. Moreover, with cable television outlets growing in number and now reaching more than half the homes in the United States, a new league has a good chance of generating some significant broadcasting revenue at the outset, unlike the two most recent entrants, the ABL and the ABA.

Even if the NBA continues to expand, entry may occur anyway. The established league is not likely to expand into markets where it already has a team, and in some cases these may be capable of supporting a franchise in a new league. Historically, new leagues have not fared well in cities that already have an established league team, but this tendency is not necessarily permanent. Growing demand and increasing cable penetration improve the prospects for additional teams in these markets, and new leagues are more likely to exploit this opportunity than the NBA.

The major factor working against entry is the extraordinarily high salaries that basketball players now command. To survive, a new league will have to sign its share of stars who earn $2–3 million. On the other hand, NBA salaries for journeymen players are far higher than these players could ever hope to earn outside of basketball, and there are many more journeymen players than there are roster slots in the NBA. Thus an entrant could be expected to have substantially lower salaries for most of its players than what the NBA is paying. A team in an entering league might expect to pay $2 million each for two highly visible players, a few hundred thousand apiece for two or three more good players, and another few hundred thousand for eight or nine additional players to round out the roster. With other costs, this produces a "nut" of around $6 million. If the team can get $1.5 million for broadcasting and draw 400,000 fans (10,000 per game) at $10 each, it will break even. Because these revenues are only about one-third of the likely average for the NBA in 1990 and are similar to the relative earnings of the ABA when it began, they do not seem wildly implausible. More than likely, a new generation of yuppie pick-up basketball players, maybe even in Orange County, will soon be making similar calculations, concluding that they, too, can live out their fantasy.

NOTES

1. The first intercollegiate basketball game, played much as the game is played today, saw Yale beat Pennsylvania, 32–10, on March 20, 1897.

2. The Memphis team eventually moved to New Orleans, and Washington played for awhile as the Virginia Squires, located primarily in Hampton–Newport News.

3. Carolina played its 1970–71 season in Greensboro (18 games), Raleigh (12 games), and Charlotte (12 games); the Florida team played 27 games in Miami, 6 in Jacksonville, 5 in Tampa, and 1 in West Palm Beach.

4. Around 1970 the marginal income tax rate for wealthy persons was 70 percent. The conventional practice in all sports at this time was to claim virtually the entire purchase price of a team as an investment in player contracts and then to claim "depreciation" of these contracts over the next few years. The net effect was that 70 percent of the purchase price of a team was paid by the federal government in tax reductions to owners. For details on the practices in basketball, see Roger G. Noll and Benjamin A. Okner, *The Economics of Professional Basketball,* Reprint 258 (Washington, D.C.: The Brookings Institution, 1972). Subsequent legislation has eliminated most, but not all, of this tax advantage. The Tax Reform Act of 1976 effectively placed a ceiling of 50 percent on the fraction of the sales price of a team that could be allocated to player contracts and depreciated. The 1986 tax reform, by reducing marginal tax rates to about half the 1970 level and by preventing the use of passive losses to offset active income, cut the tax advantage further.

5. Each ABA team was to pay $62,500 upon consummation of the deal, another $62,500 when the merged league signed a TV agreement (probably in the spring or summer of 1972), and $125,000 per year thereafter until the total reached $1,250,000. Because the ABA could expect much higher TV revenues after merger, the actual point of the $125,000 payment was to skew the sharing of revenues from national TV in favor of the NBA clubs.

6. In the early 1970s ABA teams drew about half as many fans as NBA teams and charged about half the price the NBA teams did for tickets. See Noll and Okner, *The Economics of Professional Basketball.*

7. Basketball does not differ from other sports in the extent to which new leagues tend to be underrated. Recall the astonishment of fans and sports writers when Joe Namath's Jets won Super Bowl III. A similar reaction took place when the Western League changed its name to the American League, declared itself to be a major baseball league, and promptly dominated the World Series for the next two decades, as well as outdrawing the senior circuit at the gate.

8. The tendency for teams in large cities to draw more fans and have better playing records has been documented for all sports. See, for example, Roger G. Noll, ed., *Government and the Sports Business* (Washington, D.C.: The Brookings Institution, 1974), especially chapters 2 and 4.

9. Obviously, drawing the line between contenders and also-rans is somewhat arbitrary; however, these basic findings remain unchanged if one adopts any reasonable standard. The reason is that the three best teams, Los Angeles, Detroit, and Boston, all played in very large metropolitan areas.

10. In 1988–89 the four semifinalists for the NBA championship were Chicago,

Detroit, Los Angeles, and Phoenix. Only the Phoenix team was from a smaller city.

11. The NBA is divided into two conferences, each of which has two divisions. Division champions are determined by won-lost records during the regular season. Conference and league champions are determined by the playoffs.

12. Only two moves are surprising—the two in which a team left a larger city for a considerably smaller one. The Chicago Zephyrs moved to Baltimore in 1963, and the Kansas City Kings moved to Sacramento in 1986. Baltimore later made a partial correction by moving to Washington, D.C. The Kings had made two prior moves in the predicted direction: Rochester to Cincinnati, and Cincinnati to Kansas City.

13. Both the NBA and the NFL also argued in court that the value of an expansion franchise was higher in Los Angeles than elsewhere, so that the other members of the league were damaged by the loss of potential expansion revenues when the Clippers and Raiders relocated. In reality, neither league has ever expanded into a city where it already had a team. (All multi-team markets are the result of mergers or relocations.) Moreover, neither league has ever charged different expansion fees for teams entering markets of different sizes. Not surprisingly, no court has ever bought the NBA-NFL argument.

14. An increase of such magnitude is not likely, but it is not implausible given basketball's rising audience ratings on television. It now attracts roughly as large an audience as baseball, but, of course, for fewer televised games. A significant increase in the number of games telecast might reduce the average audience and hence keep basketball's television rights fees below baseball's. Nonetheless, continued rapid growth in national broadcasting revenues is a virtual certainty for basketball.

15. The agreement was worded to convey the impression that the owners had never intended to use compensation as a means for preventing competition for free agents; however, as a practical matter, the agreement lowered compensation awards and led to much greater movement of free agents to new teams.

16. In the 1984–85 season most teams had a cap of either 53 percent of average team revenues or $3.6 million, whichever was greater, But the following specific exceptions were allowed: Los Angeles Lakers, $5.2 million; New Jersey Nets, $3.75 million; New York Knicks, $4.6 million; Philadelphia 76ers, $4.5 million; Seattle Supersonics, $4.6 million.

17. In sports with more experience with free agency, such as baseball and basketball, it is not unusual for a player to accept an offer other than the highest bid. The most extreme example is Andre Dawson, who accepted a 70-percent pay cut when he moved from the Montreal Expos to the Chicago Cubs; however, this move was no doubt partly strategic in that Dawson realized that he was building a case to prove owner collusion against free agency and could reasonably expect to get a subsequent arbitration award that would compensate him for his pay cut.

18. Even the 1950s are not statistically significantly different from the other periods, despite the effect of dropping off the weak teams.

19. Starting the 1951–67 period of monopsony earlier than 1951 would have added a large number of teams that had never won a championship and had folded by 1951. Expanding the period would have made it appear more unbalanced by

decreasing the frequency of winning teams by more than the theoretical chance of winning. The pre-1951 period in professional basketball was unlike any subsequent era because the sport was unstable in structure then and rapidly shrinking. This unstable period cannot accurately be incorporated into any other period.

Sport as TV Product: A Case Study of "Monday Night Football"

2

Joan M. Chandler

Commercial U.S. TV networks are in the business of making money. Examination of the effect television has had on sport is a relatively new enterprise, and writers are by no means in agreement, but no one would deny that the commercial TV networks can continue to televise only those sports that advertisers will subsidize.[1] Whether an audience is large or rather small ultimately matters less than that audience's demographic characteristics and the cost of producing particular events; golf tournaments, for instance, have perennially low ratings but are watched by the wealthy, and they are not nearly as costly to produce as football games. TV networks, then, must regard sport as they regard anything else they televise—as a product. The question TV executives must ask is, "Who can be persuaded to watch this sporting event, and what are they worth to advertisers?"

Once the decision has been made to televise a particular sporting event, however, TV executives are faced with a problem peculiar to sport: a sporting contest has no script, no program. A live football game cannot be made less one-sided by clipping, juxtaposing, or otherwise editing footage. No rehearsals are possible. And while the stadium crowd may be kept waiting while commercials are shown at home, the TV producers cannot make any team or player perform in any specific fashion—or even hurry the replay officials. TV executives and producers must therefore hope and pray that the intrinsic excitement of the event itself will hold an audience's interest.

Certainly a football game, like any other product, can be packaged. But in using football (or any sport) as a product, TV executives are tapping into emotions and attitudes associated not simply with the game they are telecasting but with all the games of that particular sport, and with perceptions of what sport itself means in the context of any viewer's life. A football game can be hyped and presented with great visual and oral skill, but if viewers have lost interest in the game itself or feel betrayed, no amount of fancy wrapping can persuade them to find out what's inside the box.

The case of "Monday Night Football" illustrates the paradoxical nature of sport as a TV product. For it is the very integrity of sport, resistant to manipulation by entrepreneurs, that gives it the properties of a successful TV product.[2]

In 1969 ABC was trailing CBS and NBC in prime time ratings. ABC had lost coverage of the American Football League to NBC in 1965; and while CBS and NBC claimed publicly that they had found football profits marginal, neither network was anxious to abandon Sunday afternoon football.[3] Commissioner Pete Rozelle, ever on the lookout for ways to expand the market for the NFL's product, had been trying for some years to persuade a network to televise football games in prime time. In the fall of 1970 the merger of the NFL and the AFL was to take place, entailing some franchise shifts and realignment of fan loyalty; ABC had little to lose, therefore, and much to gain by offering a prime time football package in June 1969. So eager was Rozelle to get the NFL into prime time that he committed the league to put on its best match-ups on Mondays, although the contracts with NBC and CBS for the traditional Sunday game had still to be negotiated.[4]

In 1969, then, we had what the demythologizers of sport have taught us to think of as a business-as-usual contract between the TV and football industries, in which both sets of negotiators regard sport simply as a marketable commodity. The NFL got an estimated $8.5 million a year for three years (later extended to four), and ABC got the chance to charge $65,000 a minute for commercials on Monday nights. By April 1970, 80 percent of this time had been sold; by May, it had all been sold. At the same time, sales connected with ABC's National Collegiate Athletic Association (NCAA) football had dropped off. CBS and NBC were having trouble with all their football packages.[5]

In spite of its good selling record, ABC left nothing to chance. Production costs had originally been estimated at $654,000 a game. But before the first game went on the air, ABC decided to use two production units—one for live coverage and one for technical effects such as instant replays—thus increasing the costs for each game by 25 percent.[6] Those cameras, directed by Chet Forte, focused on the human drama inherent in football, not only on its territorial and statistical qualities. The players under the helmets were made personal through the use of lingering close-ups. To introduce the first game between the New York Jets and the Cleveland Browns, Howard Cosell interviewed Joe Namath; then Cosell introduced a film montage of Don Meredith's playing days, showing "some of his most inglorious moments as a Dallas Cowboy."[7]

These introductions set the tone for "Monday Night Football"—it was to be entertaining. Roone Arledge personally chose Howard Cosell as one of the show's three (not two) commentators precisely *because* he was not a run-of-the-mill NFL announcer. Arledge stuck with Cosell, even when Henry Ford wrote to the ABC board of directors demanding his dismissal.[8] In that first year, Keith Jackson gave the game statistics Sunday afternoon fans had become accustomed to, while Cosell and Meredith played off each other's differences—the Jewish sophisticate and football ignoramus from New York versus the folksy former Dallas Cowboy quarterback from Texas.

ABC was also aware that women were far less enthusiastic viewers of Sunday football than men. Would women, tolerant of male weekend viewing, be prepared to change their habitual prime time weekday patterns and watch a football game instead? In July 1970 a booklet on football was designed especially for women, and ABC commissioned a special interview study of women to be carried out during the first game on September 21. In October the network was relieved to be able to publish results showing that three-quarters of the women interviewed did not mind the game's monopolizing the family TV set. ABC was then able to assure advertisers not only that football attracted the under-fifty male audience, but that their wives and girlfriends would not resent their Monday-night viewing.[9]

ABC's gamble paid off. In the week ending October 18, in the Nielson 70-market MultiNetwork Area, NFL football was ranked fourteenth of the top fifty prime-time shows.[10] By the end of the season Dandy Don had won an Emmy, and the Carol Burnett Show was moving out of its Monday night slot. Prime-time football had arrived.

In 1980 "Monday Night Football" won its second Emmy as the Outstanding Live Sports Series.[11] Its Nielsen ratings surged from 18.5 with a 31 share on average in 1970 to 21.7 in 1981 with a 36 share, although they slipped slightly in 1974, 1978, and 1979.[12] These ratings are the more remarkable when compared with those for other regularly scheduled sports events; ratings for CBS NFL games declined between 1971 and 1975, for instance, while Monday night baseball in 1975 produced ratings of about 12, and NBA basketball games about 8.5. In 1977 the first three games in baseball's World Series garnered a 23.9 average rating and a 39.4 share for ABC; meanwhile "Monday Night Football" was averaging a 21.5 rating and a 37 share. In 1980 the final episode of "Dallas," in which J. R. Ewing was shot, had a 35.7 rating and a 56 share, but that same week "Monday Night Football" was eighth in the overall ratings with a 22.8 rating and a 38 share.[13]

Given such ratings for the show, advertisement charges were correspondingly high. In 1974 commercial minutes were sold for $100,000, "higher than any other regularly scheduled ABC show"; by 1977 rates were up to $124,000. In 1978, twenty-two instead of twenty commercial minutes were shown at each game, at $170,000 apiece. In 1980, 30-second spots were being sold for $110,000; in 1982, a single 30-second spot was priced at $185,000.[14]

The popularity of "Monday Night Football" was evident in other ways. For example, the *New York Post* surveyed local police records for the nights on which the games were telecast in 1974 and found that arrest rates were about 20 percent lower than on previous Monday nights. And in 1979, a campus of the Miami-Dade Community College system offered a course entitled "Understanding and Enjoying Monday Night Football."[15]

How can one account for such national interest in a football game? Unfortunately, we have almost no hard evidence about what prompts people to watch sporting events, much less about why they watch televised sport. As Allen Guttmann puts it, "Why then *do* people watch? No matter how complex the response to this five-word question, no answer will be universally valid."[16] What follows must therefore be conjectural; it is suggestive, however, of the kinds of investigation that must be undertaken if we are to understand spectators' perceptions of sport.

The TV ratings evidence suggests that viewers expect a football game to mean something. In 1974 NFL players were on strike for the Hall of Fame game; instead of the 8.5 rating it had garnered in 1973, the game got only a 5.5. Two exhibition games without the regulars averaged ratings of only 3.3; but when the veterans were back, one of the pre-season games they played got a 10.6 rating.[17] Precisely the same sort of ratings slump happened during the 1982 and 1987 NFL players' strikes, and televised games of the United States Football League made a disastrous showing.[18] "Monday Night Football" was part of the proper NFL season; since each game counted in the competition for the play-offs and the Super Bowl, they mattered.

Viewers also want to "see" the football game they are watching. Throughout the time "Monday Night Football" has been on the air, ABC has developed and refined its coverage.[19] By 1985 thirteen cameras were in use; graphics had become more sophisticated. Viewers were able to see more and more of each game's pattern. In a 1987 game, for instance, the players were often shown from above and at a distance as they gathered on the scrimmage line. Then, the camera changed focus from the group of players first seen to a close-up of the play's climax. To avoid monotony, viewers were given a variety of camera angles, from eye-level in front of the center before the snap, from the side, from above. Before a replay, yellow lines were drawn on a frozen shot, while the commentators told viewers exactly how to follow the action of the replay itself. The coverage was designed to draw into the game viewers who had little previous knowledge of football, instruct them in its rules and strategies, and turn them into fans.

More casual viewers were also encouraged to keep up with the game. In a 1987 game, statistical tables were shown in up to four colors; easy-to-read white printing along the bottom of the screen gave additional information about the state of the play, individual players, and comparisons with previous games and seasons. When a player had done something outstanding, his framed photograph appeared on the screen stylishly posed as an art shot.

ABC takes pains to make the audience at home part of the stadium audience; the cameras show the stadium crowds, good-tempered, enthusiastic, having fun. When the home team scores a touchdown, there are the fans, jumping up and down, arms outstretched, roaring their approval. The camera also shows the creativity of the spectators, as it zooms in on illustrated banners designed at home and brought to drape over the stands.

Further, ABC shows the football stadium to be a safe place; a cute toddler, often dressed in a team uniform, appears in close-up, reminding viewers that football is family entertainment. Whatever stresses and strains may threaten the fabric of U.S. society, "Monday Night Football" reminds us that at least some of our activities unify us. "Monday Night Football" is intended to make viewers feel good not just about the game but about themselves and their world.

Professional football games are shown to be lawful; violence only takes place within the sport's rules. In one 1987 Monday-night game between the Miami Dolphins and the New York Jets, for instance, the tractor had to remove injured players three times. But the cameras never show the sort of wanton, random violence of which many citizens now are all too aware; rather, close-ups of football officials in their distinctive uniforms, equipped with microphones so that we can all hear their judgments, show them to be in undisputed control. However much individual players dislike a call, and whatever the coach thinks of it, chaos and mayhem are kept at bay. "Monday Night Football" epitomizes societal stability; penalties follow transgressions in a predictable and impartial fashion.

"Monday Night Football" also resolves one of the perennial problems of U.S. society: the conflicting claims of the private and public good. On the football field the balance between the individual and the community is carefully structured and maintained; the cameras allow a viewer to see that although an individual player may be outstanding in his own right, his success nevertheless depends on teamwork. The cameras focus on a Stradford or a Humphery as he trots back to the huddle having made a spectacular play, but the commentators continually remind us of the protection the quarterback is being given by his line, the blocking preceding the runner, the extra coverage given by an alert defender. Players are shown celebrating as a team; they are alone, isolated, heads hanging, only in defeat. However competitive the ethic of individualism would have us be, "Monday Night Football" reflects the societal fact that to get we each have to give.

At the same time, no viewer can be unaware that U.S. society is hierarchical. The close-up of an outraged coach disgusted by a player's shortcomings, the dispatching of plays into the huddle, the assistants (many of them plugged into electronic equipment) surrounding the head man on the sideline, leave no doubt of that. Yet even the intricate chess game of football, in which every move a player makes is theoretically predetermined, cannot be played by robots. It is a player's job to "make something happen"; the boss can command, but his orders depend on his underlings' actions. Because football is a game of territory, it has often been described as war; I suspect it is just as easy for a viewer to watch it in quite other terms.[20] It is hard for the U.S. public to believe that modern soldiers seek combat, but every viewer knows that virtually all NFL players have dedicated their lives from junior high school onward to getting onto the field in an NFL game. (Indeed, one of the reasons for a loss of interest in football may be that many viewers have decided players are more concerned with their paychecks than with their game.)[21] What "Monday Night Football" may reflect for a good number of viewers is the world of work as they experience it; someone in charge tells others what to do and may lose his job if his underlings do not or cannot produce results that are satisfactory to the head office.

Although ABC steadily developed the visual possibilities of "Monday Night Football," the show's commentary was inconsistent. Meredith dropped out after the 1973 season to reappear in 1977; Cosell left after 1983. The original irreverence of the first four seasons was never quite recaptured, and in any case, there is a limit to what commentary can do to enhance TV football coverage. Nevertheless, commentators certainly can underline each game's importance—"If X loses they're out for the season, if Y wins they clinch a play-off spot." They can also remind viewers that they are watching a game in which players have a pedigree—"Can either of you ever remember a Dan Marino game where he threw so many short passes?" An Al Michaels or a Frank Gifford can underline the aesthetic quality and skill of football—"That's beautiful. There aren't many people that could throw it like that." Clips of past games can be introduced to remind viewers that football has a heritage; the performances of contemporary players and teams can be compared to the glories of the past.

A commentator, however, can do very little about a game that is one-sided or poorly played. And while the Cosell-Meredith act was entertaining for a few seasons, especially for viewers who had little real understanding or love of football, as the audience became more sophisticated it may well have seemed that the game was being used as a foil by those who were being paid to explain it. The ratings for "Monday Night Football" slipped in both 1982 and 1983 before Cosell left; they picked up slightly in 1985 after another poor year in 1984. By then, the price of 30-second commercial spots had fallen by $10,000 apiece, and even then, they were often not sold until the Sunday before the telecast.[22]

For "Monday Night Football" was not an independent creation, however its producers may have dressed it up. It was an integral part of the NFL, an organization that was having its own troubles. Advertising sales from NFL games in 1985 had slumped at least 25 percent from 1984, "resulting in an estimated $50 million loss for the three networks combined." In 1987, for the first time since Pete Rozelle had become commissioner in 1960, the networks were not interested in increasing the amount they paid to televise football; they reduced their payments when they negotiated new contracts, and Rozelle was forced to turn to the underdog Entertainment and Sports Programming Network (ESPN) to make up the shortfall.[23]

In September 1986 ABC let it be known that "Monday Night Football" was in danger of cancellation because it had lost around $20 million in the 1985 season. The show was allowed to survive, but ABC pulled its other prime-time football games in 1987. The 1987 strike was no help to the NFL; the Super Bowl ratings declined for the second consecutive year, to their lowest point since 1976.[24] Nevertheless, in spite of these declines and the show's increased costs (now up to $130 million a year), ABC decided to persevere with "Monday Night Football," and for the 1989 season it raised the show's advertising rate for a 30-second spot to between $225,000 and $250,000.[25]

These increased charges may well backfire, however, because "Monday Night Football" viewers are no longer the demographically appealing group they once were. An advertisement in *Broadcasting* in November 1970 stressed ABC's power to reach adults under fifty years of age and cited "Monday Night Football" along with five other shows. In 1982 *Business Week* pointed out that NFL audiences contained "young, well-to-do males." But by 1985, these viewers appeared to have gone elsewhere—presumably to cable. And since 1985 the show's ratings for men in the 25–54 age group have gone down 28 percent.[26]

ESPN also may find that in purchasing TV broadcast rights to NFL games it has bought itself a fading star. For what the demographic change in viewers of "Monday Night Football" may tell us is that football may no longer represent what it once did to viewers and that viewers may have decided to seek elsewhere what the game once offered them.

Because we have not hitherto thought it important to find out, we do not know why U.S. fans made football the nation's most popular winter game on television. We must therefore conjecture. When football began in the 1870s, it was sponsored by the elite; then it was used as a marketing tool by colleges intent on improving their national image. From its earliest days, its promoters made great claims for it. As Walter Camp put it in 1896, football "calls out not merely the qualities which make the soldier . . . , but equally that mental acumen which makes the successful man in any of the affairs of life."[27] Camp also realized that the game's complexity meant that the game would remain compelling, praising "its practically unlimited field of tactical development. The fascinating study of new movements and combinations is never exhausted. It is this tactical possibility which has elevated football in popular esteem above all other sports."[28] Percy Haughton, Harvard's coach from 1908 to 1916, wrote in 1922 that "football is inherently an American game and essentially a college game. In it we find most of the red-blooded ideals which we are proud to believe are particularly American."[29]

These and other proponents of football were aware of the criticisms the game attracted as the colleges commercialized it. But they insisted that the problems the critics complained of were peripheral to the game itself. Alonzo Stagg, who coached at the University of Chicago for thirty-five years, presided over the change from a homemade football stand, which had been built in 1894 and seated about 1,200, to "a new concrete stand, seating 17,000" in 1926 and a ground that could hold 48,000. Stagg had no time for the professional game. In 1927 he wrote, "Once the college game becomes a nursery for professional gladiators, we shall have to plough up our football fields. Now it is a training in character and a moral asset to the school. The day boys play with one eye on the university and the other on professional futures, the sport will become a moral liability to the colleges."[30]

Somehow, in spite of the critique in the 1929 Carnegie Report on football and books such as *King Football,* in which Reed Harris pointed out precisely why "football, as conducted in college, is a racket," spectators managed to concentrate on what happened on the field and to ignore the larger context of college football.[31] As years went by, spectators also ignored the seamy side of the professional game. And indeed, even today, provided one concentrates on the game itself, football is a marvelous sport—dramatic, tension-filled, complex, and spiced with unexpected moments of dazzling athleticism and grace.

But the nation's infatuation with football may be over. In 1970 when "Monday Night Football" began, most NFL viewers had no idea that players were indulging in anything more than the alcohol athletes had always enjoyed. Arthur Mandell, the psychiatrist hired by the San Diego Chargers in 1972, was shocked to discover the extent of drug usage on the team; his efforts to help individual team members brought down on him the full powers of the NFL because Rozelle was only too well aware of what a drug scandal could do to football's public image. By the time Mandell's book, *The Nightmare Season,* was published in 1976, the fact of NFL drug abuse had begun to filter into the public's awareness.[32] TV viewers might by then have begun to think about the ways in which drug use might be affecting the actual games they were watching.

Although viewers could readily dismiss attacks on football as a sport when outsiders criticized it, they soon became aware that players were beginning to say the same things. During the 1970s players themselves began to publish books critical of the game—books that were reviewed in magazines the NFL audience was likely to read. At first, no matter what a reviewer wrote, it was easy to ignore what these players were saying. Dave Meggyesy could be characterized as an ungrateful pill-popper, and what had Bernie Parrish ever achieved?[33] Lance Rentzel's 1972 autobiographical account of the damage football had done to his character could perhaps be discounted as retrospective whining, an attempt to pass the buck.[34] The inside story of University of Texas football published the same year could be dismissed because Gary Shaw was never a starter.[35] Yet to a public used to hearing only from players like Jerry Kramer and accustomed to living in an age of cynicism, the message finally began to get through.[36] Jack Tatum's 1979 apologia seemed to underscore what televised football had made abundantly clear—the game was violent and corrupt, and players were pawns.[37]

Further, college football became even more grossly tainted during the 1980s. When so-called student-athletes were largely white, their presence on campus was not immediately obvious. When black athletes were imported just to play collegiate football and basketball, however, the purposes of athletic directors became visible. While "the big game" retained its hold on some campuses, the use of steroids and other drugs, the blatantly illegal recruiting and payment of players, the unethical use of young bodies and minds to make millions for colleges that accepted no responsibility for their players, the autonomy and the fat salaries of coaches all were publicized in sources ranging from the *Journal of Sport Sociology* to *Sports Illustrated*. Every mention of a player's college on an NFL telecast called to mind not an intellectual enterprise, but a corrupt minor league. And if the wellsprings of a game are corrupt, how pure can any sample of it be?

Meanwhile, the human rights movement had made some members of the U.S. public much more sensitive to the chattel status of NFL players. Certainly they were well paid, but viewers had been encouraged by TV to adopt an "up close and personal" stance toward the players. In 1970 I do not think it would have occurred to a "Monday Night Football" commentator to make the remark Dan Dierdorf did in 1987 as an injured player was hauled off the field. "I'm sorry . . . is there not a more humane way to remove a football player from the field than on the back of a tractor that's not big enough for a guy to lay down?"

The violent nature of football has always been a subject of debate. Now, in addition, the U.S. public is paying lip service—and sometimes more than that—to the ideal of physical fitness. Further, the demographically appealing men are now supposed to be sensitive, not macho. They are expected to be concerned with individual growth and development, not learning how to be disciplined team players, sacrificing their individuality to a domineering coach. On all these grounds, football is passé.

In 1970 soccer had not captured the imagination of boys and girls across the nation; today there is scarcely a high school in which it is not played, although professional soccer is languishing. The NFL developed its adult audience from the men who had learned to play and watch football in high school, but today's high school students may not be developing an emotional commitment to football. If they do not, they may well not find it attractive as a spectator sport when they become adults.

The NFL, then, would do well to look to its laurels. For although no sport, amateur or commercial, has ever been as pure as its promoters averred, any sport that has captured its fans' allegiance for a long period must have epitomized some or all of those very qualities promoters have touted. If football is ever perceived simply as a brutal game played by dummies beefed up on steroids, rather than as a fair contest featuring intricate patterns drawn by strong, well-conditioned athletes, no TV packaging will be able to make the product appealing.

For television shows us more than we can discern at the stadium. The late hit, the cheap shot, the lack of effort are as obvious on the TV screen as the brilliant catch, the amazing run, the dazzling and unexpected interception. Today no game can be turned into something spectacular (or even sportsmanlike) by newspaper writers or commentators as it could in the days before television; viewers see for themselves, and they judge for themselves. Stars to some extent now create their own image; the public's perception of Joe Montana or Herschel Walker was not manufactured by media moguls.

The product a TV network sells when it sells sport is not simply the event itself. To watch "Monday Night Football" is to watch a ritual, a historic performance, a tradition, a myth, not simply an isolated game. A sporting event is a form of communication with its own codes. "Monday Night Football" was deliberately encoded in new ways, but it may well be decoded in habitual patterns by football fans, and in unexpected and idiosyncratic fashion by casual viewers who bring their own perceptions to the game.

"Monday Night Football" was a success because it made football accessible to millions who had never really cared about it or perhaps had never had the opportunity to understand it. The show, however, did not tamper with the game's essential elements, nor its organizational structure, nor the societal values it epitomized. If anything, TV producers heightened awareness of the aspects of the game its promoters had always stressed—its discipline, manliness, complexity, and athleticism. For whatever business transactions have been involved between ABC and the NFL, the product that both have been marketing transcends them. As long as the U.S. public reveres, not just enjoys, football, "Monday Night Football" can endure. But if viewers have ceased to believe that football is more than a game, if they have ceased to accord it love and veneration—if, in fact, football has become simply a commercial product—"Monday Night Football" has no future.

NOTES

1. See, for instance, William O. Johnson, *Super Spectator and the Electric Lilliputians* (Boston: Little, Brown and Co., 1971) and Ron Powers, *Supertube: The Rise of Television Sports* (New York: Coward-McCann, 1984). Benjamin Rader believes television has "trivialized the experience of spectator sports"; see *In Its Own Image: How Television Has Transformed Sports* (New York: Free Press, 1984). On the contrary, I believe it has simply continued long-standing traditions in the commercialization of sport. See Joan M. Chandler, *Television and National Sport: The United States and Britain* (Urbana: University of Illinois Press, 1988).

2. This is not the place to discuss what, if anything, television has "done" to sport. See references above.

3. *Broadcasting*, May 19, 1969, 26; June 2, 1969, 66.

4. CBS had broadcast five NFL games in prime time since 1966. Rozelle told ABC affiliates in May 1970 that he was confident "Monday Night Football" would succeed, based on the ratings for the CBS games. *Broadcasting*, May 18, 1970, 26.

5. *Broadcasting*, April 13, 1970, 44; May 18, 1970, 26.

6. *Broadcasting*, September 14, 1970, 56.

7. Howard Cosell, *Cosell* (Chicago: Playboy Press, 1973), 283–84.

8. Powers, *Supertube*, 130.

9. *Broadcasting*, March 23, 1970, 34; July 20, 1970, 21; October 5, 1970, 57.

10. *Broadcasting*, October 26, 1970, 9.

11. *Broadcasting*, May 24, 1980, 21.

12. Whether Nielsen ratings accurately reflect what viewers are actually watching or not is a vexing question that cannot be discussed here. It seems probable, however, that the ratings indicate at least the relative popularity of prime time

shows, however unlikely it may be that viewers are really attending faithfully to a TV set that happens to be switched on.

13. *Dallas Morning News,* September 8, 1986, A8. See also *Broadcasting,* September 22, 1975, 48, 49; October 24, 1977, 26; November 24, 1980, 50.

14. *Broadcasting,* July 22, 1974, 42; August 1, 1977, 27; November 31, 1977, 21; August 4, 1980, 58; August 5, 1985, 34.

15. *Broadcasting,* February 10, 1975, 34; Cosell, *Cosell,* 274; Powers, *Supertube,* 186–87.

16. Allen Guttmann, *Sports Spectators* (New York: Columbia University Press, 1986), 176.

17. *Broadcasting,* August 12, 1974, 28; August 26, 1974, 10.

18. Although the United States Football League (USFL) started its life in 1983 with ABC and cable contracts, the ratings for its televised games (never high) declined almost steadily, and on June 17, 1983, the USFL game got the second lowest rating in TV history for a prime time sports event. The average rating for the whole 1984 season was 5.5. *Dallas Morning News,* July 8, 1983, B1, 10; July 6, 1984, B12.

19. William Taafe suggested that budget cuts for sports programming have brought networks dangerously near to undercutting production quality. *Sports Illustrated,* October 12, 1987, 50–54, 73. Chet Forte, however, speculated that independent companies can now produce sports events so well that the days of the network sports division are probably over. *Dallas Morning News,* September 8, 1986, A8.

20. From its earliest days, football has been compared to warfare. See, for instance, chapter 8 in part 2 of *Football,* by Walter Camp and Lorin Deland (Cambridge, Mass.: Riverside Press, 1896); Chapter 2, entitled "Football and Warfare—Similarities and Differences," in Herbert Reed's *Football for Public and Player* (New York: Frederick A. Stokes Company, 1913); and Percy D. Haughton, *Football and How to Watch It* (Boston: Marshall Jones Company, 1922), 145–46.

21. Seventy-six percent of the respondents to a study sponsored by the Miller Brewing Company "strongly agreed" with the statement that "professional athletes are overpaid"; only 42 percent "strongly agreed" that "professional athletes are more dedicated to the game than they are to their own gain," while 50 percent "somewhat disagreed." *Miller Lite Report on American Attitudes* (Milwaukee: Miller Brewing Company, 1983), 75, 77.

22. *Broadcasting,* August 5, 1985, 34.

23. *Broadcasting,* December 23, 1985, 60; *Dallas Morning News,* March 23, 1987, B3.

24. *Broadcasting,* February 8, 1988, 51; *Dallas Morning News,* September 8, 1986, A1, A8.

25. *Wall Street Journal,* October 11, 1989, B1.

26. *Broadcasting,* November 9, 1970, 35; *Business Week,* October 18, 1982, 52; *Wall Street Journal,* October 11, 1988, B1.

27. Camp and Deland, *Football,* iii.

28. Ibid., iv; see also, for instance, Paul Zimmerman, *A Thinking Man's Guide to Pro Football,* rev. ed. (New York: E. P. Dutton, 1971).

29. Haughton, *Football,* 210–11.

30. Amos Alonzo Stagg in Wesley Winans Stout, *Touchdown!* (New York: Longmans, Green & Co., 1927), 170, 172–73, 296–97.

31. Howard J. Savage et al., *American College Athletics,* Bulletin No. 23 (New York: Carnegie Foundation, 1929); Reed Harris, *King Football: The Vulgarization of the American Colleges* (New York: Vanguard Press, 1983), 8.

32. Arnold Mandell, *The Nightmare Season* (New York: Random House, 1976).

33. Dave Meggyesy, *Out of Their League* (Berkeley, Calif.: Ramparts Press, 1970); Bernie Parrish, *They Call It a Game* (New York: Dial Press, 1971).

34. Lance Rentzel, *When All the Laughter Died in Sorrow* (New York: Saturday Review Press, 1972).

35. Gary Shaw, *Meat on the Hoof: The Hidden World of Texas Football* (New York: St. Martin's Press, 1972).

36. Jerry Kramer, *Instant Replay* (New York: World Publishing Co., 1968).

37. Jack Tatum with Bill Kushner, *They Call Me Assassin* (New York: Everest House, 1979).

Player Compensation in the National Football League

3

Dennis A. Ahlburg and James B. Dworkin

In recent years professional football has been rocked by strikes. The National Football League Players Association (NFLPA) launched two strikes during the 1980s against the National Football League. On September 21, 1982, the NFLPA called the first in-season strike in the history of the NFL, which lasted fifty-seven days and forced the cancellation of seven weeks of the 1982 season. The third collective bargaining contract between the NFLPA and the NFL had expired on July 15, 1982, without the parties being able to come to terms over the issue of money. Bargaining efforts had continued but to no avail.

The NFLPA's main complaint was that player salaries in the NFL were too low compared to the salaries of other professional athletes. In 1970 football players' average salaries had ranked second to those of basketball players, but by 1980 the nominal average salaries of other professional athletes had increased by a factor of five while those for football players had only doubled (see Table 3.1). In fact, the real-dollar average salaries of professional football players had actually declined from 1970 to 1980. The contrasting growth of football's gross revenues, which had climbed above those for other professional sports by 1982 only served to exacerbate the players' concern that they were underpaid.

The NFLPA accused team owners of acting in collusion when setting player salaries instead of bargaining with individual players based on their field performance. "The owners operate in secret sessions to set wages. With few exceptions, an individual player has no chance against that system. Since we have examined all player contracts, there is no doubt that management establishes your salary by (1) the round you were drafted in, (2) your position, and (3) your years in the League. Salaries are not determined by your merit or your value to a team."[1] The players proposed a radical solution.

Table 3.1 Average Player Salaries 1970, 1980, 1982, 1987

		Baseball	Basketball	Football	Hockey
1970	Nominal	$ 29,000	$ 40,000	$ 34,600	$ 25,000
	Real	24,936	34,394	29,751	21,496
1980	Nominal	150,000	190,000	70,000	110,000
	Real	60,728	76,923	28,340	44,534
1982	Nominal	235,000	215,000	95,000	120,000
	Real	81,006	74,112	32,747	41,365
1987	Nominal	412,520	450,000	203,565	160,000
	Real	121,329	132,353	59,872	47,059
1982	Gross revenues	400 million	120 million	550 million	120 million

Sources: Salary data are from *Business Week*, February 22, 1982, 122. Real salaries are in 1967 dollars. The gross revenue estimates are from *U.S. News and World Report*, October 11, 1982, 74–75. The 1987 salary data are from *Sport*, June 1987, 38.

Instead of arguing for liberalized free agency benefits, the NFLPA demanded that the NFL owners turn over to the union 55 percent of the gross revenues earned by the teams. The union wanted to use these funds to establish a salary schedule for players based on years of experience, a bonus system to reward superb performance, fringe benefit improvements, drug counseling services, and improved benefits for retired players, among other things.

Management strongly denied the players' contentions. The NFL insisted that player salaries had always been set through individual negotiations, not collusion, and that they clearly reflected performance differentials. The owners also were adamant in denouncing the players' claim for a set percentage of the gross revenues of the game. Jack Donlan, chief negotiator for the NFL Management Council, put it bluntly: "Giving away a percentage of the gross is a concept alien to America. It's a control issue, and the owners aren't going to give up control."[2] Donlan's advice was indeed followed by the NFL owners.

The strike of 1982 ended, but the players lost their fight for a percentage of gross revenues. Although a new contract was signed, the players' concerns over their relatively low salaries and the unfair manner in which they thought their salaries were set lingered long after the strike was resolved. By the time the new contract expired on August 31, 1987, the average player's salary in the NFL had increased to $203,000. Much of this increase was spurred by competition with the now-defunct United States Football League (USFL), which had afforded players an alternative to the NFL and had led to a bidding war. Nevertheless, the nominal average salaries of football players in 1987 were a couple hundred thousand dollars below that for basketball and baseball (see Table 3.1). Although they were a bit higher than hockey players' salaries, the difference was probably due to the fact that the National Hockey League has much lower gross revenues than the NFL because it has no national TV contracts.

The NFLPA focused squarely on the issue of free agency in the 1987 negotiations. The players wanted to liberalize the free agency system, hoping that freedom of movement from team to team would increase their bargaining power and cause salaries to escalate. The owners were willing to make minor modifications to the free agency system but clearly wished to avoid unfettered free agency. The issue was much debated, but Jim Finks, president and general manager of the New Orleans Saints, summarized the feelings of many observers when he asserted, "Ultimately, it will come down to M-O-N-E-Y. Free agency is a smoke screen."[3]

The regular season of 1987 started as usual, but the NFLPA quickly set up a strike deadline for September 22, 1987. As expected, a settlement could not be reached, and the second NFL strike in five years began after just two weeks of the regular season had been completed. A major difference between this strike and the earlier one was that each team rostered a squad of strikebreakers so that only one regular season game had to be canceled. The substitute squads played for three weeks before the strike was settled and the regular players returned to their teams.

The second strike lasted twenty-four days, and at its conclusion the NFLPA filed an antitrust suit against the NFL in federal court in Minneapolis. The players returned to work without a new agreement. Thus the major issues that had precipitated both strikes—relatively low player salaries and their determination—have yet to be resolved. The positions of the opposing sides in these two NFL disputes have been clearly expressed. The players have consistently maintained that their compensation is based upon experience, position, and draft round and that their pay is unaffected by how well they perform. The owners maintain that player compensation levels do reflect performance factors. The question is, which side is correct?

Empirical Results

To test the competing claims of the NFL players and owners, we compiled salary data for the years 1982, 1986, and 1987. For 1982 our sample size was 1,277 players. For 1986 and 1987, we were only able to secure salary data on 317 and 244 players respectively. Since the sample sizes were so small, we decided to focus our study on the cohort of players from 1982 (see Table 3.2). We used the following equation to estimate the determinants of player salaries for 1982:

(1) $\text{Ln Sal}_i = \beta_0 + \beta_1 \text{Sen}_i + \beta_2 \text{Sen}_i^2 + \beta_3 \text{Draft}_i + \beta_4 \text{Perf}_i$

$$+ \sum_{j=5}^{11} \beta_j \text{pos}_{ij} + \epsilon_i$$

Where Ln Sal = log of 1982 salary
Sen = number of years in NFL
Sen^2 = number of years in NFL squared
Draft = round in which player was drafted
Perf = player performance
Pos = set of player-position dummies (kicker is the excluded category)
ϵ = error term (with the usual properties)

Because the players argued that longevity in the NFL pays off, we included an independent variable (Sen) to capture the effect of years in the league. If the players' contention is correct, the seniority coefficient should be positive ($\beta_1 > 0$). Although the players did not contend that the rate of return to seniority would eventually decline with increased seniority, we tested for this possibility by including a Sen^2 term in our equation. If our hypothesis is correct, this coefficient should be negative ($\beta_2 < 0$).

The players also argued that draft round is an important determinant of their salary levels. The lower the draft round (first round is best), the higher will be the player's salary ($\beta_3 < 0$). It is not immediately obvious why play-

Table 3.2 1982 Full Sample Descriptive Salaries

Position	N	%	Salary $\overline{X}$	Salary σ	Seniority $\overline{X}$	Seniority σ	Draft Round $\overline{X}$	Draft Round σ
RB	146	11.4	$106,527	65,901	3.64	2.39	7.12	6.76
QB	75	5.9	175,013	120,370	5.04	3.84	6.28	5.51
OL	240	18.8	98,658	47,186	4.67	3.20	6.30	5.86
DL	175	13.7	99,931	51,749	4.14	2.87	5.85	5.73
DB	198	15.5	88,096	41,817	3.91	2.78	7.99	6.97
R	193	15.1	99,813	55,280	4.16	2.81	7.11	6.43
LB	199	15.6	91,930	49,834	4.11	2.79	7.81	6.90
K	51	4.0	74,823	27,902	4.86	3.38	12.29	7.13

Note: RB = running back; QB = quarterback; OL = offensive lineman; DL = defensive lineman; DB = defensive back; R = receiver; LB = linebacker; K = kicker. N = 1,277; $\overline{X}$ = mean; σ = standard deviation

ers with a lower draft round should be paid more. If draft round is merely a signal for expected performance, then the coefficient on draft round should be insignificant once performance data are included in the equation, but this was not the case. Draft round continued to be a significant determinant of player salaries even when performance variables were included in our model. It may be that draft round measures ability or promise, which is rewarded whether or not a player performs as hoped for.

In terms of equation (1) above, if the players' contention is true that salary is based solely on seniority, draft round, and position played, then we should find that $\beta_1 > 0$ and $\beta_3 < 0$, and that β_j is significant. If the players are right that performance is not an important determinant of salaries, then we would expect $\beta_4 = 0$. If, however, $B_4 > 0$, then the owners' contention that performance is important is correct. Obviously, both positions may have some validity.

The most significant problem in testing the opposing models of salary determination was how to measure performance. The fact that football players are to a large extent specialists precluded the use of a global measure of performance. As an alternative we constructed position-specific measures of performance. For example, for quarterbacks we had twenty-one variables to measure lifetime performance and previous year's performance. The variables included completed passes, attempted passes, interceptions, fumbles, rushing attempts, games played, touchdown passes thrown, and touchdown passes completed. For running backs we had fourteen measures; for offensive linemen, six; defensive linemen, eight; defensive backs, nine; receivers, six; linebackers, six; and kickers, twelve.[4]

The position-specific performance measures were extracted from the performance data by principal factor analysis, which is the simplest, most commonly used, and computationally most efficient method of common factor analysis. Factor analysis is a technique designed to uncover unobservable hypothetical variables, called factors, that contribute to the variance of the observed performance variable. Using the traditional rule of extracting factors with eigenvalues greater than unity, we extracted four measures of performance for quarterbacks and running backs, three for defensive linemen, two for kickers, and one each for the other positions. A commonly used rule of thumb for identification is that there should be at least three variables per factor extracted. This rule held for all factors other than the third and fourth factors for quarterbacks and running backs, the first and third factors for defensive linemen, and the factor for linebackers. These factors were underidentified.

When based on multiple factors, the performance measures extracted tended to represent either total career performance or previous season's performance; when based on only a single factor, they tended to represent ca-

Table 3.3 Determinants of 1982 NFL Player Salaries

Variable	Coefficient	Variable	Coefficient
Seniority	0.181	DL	0.045
	(0.007)**		−(0.027)
Seniority^2	−0.006	DB	−0.009
	(0.001)**		(0.026)
Draft	−0.023	R	0.041
	(0.001)**		(0.026)
QB	0.406	LB	0.000
	(0.038)**		(0.000)
RB	0.142	Constant	3.996
	(0.028)**		(0.024)**
OL	0.003	$\bar{R}^2$	0.681
	(0.015)	F	347.633**

**Statistically significant at the .01 level.
Note: N = 1,277; the dependent variable is Logarithm of Annual Salary (SAL); absolute value of t-statistics are in parentheses.

reer performance. It is interesting to note that when multiple factors were identified, the lifetime career factor explained two to four times as much of the common variance in the performance data as did previous season's performance. The one exception was for kickers, in which case this order was reversed.

The estimation of equation (1) for all players (see Table 3.3) confirms the players' claim that salary is significantly related to seniority, draft round, and position. In addition, the rate of return declines with increasing seniority. Based on a mean of 3.5 years in the league, an additional year of experience is worth a 14-percent higher salary. For each higher round in which a player is selected in the draft, his salary is 2.3 percent lower. The players' claim that position matters is only partially supported by the data since only quarterbacks and running backs earn higher salaries than other players, but these differentials are large. Quarterbacks earn 40 percent more than other players, and running backs earn 15 percent more. These estimates assume that performance is unrelated to seniority, draft, and position—a reasonable assumption as it turns out, since few of the performance factors are significantly correlated with seniority or draft round (the highest correlation is .44).

For all positions, salary was significantly related to seniority and draft round, as the players claimed (see Table 3.4). If our performance measures capture what the players referred to as "merit or value to the team," then the empirical evidence also supports the owners in their contention that

Table 3.4 Determinants of NFL Player Salary by Position

	QB	RB	OL	DL
Seniority	0.157	0.150	0.223	0.196
	(0.043)**	(0.033)**	(0.017)**	(0.028)**
Seniority^2	−0.008	−0.009	−0.010	−0.011
	(0.003)**	(0.004)*	(0.001)**	(0.002)**
Draft	−0.028	−0.020	−0.018	−0.012
	(0.008)**	(0.004)**	(0.003)**	(0.004)**
Performance 1	0.298	0.212	0.038	0.008
	(0.078)**	(0.044)**	(0.012)*	(0.021)
Performance 2	0.175	0.048	—	0.188
	(0.049)**	(0.023)*		(0.065)**
Performance 3	−0.004	0.209	—	0.003
	(0.047)	(0.024)**		(0.024)
Performance 4	0.156	0.105	—	—
	(0.052)**	(0.025)**		
Constant	4.615	4.274	3.869	4.015
	(0.146)**	(0.079)**	(0.511)**	(0.079)**
$\bar{R}^2$	0.727	0.760	0.699	0.687
F	29.090**	66.591**	139.530**	64.675**
N	75	146	240	175

	DB	R	LB	K
Seniority	0.156	0.147	0.173	0.231
	(0.022)**	(0.029)**	(0.024)**	(0.027)**
Seniority^2	−0.012	−0.006	−0.006	−0.014
	(0.002)**	(0.002)**	(0.002)**	(0.002)**
Draft	−0.018	−0.008	−0.016	−0.006
	(0.003)**	(0.004)**	(0.003)**	(0.004)
Performance 1	0.296	0.226	0.070	0.015
	(0.036)**	(0.036)**	(0.025)**	(0.027)
Performance 2	—	—	—	0.120
				(0.048)
Performance 3	—	—	—	—
Performance 4	—	—	—	—
Constant	4.188	4.075	3.970	3.661
	(0.064)**	(0.075)**	(0.062)**	(0.087)**
$\bar{R}^2$	0.700	0.651	0.667	0.759
F	115.937**	90.624**	100.297**	32.440**
N	198	193	199	51

*Statistically significant of the .05 level.
**Statistically significant at the .01 level.

player salaries already reflect performance, since salary differences clearly reflected performance differences across all positions.

As for seniority, the rates of return (evaluated at the means for each position) varied from a low of 6.2 percent for defensive backs to a high of 12.9 percent for offensive linemen (see Table 3.5). The number of years of seniority at which the rate of return to seniority was maximized varied by position, from a low of 6.5 years for defensive backs to a high of 14.4 years for linebackers. For four positions the maximum was twice the mean, and for the other four it was roughly three times the mean. The rate of return to draft round also varied by position. Quarterbacks received a return of 2.8 percent for each lower draft round in which they were picked while receivers were paid only 0.8 percent more for each lower draft round.

Since the performance factors were standardized (zero mean, unit variance), their contribution to salary cannot be straightforwardly evaluated. First all variables must be standardized and then standardized coefficients or beta weights compared.[5] Since each variable in the regression has the same standard deviation and mean, the beta weights tell us the rank order of importance of the independent variables, and the ratio of the squares of the beta weights tells us their relative importance.

An analysis of the beta weights of the performance factors shows that for all positions other than offensive linemen and linebackers, the single most important measure of performance for each position is between two and five times as important as draft round in contributing to salary (see Table 3.6). For offensive linemen, performance is only one-third as important as draft round, and for linebackers only 40 percent as important. Because of the squared term on seniority, we were unable to compute the contribution of performance relative to that of seniority.

Discussion and Conclusions

The results of the preceding empirical analyses indicate that neither the positions of the NFLPA nor the NFL are entirely correct when it comes to the issue of the determinants of player salaries. The owners' assertion that players do receive differential compensation based upon their performance lev-

Table 3.5 Rates of Return to Seniority and Draft Round by Position

	QB	RB	OL	DL	DB	R	LB	K
Seniority	7.7	8.5	12.9	10.6	6.2	9.7	12.4	9.4
Draft	2.8	2.0	1.8	1.2	1.8	0.8	1.6	0.6
Max[a]	10.5	8.3	11.2	8.9	6.5	12.3	14.4	13.6

[a]Number of years of seniority at which the rate of return to seniority was maximized.

Table 3.6 Beta Coefficients for Regression of Log Salary on Draft
and Performance

	QB	RB	OL	DL	DB	R	LB	K
Draft	.22	.24	.23	.14	.27	.10	.23	.10
Performance 1	.42	.37	.07	.02	.60	.41	.14	.04
Performance 2	.24	.08	—	.34	—	—	—	.31
Performance 3	.00	.37	—	.01	—	—	—	—
Performance 4	.21	.18	—	—	—	—	—	—

els is borne out through the individual position regressions. In every case, position by position, performance does count. It is also true, however, that for each position cohort, nonperformance factors such as seniority and draft round are also significant explanatory factors in the salary determination process. Both parties are partially correct: both performance-related and nonperformance-related factors do in fact matter.

Meanwhile, the matter of labor peace in the NFL has yet to be resolved as the NFL Players Association continues to challenge the league on what it contends are violations of antitrust law. Separate suits have been filed against the league's restrictive free agent system and the management-implemented developmental squad, which was in effect during the 1989 season. In a recent decision, the U.S. Eighth Circuit Court of Appeals ruled in November 1989 that the NFL's free agency restraints were immune from antitrust prosecution because the union remained in place for the purposes of collective bargaining. To combat this decision the NFLPA decertified itself as a bargaining agent, and appeals have been filed. Most recently, former NFL player Larry Csonka has spearheaded an attempt to form a new union to represent the players, the so-called United Players of the National Football League. As of this writing, the outcome of all these maneuvers is very hard to predict.

No easy solution to the current impasse appears to be in sight. The one thing we know for certain is that the instant dispute revolves around money. Players in the NFL feel that their salaries are too low, while the owners argue that player salaries are fair at their current levels. Although we did not address the issue of whether professional football players are underpaid, we did establish that player salaries are determined through a combination of factors, some performance-related and some not. Hopefully the two sides will be able to resolve their current impasse and future problems through collective bargaining or some other conflict resolution procedure. Obviously, football fans throughout the nation would much rather watch professional football games played by real professional players rather than to have to endure yet another strike.

NOTES

1. National Football League Players Association, ''Why a Percentage of the Gross?'' September 1981, 3.

2. ''They're Playing for Keeps,'' *Newsweek*, September 20, 1982, 72.

3. Hal Lancaster, ''NFL Labor Contract Expires Tonight: Players Union to Consider Strike Date,'' *Wall Street Journal*, August 31, 1987, 20.

4. The full set of variables is available from the authors upon request.

5. See Samuel K. Kachigan, *Multivariate Statistical Analysis* (New York: Radius Press, 1982), 193.

Racial Discrimination in the National Basketball Association

4

Lawrence M. Kahn and Peter D. Sherer

The National Basketball Association appears to be an example of racial progress. Blacks comprise roughly 75 percent of the players and about 80 percent of starting players. Black coaches are more common in the NBA than in other professional sports (Berry, Gould, and Staudohar 1986). Many of the most highly paid players are black: the top three NBA salaries for the 1985–86 season went to Earvin Johnson ($2,500,000), Moses Malone ($2,145,000), and Kareem Abdul-Jabbar ($2,030,000). Several other black players earned over $1 million: Ralph Sampson ($1,165,000), Marques Johnson ($1,100,000), Otis Birdsong ($1,100,000), Julius Erving ($1,485,000), and Patrick Ewing ($1,250,000).[1] Blacks have traditionally held leadership positions in the National Basketball Players Association (NBPA), although its director has always been white.[2]

Despite this high level of economic reward, blacks remain a small, though growing, minority of coaches and executives. In 1986, among the twenty-three teams in the NBA there were only two black head coaches and one black general manager; by the 1987–88 season, there were only four black head coaches and two black general managers.[3] The issue of racism in professional sports has been heightened by the well-publicized remarks of Al Campanis (a former executive with the Los Angeles Dodgers) and Jimmy Snyder (a former television commentator on NFL football) that many took to be racially inflammatory.

Racial discrimination in the NBA has not gone unnoticed by the players and inside observers. Bill Bradley, in *Life on the Run*, quotes a reporter's view of the racial sentiments and actions of basketball fans in the early 1970s: "Take the ordinary ethnic, white, working stiff. . . . There he sees Frazier, this black . . . who is making $300,000 a year for playing. . . . Then there he is, playing poorly. . . . I have watched crowds and those boos for Frazier were vicious" (Bradley 1976, 204). Bradley also alleges in several instances that blacks were discriminated against in the 1960s. Consider the case of Bill Russell: "Russell never got as much recognition as he deserved. Race was undoubtedly a reason" (ibid., 185). Or the case of Dick Barnett, Bradley's teammate on the New York Knicks in the 1960s: "After a few swings around the league, [Dick] realized that he really was as good as most of the white stars he had read about. He also knew he was not equally paid" (ibid., 18). More recently, David Halberstam reports that Maurice Lucas, a Portland Trail Blazer, in 1979 "did not believe that Portland would pay a black star as much as it paid a white star" (Halberstam 1981, 44). Racial prejudice may well adversely affect NBA players just as it has led to racial inequality in the labor market at large.

Just what does the anecdotal evidence add up to? Is there a pattern of racial salary differentials in the NBA? Do the stories about fan prejudices reflect actual attendance records? We obtained provisional answers to these questions by investigating NBA salary determination for the 1985–86 season and the determinants of home attendance for each NBA team for the period 1980–1986.[4]

We find that although black and white players earn comparable average salaries, when we control for performance, league seniority, and market-related variables, blacks are paid less than whites by about 20 percent, or about $80,000 per year. This finding is robust to a variety of independent variable specifications and estimation techniques. Our estimate of a 20-percent black salary shortfall (all else equal), while not direct proof of discrimination, is similar to the evidence presented in federal courts in pay discrimination cases under Title VII of the Civil Rights Act of 1964. Further, recent evidence for the economy at large suggests that the pay gap in the NBA between equally qualified black and white players is similar in percentage terms to the pay gap between blacks and whites in the general labor force.[5]

Regarding fan attendance, when we control for other influences on attendance, we find that white players add fans. Replacing a black player with a white player who performs equally as well raises home attendance by 8,000 to 13,000 fans per year. This finding suggests that at the margin, fans would rather see white players. The salary and attendance results are consistent with a pattern in which white players create extra entertainment value because of their race and receive at least some of this added value in the form of a salary premium.

Labor Relations and Salary Determination in the NBA

The NBA players have been represented by a union since the 1960s.[6] As in other professional sports, collective bargaining agreements in basketball set the rules for salary determination instead of specific salary scales.[7] The era of free agency in the NBA began with the 1976 collective bargaining agreement, which addressed two distinct periods—1976–81 and 1981–87. During 1976–81, a player could become a free agent when his existing contract expired. If he were bid away by another team, the two clubs involved needed to agree on compensation; the NBA Commissioner acted as an arbitrator in the event of no agreement. In 1981 this system was replaced by one in which the teams were given the right of first refusal: a team could keep a player's contract by matching the bidding team's offer.

By greatly reducing employer monopsony power, the free agency system appears to have led to a rapid escalation of salaries. According to Berry, Gould, and Staudohar (1986), the average player salary was $109,000 in 1976; our data for 1985–86 show an average of about $380,000.[8] At the same time, perhaps as a result of this salary escalation, the owners began reporting severe financial difficulties. In 1982 it was claimed that the average team lost $700,000 and that only six of the twenty-three were making profits (ibid., 181). As a result, in 1983 a cap on total team salaries was agreed upon by the owners and the NBA Players Association. Although the salary cap is very complicated, with multiple qualifications and clauses, its intent is clear—to slow down the spiral in player salaries.[9]

Collective bargaining in professional basketball, as of April 1988, was moving toward a relaxation of restrictions on free agency.[10] The 1976 union contract discussed above expired in June 1987 and was renegotiated in April 1988. The players wanted to get rid of the college draft, the teams' right of first refusal on free agent offers, and the salary cap, and their union filed suit against the league, alleging that these three provisions constituted violations of the antitrust laws. The new contract lasts for six years and contains some gains for the players. The college draft was cut from seven to three rounds in 1988 and to two rounds after that. Undrafted players, of whom there would be many more than before, would be free agents. The salary cap remains in force, but with stipulated minimum annual increases in the cap that were anticipated to allow a doubling of players' salaries over the 1988–93 period. Finally, teams no longer have the right of first refusal over players with at least seven years of league seniority (this figure eventually falls to three) who had previously signed at least two NBA contracts. In return for these concessions, the players dropped their antitrust suit against the league.

It is probably too early to tell whether the salary cap has had any impact on overall salaries.[11] Its existence, however, poses no obvious difficulty in comparing players' salaries. In 1985–86, NBA salaries, at least for experienced players, were basically market-determined: players used the free agent system to find the best offer. As noted, events in basketball during that time appeared to be moving the system toward a freer labor market.

Theoretical Considerations, Estimation Methods, and Data

Since 1957 economists have been concerned with the economic implications of labor market discrimination.[12] We take discrimination to mean unequal pay for equally qualified workers, although it may also take the form of discriminatory access to high-paying jobs. Economists have identified at least three kinds of discrimination: that based on employer prejudice, worker prejudice, or customer prejudice. In the case of race, employer prejudice may manifest itself in the unwillingness of firms to hire minorities unless they are willing to work for less pay than whites; worker prejudice may result in a demand by whites for a pay premium to compensate them for working with groups they do not like; prejudiced customers are willing to pay more for the services of workers from groups they like.

Applying economic theory to discrimination, one may conclude that unregulated competitive forces tend to diminish the first two kinds of discrimination but may not reduce the third. To understand this result, consider the prejudiced employer in a competitive industry, that is, one in which there is free entry of new firms. The firm, by assumption, is paying higher wages for whites who are no more qualified than black workers. With free entry and the existence of a sufficient number of profit-maximizing firms, the prejudiced firm will be undercut by lower-cost competitors. In the case of worker prejudice, firms with all-white or all-minority workforces will have lower costs than integrated firms; if the firms are profit-maximizers, then competitive pressures presumably will lead to equality of pay for equally qualified workers. Of course, if there are no profit-maximizing firms (meaning all firms are prejudiced), or if entry into the industry is restricted (profit-oriented investors cannot, for some reason, buy out the discriminatory firms), then employer or worker prejudice can result in permanent racial differences in pay for equally productive workers.

When customer prejudice exists, the consumer is willing to pay a premium to be served by members of particular groups. In the case of the NBA, fans may be willing to pay extra (or more fans are willing to buy tickets) to see white players. The white fan acts as if the white player is producing more entertainment value than a comparable black player. In this case, it may be a profit-maximizing decision for a team to make higher salary offers to whites than to comparable blacks. If blacks do not have better opportunities in labor market sectors in which there is no contact with prejudiced consumers, then a black-white pay gap will not be eroded by competition. Because most black NBA players (as well as whites) undoubtedly have far worse-paying opportunities outside basketball, the customer discrimination argument may be particularly relevant here.

These considerations suggest that we should compare the compensation of equally productive black and white NBA players in order to test for the existence of discrimination. Using a variety of regression models will illustrate the robustness of our results. Unfortunately, we do not have data on "true" productivity; instead, we must find proxies for productivity by using a vector X of measurable performance, team, and local market characteristics.[13] We estimate the following equation:

(1) $lnS = B'X + \delta R + \epsilon_1$, where for each NBA player,
      S = the player's compensation for 1985–86, including an imputation for deferred payments,
      B is a coefficient vector,
RACE = 1 for white players, 0 for black players, and
      ϵ_1 is an error term summarizing unmeasured influences on player compensation.

The interpretation of δ, the coefficient on RACE, includes the sum of the effects of the types of discrimination discussed earlier. For example, a finding of $\delta > 0$ indicates that at the same level of measured performance and market-related characteristics, whites earn higher compensation than blacks. Such a finding is due either to one or more types of discrimination (employer, employee, or customer) or to a systematic mismeasurement of salary or productivity. (The issue of mismeasurement will be discussed later.)

To estimate the compensation model, we merge three data bases: (1) player salary data, (2) individual player performance data, and (3) team and metropolitan area data. The player performance and team data are taken from the 1985–86 editions of *The Sporting News NBA Guide* and *NBA Register*. The metropolitan area data for each player's team are taken from the U.S. Department of Commerce (1984–85). Player salary data for 1985–86 are taken from a survey of the entire NBA by a team of newspapers including *The Sporting News, Houston Chronicle, Phoenix Gazette, Detroit Free Press,* and *New York Daily News*.[14] The salary data include an imputation for the value of deferred compensation (as well as bonuses), including "base salary, signing bonuses, 'reasonably attainable' performance bonuses, and deferred payments" (*New York Daily News* 1985, 100). Although the newspapers' survey made a serious attempt to go beyond a base salary measure, our compensation variable does not include future deferred payments, and it is impossible to break down current compensation into salary and nonsalary components. Further, if more black players come from poorer families compared to white players, they may be more likely to have liquidity problems, leading them to take more of their compensation as salary rather than deferred payments. The lack of data on future deferred payments, then, may cause us to understate white compensation. Finally, the bonus component (which obviously is not separable in our sample from deferred payments) is not an actual "piece rate," but an estimate of what the surveyors thought was reasonably attainable by any player. It should, therefore, be thought of as a deferred payment. We use the log of salary in view of the large body of labor economics literature arguing that this is the appropriate form of the dependent variable (Willis 1986). When we use salary (not its log), the results are unchanged.

The vector X of explanatory variables includes the following (measured for the start of the 1985–86 season):

CONSTANT term
SEASONS = total seasons played[15]
MINS = average minutes played per game
GAMES = average games played per season
FTPCT = career free-throw percentage (fraction made)
FGPCT = career field-goal percentage (fraction made)
POINTS = career points scored per game
CENTER = dummy variable for centers[16]
FORWARD = dummy variable for forwards
OFFREB = career per-game offensive rebounds[17]
DEFREB = career per-game defensive rebounds
ASSISTS = career per-game assists
PFOULS = career per-game personal fouls
STEALS = career per-game steals
BLOCKS = career per-game shots blocked
HOMEATT = 1984–85 home attendance of player's 1985–86 team
RACEMSA = 1980 percent of Standard Metropolitan Statistical Area (SMSA) population that was black in the SMSA where player's team was located
POPMSA = 1980 population of SMSA of player's team
INCMSA = 1983 real per capita income in the team's SMSA[18]
DRAFTNO = number a player was picked in the draft (e.g., the top player was picked number one)
WINPCT = 1984–85 winning percentage of player's 1985–86 team

Longevity (SEASONS) combines a pure seniority effect and the value of a sustained level of per-game and per-season performance. The position variables (CENTER, FORWARD) are included to control for the possible differential value of these positions, especially for centers since it is often alleged that a good center is of special importance and that the best teams usually have a dominant center. Similarly, good forwards may be more scarce than good guards. By including CENTER and FORWARD, we test for the notion that the measured performance variables may not completely control for this position phenomenon. Minutes per game (MINS) measures a player's importance, but it may also be a negative productivity indicator since we control for per-game statistics (e.g., more minutes for the same points per game). Games per season measures freedom from injury or willingness to play while injured.

The team-related variables HOMEATT, RACEMSA, INCMSA, and POPMSA all capture market factors. The customer discrimination argument would suggest that RACEMSA would interact with RACE, that is, we would expect the premium paid to white players to be a negative function of the proportion of the local population that is black, and this test was attempted (see below). WINPCT is included to test for the idea that the team "settles up" with its players on the basis of their past year's performance.

Finally, DRAFTNO is included as a further indicator of a player's quality, potential, or fan appeal. It is an inverse ordinal measure of the league's desire for a given player as he entered the NBA. Unfortunately, although player quality should be controlled for as completely as possible, DRAFTNO may confound player quality and racial aspects of fan appeal. The customer (as well as team/player) discrimination model would suggest that, all else equal, white players would be drafted before black players:

(2) DRAFTNO = $\alpha'Z + B l\hat{n}S + \epsilon_1$, where Z includes
RACE (defined earlier)
     EARLY = dummy variable for those who left college as underclassmen
SEASONS as a pro (defined earlier)
 COLLSEA = college seasons
 CGAMES = total college games played per season
    CPTS = total college points scored per game
  CFGPCT = college field-goal percentage
  CFTPCT = college free-throw percentage
    CREB = total college rebounds per game (data on offensive and defensive rebounds were not available)
 CAWARDS = number of times named to *The Sporting News* first or second All-America team or won its College Player of the Year Award
     $l\hat{n}S$ = predicted log compensation from a reduced form model (the raw lnS is used in OLS versions of this equation)

In the DRAFT equation we include measures of college performance plus SEASONS (as a pro) in order to control for cohort effects in the player draft. If discrimination affects the draft, then at the same price (i.e., compensation) whites should be drafted before blacks. Therefore the DRAFT equation is estimated by including predicted log compensation as a measure of anticipated cost of a player at the time of the draft. In addition, because equations (1) and (2) both have an endogenous variable on the righthand side, we report two-stage least squares (2SLS) results, as well as ordinary least squares (OLS).

Performing a salary regression can shed light on racial differences in compensation when qualifications are controlled for. The techniques involved do not provide direct tests of discrimination, although their results can be suggestive. To shed light on fan preferences (and, implicitly, the idea of customer discrimination), we estimate a model of home attendance, using data on home attendance for the six-season period 1980–81 through 1985–86 (collected from *The Sporting News NBA Guide* for each season). We then pose the following equation (the unit of observation is a team in a given year):

$$
\begin{aligned}
(3) \quad \text{ATTEND} = {} & m_0 + m_1 \text{ YEAR} + m_2 \text{ WINPCT} + m_3 \text{ STARS} \\
& + m_4 \text{ ARENA} + m_5 \text{ RACEMSA} \\
& + m_6 \text{ POPMSA} + m_7 \text{ TEAMS} + m_8 \text{ PRICE} \\
& + m_9 \text{ INCMSA} + m_{10} \text{ PCTWHITE} + \epsilon_3, \text{ where}
\end{aligned}
$$

ATTEND = team's home attendance for a given year
YEAR = time trend (i.e., 81 for 1980–81, . . . , 86 for 1985–86)
WINPCT = team's winning percentage for a given year
STARS = number of team members on first or second All-NBA Team (chosen by *The Sporting News*)
ARENA = arena capacity
TEAMS = number of other major league sports franchises in the area
PRICE = minimum ticket price in 1967 dollars
PCTWHITE = fraction of team members who were white
(RACEMSA, INCMSA, and POPMSA are already defined)

The estimation of equation (3) tests the idea of customer discrimination. The PCTWHITE coefficient tells us the impact on attendance of adding white players of equal ability to the black players replaced. WINPCT and STARS are further indicators of team fan appeal; ARENA controls for the upper limit on attendance; and RACEMSA, INCMSA, POPMSA, and TEAMS are demand-related variables. Minimum ticket price data must be used since average ticket price data are unavailable.[19] Since teams choose ticket prices, PRICE is likely to be endogenous. Therefore, equation (3) is also estimated in a reduced form, with PRICE omitted. Even in this context PCTWHITE may yield interesting information about fan preferences.

Empirical Results

In the sample used in the wage and draft regressions black players make up 74.3 percent of the sample, a figure very close to Berry, Gould, and Stau-

Table 4.1 Mean Values of the Wage and Draft Regression Sample

Variable	Whites	Blacks
SEASONS	4.4140	4.8571
FTPCT	.7290	.7370
FGPCT	.4860	.4900
MINS	20.8620	25.4460
POINTS	8.6900	12.1100
GAMES	66.1700	71.0900
CENTER	.3450	.1730
FORWARD	.4480	.3990
OFFREB	1.3720	1.6340
DEFREB	3.0520	3.1420
ASSISTS	1.8580	2.6650
PFOULS	2.4570	2.6990
STEALS	.6260	.9710
BLOCKS	.6480	.6380
HOMEATT	473,540	454,080
RACEMSA	11.0%	13.6%
POPMSA	271.5×10^4	314.8×10^4
DRAFTNO	29.1000	24.8000
WINPCT	.5240	.4910
INCMSA	$ 9,410.9000	$ 9,640.7000
EARLY	.1207	.1905
COLLSEA	3.8103	3.5774
CGAMES	27.2920	27.9930
CPTS	13.2710	16.1550
CFGPCT	.5393	.5243
CFTPCT	.7201	.7051
CREB	6.6063	7.3616
CAWARDS	.3793	.4167
S	$396,570.0000	$407,190.0000
*ln*S	12.5700	12.6700

Note: N = 58 for whites; N = 168 for blacks.

dohar's (1986) estimate of 75 percent. An analysis of the mean values of the sample (see Table 4.1) shows that blacks on average have a $10,620 compensation advantage (2.7 percent) over whites, while the difference in mean log compensation implies a 10.5-percent black advantage ($e^{.1} \approx$ 1.105). But blacks on average have more experience (both seasons and minutes per game), better shooting statistics, more points per game, more points per minute, and are drafted earlier than whites. Blacks are more likely to leave college before using up their eligibility, score and rebound more as collegians than whites, and win more college awards. On the other hand, whites play for teams with better records, a possible Celtic effect.[20] The other team-related variables suggest that whites play for teams with higher home attendance that are located in smaller metropolitan areas with a greater percentage of whites in the area. These team variable means are consistent with the customer discrimination idea, as teams with more white players draw more fans and are located in relatively white areas. (The effect of white players on home attendance is tested more formally below.)

Compensation Regression Results

Although at first glance blacks seem to have a slight salary advantage over whites (Table 4.1), the regression results suggest that, all else equal, they are paid significantly less than whites in the NBA (Table 4.2).[21] First, the OLS and 2SLS race effects for *ln* (COMPENSATION) (see Table 4.2) are highly significant and amount to a white premium of about 20 percent. Although the raw means of log compensation show a 10-percent advantage for blacks (Table 4.1), when we control for individual performance, the result is a significant 20-percent black compensation shortfall. This effect holds with the inclusion of DRAFTNO, WINPCT, and the market-related variables.

Among other regression results, scoring appears to strongly affect salary. For example, a ten-point-per-game scoring differential contributes to a 40 to 50-percent compensation premium (all else equal). Longevity (SEASONS) and durability within a season (GAMES) both contribute to salaries, although these variables may indicate playing ability: the coach (or general manager) chooses to keep the better players on the court. Players in large markets (POPMSA) make a clear salary premium. For example, moving from an area the size of Washington, D.C., to one as large as Los Angeles raises salaries about 18 percent. This finding may indicate that in more lucrative markets the same levels of player and team performance are worth more than in less lucrative markets. Finally, the negative effect of DRAFTNO suggests that this variable is a further indicator of player quality or fan appeal, beyond what is measured by the performance statistics.[22] The effect is negative since a low DRAFTNO means that the player was an early draft choice.

Alternative Specifications of the Salary Model

The race effect on compensation is robust to alternative specifications. For example, inclusion of height, weight, all-star games, number of team changes, or team ability to pay (as measured by team salary minus the player's salary) does not affect the race results. In particular, the nonsignificant effects for "ability to pay" are consistent with team profit maximization:

Table 4.2 Ordinary (OLS) and Two-Stage Least Squares (2SLS) Results for *ln* (COMPENSATION)

Explanatory Variables	OLS[a]	OLS	OLS	2SLS
CONSTANT	10.3780***	10.6600***	10.5740***	10.6430***
	(.4265)	(.4203)	(.4512)	(.4887)
SEASONS	.0300***	.0352***	.0316***	.0286**
	(.0105)	(.0102)	(.0101)	(.0111)
FTPCT	−.2191	−.3434	−.2735	−.2761
	(.4225)	(.4080)	(.3977)	(.4189)
FGPCT	1.2761*	1.4045**	1.1678*	.9052
	(.6799)	(.6597)	(.6451)	(.6751)
MINS	.0095	.0128	.0142	.0124
	(.0129)	(.0125)	(.0122)	(.0128)
POINTS	.0558***	.0470***	.0444***	.0471***
	(.0114)	(.0111)	(.0108)	(.0125)
GAMES	.0081***	.0057**	.0066**	.0097***
	(.0027)	(.0027)	(.0027)	(.0032)
CENTER	.0808	.0599	.0844	.1105
	(.1318)	(.1283)	(.1252)	(.1308)
FORWARD	−.0297	−.0175	−.0132	−.0197
	(.0915)	(.0889)	(.0865)	(.0900)
OFFREB	.1022	.0660	.0854	.1166
	(.0758)	(.0736)	(.0720)	(.0780)
DEFREB	.0491	.0464	.0352	.0288
	(.0370)	(.0357)	(.0352)	(.0366)
ASSISTS	.0396	.0296	.0281	.0250
	(.0325)	(.0313)	(.0304)	(.0322)
PFOULS	−.0732	−.0418	−.0315	−.0498
	(.0530)	(.0515)	(.0509)	(.0569)

continued on next page

teams are only willing to pay players what they are worth. Further, tests for structural differences between black and white log salary regressions accept the hypothesis of a common structure—except for the race dummy variable. In particular, interactions between RACE and RACEMSA or RACE and league experience are not significant.

Having established a finding of a significant black shortfall in compensation, all else equal, we now investigate the extent to which this finding reflects extreme values. Is our finding due to a few highly paid white players? For example, in our sample of 58 white players, a salary raise for one player from $100,000 to $2,000,000 raises the average white salary by

Table 4.2—*Continued*

Explanatory Variables	OLS[a]	OLS	OLS	2SLS
STEALS	−.0612	−.0630	−.0552	−.0488
	(.1019)	(.0982)	(.0956)	(.0993)
BLOCKS	.0184	.0342	.0389	.0426
	(.0620)	(.0604)	(.0591)	(.0625)
HOMEATT $(\%10^3)$	—	—	.00009	.00008
			(.0003)	(.0003)
RACEMSA	—	—	.0003	−.0012
			(.0040)	(.0042)
POPMSA	—	—	.0004***	.0004***
			(.0001)	(.0001)
INCMSA$(\%10^3)$	—	—	−.0092	−.0144
			(.0177)	(.0187)
DRAFTNO	—	−.0048***	−.0050***	−.0063*
		(.0011)	(.0011)	(.0033)
WINPCT	—	.0730	.0199	.0086
		(.1955)	(.2449)	(.2559)
RACE	.2065***	.1914***	.2130***	.2262***
	(.0679)	(.0660)	(.0647)	(.0674)
R^2	.7224	.7462	.7660	—
S.E.E.	.4002	.3845	.3728	.3870

Note: N = 226. The first OLS column includes only individual performance measures and race; the second OLS column adds DRAFTNO and WINPCT; the third OLS column adds these two and the market-related variables; and the fourth column presents two-stage least squares estimates that correct for the fact that DRAFTNO is an endogenous variable.
[a](Asymptotic) standard errors are in parentheses.
***Coefficient is significantly different from zero at .01 level (2-tailed test).
**Coefficient is significantly different from zero at .05 level (2-tailed test).
*Coefficient is significantly different from zero at .10 level (2-tailed test).

about \$33,000, or over 8 percent. To assess the impact of such extreme values on racial salary differentials, we use OLS to estimate the basic log salary regression but exclude players making over \$800,000 per year, that is, we exclude a total of 20 players (5 whites and 15 blacks). The race coefficient becomes .1560** (.0646). When we restrict the sample to those earning less than \$600,000 (an exclusion of 12 whites and 25 blacks), the RACE effect becomes .1293* (.0693). When we restrict the model to those earning at least \$100,000, the RACE effect is .2327*** (.0665). The findings for the samples excluding high-paid players indicate that extreme values contribute to some but not all of the all-else-equal racial compensation differential. Even among low-paid to moderately paid players (earnings less than \$600,000), there is a race effect of about 13 percent that is significant at 6.1 percent (two-tailed test).

Earlier we suggested that the vector X of explanatory variables may not truly capture a player's productivity and that there may be errors in the compensation variable as well. Our race findings may not reflect discrimination if black compensation is systematically understated in our data relative to that for whites. We have argued that, if anything, the opposite may be true: white players may be less likely to have liquidity problems (because they presumably come from wealthier families than blacks): a larger share of white compensation may be "hidden" from us in the form of future payments. However, even with no errors in the compensation variable, if average "true" white playing ability is greater for a given level of the X variables than that for blacks, then our race results could in part reflect ability differences rather than discrimination. Of course, if average true black playing ability for a given X is greater than that of whites, then we have understated discrimination.

To measure discrimination when proxy variables are used for true productivity, some have suggested using an alternative technique called reverse regression (Roberts 1980). In this method, we regress the qualifications variables X (or a linear combination of them) on *ln*S and RACE: in effect we ask whether blacks, in order to achieve a given salary level, need to attain higher performance levels than whites. This technique has its advocates (ibid.) and its detractors (Goldberger 1984); we use it as an additional check on our results. As suggested by Roberts (1980), the dependent variable is the predicted value of *ln*S when RACE = 0, using the OLS log salary model from the third OLS column of Table 4.2. The coefficients are

*ln*S	.7652***
	(.0283)
RACE	−.2359***
	(.0476)

The result for RACE indicates that whites have significantly lower levels of qualifications than blacks at the same salary level. While productivity or salary mismeasurement may still be responsible for the race results in Table 4.2, the reverse regression technique does not indicate this to be true.

A final modification of the basic salary equation is to use OLS to interact league seniority and DRAFTNO. The coefficient is .0001 (.0003), a result of very low magnitude and a low significance level. In other words, the effect of draft number on salary does not decay over time. Evidently, DRAFTNO is a "fixed" effect, controlling for the other variables. Comparing two hypothetical players with the same performance but different draft numbers, we conclude that the league drafted the earlier player because of some unmeasured playing ability or fan appeal.

Table 4.3 OLS and 2SLS Results for Position in Draft Dependent Variable

Explanatory Variables	DRAFTNO		ln (DRAFTNO)	
	OLS	2SLS	OLS	2SLS
CONSTANT	320.0700***	325.7100***	17.2250***	17.6380***
	(39.3350)	(45.9100)	(2.1234)	(2.3019)
SEASONS	.5322	.6143	.0528*	.0604**
	(.7589)	(.8433)	(.0268)	(.0302)
EARLY	−8.4788*	−8.2754*	−.4023**	−.3832**
	(4.6858)	(4.9020)	(.1714)	(.1812)
COLLSEA[a]	−6.0410**	−6.0382**	−.1727*	−.1733*
	(2.7404)	(2.8307)	(.0994)	(.1038)
CGAMES	−1.4035**	−1.3759**	−.9635*	−.9054
	(.6033)	(.6319)	(.5684)	(.5998)
CPTS[a]	−.1737	−.1648	−.0574	−.0542
	(.4881)	(.5055)	(.2350)	(.2455)
CFGPCT	6.3856	8.8789	−.9577	−.7437
	(41.8450)	(44.2550)	(1.5240)	(1.6234)
CFTPCT	−34.4880	−34.7100	−.8758	−.8752
	(24.4640)	(25.2910)	(.9126)	(.9530)
CREB[a]	.8441	.8445	.0611	.0684
	(.5827)	(.6019)	(.1383)	(.1448)
CAWARDS	−3.5230*	−3.4365*	−.4573***	−.4480***
	(1.9739)	(2.0656)	(.0708)	(.0752)
RACE	3.1735	3.1728	.1997	.1987
	(3.8542)	(3.9823)	(.1439)	(.1502)
ln (COMPENSATION)	−17.0850***	−17.7310***	−.7573***	−.8192***
	(2.7646)	(3.7618)	(.1007)	(.1401)
S.E.E.	22.7540	23.5110	.8301	.8668
R^2	.3244	—	.5109	—

[a]These variables are logged when the dependent variable is ln (DRAFT).

Draft Position Results

An analysis of the OLS and 2SLS results for the determination of a player's draft position (Table 4.3) shows that in all specifications, white players are drafted later than black players, other things equal, although the RACE coefficient is never significant. Such a finding does not suggest racial discrimination. Further, the compensation effect is negative and significant in all cases: in the case of the 2SLS models this result means that predicted compensation is related to being selected earlier in the draft. Clearly, the compensation variable is not acting as a price term, which should have a positive coefficient, controlling for ability. It is likely that compensation (or its predicted value) is really a measure of player quality.

The overall results for the draft equations are disappointing. Other than compensation, the only significant coefficients are EARLY, COLLSEA, CGAMES, and CAWARDS. To make a full study of the draft process, we would need college statistics and draft numbers for all players drafted and for those not drafted. Our sample includes only those who were both drafted and selected to join an NBA team. Unfortunately, complete data on the draftable population are unavailable.

Home Attendance Results

In the regression results for the determinants of home attendance (Table 4.4), we report both OLS and generalized least squares (GLS) coefficients—the latter correct for serial correlation in our time series using a method proposed by Pindyck and Rubinfeld (1976). We interpret the GLS results with caution due to the short time series used. In both OLS specifications, PCTWHITE has positive significant effects on home attendance (at 2 percent in the first column and 11 percent in the second column on two-tailed tests). These OLS results imply that going from an all-black to an all-white team increases attendance by 137,885 fans (the third column's coefficient applied to the mean attendance level) to 157,040 fans (the first column). At ten dollars a head (a conservative estimate of average ticket price plus concession revenue) and twelve players per team, these estimates imply an arena revenue effect of $114,904 to $130,887 per white player. This estimate is somewhat higher than the 20-percent all-else-equal racial salary differential (about $80,000) (Table 4.2), suggesting that teams and white players share in the gains from serving fans' desires to see white players. The GLS results show positive but smaller and less significant effects of PCTWHITE on attendance (or its log). The effect on ATTEND is still significant at 11 percent (2-tailed test), however, and suggests a per-player revenue effect of $80,000.

The home attendance regression results also indicate that teams playing in large arenas, with high winning percentages, and in areas with small numbers of blacks and high incomes have higher home attendance, other things equal. The effect of price is small, and much smaller than its standard error. Price is obviously an endogenous variable, and it may be picking up demand effects, although excluding price does not affect the results. Finally, when PCTWHITE is interacted with other variables, there is no evidence that the impact of white players on attendance varies with the racial composition of the market.[23]

Table 4.4 Ordinary Least Squares (OLS) and Generalized Least Squares (GLS) Annual Home Attendance (1980–81—1985–86)

Explanatory Variables	Dependent Variable			
	ATTEND(%10³) (Mean = 440.10³)		*ln* ATTEND (Mean = 12.952)	
	OLS	GLS	OLS	GLS
CONSTANT	−1254.1000***	−1247.4000***	3.6227**	−2.8322
	(340.4800)	(349.7600)	(1.5406)	(1.8165)
YEAR	14.0100***	14.8140***	.0344***	.0359***
	(3.9825)	(4.0703)	(.0100)	(.0104)
WINPCT	473.6700***	448.2500***	1.2532***	1.1682***
	(66.1540)	(60.9130)	(.1665)	(.1572)
STARS	18.3770	13.4790	.0230	.0134
	(16.5690)	(14.4500)	(.0418)	(.0371)
ARENA[a]	5.2067***	4.1600**	.2220**	.1385
	(1.5808)	(1.7600)	(.0893)	(.1021)
RACEMSA[a]	−2.1441*	−2.8483**	−.0067**	−.0084**
	(1.1652)	(1.3887)	(.0033)	(.0040)
POPMSA[a]	.0140***	.0170***	.1011**	.1330**
	(.0053)	(.0062)	(.0497)	(.0592)
INCMSA[a]	.0116**	.0126**	.3116***	.3313**
	(.0049)	(.0059)	(.1137)	(.1403)
TEAMS	.8327	.0971	−.0005	−.0004
	(4.7144)	(5.6476)	(.0121)	(.0146)
PRICE	13.5330	−3.8426	.0260	−.0259
	(18.1320)	(17.9260)	(.0448)	(.0458)
PCTWHITE	157.040**	96.0890	.2726	.1619
	(68.1170)	(60.8880)	(.1708)	(.1558)
S.E.E.	79.5500	65.3000	.1992	.1671
R²	.6304	—	.6079	—

Note: Units of observation are team-years for 23 teams and 6 years ; n= 138. [a]These variables are logged when the dependent variable is *ln* (ATTEND). When the dependent variable is ATTEND, these variables are in thousands.

Comparison to Other Studies of Discrimination in Basketball and Baseball

In general, early studies of racial discrimination in professional basketball either were inconclusive or did not find discrimination against black players, while studies based on the most recent data do find discrimination against blacks. For example, using a sample of 28 players from the 1970–71 season, Mogull (1974) concluded that there was discrimination, although he did not compute a discrimination coefficient or test for significant racial differences in salaries. Rockwood and Asher (1976) criticized Mogull's (1974) study on these grounds. They used his sample of 28 players to estimate a wage equation and found a small and insignificant race coefficient. Further, Markmann (1976) used a sample of 201 NBA players from the 1972–73 season and found that, controlling for points, rebounds, and assists per minute played, there were no significant race differences in total playing time. While this is interesting information, it does not bear directly on the question of salaries or attendance.

Two other studies on the NBA that do not find racial discrimination were conducted by Scott, Long, and Somppi (1985) and Schollaert and Smith (1987). The former used 1978–81 data and concluded that, all else equal, additional black players raised team revenues. Since Scott, Long, and Somppi (1985) did not use a time trend in their equation (compare Table 4.4 left) and since the share of black NBA players was rising, their race term may be picking up a trend (revenues presumably increased). Although they do include the number of years a team has been located in a particular area, this technique does not necessarily capture trends. In addition, on a sample of 26 players from the 1980–81 season, the authors found a large salary effect ($101,096) of being white, but it was not significantly different from zero. Schollaert and Smith (1987) used samples of 1969–82 and 1977–82 team data and did not find an effect on attendance of the racial composition of the team.

In contrast to these studies using data from periods included in the interval 1969–82, two studies using more recent data did find evidence of discrimination in the NBA. Wallace (1988) used 1985–86 salary and many of the same explanatory variables we do. He found roughly a 17-percent discrimination coefficient that is statistically significant, a result similar to ours. Burdekin and Idson (1987), using data from the period 1980–86, found that the racial composition of teams was significantly affected by the racial composition of their metropolitan areas (compare Table 4.1 above): an increase in black representation in the area led to an increase in black representation on the team. Further, the closer the match between these measures of racial composition, the higher home attendance was, all else equal. The authors did not, however, examine the impact of team racial composition per se on home attendance.[24]

Taking all these studies at face value, we may conclude that as the percentage of black players has increased, so has evidence of discrimination in salaries and by fans. For example, according to Schollaert and Smith (1987), in the 1970s blacks comprised 60 to 70 percent of the league, in contrast to our 1985–86 figure of 74 percent. As white players have become more scarce, an increase in their presence now has a greater marginal effect on attendance, and the market value of being white has increased. In addition, it is possible that players' salaries in the later periods more closely approximate their market value than in earlier periods (due to, perhaps, a lag in the full effects of the free agency system). Fan preferences for white players are, of course, part of a white player's market value.

Although some of our findings suggest that discrimination against blacks exists in the NBA, two recent analyses of professional baseball during the free-agency era fail to find racial discrimination there (Raimondo 1983; Hill and Spellman 1984). What accounts for the differences between our findings and theirs? We believe that the relative scarcity of white NBA players and the greater visibility of basketball players to fans (compared with baseball) account for our findings. For example, Hill and Spellman (1984) report that about 30.8 percent of major league baseball players in 1976 were black, a far smaller figure than we find in the NBA. In addition, while the all-else-equal racial compensation differential we found is large (20 percent), it exists in the context of roughly equal overall black and white salaries. Social pressures to eliminate discrimination in this situation may well be less than if a highly visible black shortfall in average salaries were the case. The fact that several black players are among the most highly paid in the league may deflect any suspicion that blacks face discrimination in the NBA.

Today's NBA Salaries in Historical Perspective

Since the 1950s, many factors have combined to raise NBA players' salaries: unionization, free agency, the increasing popularity of professional sports, television, and so on (Berry, Gould, and Staudohar 1986). To provide an indication of how far players' salaries have come, we have, based on our salary model, computed predicted 1985–86 salary levels for selected all-time great players (see Table 4.5). Of this group of players, only Wilt Chamberlain, at $2.317 million, would have been paid at the top levels of the salary structure (as he was paid during his career). All of these players actually earned in 1985 dollars considerably less money than they would have if they were playing today, in particular, Elgin Baylor, Wilt Chamberlain, Bob Pettit, Bob Cousy, and Bill Russell.

Conclusions

Our study of racial salary differentials in the NBA, using a variety of specifications and statistical techniques, indicates that, all else equal, black NBA players earn significantly less than white players—about 20 percent less. In addition, all else equal, home attendance is a positive function of

Table 4.5 Actual and Predicted Salaries of Selected All-Time Greats

Player	Calendar Year	Year of Career	Actual Salary at the Time	Salary in 1985 Dollars	Predicted Salary[b]
Elgin Baylor	1962–63	5th	$ 30,000	$ 106,656	$1,712,357
Wilt Chamberlain	1972–73	14th	450,000	1,157,143	2,317,489
Bob Cousy	1962–63	13th	50,000	177,760	956,233
Dave DeBusschere	1971–72	10th	100,000	265,622	1,021,142
Walt Frazier	1973–74	7th	300,000	726,221	946,418
John Havlicek	1969–70	8th	140,000	410,820	797,346
Elvin Hayes	1971–72	4th	87,500	232,420	1,349,803
Earl Monroe	1972–73	6th	200,000	514,286	743,270
Bob Pettit	1962–63	9th	30,000	106,656	1,506,648
Oscar Robertson	1971–72	12th	233,333	619,785	1,312,598
Bill Russell[a]	1966–67	11th	125,001	414,149	1,558,021
Jerry West	1973–74	14th	300,000	726,221	1,331,624

Sources: Koppett (1968)—Hayes and Russell; Koppett (1973)—Monroe; Hirschberg (1963)—Baylor, Pettit, and Cousy; Bradley (1976)—Frazier; Libby (1977)—Chamberlain and West; U.S. Senate Subcommittee on Antitrust and Monopoly (1972)—DeBusschere and Robertson; Halberstam (1981)—Havlicek.

Note: The results are based on wage level regressions, not log wage regressions. For superstars it may be unrealistic to say that, for example, each increase in points per game raises salary by the same percentage (as a log wage regression requires). The salary level regression produced a larger race effect ($111,590) *** (34743) than did the log wage regression.

[a]Player-coach.

[b]Based on SALARY level OLS regression and also on statistics as of the indicated year of career.

white representation on the teams. These findings are consistent with the notion of customer discrimination. On the other hand, our results for draft position do not indicate discrimination in hiring.

It is noteworthy that the estimates of all-else-equal salary shortfalls for blacks have emerged ten years after the advent of free agency in the NBA. In addition, the high losses claimed by owners (Berry, Gould, and Staudohar 1986) suggest that they are under some pressure to maximize profits. If discrimination exists in such a competitive market, then it is either profitable, or else owners are willing to take negative profits in order to indulge their preferences for white players. Our results suggest that customer (fan) discrimination may be the ultimate cause of the black shortfall. As long as fans prefer to see white players, profit-oriented teams will make discriminatory salary offers.

Should we be concerned about a 20-percent (all else equal) shortfall in salaries for a group of workers who were earning about $400,000 on the average in 1985–86? While such differentials may pose a less pressing social problem for these players than for workers earning $10,000, the forces leading to the shortfall in NBA black players' salaries are a matter of considerable concern. The results found here and in recent studies by others indicating the presence of customer discrimination suggest that the individual instances of racial prejudice described earlier are part of a general pattern. This pattern would also include recent racial incidents on college campuses and in places like Howard Beach, New York.

While black workers on average earn considerably higher real wages and salaries than they did thirty-five years ago, their progress in the labor market relative to whites appears to have slowed in the 1980s. For example, among full-time year-round male workers, median black income in 1959 was 61 percent of median white income.[25] By 1969 the ratio had risen to 66 percent, and by 1978 it stood at 77 percent. As recently as 1983 black male median income for full-time year-round workers was 76 percent of the white figure; however, by 1985 the ratio had fallen to 70 percent, the same figure that was observed in 1974 and 1980. A similar story can be told for women: the median income of full-time year-round black female workers as a percentage of that of whites was 66 percent in 1959, 80 percent in 1969, 93 percent in 1980 and 1984, and 89 percent in 1985. These income figures indicate that, especially for black men, there is still a considerable racial gap. As of now, we do not have good information on the extent to which these differentials represent discrimination, but previous research indicates that perhaps 20 to 50 percent of past racial wage differentials may be due to discrimination (Flanagan, Kahn, Smith, and Ehrenberg 1989).

At the same time that black wages relative to whites' appear to have stopped rising, the black-white unemployment gap remains substantial: in 1978 the black unemployment rate was 2.47 times the rate for whites, and in November 1987 the ratio was 2.37.[26] These figures on wage and unemployment differentials indicate considerable gaps in the labor market outcomes for blacks and whites, and these gaps do not appear to be closing. Our study of racial discrimination in the NBA serves to highlight one facet of U.S. society that may be contributing to racial labor market inequality: race prejudice among consumers.

NOTES

1. These salary figures are from our data base (described later in the chapter). The highest-paid white players include Larry Bird ($1.8 million), Jack Sikma ($1.6 million), Mitch Kupchak ($1.15 million), and Kevin McHale ($1 million).

2. Among the NBPA leaders have been black players Oscar Robertson, Paul Silas, and Bob Lanier (Berry, Gould, and Staudohar 1986).

3. See ibid. and *The Sporting News NBA Guide, 1987–88.*

4. These data came from a larger research project. For details on this project see Kahn and Sherer (1988).

5. For example, Blau and Beller (1988) found that, all else equal, black males faced a 14.5-percent weekly earnings shortfall in 1981 compared with otherwise identical white males.

6. Much of this section is drawn from Berry, Gould, and Staudohar (1986).

7. Basketball, like football and baseball, has a minimum salary ($70,000 for 1985–86). In addition, in 1983 a team salary cap was instituted in the NBA (discussed later).

8. Similar increases have been observed in baseball following the institution of free agency. See Hill and Spellman (1983). The NBA compounded average annual rate of salary increase from 1976 to 1986 was about 13 percent, a substantially higher figure than the 7 percent annual hourly wage increase from 1976–84 for the private sector. See the U.S. Bureau of Labor Statistics, *Monthly Labor Review,* January 1986.

9. The basic salary cap for 1985–86 was the maximum of $3.8 million per team or 53 percent of gross revenues. On the other hand, there were enough exceptions to the cap to put 20 out of 23 teams over the $3.8 million figure. According to Berry, Gould, and Staudohar (1986), the cap has, at the margin, caused some teams to alter their lineups to accommodate the cap.

10. The following discussion of events in 1987 and 1988 is based on Goldaper (1988) and Thomas (1988).

11. The increase from 1984–85 to 1985–86 in average salaries was about 11 percent, similar to the 13-percent average from 1976–1986 reported earlier. See Berry, Gould, and Staudohar (1986).

12. See Becker (1975); see Cain (1986) for a summary of the literature that followed Becker's (1975) seminal book, the first edition of which was published in 1957.

13. The data are described more fully later in the chapter.

14. See the *New York Daily News,* December 26, 1985, 100. This survey was further described to the authors by Mike Douchant, basketball editor of *The Sporting News.*

15. A small number of players (e.g., Moses Malone, Julius Erving, George Gervin, Artis Gilmore) had ABA experience before the NBA-ABA merger in 1976. For these players we computed the entire professional career including ABA statistics.

16. In the case of players who play more than one position (e.g., Kevin McHale plays forward and center), we code their primary position as defined by the *NBA Guide.*

17. Rebounds were not broken down into offensive and defensive categories before 1973. For players whose careers started before 1973, we imputed offensive and defensive rebounds by prorating the total rebounds for these years by the post-1973 reported percentages of total rebounds in these two categories. The number of players affected was small.

18. The data on monetary income were taken from the U.S. Department of Commerce (1985). The income figure for each player was deflated by the relative cost of

living in the area, which was calculated by inflating the 1976 budget for an intermediate living standard (for a family of four) by the area's increase in the Consumer Price Index (CPI) from 1976 to 1983. Cost of living figures were taken from the U.S. Bureau of Labor Statistics (1978, 1985).

19. For some cases even minimum ticket price is missing. In these instances we interpolated to approximate this variable.

20. With the Celtics excluded, the average WINPCT is .490 for whites and .487 for blacks, but the race coefficient in the log wage regression is unchanged. Thus our basic findings for racial pay differences are not due to the presence of high-paid white players on the Celtics.

21. The existence of a $70,000 minimum salary suggests the possibility of a truncated dependent variable. However, in our sample, those earning $70,000, for whom we have complete data on their explanatory variables, comprise less than 1 percent of the regression sample. Thus the truncation problem is not likely to be severe in this case. On the other hand, the mean salary figures in Table 4.1 are 2 to 5 percent higher than the $380,000 figure reported earlier, indicating that low-paid players are slightly less likely to have complete data than high-paid players.

22. Heteroskedasticity tests suggested by Dutta (1975) do not indicate that this problem is present in our data. In addition, regressing the squared residuals from the full OLS *ln* (COMPENSATION) model on the predicted value of the dependent variable (and a constant) yields a coefficient of .0154 (.0181).

23. With the exception of PRICE, our results for attendance are similar to those of Noll (1974), who did not include racial makeup of the team or arena size. He suggests including each variable other than RACEMSA or POPMSA as an interaction with POPMSA but with no main term. When this specification is attempted, the results are similar to those in Table 4.4. In particular, the PCTWHITE effect in the Noll (1974)-type specification is positive and significant. Finally, when we omit Celtics (due to the uniqueness of Larry Bird, Kevin McHale, and the rest), the attendance results get stronger: in OLS regressions the PCTWHITE effect becomes 188.57** (81.38) (ATTEND) and .4239** (.2048) (*ln*/ATTEND).

24. Although their study was not directly on discrimination, Vining and Kerrigan (1978) reject the hypothesis that black players were randomly distributed across teams in the 1964–77 period. The authors argue that this result may reflect racial quotas or differences in the distribution of ability among those allowed to play in the NBA.

25. These income figures are taken from Flanagan, Kahn, Smith, and Ehrenberg (1989).

26. See Westcott and Bednarzik (1981) and U.S. Bureau of Labor Statistics, *Monthly Labor Review* (January 1988): 87.

REFERENCES

Becker, Gary. 1975. *The Economics of Discrimination.* 2nd ed. Chicago: University of Chicago Press.

Berry, Robert C., William B. Gould IV, and Paul D. Staudohar. 1986. *Labor Relations in Professional Sports.* Dover, Mass.: Auburn House.

Blau, Francine D., and Andrea Beller. 1988. "Trends in Earnings Differentials by Gender: 1971–1981." *Industrial and Labor Relations Review* 41 (July): 513–29.

Bradley, Bill. 1976. *Life on the Run.* New York: Quadrangle/The New York Times Book Co.

Burdekin, Richard K., and Todd L. Idson. 1987. "Customer Preferences, Attendance and the Racial Structure of Professional Basketball Teams." University of Miami. Mimeo.

Cain, Glen. 1986. "The Economic Analysis of Labor Market Discrimination: A Survey." In O. Ashenfelter and R. Layard, eds. *Handbook of Labor Economics*, 693–785. Amsterdam: North-Holland.

Dutta, M. 1975. *Econometric Methods.* Cincinnati: South-Western Publishing Co.

Flanagan, Robert J., Lawrence M. Kahn, Robert S. Smith, and Ronald G. Ehrenberg. 1989. *Economics of the Employment Relationship.* Glenview, Ill.: Scott, Foresman.

Goldberger, Arthur S. 1984. "Reverse Regression and Salary Discrimination." *Journal of Human Resources* 19 (Summer): 293–318.

Goldaper, Sam. 1988. "Union to Pass on All-Star Game Strike." *New York Times.* February 6, p. 30.

Halberstam, David. 1981. *The Breaks of the Game.* New York: Alfred A. Knopf.

Hill, James, and William Spellman. 1984. "Pay Discrimination in Baseball: Data from the Seventies." *Industrial Relations* 23 (Winter): 103–12.

———. 1983. "Professional Baseball: The Reserve Clause and Salary Structure." *Industrial Relations* 22 (Winter): 1–19.

Hirschberg, Al. 1963. *Basketball's Greatest Stars.* New York: G. P. Putnam's Sons.

Kahn, Lawrence M., and Peter D. Sherer. 1988. "Racial Differences in Professional Basketball Players' Compensation." *Journal of Labor Economics* 6 (January): 40–61.

Koppett, Leonard. 1973. *The Essence of the Game is Deception.* Boston: Little, Brown.

———. 1968. *24 Seconds to Shoot.* New York: Macmillan.

Libby, Bill. 1977 *Goliath: The Wilt Chamberlain Story.* New York: Dodd, Mead.

Markmann, Joseph M. 1976. "A Note on Discrimination by Race in Professional Basketball." *American Economist* 20 (Spring): 65–67.

Mogull, Robert G. 1974. "Racial Discrimination in Professional Basketball." *American Economist* 18 (Spring): 11–15.

New York Daily News. 1985. December 26, p. 100.

Noll, Roger G. 1974. "Attendance and Price Setting." Chapter 4 in Noll, ed., *Government and the Sports Business.* Brookings Institution: Washington, D.C.

Pindyck, Robert S., and Daniel L. Rubinfeld. 1976. *Econometric Models and Economic Forecasts.* New York: McGraw-Hill.

Raimondo, Henry J. 1983. "Free Agents' Impact on the Labor Market for Baseball Players." *Journal of Labor Research* 4 (Spring): 183–93.

Roberts, Harry. 1980. "Statistical Biases in the Measurement of Employment Discrimination." In E. Robert Livernash, ed. *Comparable Worth: Issues and Alternatives*, 173–95. Washington, D.C.: Equal Employment Advisory Council.

Rockwood, Charles E., and Ephraim Asher. 1976. "Racial Discrimination in Professional Basketball Revisited." *American Economist* 20 (Spring): 59–64.

Schollaert, Paul T., and Donald Hugh Smith. 1987. "Team Racial Composition and Sports Attendance." *The Sociological Quarterly* 28:71–87.

Scott, Frank A., Jr., James E. Long, and Ken Somppi. 1985. "Salary vs. Marginal Revenue Product under Monopsony and Competition: The Case of Professional Basketball." *Atlantic Economic Journal* 13 (September): 50–59.

The Sporting News NBA Guide, 1981–82 through *1987–88.* 1981–87. St. Louis: *The Sporting News.*

The Sporting News NBA Register 1985–86. 1985. St. Louis: *The Sporting News.*

Thomas, Jr., Robert M. 1988. "NBA in 6-Year Pact With Players' Union." *New York Times.* April 27, p. 48.

U.S. Bureau of Labor Statistics. 1978, 1985. *Handbook of Labor Statistics.* Washington, D.C.: GPO.

———. Various years. *Monthly Labor Review.*

U.S. Department of Commerce. 1984, 1985. *Statistical Abstract of the United States 1985, 1986.* Washington, D.C.: GPO.

U.S. Senate, Subcommittee on Antitrust and Monopoly. 1972. *Hearing on S. 2373, A Bill to Allow the Merger of Two or More Professional Basketball Leagues, September 21–23, 1971.* Washington, D.C.: GPO.

Vining, Daniel R., Jr., and James F. Kerrigan. 1978. "An Application of the Lexis Ratio to the Detection of Racial Quotas in Professional Sports: A Note." *American Economist* 22 (Fall): 71–75.

Wallace, Michael. 1988. "Labor Market Structure and Salary Determination among Professional Basketball Players." *Work and Occupations* 15 (August): 294–312.

Westcott, Diane N., and Robert W. Bednarzik. 1981. "Employment and Unemployment: A Report on 1980." *Monthly Labor Review* 104 (February): 4–14.

Willis, Robert J. 1986. "Wage Determinants: A Survey and Reinterpretation of Human Capital Earnings Functions." In O. Ashenfelter and R. Layard, eds. *Handbook of Labor Economics,* 525–602. Amsterdam: North-Holland.

Serfs versus Magnates: A Century of Labor Strife in Major League Baseball

5

David Q. Voigt

Among the more cynical definitions of the historian's enterprise is one proclaiming history to be the record of events as told by the winners of ideological struggles. This definition implies that by controlling the outcome of events, a victorious interest invariably manages to consolidate its position by foisting its version of what happened on the populace. And indeed, such interpretations of events crop up in "official" histories and records, where they portray past events in ways most palatable to the interests of established orders.

Certainly the history of major league baseball lends credibility to this propagandistic interpretation of historiography. In the century-long struggle for power between players and club owners in major league baseball, it was the victorious owners who took most of the credit for forging the game into a popular and profitable sports spectacle. As portrayed by some of the official histories of the game, it was the owners who acted decisively for the good of baseball; by crushing four player union movements over the years 1885–1946, the owners are credited with having saved the game from possible anarchy. The owners were supposedly defending such necessary policies as their right to insert reserve clauses in player contracts, to sell and trade players in order to maintain "competitive balance," and to discipline players by invoking their own brand of baseball law, which they saw as essential to the health and growth of the major league game. Indeed, until recently this defense of enlightened owners' opposition to player unionism has remained strongly entrenched in official histories of the game, where it influences the minds of fans. Moreover, while the strong Major League Baseball Players Association in recent years has scored massive gains in salaries and contractual rights for players, owners and their apologists still manage to portray player unions as hell-bent on wrecking baseball.

In the Beginning Were the Players

The long-standing confrontations between major league players and owners are rooted in the formative period of organized baseball, 1845–71. In that pioneering era the players were the major catalyst behind the game's growth and development. The game's other major constituencies—the latter-day club owners, who rose to wrest control of the major league game from the players; the spectators, whose growing support would hasten the game's enduring popularity; and the sportswriters and sportscasters who fanned the game's popularity by glorifying its heroes and its stirring seasonal campaigns—all followed the player vanguard.

As the early organizers and innovators of American baseball, the players dominated the game's formative years. It was the players who formed the first clubs and, by their spirited rivalries, established the early patterns of competition. The New York Knickerbockers, one of the earliest clubs, formalized the game by publishing a set of rules, which among other innovations mandated the now-familiar diamond-shaped infield with bases set ninety feet apart. When the Knickerbockers sought to control the game after the fashion of the lordly Marylebone Cricket Club, which ruled over English cricket competition, other clubs moved against the Knicks. In 1858 some two dozen rival clubs organized the National Association of Base Ball Players (NABBP), which wrested control of the game from the Knickerbockers.

Over the next twelve years the NABBP exerted its tenuous influence over the rapidly growing sport of baseball. By 1861 some fifty clubs had joined the NABBP, and by the end of the Civil War one hundred were enrolled. Moreover, during the war years players who served as soldiers stimulated the growth of the game by staging numerous contests in wartime camps on both sides. This widespread exposure kindled the great postwar boom in baseball's popularity. By 1867, 202 clubs, mostly hailing from the East and Northwest, were part of the NABBP, and by the following year membership had swelled to 350 clubs. But this rapid growth severely taxed the NABBP; with no league structure or fixed playing schedule, it was unable to regulate competition among clubs or determine a season's championship team. To this latter end, editor Frank Queen of the *New York Clipper* began awarding gold balls to the year's best teams and players as judged by reporters like Henry Chadwick.

As the decade of the 1860s drew to a close, the player-dominated NABBP was confronted by the divisive problem of professional players upstaging the amateurs in its ranks. Strong clubs were charging admissions to games, and as early as 1860, when star pitcher Jim Creighton was paid for his sterling efforts, the professional player had begun to emerge. By 1866 the Philadelphia Athletics reportedly employed four paid players, and by

1868 sportswriter Chadwick had taken to defining a professional player as one who played baseball "for money, place or emolument." For the time being, the NABBP tolerated professional players in its ranks, but in 1869 the growing tensions between amateurs and professionals reached a breaking point when the Cincinnati Red Stockings announced their plan to field a frankly professional team that would challenge all comers. The Cincinnati Reds of 1869–70 popularized the professional game by winning some eighty games without a loss. When the Reds finally lost to the Brooklyn Atlantics in 1870, the professional movement in baseball had reached such proportions that the dominant amateur element in the NABBP took steps to oust the professionals from its ranks.

In the fall of 1870 the NABBP voted to oust the professional players, but the belated move proved to be the death knell for amateur control over organized baseball in the United States. In March 1871 the homeless professional players met in New York City, where in a single night's work they founded the first professional baseball league. Structurally, the National Association of Professional Base Ball Players closely resembled the amateur NABBP, whose constitution it modified to serve the professional teams. Like its predecessor, the professional association was run by players, whose financial interests came first, and it insisted on the right of players to sell themselves to the highest bidder in a free market.

In asserting the right to contract freely, some players jumped contracts, a practice that sportswriter Chadwick, who strongly supported the professional association, castigated as disgraceful "revolving." By no means a new practice, revolving increased so much among players during the National Association's five-year existence that it hastened the league's demise. But other problems also blighted this first professional venture. The association lacked a fixed playing schedule of games, a paid corps of umpires, and the power to discipline players, including some who were accused of consorting with gamblers to fix games. Moreover, it lacked competitive balance because of its easy entry policy, which allowed any team to join the association merely by paying a ten-dollar entry fee. Each season saw hopeful teams enroll only to drop out under the pressures of losses and lack of profits. Indeed, success in the association favored clubs that were organized and funded as joint stock companies. More solidly financed, these teams generally outclassed the "cooperative nines," whose players directly shared in gate receipts and decision making. Thus, they depended wholly on shares of gate receipts for their salaries. And since victories boosted gate receipts, the better-financed teams grew increasingly able to entice the better players.

During the association's short history, no team was better financed or better led than the Boston Red Stockings. Led by player-manager Harry

Wright, the Boston Reds lost the first season's championship race to the joint stock company the Athletics but then proceeded to win the next four races, including a crushing victory in the association's last season in 1875. Moreover, Wright's Reds were the only consistent profiteers in the association; the Reds' player salaries were unsurpassed in the successor National League of Professional Base Ball Clubs until the early 1880s.

Despite the National Association's shortcomings, it lasted five seasons and established professional baseball as a popular sport. Most of its players went on to play with the National League (NL) when it dethroned the association in 1876. From a historical perspective, it certainly seems that the pioneer National Association deserves to be recognized as U.S. baseball's first major league. The fact that such recognition has been denied it to this day poses an object lesson in the politics of historiography. The fact that the National Association was a player-dominated league—an anathema to the profit-minded promoters of the successor National League—goes far to explain the denigration of the association. To be sure, "official" sources ignore the issue of player control and resort to other reasons to deny the association's claim to major league status. For example, the editors of the *Macmillan Encyclopedia* (6th ed.) concede that the National Association was the "first professional baseball league" but follow the establishment line of belittling the association's record. After all, in 1969 the Special Baseball Records Committee denied major league status to the association, citing "gambling and bribery" as undermining the "public's confidence in this loosely knit Association," along with the association's "erratic schedule and procedures" and the "poor newspaper coverage" of its games. Thus, the *Macmillan Encyclopedia* consigns this player-run league to an inferior position and relegates the records of association teams and players to a separate section.

Club Owners Take Command: The Rise of the National League

In 1876 William A. Hulbert, a Chicago businessman and baseball promoter, pulled off a coup that ended the brief era of player domination of professional baseball. At a New York City meeting of club directors in February of that year, Hulbert presided over the formation of the National League of Professional Base Ball Clubs. The title of the new league was significant; henceforth major league baseball would be controlled by club directors, whose interests would predominate over those of the players. No longer would players function as decision makers or stockholders, as had been possible under the National Association. Indeed, cooperative nines were excluded from National League membership. Only joint-stock company clubs from cities with populations of at least 75,000 were accepted as members. And a member club had to pay an entry fee of $100 and annual dues of the same sum. A territorial monopoly went with membership, and this development led to the idea of selling and buying major league franchises. Thus the major league club owners emerged as the dominant force in major league baseball. The owners individually ruled over their respective clubs and territories; collectively, eventually they voted to admit or drop member clubs, instituted sweeping changes in rules, waged war against rival leagues, dominated the minor leagues, and subordinated players under the owners' own code of baseball law.

Under Hulbert's presidency (1877–82) the NL devised a regular playing schedule of games, and in 1880 the reserve clause was added to player contracts. The reserve clause allowed a team to unilaterally reserve a player's services for the following year. At first only five players on a team could be reserved, and players viewed reservation as a status symbol. But by 1883, when the reserve system was extended to cover all players, the players had come to see the clause as a device for holding down their salaries. When the reserve clause was expanded later to allow for the selling and trading of players to other clubs, player resentment mounted. By denying a player freedom of contract and movement, the reserve clause became a rallying issue for player reformist movements. The device of the reserve clause, a patently illegal imposition, had earlier been used by theatrical promoters seeking to bind actors and actresses to long-term contracts and had been successfully challenged by legal action. But despite court rulings barring its use in the theatrical profession, the reserve clause became an accepted part of "baseball law" and was staunchly defended by owners as necessary for the good of the game.

The NL's success in controlling its players and dominating professional baseball did not come easily, however. In the league's early years promoters faced stiff competition from the International Association of Professional Baseball Players (IA). Over the years 1877–79 this loose league of joint-stock company clubs and cooperative teams opposed the NL. In this struggle IA teams often bested NL teams in exhibition play and attendance. But NL clubs had the advantage of superior organization and finances. The IA suffered from lack of a fixed playing schedule, which made regulation of championship play difficult and contentious. Thus the NL—by dint of such tactics as forbidding its teams to play exhibition games with association teams and luring strong association teams like Providence, Buffalo, Syracuse, Troy, and Worcester into its fold—crushed its rival in 1879. By that time, too, most good players regarded playing in the NL as a status symbol.

The Brotherhood Revolt of 1890

Following the collapse of the IA, the NL enjoyed two seasons of dominance in professional baseball despite President Hulbert's obstinate refusal to allow the league to reoccupy New York City and Philadelphia. Teams had been dropped from these cities earlier for failing to meet schedule obligations, and Hulbert's order barred the league from exploiting these lucrative sites. Nevertheless, the NL's fortunes improved during its 1880 and 1881 seasons. Unfortunately, its success encouraged promoters to launch a rival venture in 1882—the American Association (AA). Several factors—the location of one of the AA's six clubs in Philadelphia, the AA's formula of a twenty-five cent basic admission price, and its acceptance of Sunday games and alcohol sales where allowed by local law—attracted fans and made for a successful first season. At the same time, the AA's opposition to the reserve clause enticed some NL players to desert to it. The following year the AA expanded to eight teams and established a club in New York City.

The NL, confronted with a formidable rival, took measures to blunt the threat. After Hulbert died in 1882, his successor, President A. G. Mills, persuaded NL owners to drop the league's Troy and Worcester clubs and replace them with franchises in New York City and Philadelphia. And in a bold move aimed at halting player desertions, Mills summoned AA president H. Denny McKnight to a peace conference, where the association's delegates agreed to allow the reserve clause to apply to all player contracts in return for major league recognition. The outcome of this baseball summit meeting was the Tripartite Agreement of March 1883. This first national agreement bestowed major league status on the AA and high minor league status upon the Northwestern League. It also recognized the territorial rights of the clubs in the National and Northwestern leagues and the AA. The decision of the two major leagues to employ the reserve clause in their player contracts effectively limited player mobility, and in 1888 the two leagues conceded the right of player reservation to several recognized minor leagues, thereby extending their control over the growing number of minor leagues in professional baseball.

Meanwhile, in 1884 another rival circuit launched a bid to gain major league status. Organized by Henry V. Lucas, a St. Louis businessman, the Union Association announced its opposition to the reserve clause and welcomed players from the established majors into its ranks. Some jumped, but in the 1884 season the unbalanced Union Association suffered a spate of dropouts, and most of its clubs had heavy financial losses. Seizing the opportunity, NL promoters administered a coup de grace to this shaky rival by persuading Lucas to bring his team, the St. Louis Maroons, into the NL. This ploy ended the Union Association threat but angered American Association promoters in St. Louis, who viewed the presence of the new club as a direct violation of their territorial rights. Moreover, the restoration of the reserve clause system sowed the seeds of unionism in the ranks of major league players.

By the mid-1880s major league players were painfully aware of their worsening financial status compared to the club owners. In the minds of many players the reserve clause was associated with lower salaries. Although player salaries rose by 30 percent over the years 1880–89, owner profits rose by as much as 300 percent. This dichotomy was the major sore point, but players also resented the owners' use of the reserve clause to trade and sell players to other clubs without obtaining the consent of the players involved and without compensating them. Player resentment mounted in 1888 when major league club owners moved to establish a salary limitation plan. As proposed by owner John T. Brush, the plan called for a maximum salary of $2,500, with four lesser categories taking salaries downward to a minimum of $1,500. Performance and conduct were proposed as major considerations in ranking a player on the salary scale. This much was inflammatory enough, but the plan also proposed a new disciplinary code that proscribed drinking and even attempted to regulate player conduct off the field. This code was to be backed by fines, peremptory dismissals, and blacklistings. Not surprisingly, thoughtful players came to see themselves as serfs arrayed against exploitive owner "magnates."

In battling to regain their lost rights, players rallied around John Montgomery Ward. An extraordinary man, Ward was a star pitcher who became a star infielder after his pitching arm gave out. In off-seasons he earned two advanced degrees from Columbia University, including a law degree. Dedicated to the players' cause, Ward borrowed the idea of forming the Brotherhood of Professional Base Ball Players from Philadelphia sportswriter William Voltz, who urged players to form a benevolent association that would offer health care, insurance, and aid to indigent former players. Ward's vision, however, was of an organization that would bargain collectively with owners for settlement of player grievances.

In October 1885 Ward drew up the charter for the Brotherhood of Professional Base Ball Players and persuaded his New York Giant teammates to enroll in its first chapter. With Ward as its leader and with the solid support of editor Francis Richter of *Sporting Life,* the Brotherhood grew swiftly. By the end of 1885, 107 major league players had joined, and by 1886 the Brotherhood fielded chapters in every NL city. Thus encouraged, Ward launched attacks on the reserve clause and urged owners to instead use long-term contracts. In an 1887 article published in *Lippincott's Magazine,* Ward called for free agency for any player who had played with a club for a number of seasons, the length of time to be determined by bargaining with the owners. Lambasting the reserve system, Ward persuasively argued that although during the lean years of 1870–82 the clause had helped owners to weather financial storms, in the ensuing profitable years it had become a device for holding down player salaries and limiting their freedom of movement. When the owners voted late in 1888 to install the hated salary limitation plan, Ward demanded that they meet with the Brotherhood to compromise on this and other grievances. When the owners stalled, Ward demanded a July 1889 meeting to discuss the matter. When this tactic failed, Ward persuaded the Brotherhood, whose ranks now numbered two hundred players drawn from both major leagues, to gird for war.

The 1890 campaign mounted by the Brotherhood against the established major leagues was the most formidable of all organized actions by players against club owners until Marvin Miller's emergence as the leader of the Major League Baseball Players Association in the late 1960s. Indeed, when Miller battled the owners in the great fifty-day strike of 1981, at one point he threatened to employ Ward's strategy of 1890 to break the deadlock. Ward's strategy was to confront the established majors with an elite Players League (PL), whose teams would be staffed by the best players in the game. To bankroll the league, Ward lined up financiers, including the resolute Arnold Johnson of Cleveland (the financiers spent an average of $25,000 each to build ballparks and locate teams in most of the cities already occupied by NL clubs). In going its own way, the Players League was to operate as an economic cooperative with teams sharing profits and owners and players sharing in decision making.

It was Ward's hope that the cooperative approach would eliminate the inequitable distribution of profits that plagued the established majors. His scheme called for the equal sharing of gate receipts and any club profits in excess of $10,000, but this profit-sharing plan was primarily intended to benefit the financiers (in reality the profit threshold was never reached). As for the players, who might also share in the profits, there was the promise of long-term contracts, guaranteed salaries for 1890, and no pay cuts in subsequent years. The hated reserve clause system was replaced by a system of three-year contracts, that granted each club a two-year option to renew a player's contract. No team could release a player without giving him a hearing, and none could sell or trade a player without his consent.

Given such a cause, the players responded with firm resolve; fewer than twenty Brotherhood men deserted the Players League. It was an extraordinary display of solidarity, with some rebel players spurning hefty salary offers to return to their former clubs. In addition to offering such bribes, the defending majors pressed costly lawsuits against selected reserve clause jumpers. The major leagues lost two of these suits in New York State, where a superior court judge and a federal district court judge each found the reserve clause to be lacking in equity and thus unenforceable.

With the best players staffing their eight teams, the Players League waged a stirring season's competition, which player-manager Mike Kelly's Boston team won by 6½ games over Ward's runner-up Brooklyns. That year a lengthened pitching distance helped batters compile a .274 league batting average, which far outshone the record of either of the established majors. The prospect of seeing higher scoring, and perhaps the presence of two working umpires, enticed fans to PL games. The Players League outdrew the National League by more than 100,000 admissions and far outclassed the depressed American Association. As the dust of the 1890 campaign settled, a few PL teams were staggering financially, but four AA teams and two NL teams were reported to be bankrupt.

But although the Players League may have won the battle of 1890, the Brotherhood lost its war for independence before the year was over with the stunning collapse of the league. The collapse came as a result of pressures from the NL war committee against the rebel players and their nervous financiers. Drawing from a $250,000 war chest, Albert G. Spalding, a former player and now a powerful NL club owner and sporting goods entrepreneur, headed the NL's war committee, which waged a ruthless campaign against the PL. Invoking the antilabor rhetoric of the day, Spalding excoriated the members of the Brotherhood as anarchists, socialists, and radical conspirators. Such verbal assaults scored, since neither Ward nor his followers and financiers wanted to be branded as a labor union. Seeking a respectable middle-class image for their cause, the PL leaders opted for a 50-cent basic admission price and banned spirits and Sunday games from their parks. But this stance probably cost them the potential support of working-class fans. Indeed, the PL lost the enthusiastic support of the fledgling American Federation of Labor when some of its clubs employed nonunion contractors in their ballpark construction. Moreover, Spalding's committee, by threats to withdraw advertising, neutralized much of the early press support for the players' cause.

By holding the top minor leagues in line, Spalding's committee also neutralized the PL talent advantage. By extending player reservation privileges to the minor leagues and by paying higher prices for players drafted from minor league clubs, the major leagues were able to fill vacant ranks with enough good players to carry on the season's competition. And in a bold move, the NL waited until the PL published its playing schedule and then scheduled games in direct competition with the rebel league. The resultant head-to-head competition produced a surfeit of games, with the rivals swelling attendance by supplying free tickets to fans. With three major leagues vying for public support (NL, AA, and PL), it was hardly surprising that a new record for overall attendance was set. Nevertheless, the revenues from the 1890 games were so thinly spread that all three leagues suffered losses. NL teams lost an estimated $230,000; the AA, with four nearly bankrupt teams, suffered the worst; as for the PL, it lost an estimated $125,000, with only its Boston team showing a clear profit. Combined with an initial outlay of $215,000 for ballpark construction, these losses persuaded some PL owners to give up the struggle.

Concealing his own league's heavy losses, Spalding took advantage of the defeatist mood among PL financiers, whose losses were well publicized. Smelling a victory, in the fall of 1890 Spalding invited PL promoters to a peace conference to be held without the participation of Ward and the other Brotherhood leaders. The ploy broke the tottering alliance between the players and their backers and speeded the league's demise. The financiers were bought off by allowing some of their clubs to enter the major leagues; of these, three joined the NL, and one entered the reconstructed AA. The rest of the PL clubs either disbanded or were merged with the established majors, and the players were welcomed back with a promise of no reprisals. The players' defeat was sweetened somewhat by the scrapping of the salary classification plan, the modification of the reserve clause to include a vague "option to renew" clause in player contracts, and a false promise of improved working conditions. But these will-o-the-wisp reforms vanished in little more than a year.

In 1891 the NL waged a destructive war against the AA, which ended with the breakup of the association. In the aftermath of the 1891 war, at a cost of $131,000, the NL owners bought out four AA clubs and admitted the remaining four into the newly established National League and American Association of Professional Base Ball Clubs. Over the next eight seasons this twelve-club "big league" monopolized major league baseball. While it lasted, the major league players suffered the consequences of their 1890 defeat. By 1892 player salaries had been slashed and their travel budgets reduced. The reserve clause had been fully restored, the selling and trading of players continued, and strict disciplinary codes were in force. Under the Brush code of 1898 some twenty-one player "crimes," including swearing and insubordination, were punishable by fines or by dismissals and blacklistings. Worse still, in 1893 it was reported that only 54 of the 128 players who had played with PL teams remained in the majors. By then a salary limitation plan was in place that established the maximum pay for a star player at $2,400 per year, about half of what a star player made three years earlier.

On the other hand, the eight seasons played under the monopoly big league were financially disappointing to the club owners, mainly because of a national depression and the lack of competitive balance in the league. Nevertheless, the owners basked in their illusory power and glory. Styling themselves as magnates, the owners were lionized by the press, which made celebrities of men like John Brush of Cincinnati, Jim Hart of Chicago,

A. H. Soden of Boston, Charles Byrne of Brooklyn, and the notorious Andrew Freedman of New York. But the magnates were a disunited lot; contentious and individualistic to a fault, they battled one another for advantage. The poorer owners fought for an even split of gate receipts and the right to play Sunday games. Freedman loudly and vainly pursued his controversial baseball trust plan, which called for the annual redistribution of players with special advantages for his strategically located New York club. And in 1899 two owners each acquired control over two clubs and launched destructive syndicate baseball schemes. By the end of the 1899 campaign the quarreling owners agreed to drop four of the league's weaker clubs and return to an eight-club format. This move saddled the remaining eight clubs with a collective debt of $110,000—the price paid to buy off the four discarded clubs.

As the new century dawned, a rival league rose to contest the NL's monopoly of major league baseball. This latest challenge came from the strong Western League, an elite minor league circuit whose president, Byron B. Johnson, resented the NL's player drafting policies. In 1900 after the NL cut back to eight teams, Johnson's teams snapped up surplus NL players. The Western League was renamed the American League (AL), and franchises were planted in Chicago and Cleveland. The following year, Johnson demanded major league status for the AL. When he was rebuffed, his clubs raided NL rosters, enticing players with offers of higher salaries. This move ignited an all-out war, and over the 1901 and 1902 seasons the NL and AL dueled after the fashion of the baseball wars of the nineteenth century. Such interleague wars had always disrupted the reserve clause system, and this one was no exception. While the American League war raged, the players enjoyed a brief respite from the reserve clause and also scored limited gains in salaries and working conditions.

The Players Protective Association of 1900–1903

The outbreak of the American League war coincided with a renewed attempt by major league players to launch a collective bargaining movement against NL owners. This second union movement was precipitated by the NL owners' decision to cut back to eight teams for the 1900 season. Some sixty players lost their jobs through this cutback, which fanned a wave of unionist sentiment among the league's players. Moving secretly because of fears of owner reprisals, selected NL player delegates met in New York City in June 1900 and formed the Players Protective Association. At this meeting, three veteran players were chosen to head the association: Charles "Chief" Zimmer was named president, and Clark Griffith and Hugh Jennings became vice presidents. On hand to lend advice to the organizers was

Dan Harris of the American Federation of Labor, but the players decided against affiliating with organized labor or using the strike weapon to advance their cause. Their caution won the organization early press support, and one month later a second meeting was attended by one hundred players, including some from the American and Eastern leagues.

At this meeting Harry Taylor, a former major league player turned lawyer, surfaced as the chief strategist of the association. Taylor pledged to help the players in their struggle by working to modify the reserve clause, to improve salaries and working conditions, and to seek reforms in such matters as player sales and the farming of players to the minor leagues. That fall Taylor was named counsel and spokesman for the association, and one of his first moves was to urge all members to refrain from signing 1901 seasonal contracts until the NL owners agreed to consider the association's demands. These demands included the expansion of the ten-day release clause in player contracts to allow a player (as well as an owner) to opt for his release within ten days of giving notice of his intent. Moreover, Taylor demanded that no player be sold, traded, or sent to the minors without giving his consent.

Although the NL owners branded Taylor as a dangerous radical, the threat from the American League prompted them to treat with the Players Protective Association. When the two sides met in December 1900, however, the owners' committee advised the player delegation that it was not empowered to grant any concessions. Following this rebuff, Taylor's strategy of persuading NL players to sign no contracts for the 1901 season failed. That year nearly one hundred NL players either contracted with AL teams or accepted higher salary offers from nervous NL clubs. The players' opportunistic actions undermined Taylor's strategy of using the association's united front against NL owners and soon made the association a pawn in the struggle between the NL and the AL. Mindful of this fact, AL president Johnson appeared to recognize the Players Association when he promised not to farm a player to the minors without the consent of the player.

Johnson's tactics persuaded NL owners to try to win the support of the Players Association in their struggle against the AL. In February 1901 the NL owners requested a meeting with the association, provided that counselor Taylor not attend. Promising to keep Taylor informed of the proceedings, Zimmer headed a player delegation that met with the owners. At the meeting the NL owners agreed to recognize the association if the association would promise to expel any of its members who jumped to the American League. This condition was accepted by the players, who also won other concessions. Among them, the owners agreed to modify the reserve clause along the following lines: there would be a one-year option to renew a player's contract; no player could be assigned to the minors without his consent; and, if sent to the minors, a player would receive a fixed salary.

These limited concessions failed to satisfy most players, nor did they prevent association members from jumping to the American League. By failing to hold its players in line, the association lost its credibility as a bargaining agency. As the association's fortunes sank, Taylor devoted most of his time to his legal affairs, and the discredited Zimmer lost his post as association president. Zimmer's successor, Tom Daly, jumped to the AL in 1902, leaving the association leaderless and dying. The collapse of the Players Association coincided with the end of the American League war. Under the National Agreement of 1903 the American League was recognized as a major league, and the NL and the AL agreed to respect each other's territorial rights and player contracts, including the reserve clause. A three-member National Commission on Baseball was empowered to rule on disputes arising between the major leagues, but no provision was made for player representation or input on the commission. AL president Johnson became the most powerful member of the National Commission, and he strongly opposed player unionism. So did most players, who for the time being rejected unionism as a solution to their continuing grievances. Fear of owner reprisals was a major deterrent, but rampant individualism and unwillingness to be linked with labor organizations also mitigated against the rise of collective action by players. Under the press of cumulative grievances, however, union sentiments rose again in the second decade of the twentieth century.

The Baseball Players Fraternity, 1912–17

The dual major league system, with its profitable World Series format, ushered in an era of stability and prosperity for major league baseball. From 4.7 million admissions in 1903, major league game attendance rose to 7 million in 1908 and peaked at 10 million in 1911. Rising revenues sparked a ballpark building boom. New stadiums, capable of accommodating an average of 30,000 spectators each, appeared beginning in 1909. By then the annual World Series games between the league champions helped swell annual revenues by as much as $500,000. At the same time expanded newspaper coverage boosted the popularity of the "national game."

During these prosperous years player salaries rose slowly. By 1910 superstar Nap Lajoie was paid $12,000 a season, but the average player salary was $2,500, and some players still received less than $1,000. Not surprisingly, players groused over their modest shares of the profits and other long-standing grievances. These included abuses of the reserve clause, harsh disciplinary codes, poor working conditions, and peremptory dismissals or assignments to minor league teams. What is more, at this time players often did not receive copies of their seasonal contracts and were also obliged to pay for their uniforms.

In need of a leader to advance their cause, the players found one in David Fultz, another former player turned New York lawyer. Although prudishly critical of easygoing, spendthrift players, Fultz nevertheless won the respect of several players whom he had advised on contract matters since 1908. By 1910 some of them were urging Fultz to help them organize for collective action against the owners.

In May 1912 a playing-field incident precipitated the formation of the third organizational movement by the major league players. In a game at New York, Detroit star Ty Cobb attacked and beat an abusive fan and drew a ten-day suspension without pay from AL president Johnson. Rallying behind their volatile and generally unpopular teammate, the Detroit players demanded Cobb's reinstatement and a formal hearing on the incident. When Johnson refused, Cobb's teammates refused to play a game in Philadelphia, forcing the Detroit owner to field a team of semiprofessional players against the Athletics. In the aftermath of this famous one-day "strike," Cobb persuaded his teammates to return to action. Cobb served his ten-day suspension, and his striking mates were fined fifty dollars each. But the episode fanned union sentiment among players in both leagues.

The following September, player representatives met in New York City and chose Fultz as their leader. At this meeting Fultz formally chartered the Baseball Players Fraternity as a New York State corporation. Fultz became president of the fraternity, and two players from each major league were named as vice presidents. Player representatives from each team staffed a board of directors. By the end of 1912 nearly three hundred players had paid annual dues of eighteen dollars to join the fledgling fraternity.

As envisioned by Fultz, the Players Fraternity was to be a professional association and not a labor union. To this end Fultz urged the membership to conduct themselves as professionals and pointedly disavowed any comparisons with the ill-fated Brotherhood movement. Moreover, Fultz rejected both the strike weapon and any thought of creating a rival major league. In a published article Fultz summed up the major player grievances that he proposed to redress and called for higher salaries for professional players at all levels.

Over the years 1913–14, Fultz concentrated on swelling the ranks of the fraternity, which by the end of 1914 boasted 1,100 members and $10,000 in funds. The fraternity's outreach extended to minor league players whose grievances made for a common cause in the mind of the altruistic Fultz. Unfortunately, the inclusion of minor league player concerns ultimately undermined the fraternity and greatly contributed to its demise. Later organizational movements by major league players would exclude minor league players from membership.

In 1914 the National Commission recognized the fraternity, and the major league owners conceded eleven of its seventeen demands, but little of substance was won by the players. Among the concessions granted, the owners agreed not to discriminate against fraternity members, to give written reasons for suspending a player, to give players copies of their annual contracts, to furnish free uniforms, to give unconditional release to ten-year veterans if requested by those who qualified, and to paint outfield fences green. This last concession was regarded as an important safety measure by players, one that would diminish their chance of being hit by pitched balls by giving batters a better view. But the owners refused to give ground on major issues. They refused to guarantee the contracts of players sent to the minor leagues or to publish waiver lists of players who were being shopped for trade or sale to other clubs. Nor would the owners modify the reserve clause. Although Fultz accepted the reserve clause as a necessary part of the baseball business, he had hoped to harmonize the clause with existing civil laws; failing that, he had hoped to at least limit the application of the reserve clause to five years, after which time a player would have been free to sell his services anew.

The decision of the major league owners to recognize the fraternity and grant it some concessions owed more to the threat from a strong rival league than any threat posed by the organized players. In 1914 the rival Federal League launched its move for recognition as a third major league. By dangling higher salary offers and promises of better working conditions, the Federal League promoters enticed some eighty players to jump their contracts or their reserve clauses and join its ranks. When the established majors sued some of the reserve clause jumpers, the Federal League owners won an important legal ruling against the reserve clause. Moreover, the Federal League owners struck back by filing a federal antitrust suit against the established majors. The Federal League folded after two seasons of play (1914–15), however, and its owners settled their antitrust suit out of court at a cost of $600,000 to the established major leagues. Despite these developments, the disgruntled Baltimore club promoters of the Federal League pressed on with another antitrust suit against the majors, and in December 1922 the U.S. Supreme Court ruled against the claim.

The Federal League settlement of 1915 hastened the collapse of the Players Fraternity. Like all player movements thus far, the fraternity had drawn strength from interleague warfare; once this opportunistic menace was gone, the fraternity, like its predecessors, stood alone and woefully vulnerable. Still, the fraternity managed to claim 1,215 members in 1916, even though it faced the combined opposition of the established majors and the

National Association of Professional Baseball Leagues, which represented the minor league promoters. Although the fraternity managed to score a few gains—including winning the reinstatement of players who had jumped to the Federal League and continued pay for any player injured in the line of duty—the organization suffered a major defeat in its effort to win improved playing conditions for minor league players. Stung by rebuff on this issue, Fultz threatened to merge the fraternity with the American Federation of Labor and to lead a strike against the majors in 1917. But AFL leader Samuel Gompers withheld the welcome mat from the association, and Fultz's major league supporters showed little interest in affiliating with the AFL or striking on behalf of minor league players. Thus isolated, Fultz lost control of the fraternity, which soon expired. The national commission's withdrawal of recognition was a death blow; in its wake the players' fear of reprisals by owners led to a severe decline in fraternity membership. Thus, it was Fultz's quixotic strike call that spelled the end of the fraternity; by the end of 1917 it had vanished.

In the aftermath of the fraternity's collapse, the United States' entry into World War I posed serious problems for organized baseball. After two seasons of financial austerity, major league baseball rebounded in 1919. But that season also produced the Black Sox Scandal, which threatened the game's public image once its revelations came to light in 1920. In this episode eight Chicago White Sox players, who were motivated in part by owner Charles Comiskey's pinch-penny salary practices, were charged with accepting bribes from gamblers to throw the 1919 World Series. The fallout from this widely publicized scandal ended the reign of the National Commission in the major leagues in 1920. The following year, federal judge Kenesaw M. Landis was named sole Commissioner of Baseball.

The Long Hiatus, 1920–45

Over the years 1920–45, organizational movements by major league players were at a standstill. Strong public antilabor sentiment in the 1920s affected major league players, who viewed themselves as professional individualists. When attorney Ray Cannon of Milwaukee attempted to organize a National Baseball Players Association in 1922 with the avowed goal of enabling players to share in the governance of the game, few players were interested. Amid gales of hostile publicity, Cannon's association was stillborn. In 1924 an Association of Professional Ball Players was organized in Los Angeles, but it was only a mutual benefit organization dedicated to assisting sick and indigent former players. Open to major and minor league players and umpires, the association attracted 2,000 members by 1926. Eventually, the commissioner's office lent some financial support to the association, which in an average year assisted some fifty needy veterans.

Meanwhile, players of the 1920s nursed familiar grievances, especially against the reserve clause system, which made possible the brisk market in selling and trading players. In 1925 New York Congressman Fiorello La Guardia introduced a bill in the House of Representatives calling for a 90 percent federal tax to be levied on any player sale in excess of $5,000. The tax would be assessed only if the bartered player was not paid the full purchase price. Not surprisingly the bill failed to become law. If it had, it might well have ended the abuse of the reserve clause. Still, the bill was one of the early harbingers of increasing congressional interest in curbing abusive practices by major league owners. The suggestion that any federal action against major league baseball practices must come from Congress was one of the signals sent by the U.S. Supreme Court, which ruled in 1922 that the major league owners were not liable to prosecution under existing antitrust laws.

During the 1920s rising salaries dampened player interest in organizing to better their lot. From an average of $5,000 in 1923, major league salaries rose to an average of $7,000 in 1930, with superstar Babe Ruth's $80,000 salary leading all players that year. By 1930 an estimated 35 percent of club revenues went for salaries. Thereafter this percentage steadily declined, reaching 22 percent in recent years.

But if player salaries were better in the 1920s, they were also unequally distributed. In 1929 team payrolls ranged from more than $300,000 for teams like the Yankees and Cubs to little more than $140,000 for teams like the Pirates and Phillies. Comparative salary information was unavailable to players for use in their individual salary negotiations, but owners shared this information and used it to browbeat players in negotiations. Forced to negotiate as individuals, players were usually confronted with take-it-or-leave-it demands. Star players might stage holdouts for more money, but this ploy incurred the wrath of fans. Fans were incited by sportswriters, whose expenses were often paid by club owners.

During the Depression era and World War II, nothing stirred on the labor front in major league baseball. During the 1930s average salaries fell to $6,000 in 1933 and only regained the $7,000 mark in 1939. Meanwhile, New Deal legislation, especially the Wagner Act of 1935, which created the National Labor Relations Board (NLRB), defended and strengthened the rights of workers to organize for collective bargaining. In time the NLRB policies would be used to good advantage by union-minded major league players, but not during the Depression. With a surplus of hungry players in the minors aspiring to major league playing positions, major league players were unwilling to risk the anger of owners with collective demands for reforms.

The far-reaching military drafts of World War II reversed the situation and confronted owners with a talent shortage. Nevertheless, player salaries actually declined during the war years. Sagging attendance in 1942–43 and federally imposed wage freezes combined to lower salaries to an average of $6,400 in 1943. And despite rising attendance in 1944–45, player salaries remained low under wartime wage freeze policies. In the first full year of peace, 1946, the wage and price restrictions were lifted, unleashing nation-wide demands for higher wages. During this banner year for strikes in the United States, union membership soared to nearly fifteen million.

The American Baseball Guild of 1946

Major league baseball owners were caught up in the labor turmoil that swept the nation in 1946. Former players returning from military service complained about low salaries, travel problems, night games, and working conditions. Invoking a provision of the Veterans Act that allowed a worker to return to his former job at his original salary, dozens of players forced owners to pay cash settlements for illegal demotions. At the same time, promoters tempted players with high salary offers to join Mexican League teams. When a handful of major league players jumped, Commissioner A. B. Chandler retaliated with expulsions and blacklistings. But Chandler's invocation of "baseball law" provoked a formidable challenge from one recalcitrant player, former New York Giant outfielder Danny Gardella. In jumping to the Mexican League for $13,000 in salary and bonus payments, Gardella had refused to sign a proffered Giant contract. He was suspended for five seasons and blacklisted for jumping his reserve clause. In 1947 lawyer Frederic Johnson persuaded Gardella to sue Chandler and major league baseball for conspiracy to deny a player his livelihood. When this challenge to the reserve clause and "baseball law" was rejected by a fed-eral district court in 1948, Johnson filed an appeal. A federal appellate court in New York voted 2 to 1 to grant Gardella a trial. The appellate judges were moved by Johnson's argument that income from radio and tele-vision broadcasts brought major league baseball under the control of inter-state commerce laws. The ominous implications of this decision persuaded the owners to settle Gardella's case out of court in 1949. Although they avoided a legal battle, the case alerted congressional subcommittees. Over the next decade congressional inquiries into baseball's status under the an-titrust laws were to harry the fearful owners.

The Mexican League incident also inspired another movement to organize major league players. Early in 1946 Robert Murphy, a lawyer and former National Labor Relations Board examiner, reacting to the punishment of Mexican League jumpers and to the grievances of all major league players, moved to organize the players. In April Murphy chartered the American Baseball Guild in New York and proposed a wide-ranging list of reforms.

The guild's platform called for a $6,500 minimum salary, impartial arbitration of salary disputes, the replacement of the reserve clause system with a system of long-term contracts, and the elimination of the ten-day release clause from player contracts. Furthermore, players sold to other clubs were to receive half of the selling price and, if traded, were to be compensated with hefty salary increases.

To force the major league owners to deal with the guild, Murphy alerted the NLRB of his intent to use its established procedures. These included holding elections for players to decide if they wanted to join the guild. Having met with players on the Pittsburgh team, Murphy proposed to use that team's vote as a first test of overall player support for the guild. To this end, Murphy served notice on the Pittsburgh owner of his intent to hold an election in June. When the owner hedged, guild supporters on the Pittsburgh team threatened to strike. But the strike was averted by the owner's emotional appeal to players. Although twenty players voted to strike, this was too narrow a majority to qualify under NLRB policy. Still, Murphy kept the pot boiling by filing an unfair labor practice complaint with the NLRB against the Pirates and against five other major league teams.

While awaiting the decision of the NLRB, the major league owners took steps to undercut the guild movement. In June a committee representing the club owners met with player representatives and listened to their demands. In July the owners' committee offered the following concessions—a minimum salary of $5,500, a spring training allowance of $25 a week per player, and a pension program to be funded by contributions from players and owners. For the while, these sops had the desired effect of hobbling the guild. In August an election called by the NLRB to vote on the guild issue resulted in the Pittsburgh players rejecting the union. In the aftermath of the guild's defeat, the owners reduced their minimum salary concession by $500 and inserted a disclaimer clause in player contracts that deprived a player of legal recourse in any contract dispute. By leaving the pension promise intact, however, the owners sowed the seeds of a future harvest of labor unrest.

By linking the funding of the pension program to the sale of national television and radio rights, the owners established a precedent that their contemporary successors would rue. And by not informing the unorganized players of the pension program, the owners ended up confronting another labor movement in 1953. Although its early years were precarious, in time the Major League Baseball Players Association would become a powerful countervailing force on behalf of the players in major league baseball. Indeed, the successes scored to this date by this fifth players' organization surely have exceeded the wildest dreams of baseball's pioneer labor leader John Montgomery Ward.

BIBLIOGRAPHIC ESSAY

The best history of union movements by major league players is Lee Lowenfish and Tony Lupien's volume, *The Imperfect Diamond* (New York: Stein and Day, 1980). The early struggles of players to organize against owners are treated by Ted Vincent, *Mudville's Revenge: The Rise and Fall of American Sport* (New York: Seaview Books, 1981). Insights into John Montgomery Ward, the founder of the Brotherhood of Professional Base Ball Players, are to be found in a pair of articles: Cynthia Bass, "The Making of a Baseball Radical," *National Pastime* 2 (Fall 1982): 63–65, and Lee Lowenfish, "The Later Years of John M. Ward," ibid., 67–69. For sketches of post-World War II club owners, see Harold Parrott's, *The Lords of Baseball* (New York: Praeger, 1975).

Multivolume histories of the major league game that place player organizational movements in the context of the history of the game itself include Harold Seymour's two volumes, *Baseball: The Early Years* (New York: Oxford University Press, 1960), and *Baseball: The Golden Age* (New York: Oxford University Press, 1971). Seymour covers the early player movements up to 1930 in considerable depth. See also my own three-volume study, *American Baseball* (University Park: Pennsylvania State University Press, 1983), which extends the historical coverage of the major league game to 1982, and *America through Baseball* (Chicago: Nelson-Hall Press, 1976), which contains an essay on player union movements from the early years to the formation of the Major League Baseball Players Association.

Marvin Miller and the New Unionism in Baseball   6

Charles P. Korr

When the 1987 strike by the National Football League Players' Association collapsed with no apparent gains for players, many commentators took the opportunity to compare its failures with the long record of successes (seemingly two decades long) by the Major League Baseball Players Association (MLBPA). Even a casual observer of sports might be able to list some of the changes that have taken place in baseball as a consequence of the MLBPA: high player salaries, limited control by players over being traded or sold, an excellent pension plan, and impartial arbitration concerning salary disputes and grievances. The MLBPA's most significant victory was one that most observers had thought was impossible—gaining the right of players to become free agents and to sell their services to the team of their choice (as limited by the agreement negotiated between the association and the owners). In slightly more than a decade, the MLBPA overturned almost a century of baseball's traditions and business practices, effectively ending management's dominance, which had been sanctified by the U.S. Supreme Court. The executive director of the association, Marvin Miller, in many ways became a more important figure in baseball than the owners, the league presidents, and even the Commissioner of Baseball.[1] How did Miller operate during the first few years of his tenure in order to gain the confidence and support of the membership, and how did he ensure that the MLBPA would assert itself as a force to be taken seriously by management?

Since the MLBPA was formed after many unsuccessful efforts to organize baseball players for collective action before 1966, it is easy to describe its success as nothing more than the one-man victory of Marvin Miller over the joint efforts of the entrenched owners. That analysis of the United States' "National Pastime" has the appeal of the Western film legend in which the hero faces down the assorted villains in a one-man crusade. But

Miller was not a film character nor a lone warrior. His policies were rooted firmly within the context of his long career as a labor official. His actions were based on his ability to understand that he was employed by an association that had the potential to become something more than a loosely known fraternal order and "company union" whose main purpose was to deal with a pension fund.

In 1953 efforts by players Ralph Kiner and Allie Reynolds to give new meaning to the MLBPA had been opposed by both owners and former players. Bill Terry (who had said of baseball in 1941 that "no business has ever made money with poorer management")[2] warned that he was "absolutely against the players association" and that Reynolds and Kiner "will find themselves in a bad spot if they do not halt right now." Terry feared that even though the players said they were not heading toward unionism, they did not understand the dangers: "Not that the union principle is wrong, but it is not for ball players and baseball."[3] Reynolds tried to calm that fear in an article in the semiofficial house organ of baseball management, *The Sporting News.* "I have nothing against unions in industry. But if I had any suspicion that we in baseball were moving towards a union, I would not have anything to do with the enterprise."[4]

Those sentiments did not wear off easily. In 1963, almost ten years after Reynolds's declaration, Bob Friend, the National League player representative for the MLBPA, published a "rebuttal" to a forthcoming article entitled "Unionization and Professional Sports" in which the author had claimed that unionization might be the best way for players to achieve economic strength and that the MLBPA was ineffective because of its lack of funds and stale leadership.[5] Friend stated that the association already had enough money and good enough leadership. Those comments are worth remembering in light of the situation three years later, in 1966, when Friend participated in the meeting at which Miller was selected to head the association.[6] In 1963 Friend went beyond simply defending his association to justifying the status quo in baseball: "The reserve clause is an absolute must for the survival of baseball, and during the thirteen years I have been in the National League I know of no player who has been exploited." Friend's conclusion was that the players were getting more than they ever would with a union. To the charge that the players were relying on the "benevolence" of the owners, Friend replied that a union "would not fit the situation in baseball [because] players and management work closely together. It would destroy baseball if fans were exposed to the spectacle of someone like Stan Musial picketing a ball park." Any change—even steps in the direction of unionism—would be dangerous, and it could not help the players, who had made great strides through the present system with the minimum salary and expenses and had a good pension plan.[7] The benefits that Friend pointed to with pride in 1963 were precisely those Miller used in 1966 to rally the support of the MLBPA's player representatives against proposals by management that might have restricted the right of the association to act as the bargaining agent and representative of the players.[8]

Despite Friend's views, as early as 1960 Robin Roberts (one of the players' spokesmen on the Pension Fund Committee, which was composed of an equal number of player and owner representatives) had been invited by several player representatives to discuss the possibility of creating a permanent office for the MLBPA with a full-time staff. The issue was not who would lead the association, but whether there was any need for an office at all. Before the meeting, a group of players (who had been elected by other players to work in their interests) had obtained the commissioner's approval of the discussions about how to reshape their organization.[9] The essence of Roberts's presentation was that the association's workload warranted a full-time director and a full-time legal representative who would be empowered to deal with the pension fund and "all business matters pertaining to baseball players." However strange the pairing of something as specific as the pension and as general as "all business matters" might seem, it foreshadowed the future concerns of the association.[10] Two days later, after a lengthy discussion on the possibility of organizing a permanent office, another meeting of the player representatives was held, at which the motion to hire a full-time administrator was tabled by a unanimous vote. This decision was not taken thoughtlessly. The Executive Committee reported that a major concession was about to be granted by the owners. They would *permit* (my italics) Judge Cannon, the MLBPA's legal advisor, to sit as an advisor to the players on the pension committee. That change supposedly negated the need for a full-time advocate. The 1960 discussion revealed much about the players' concerns, the association's needs, and the relationship between the players, the owners, and the commissioner. It makes it easy to understand how Bob Friend's position in 1963 represented the prevailing concerns of his fellow players and their organization.

A few years later, Marvin Miller made an interesting reply to a reporter from the *Chicago Tribune* who had quoted Judge Cannon as saying that during his time, baseball had "the finest relationship between players and management in the history of sport."[11] Miller responded that whatever the relationship had been under Cannon, it "had a steep price, all of it paid by the players in the form of failing to achieve progress merited by the circumstances."[12] Miller and Cannon did not simply disagree; they had a basic philosophical difference. Cannon saw himself as representing the interests of one part of a larger entity known as baseball, a sport that had a recognized hierarchy and in which individual players had no vested interest and no permanent stake. Miller saw himself as the negotiator for one side in what he viewed as a classic two-sided management-labor relationship. Miller also saw the history of baseball in a very different way from his predecessor. When someone cautioned him that players come and go but the owners remain forever, he responded that players remain forever in the game, even if their names keep changing.[13] It was, after all, players on the field that attracted the paying customers, and it was generations of players that had given baseball the sense of tradition and continuity that made it special.

The symbolic passing of the torch of leadership from Robert Cannon to Marvin Miller took place at a special meeting of the MLBPA held in Miami on March 5, 1966, to discuss the candidates for the position of executive director and for the player representatives to nominate one man for approval by the membership of the association. (A few months before this meeting Cannon had been offered the position and had rejected it.) The elected player representatives were joined by Frank Scott (the director), Robert Cannon (legal advisor), Robin Roberts, Bob Friend, and Harvey Kuenn. The meeting also included General William Eckert, the commissioner of baseball, and Lee McPhail, his assistant. No one at the meeting was surprised when Eckert and McPhail took part in the discussion but not in the voting.[14]

Commissioner Eckert recommended discretion in the selection of the executive director and stated that he would cooperate fully with the new man. Any definition of cooperation must be understood in light of his opening remark that the office of commissioner "was intended to represent the players, *as well as* the owners" (my italics).[15] It is easy to joke about William Eckert's ineffectiveness as commissioner, but in this instance he was simply acting in the tradition of his predecessors and in the pattern that was adopted by his successor, Bowie Kuhn. The concept of the commissioner as the one spokesman for all the constituent parts of professional baseball was part of the history of the game, but not something that Marvin Miller, who was to become the main topic of conversation at the meeting, was going to accept.

Robin Roberts had been the impetus behind the decision to set up a permanent office and to hire a full-time executive director. His role in the process had hardly endeared him to the owners, many of whom regarded him as some kind of agitator. His most important contribution to changing the association had been to bring the name of Marvin Miller before the screening committee. Miller had been recommended to Roberts by George Taylor, a distinguished professor at the Wharton School of the University of Pennsylvania. When Roberts wrote about the episode almost three years later, he recalled that he had sent the whole list of possible candidates to Commissioner Eckert and had asked him to run a check on the suitability of each of them for the position. Roberts concluded his call to Eckert with the comment, "If there is anyone on the list you think we should not choose because he might be bad for the game, then he won't be chosen."[16] If that was the philosophy of the man who prodded his fellow members into recognizing the need for a permanent representative, why should there be any surprise that the majority of the players were tepid in their beliefs about the autonomy of their organization and that Eckert's comments and Cannon's philosophy scarcely created any stir?

The day before the March 5 selection meeting of the MLBPA, the pension committee (the joint group) had met and approved two-year funding for the permanent office. General Eckert referred to this decision at the selection meeting, reminding the players that "the allocation recommendation by the Pension Committee would have to be approved by all of the owners."[17] Eckert was not making a veiled threat but was simply describing the unvarnished realities of an association that until this time had been dependent on the good graces of the owners to approve its funding. Could such an organization function as anything more than a part-time operation working out of some player's hotel suite? The commissioner concluded by saying that if the players had any questions concerning the pension committee's decision to fund the permanent office, they could direct them to "the Commissioner's Office at any time."[18] Eckert was not making policy but merely relaying the realities of the situation, just as his presence at the selection meeting spoke volumes about the independence of the association.

When the voting took place for the candidates brought forward by the screening committee, Miller was chosen on the first ballot. Plans were made to distribute his name and biography to the press and tell them that similar information would be sent to all the teams so that their members could vote on his acceptability. The voting would take place after Miller had toured all of the spring training camps in the few weeks following the nomination meeting to give players a chance to question him and get an idea about his ideas and style.[19] The players did not know anything about Miller except what they could learn from his biographical sketch and whatever their player representatives and management said about him. The facts about him were clear but open to different interpretations. He was a labor expert, and much of his career had been spent in the employ of the Steelworkers Union. Immediately after his nomination, some players and writers raised questions about what impact he might have on baseball. What did his background or his abilities have to do with the sport and its unique history of paternalistic player-management relationships?

There were no doubts about Miller in the mind of one of the three men on the screening committee. Jim Bunning, now a Republican congressman from Kentucky, was a veteran pitcher in 1966 who had been active in the association and in pension-related matters for years. He had served as a player representative for both the Tigers and the Phillies and had been involved in the decision to create the permanent office and to name a full-time executive director. The issue of the permanent office had been important to him because he had felt the players "needed continuity" to get anything out of the owners. Bunning, twenty years after the fact, reflected that he had not been "particularly disappointed" when Judge Cannon turned down the job, and he was convinced from the start that Miller had exactly the qualities that the "players' group" needed at the time. Bunning understood that Miller's background with the Steelworkers might frighten some people in baseball, players and management alike. This fear was overcome in Bunning's mind by the belief that it "wouldn't take him long to learn the answers," and there was no question that shortly he "would know more about baseball than ownership did." The important feature about Miller was that "he knew labor-management law better than anyone the other side ever hired." If Miller had even a slight resemblance to "the hired gun" portrayed by his opponents in the press and management, we have to assume that players like Bunning recognized that they might be heading toward a confrontation with the owners. In Bunning's opinion, Miller did not maneuver the Executive Committee and the association into going in his direction; he was hired because players already knew that they had to do something to change the status quo.[20]

One reason to employ an expert like Miller was the vast amount of money coming into baseball. Bunning was concerned that the players were not getting "their share."[21] Bunning's sense of injustice was heightened by recent changes in ownership that had ended some of the old-style paternalism and encouraged some players like him to look more closely at the business side of baseball. Taking a chance on a permanent executive director seemed to be a logical alternative. Bunning's description sums up the case for Miller and the association's new approach: "The only way that we ever presented anything was at the joint meetings with the owners and we'd take our requests there and they would just laugh at us and say, 'Sure, we'll look at it,' and that was the end of it. We didn't know labor law, we didn't know collective bargaining." Most of the players did not want confrontation, but their leadership wanted to act to make them understand the realities of the situation. The players' group "needed someone to pull away that friendly fatherly image" with which the owners had controlled the players.[22]

No doubt the Executive Committee's feeling, as represented by Bunning, was a combination of self-interest and annoyance with the association's inability to change things. After all, "it gets a little frustrating after a while, not being taken seriously when you know that they're the capital, but without the players there is no franchise." If management had no idea in 1966 that many established veterans who could scarcely be called malcontents were dissatisfied with the system, it was even less aware that there were ordinary players who shared that feeling. It took a long series of annoyances for the MLBPA to get to the point it reached in 1966, but "we knew that when the mounds in the bull pen in Yankee Stadium were on the agenda for the annual joint meeting with the owners, then something was screwed up. It was another matter to have some idea about how to fix them." Miller's role, according to Bunning, was to "coldly explain" to the players what their options were.[23]

During his visits to the training camps in 1966 Miller had fielded questions about his background in organized labor. Management had inspired rumors that he was a "labor goon." The players also wanted to know what he thought were the issues confronting baseball. The most serious charge leveled against Miller was that he could not understand that ball players were individual talents who could not operate outside a system that employed a wage scale and paid a premium for seniority. In 1963 Bob Friend had written off the idea of a union because it "would antagonize the owners" and because "ball players could not submit to pay scales like bricklayers. . . . They are individualist. They don't contribute the same."[24] Miller went out of his way to remind the players that he was going to be the executive director of their own association, not the leader of some union that happened to include baseball players. He could not have disowned his past (nor would he have tried to).

The doubters among the players had to be convinced, as Bunning and Roberts had been, that his particular skills were just what they needed to address the problems they faced.[25] Before Miller could use his noted powers of persuasion, the players first had to have a sense that problems existed.[26] Miller spent most of his time listening to players, realizing that to address the inertia among them, he had to understand what mattered to them. At virtually every training camp the players expressed the same concerns—the season was too long; the travel schedule was brutal; playing conditions in certain ballparks were terrible and had not been improved despite complaints by the association. Most of all, players stated, the pension fund was good but had to be protected, and hopefully it could be improved.

The importance of the pension fund to the history of the MLBPA cannot be overestimated. In 1966, as far as most players were concerned, the pension was the association and vice versa. Miller discovered that most of the players had no idea how the fund operated or how it compared to retirement programs in other industries. From his perspective, this ignorance showed just how little most of the MLBPA's members had ever thought about the possibility of doing more for themselves through the association.[27] But the spring of 1966 was not the time for Miller, or the Executive Committee, to think about philosophical questions. First, Miller's selection by the members had to be ratified by a vote of the membership of the association, and the permanent office for the association had to be established. Between March and July, Miller demonstrated the style that would be the mark of his tenure as the executive director. He dealt with specific problems and waited until issues could be formulated in a way that the majority of the players could identify with, and he was careful not to get too far ahead of where the membership seemed to be heading. His determination to keep the players informed was based on a belief that once the players knew what was going on around them, they would reject the past practices of the owners.

Many commentators have noted that Miller was fortunate in having as his opponents a collection of men who were used to getting their way. The owners were unprepared to cope with an opponent who did not accept their premise that nothing was wrong in baseball and that the players' best interest was always one of the owners' main concerns. Miller could not imagine that even before he had an office of his own, the owners would present him with an almost perfect case to show the players the need for a strong association and to prove to the owners that he would not back away from a fight. The irony of the first struggle between Miller and management was that the latter brought up the one issue guaranteed to mobilize the energies of the players: the integrity and independence of the pension fund.

On June 6, 1966, Johnny Edwards presided over a specially called meeting of the player representatives on the Executive Committee to discuss and "work out" matters concerning the "financing of the permanent office."[28] The phrase "permanent office" had become a catchphrase implying that the players were establishing an organization that might be expected to be more active in pressing for the concerns of its members than had been the case with the part-time collaboration of Judge Cannon and Frank Scott. An even greater concern to some of the owners was that a full-time director might find or create divisive issues as a means of justifying his existence and that of the permanent office. The player representatives were joined at this June 6 meeting by Miller, Scott, Cannon, Roberts, and Kuenn. Miller's report provided the focus for the special meeting and set the scene for a tumultuous later meeting that day with representatives of the owners.

Miller started by reminding everyone that the pension committee (in December 1985) and the association's Executive Committee (in March 1966) had each approved the principle that once the permanent office was established it would be paid for out of money paid into the pension fund. As a result of these decisions, he reminded them, the player representatives had then voted on March 5, 1966, to establish the office and to name an executive director, subject only to ratification by the players. These decisions and the selection of Miller had been ratified by an overwhelming vote of the players in April 1966. But now the plans were beginning to unravel. Miller reported that the pension committee had the right to approve the financing of the office and that the commissioner had approved it, "but on May 3rd the owners attempted to assert a veto by reversing the actions of the Pension Committee and the recommendation of the Executive [Committee]."[29] Miller had met with the commissioner a few days after this attempt to question the decision of the owners and had been informed that their action was based on their counsel's view that financing for the office was prohibited by the Taft-Hartley Law.[30] The spectacle of Commissioner Eckert lecturing Marvin Miller on the subtleties of Taft-Hartley would be hilarious were the issue not so serious. The owners' position, simply put, was that they were doing nothing more than backing away from a previously illegal position. Many of the player representatives must have been surprised by the owners' eager admission of past ineptitude or quasi-illegal conduct, especially since they had consistently asserted that the players did not need a strong organization because they could trust both the owners' judgment and instinct to do what was best for everyone. The timing of the owners' "mea culpa" regarding the Taft-Hartley Act gave Miller the opportunity to question their sincerity, their ability as businessmen, and the scope of their paternalistic control of the sport—and to do it with an issue that had been raised by the owners, not the association.

Miller's June 6 presentation stressed that the financial problem could be solved. The real issue was what the owners were trying to do and why. Miller pointed out that Taft-Hartley forbids payment of money by an employer to employees' organizations. By using the Taft-Hartley argument, the owners were assuming that "baseball was an industry affecting commerce," that the association had been a labor organization under the definition of the law, and that all of the money going into the pension fund belonged to the owners.[31] The first point struck at baseball's long-cherished exemption from antitrust legislation, and the second provided additional legitimacy to the association. The last point was less dramatic, but it was Miller's real weapon. He pointed out that regardless of the first two claims, it was not true that the players' contribution to the pension fund was "Owners' Money."[32] He was in a position to attack the owners' good faith and set himself up as the defender of the pension. Miller could not have choreographed a better situation for himself than the one he had been presented by the owners.

The owners' position might have been on firmer ground if it had described a pension fund that was not partly based on employee contributions; some fine points of labor law might have been argued. But it was the method and timing of the presentation, not the legal issues, that infuriated many of the player representatives. The owners were so used to getting their way without being challenged, they were unprepared for Miller's counter-attack. Once Miller started on the owners, he was not going to let them off the hook. If their contention was correct that baseball was covered by Taft-Hartley, then several conclusions followed: the law had been violated for years before 1966; the owners and their lawyers had ignored it; and, more-over, the players had "certain rights and privileges" given them by the law.[33] No doubt these conclusions were as surprising to the owners as they were unacceptable to them.

When the player representatives turned their attention to how the associ-ation should be financed, some of the players raised questions about using their two-dollar-per-day contribution versus taking $150,000 per year from the proceeds of the All-Star Game. A resolution was passed to discuss var-ious alternatives with the owners' committee in the meeting that was to follow immediately.[34] The controversial joint meeting opened with a state-ment by Commissioner Eckert that summarized the May 3 actions of the owners and presented a written proposal to amend the benefits plan by elim-inating the two-dollar contribution as well as terminating the reimburse-ment of player representatives for their expenses incurred while attending meetings. Miller replied by asking for a discussion of the proposal drawn up by the players. Eckert said that the owners would need more time to discuss it, but Walter O'Malley said there was no reason to consider the proposal since some representatives of the twenty clubs were absent from the meet-ing. In any case, O'Malley said, the owners would have to look into the legality of the proposal before discussing it. When Miller pointed out that the owners present were accompanied by their lawyers and that the issues had to be taken care of quickly, Tom Haller followed by asking if any of the owners would like to respond to the proposal made by Miller "on behalf of the player representatives"—the phrasing of the question made clear that Miller and the association were united. The answer by the owners was com-plete silence. Then Donald Grant, a New York Mets executive, suggested that since it had been so difficult to arrange the joint meeting, rather than terminate it "with little accomplished," the owners, commissioner, and counsel should caucus and meet later with the players.[35]

During the recess, the players returned to their own room to discuss what had happened. In the official minutes that were distributed later to the membership of the association it was noted that the representatives ex-pressed the opinion that "a meeting such as just had been held was a farce. . . . It was clear that the Commissioner and the League President and the owners felt they had no authority to work out a solution with the Players Association. They had been given the authority to present their own proposal, but not to consider any other."[36] There was more than pique involved in the reaction of the player representatives. The outcome of the first part of this joint meeting convinced them that their decision to hire an assertive executive director had been correct. The players turned from anger to working out a set of specific proposals that went beyond anything they had prepared before. The vote was sixteen in favor, with one abstention, for a plan to work out the funding for the office (meeting only with the player members of the pension committee) that would take $150,000 from either the pension fund or the All-Star Game.[37]

The reconvened joint meeting gave the players even more reason to distrust the reaction of management to the creation of a permanent office. Paul Porter, counsel for the owners, reasserted that the proposed funding was illegal and that the owners "considered All-Star Game funds to be legally the property of the clubs." The statement must have been the beginning of the end for any illusions held by the members of the association that the supposed benevolence of the owners held any assurances for the future. The players had been shown the business equivalent of "the Lord giveth and the Lord taketh away." But Porter was not wholly negative; he proposed a "proper, lawful and legitimate" way to finance the office—a two-dollar contribution by the players. The owners were suggesting the equivalent of a "checkoff system on the basis of a voluntary revocable plan."[38] In a few sentences, the attorney had destroyed whatever faith existed in the charity of the owners, had discussed the association as though it were a union, and had suggested precisely the source of funding that Miller thought the association needed to ensure its ability to challenge the owners in the future.

On the face of it, there are two plausible explanations for Porter's remarks. Either his employers were convinced that nothing could be worse than providing an income from the pension fund for the association, or they thought that a voluntary checkoff system would not attract enough players to create a viable organization. In either case, the owners' calculations were incorrect. They gave Miller the mechanism to run the association and the issue with which to create solidarity among its members.

When Miller spoke at the reconvened meeting, he reviewed the history of the discussions to use the $150,000 to finance the association. He pointed out that during two years of meetings and correspondence no attorney for the owners had even suggested that the proposed set-up was a violation of the law. How could they account for the sudden concern over legal problems? The question was rhetorical, and Miller followed with the answer. His statement is worth quoting in its entirety since it marked the gloves-off, no-false-respect-for-existing-authority approach that set the pattern for Miller's career: "It had not escaped the attention of the players that the 'legal' problems allegedly present first came to light when it appeared that the new Executive Director of the Players Association was to be someone whom the owners were unable to hand pick. These 'legal' problems which counsel, Mr. Porter, admitted had been ignored for years by the owners, suddenly became a matter of concern when the players decided to name their own choice for the new job.'' The minutes of the meeting do not give any way to be sure about the tone in which these remarks were delivered, but Miller's sense of sarcasm seems evident. It should also be noted that since Cannon was present at the meeting, he could not have missed the references to his relationship with the owners.[39]

The response to Miller's statement was a comment by the counsel for the National League that the lack of diligence in discovering the Taft-Hartley problems was not a sign of bad faith. Commissioner Eckert followed, remarking the ''no one questions the actions of the players in selecting a man of their choice.''[40] These replies only intensified the wariness of the players and convinced them that they needed to press for answers and demand the right to take their own course of action. Ed Fisher was not challenged by any of his colleagues when he said that ''not a single thing had been accomplished and that the Player Representatives would like to know when our proposal would be considered.'' The commissioner's answer—that a decision would be made at an early date— did little to clear up the real question: what did the owners intend to do to show they were acting in good faith?[41]

Fisher was wrong—something surely had been accomplished during the five hours and forty-five minutes taken up by the joint meeting: the players had asserted their independence; their executive director had shown that he was not going to hold back in his attacks on management or the commissioner if he felt they were useful; and the attorney for the owners had opened the door for the association to operate in the way in which Miller could gain the greatest independence of action for it. After this June 6 joint meeting Miller would use the words and actions of the owners and their representatives as his most potent weapon to form a united front in the MLBPA. From that time, Miller went on the attack against the notion that the players could place any faith in the good will or generosity of management.

The player representatives found it easier than before to convince the players that the only way they could solve their problems was through their own organization and their ability to stick together. For his part, Miller had to provide leadership and focus. He recognized that he had to pick his targets carefully. Nothing could be more harmful to the uncertain future of the association than charging out in a quixotic fashion and showing the players that they had either an idealogue or an ineffective negotiator to lead them. Miller concentrated on two sets of projects in his early years as executive director—specific issues such as minimum salary, grievances, fines, and the pension fund and the broader goal of asserting that the association was both the necessary and the legally established representative of the major league baseball players. Much of Miller's success was his ability to see that the more effective he was in getting the owners to show their opposition to the association's specific programs, the easier it would be to build a strong association that could then challenge portions of the status quo that management had formerly thought were inviolable.

The basis for the MLBPA's successful efforts to raise the minimum salary, create an impartial arbitration system for grievances, and institute free agency was laid during the first two years of Miller's tenure as executive director. Commentators favoring the status quo in baseball have accused Miller of driving a wedge between the owners and players. Miller would probably argue that he has done everything possible to bring an already existing division out into the open. He was interested in establishing something more than just a "fair chance" for the players to be heard. His job was to make sure that his men and their organization obtained the benefits that they thought were reasonable as part of the industry of baseball. The association had hired a man from the labor movement, and baseball's hierarchy was going to have to learn how to deal with him. From the beginning of his tenure as executive director, Miller demonstrated the skills of an experienced negotiator by ensuring that he did not get too far ahead of his own constituency. His job was to identify ways in which the association might better represent the interests of its members and then to convince them of the need for action to implement those goals. Despite the comments of some prominent sports writers, it does not appear either that Miller exercised some kind of Svengali-like power over the Executive Committee or that he tried to substitute his judgment for that of the players. In one important area, however, he had great freedom of action: the style of leadership that he brought to the association in its relationship with management.

One episode may suffice to show how Miller, with the support of the Executive Committee, demonstrated the change in the association, both to the members and the owners. It was a seemingly minor problem in the way dues were processed. On May 3, 1967, a check for $1,032 was returned by the association to Arthur Allyn, owner of the Chicago White Sox. The check had been sent by the White Sox in lieu of dues for three members of the association—the club's manager, Stanky, and two coaches, Farrell and Grissom. Miller sent a curt note to Allyn that the method of payment did not "conform to your obligations" under the agreement of December 1, 1966, which was to deduct dues from members' salaries, and that the delivery of the money violated Section 302 of the Labor Management Relations Act. In order to emphasize his point, Miller explicitly stated that the "money is incidental. . . . the issue at hand is the obligation of the owners." Allyn's assertion that the club "cannot permit coaches and managers to pay dues or to be active members of the Association represents a position which constitutes unfair labor practices under the law."[42] Once again, Miller based his position on the legal position of the association. The owners might not like the association, but they were going to have to learn to coexist with it. In case Allyn did not get the message, Miller concluded with the comment that the MLBPA was willing to initiate the appropriate legal action to rectify the situation.[43]

The actions of the White Sox gave Miller another opportunity to state the case to the players and solidify the membership. He sent a lengthy letter to the club in which he reminded the players of the struggle over the establishment of the permanent office and that the membership had agreed to a checkoff system, which was important to the continued existence of the association. Miller was hitting two points he thought would touch most of the members—the security of the association and the presumption that the owners were trying to sabatoge it. He reviewed the history of the checkoff arrangement, which had existed for years before the creation of the "permanent office." The 1966 agreement between the owners and the association established the formal mechanism by which the clubs would deduct the association dues from the salaries of those employees of the club who chose to be members. Employees were defined as "players, managers, coaches and trainers." The owners had drafted the original agreement, too, including these provisions. Miller added that it was up to each individual (no names mentioned) to decide whether to "accept all the benefits and have the costs met by others. . . . Whether it is fair or not is for each individual to decide for himself."[44] Miller was countering charges that he was trying to bludgeon unwilling managers and coaches, let alone players, into the association. But if anyone reading the memorandum wanted to assume that the owners were encouraging a selfish attitude on the part of some members who benefited from the association, that was a conclusion that was up to them.

Miller went out of his way to make the point that the White Sox were trying to ignore their contractual obligations and to change an arrangement that had been suggested by the owners. He was playing on the fact that his constituency was used to constant reminders from owners that rules were rules, that rules could not be changed at the whim of one party, and that fair play meant playing within the rules. Miller might have felt it necessary to counter the charge made by some of the owners and many journalists that somehow a slick labor negotiator (with no knowledge or appreciation of the unique qualities of baseball) had talked honest, well-meaning, but somewhat naive sportsmen who owned clubs into doing something against their interests and those of baseball. Arthur Allyn's action gave Miller a perfect object lesson to use for his members—the White Sox were tampering with an arrangement that had been agreed to by both sides for the benefit of both sides.

In a lengthy conclusion to the memorandum, Miller analyzed what he thought was the importance of the issue. It is useful to quote part of it to understand both where Miller was leading the association and how he intended to gather the membership behind him:

> If a formal written contract can be rendered meaningless by one party to the contract, then all contracts are in jeopardy—including the Major League Baseball Players Benefit Plan which, after all, is merely a piece of paper that is given meaning only through the signatures of the parties and their carrying out the agreement expressed in that piece of paper. . . . The matter of whether or not a few persons do or do not pay membership dues is not of overriding importance. The matter of whether or not a contract agreed upon in good faith is to be complied with or violated *is* of very great importance.[45]

Miller hit upon the greatest fear of the players—that even the hitherto sacrosanct pension fund might not be safe from the efforts of owners to break the association. He was doing more than sowing the seeds of distrust among the members, though. He was showing them how their latent distrust of management—the very reason they had turned to someone like him to be executive director—had a strong basis in fact. The actions of the White Sox might be explained by the club or other owners as just an administrative problem, a misunderstanding or a good-faith effort to enable three men to handle their objections to the checkoff system of the MLBPA. Judge Cannon might have been willing to give the owners every benefit of every possible doubt, but Miller was not.

We can get some idea about Miller's agenda by looking at interviews he gave early in his tenure. In February 1967 he outlined many of the association's concerns to Jim Kilgallen. They included the length of the season playing schedule, the $7,000 minimum salary, split doubleheaders, the unsatisfactory travel schedule, and the need to modernize the standard players' contract.[46] Neither free agency nor strikes were mentioned, but Miller's agenda was a long way from where the association's agenda had been four years earlier. The agenda for the December 1963 joint meeting with the owners (the time at which the players presented the issues that meant the most to them) included the following demands: that the players' per diem be raised to thirteen dollars, that more getaway games be played during the day, that up to eight warm-up pitches be allowed, that backdrops be provided in all spring training camps, and that each major league park have "standard foul poles."[47] The 1967 and 1963 lists might seem worlds apart, but they share two essential ingredients. Both dealt with specific conditions of employment that affected the individual members of the association. They did not speak to any changes in the reserve system.

Miller certainly expanded his efforts beyond the specific points he discussed in his first tour of the training camps. He listened to the members, determined what they wanted, and then made suggestions not only about tactics but also about goals. When the players hired Miller, they were not getting just a sounding board, a man who would go to them for every instruction and who would go no further than their clearly enunciated goals. They had purposely hired an expert in labor law and negotiations. They had also brought in a form of "hired gun" and assumed that he would outperform the men who did that job for the other side.[48] The most striking feature about the early years of Miller's administration was not that the players went along with his suggestions and tactics, but that the owners, their representatives, and the commissioner did not seem to realize that the administrative and business structure of baseball had been transformed. Maybe they were mesmerized by their adherence to the belief that the status quo could never change. Perhaps they were so used to players always asking permission for any proposed change that they could not see what was going on.

Miller certainly took every opportunity to remind the players of his philosophy of unionism—that only through solidarity could the players achieve any significant changes in their situation vis-à-vis their employers. He made no apologies at any time for pointing out the differences that existed between the two sides, nor did he feel any need to. If we look at the structure of professional baseball through the eyes of one of its long-term employees, Bowie Kuhn, we might get a better understanding of what Miller did in his first few years as executive director of the MLBPA. "Our repeated attempts to create a good relationship with the Association never really worked and never would so long as Miller was there."[49] The key to interpreting this assessment is understanding that Miller and Kuhn did not share a common definition of a "good relationship." Kuhn did not share Miller's view that the history of organized baseball gave him every reason to think that there were two sides in baseball and that the role of the MLBPA was to act as the advocate of its members. The job of its executive director was to seize every possible legal and ethical advantage. In his memoirs, Kuhn described the relationship between Miller and General Eckert as trying to get the lion to lie down with the lamb and that Miller, the lion, would devour the lamb before morning.[50] If Miller had resorted to biblical analogies, he might have described the situation in terms of sheep and goats. The association was one party and expected opposition from the organized force of the owners. Baseball traditionalists, especially in management, had every reason to see no conflicts in baseball—that was part of their heritage. It also was in the interests of the owners, who had no reason to recognize the need for change until the association could challenge them successfully on issues that mattered to both sides.

The task facing Miller in his first few years as executive director was to convince the MLBPA's members that real issues divided them from the owners, that something could be done about them, and that the MLBPA was the only way to improve the players' situation. That meant bringing issues to the forefront that dramatized the differences between the two sides and showing that the association was capable of beating the owners at what had been their own game. Even if the owners had tradition and legal precedent on their side, it was possible to tap the competitive instincts of the players if they could be convinced that there were realistic opportunities to change things and that the new executive director was the man to lead the movement.

If the officials charged with the maintenance of the status quo in baseball did not notice what was happening in their industry, Miller gave them repeated lessons. Threatening legal action against the White Sox, intervening in disciplinary cases, and making demands based on the strict interpretation of labor laws were only a few examples of how Miller asserted both the legitimacy of the association and its power to work for its members.[51] At no time was the new situation stated in more unambiguous terms than in a series of letters Miller sent to Commissioner Bowie Kuhn in the summer of 1969. In the first letter Miller volunteered the advice of the association on matters affecting the welfare of the players and reminded the commissioner that "the Players Association, as the duly authorized representative of the players, is always interested in receiving your views or those of any other responsible representative of management at any mutually convenient opportunity."[52] So much for the supposedly exalted position of the commissioner as the impartial representative of baseball, charged with looking out for the welfare of the game. Miller, speaking for the association, described the new commissioner as just another member of management and made it clear that any discussion in the future would have to be on mutually agreeable terms. In case Kuhn was the least bit confused about the attitude of the association toward him, a month later Miller wrote him: "The players do not regard the Commissioner as being their representative or having the role of an impartial neutral in matters of player-owner relationships. The reasons are quite simple. The Commissioner is not selected by the players. The Commissioner is selected exclusively by the owners."[53] Miller hastened to point out that Kuhn should not take the comment personally and that circumstances had been the same during the tenures of Landis, Chandler, Frick, and Eckert. The difference in 1969 was that the players recognized the commissioner's real role. They wished the new commissioner well and looked forward to working with him in a spirit of cooperation for the best interests of baseball. But the MLBPA was putting him on notice that any of his efforts based on the old notion of his power were doomed to failure. They were not going to allow him the power to unilaterally define the best interest of baseball.

It is impossible to know just how all the players felt about this interpretation, but there is no evidence that there was any significant oposition to it. By the end of the 1969 season, the year of the first divisional races and the triumph of the Amazing Mets, an even more dramatic change had surfaced in major league baseball. A new philosophy of self-assertive unionism had come to the Major League Baseball Players Association, and its impact would transform baseball radically over the next ten years.

NOTES

I want to express my appreciation to the MLBPA, including Donald Fehr, Eugene Orza, Arthur Schack, Mark Belanger, Lauren Rich, and Marvin J. Miller, for allowing me access to their files and correspondence. Thanks are also due to Jim Bunning, Milt Pappas, and other former members of the association for their valuable comments. Dr. Edwin Fedder, Director of the Center for International Studies, Dr. Dennis Judd, Director of the Center for Metropolitan Studies, and Dr. Thomas Jordan, Dean of the Graduate School, University of Missouri, St. Louis, provided the funding that allowed me to complete the research for this chapter.

1. For a brief appreciation of Miller's role, see David Q. Voigt, "They Shaped the Game: Nine Innovators of Major League Baseball," *Baseball History* 1 (1): 19–21. For a more detailed look at the history of unionism in baseball, see Lee Lowenfish and Tony Lupien, *The Imperfect Diamond* (New York: Stein and Day, 1980).

2. Lee Lowenfish and Tony Lupien, *The Imperfect Diamond,* 157.

3. *The Sporting News,* September 1, 1954.

4. Ibid.

5. *The Sporting News,* August 3, 1963.

6. Minutes of MLBPA Player Representatives Meeting, March 5, 1966, the offices of the MLBPA, New York.

7. *The Sporting News,* August 3, 1963.

8. Minutes of Player Representatives Meetings, July 11, 1966, October 3, 1966, and November 29–30, 1966.

9. Robin Roberts, "The Game Deserves the Best," *Sports Illustrated* (February 24, 1969): 46–47.

10. Ibid., 47.

11. Letter from Marvin Miller to R. Dozier, April 17, 1969.

12. Ibid.

13. Letter from Marvin Miller to Watson Spoelstra, December 14, 1969. All letters are from the offices of the MLBPA in New York.

14. Minutes of Player Representatives Meeting, March 5, 1966.

15. Ibid.

16. Robin Roberts, "The Game Deserves the Best," 47.

17. Minutes of Player Representatives Meeting, March 5, 1966.

18. Ibid.

19. Ibid.

20. Interview by the author with Jim Bunning, June 30, 1987.

21. Ibid.

22. Ibid.

23. Ibid.

24. *The Sporting News,* August 3, 1963.

25. Robin Roberts, "The Game Deserves the Best," and Bunning interview, June 30, 1987.

26. Interviews by the author with Marvin Miller, February 5 and November 2, 1987. The most often quoted opposition view of Miller was that of Dick Young, who commented that Miller was a "smoothie . . . who runs the players through a high pressure spray the way an auto goes through a car wash, and that's how they come out brain washed," *New York Daily News,* March 23, 1972. This quotation became the basis for others who labeled Miller as a Svengali.

27. Interview by the author with Marvin Miller, November 2, 1987.

28. Minutes of Special Meeting of Player Representatives, June 6, 1966.

29. Ibid.

30. Ibid.

31. Ibid.

32. Ibid.

33. Ibid.

34. Ibid.

35. Ibid.

36. Ibid.

37. Ibid.

38. Ibid.

39. Ibid.

40. Ibid.

41. Ibid.

42. Letter from Marvin Miller to Arthur Allyn, May 3, 1967.

43. Ibid.

44. Letter from Marvin Miller to Player Representatives, May 4, 1967. The checkoff arrangement provided a mechanism by which the dues for the association were taken directly out of the players' wages and sent to the association by the clubs. It assured that the funds would come in at a regular time and relieved the players of the individual responsibility for a payment. The arrangement that was set up in 1966 provided for the payment of dues of $2 per day (to a maximum of $344 per season). It took the place of the money that the players had formerly paid into the pension fund. The new arrangement cost the players $50 less per year and also gave them the right to claim the $344 as a tax-deductible expense.

45. Ibid. By 1972 Player Representatives were writing to Miller in terms similar to those he used to Arthur Allyn. When a grievance was filed about a violation of

scheduling rules, two of the comments sent to Miller were: "It's quite simple; agreements are not reached to be broken. . . . I'll say one thing for them [the owners], they break agreements, admit they did and just stick it in your face to see what reaction we have" (Bob Barton, San Diego, May 1972); and "can't let violations continue or the contract will be nothing more than a piece of paper" (Jay Johnstone, Chicago White Sox, May 1972).

46. Letter from Jim Kilgallen to Marvin Miller, February 22, 1967.

47. Minutes of Joint Meeting, December 3, 1963.

48. Comments by Milt Pappas in an interview with the author, June 29, 1987.

49. Bowie Kuhn, *Hardball: The Education of a Baseball Commissioner* (New York: Times Books, 1987), 158.

50. Ibid., 29.

51. For example, the MLBPA demanded that the owners honor their contractual obligation to provide first-class air travel and hotel accommodations for the players (letter from Marvin Miller to Player Representatives, May 31, 1968); it intervened when Charlie Finley attempted to fine Lew Krausse and other players for their alleged misconduct on a team flight (letters from Richard Moss to Commissioner Eckert, August 21, 28, and September 23, 1967, and Marvin Miller to Commissioner Eckert, August 28, 1967); and it insisted on the strict interpretation of regulations concerning unconditional releases and termination pay (memorandum from Marvin Miller to Player Representatives, February 22, 1971).

52. Letter from Marvin Miller to Bowie Kuhn, August 1, 1969.

53. Letter from Marvin Miller to Bowie Kuhn, September 3, 1969.

Professional Sports and the Antitrust Laws $\quad$ 7

Gary R. Roberts

Perhaps no area of law has impacted professional sports more over these past twenty years than antitrust. Since 1966 the National Football League alone has had to defend over sixty antitrust suits. The National Basketball Association, and the National Hockey League, and even upstart leagues like the now-defunct World Hockey Association (WHA), American Basketball League, and the United States Football League (USFL), have also been frequently hit by such suits. Only major league baseball, which enjoys a broad antitrust immunity as a result of three U.S. Supreme Court decisions, has been able to operate without the substantial risk and expense of antitrust litigation.[1]

Although antitrust law seems mysterious and complex, its source is surprisingly simple. Except for the statute governing mergers of two firms, the overwhelming bulk of antitrust law derives from the first two sections of the 1890 Sherman Act. Section 1 prohibits "every contract, combination, . . . or conspiracy in restraint of trade or commerce," while section 2 makes it illegal to "monopolize, or attempt to monopolize, or combine or conspire . . . to monopolize" trade or commerce. Virtually all sports antitrust cases involve one or both of these vague statutory proscriptions—conspiracies to restrain trade and monopolization.[2]

Antitrust cases against professional leagues or their member clubs generally are of two types. The first involves disputes between two different leagues or between member clubs of different leagues. The second, and more significant, category includes all cases brought by anyone having a dispute with a league and alleging that a league rule or decision constitutes an unlawful section 1 conspiracy among the individual member clubs of the league. It is the second type of cases—those involving so-called intraleague conspiracies—that has been the most frequent and problematic, and it has had the greatest impact on professional sports.

The Interleague Dispute Cases

The interleague type of case is typically brought by a young struggling league claiming that an older and more established league monopolized or attempted to monopolize some part of the sports entertainment market in violation of Sherman Act section 2. To win such a claim the plaintiff must prove two things: (1) that the defendant has, or is close to having, monopoly market power in some relevant market or line of commerce, and (2) that the defendant has acted improperly in acquiring or maintaining that monopoly power. Because these issues are economically complex and often very difficult to prove, plaintiffs also often allege that the defendant league's conduct involved a section 1 conspiracy in restraint of trade. But regardless of the legal theory, the essential claim is always that a well-established league or its teams acted to cripple or destroy a rival league or teams in order to maintain a monopoly position.

As suggested above, antitrust cases between leagues have been few and have had relatively little impact on the structure or operation of professional sports. The most recent example is the highly publicized case the USFL brought against the NFL, which primarily claimed that the NFL's contracts with the three major television networks unlawfully monopolized professional football. After a lengthy trial in 1986, a Manhattan jury found that the NFL had monopolized professional football; however, apparently because the jury believed that the USFL went bankrupt primarily because of its own mismanagement, it awarded the USFL damages of only one dollar (which by law were automatically trebled to three). When the verdict was affirmed on appeal, the demise of the USFL became permanent (*USFL v. NFL*, 842 F.2d 1335 [2d Cir. 1988]). In a similar case in 1962, the old American Football League claimed that the NFL monopolized professional football by putting teams in Dallas and Minnesota and threatening to expand in other cities in order to disrupt the AFL's initial operations. The case resulted in a verdict for the NFL (*AFL v. NFL*, 205 F. Supp. 60 [D. Md. 1962], aff'd, 323 F.2d 124 [4th Cir. 1963]).

The WHA was more successful in its suit against the NHL in the early 1970s. The essence of this claim was that the NHL monopolized professional hockey by including a clause in all of its clubs' player contracts giving the club a permanent renewable option on the player when the contract term ended, which prevented a player from playing for any other hockey club until his NHL club no longer wanted him. Thus the WHA was unable to employ good hockey players if they had ever played in the NHL and, as a result, could never seriously compete with the NHL. In 1972 shortly after the case was filed, the district judge issued a preliminary injunction against the NHL's enforcement of these "lifetime reserve clauses" based on his finding that at trial they would probably be found to constitute unlawful monopolization (*Philadelphia World Hockey Club v. Philadelphia Hockey Club,* 351 F. Supp. 462 [E.D. Pa. 1972]).

Unfortunately, the injunction was of little help to the WHA; by 1979 all of its clubs were insolvent and had disbanded except for the teams in Hartford, Winnipeg, Edmonton, and Vancouver, all of which joined the NHL. The case did, however, lead to a settlement between the two leagues and their player unions under which the NHL's lifetime reserve clause was replaced with a much less onerous "free agent compensation system" that allowed a player to sign with any hockey team when his contract expired, subject only to the new club giving some arbitrated compensation to the old club, but only if both clubs were NHL members.[3]

Another group of interleague cases has involved stadium lease or arena lease provisions that give the leasing club an exclusive right to use the facility for its sport. If a facility is realistically the only one in the area capable of housing a professional team, the exercise of the exclusive rights clause forecloses other leagues from putting a competing team in the city. Several cases have involved plaintiffs who were trying to obtain franchises in upstart leagues who alleged that such lease provisions allowed the established local team to monopolize the local market in its sport. These plaintiffs have generally been unsuccessful, either because alternative facilities were available or because the team could not show that they would have obtained a franchise in the new league even if the stadium had been available. The only such case to result in a published opinion was eventually settled for $200,000 after thirteen years of litigation. The ruling in this case makes it reasonably clear that the Sherman Act is violated if a new league is excluded from a city because of such a lease provision, at least unless very strong business justifications exist for restricting the newcomer's access to the facility (*Hecht v. Pro-Football, Inc.,* 570 F.2d 982 [D.C. Cir. 1977], cert. denied, 436 U.S. 956 [1978]).

Another interleague case involved a challenge by the North American Soccer League (NASL) to the NFL's proposed by-law that would have prohibited majority owners or chief executive officers of NFL teams from owning an interest in franchises of other sports leagues. Specifically at issue was the NFL's efforts to force Lamar Hunt, who owns the NFL's Kansas City Chiefs, and Joe Robbie, who owns the Miami Dolphins, to divest their interests (or in Robbie's case, his wife's interest) in NASL franchises. Because of the shaky financial position of the NASL, the divestment, combined with the paucity of non-NFL owners willing to invest in the NASL, might have pushed the NASL over the financial edge (over which it eventually went anyway). Curiously, the primary claim in the case was not that the NFL monopolized any relevant market, such as the league sports autumn entertainment market, but that the NFL clubs unlawfully conspired among themselves under section 1 to restrain trade. After the district court in New York granted a summary judgment for the NFL, the court of appeals reversed and entered a judgment for the NASL on the grounds that the NFL clubs had conspired to restrain the previously unheard-of sports capital investment market (*NASL v. NFL*, 670 F.2d 1249 [2d Cir.], cert. denied, 459 U.S. 1074 [1982]).

The *NASL* decision has been severely criticized, not only because of its result but because of its doctrinal justification. Justifying the decision on conspiracy grounds rather than monopolization grounds seems totally at odds with standard section 1 principles, which encourage vigorous independent competition between separate entities, such as two different leagues. Thus, although the decision clearly invalidated the NFL's cross-ownership ban when applied against the struggling NASL, it is probably limited to its specific facts—that is, the ban probably does not violate the law when applied by the NFL against cross-ownership in established sports leagues like the NHL, NBA, or major league baseball, or rival leagues in the same sport, like the WFL or USFL.

Generally, with the possible exception of the anomalous *NASL* case, the decisions in these interleague cases have been unsurprising and unremarkable, and they have had little impact on either the law or the structure of professional sports. Most doctrinal principles relating to monopolization are reasonably clear and have not changed, and in each of the cases the outcome primarily turned not on the interpretation or application of the law, but on what the juries believed were the real facts of the case. While jury findings of fact usually are significant for a particular case, they generally have little or no impact on future cases or the general state of the law.

The one legal issue in these sports monopolization cases that is problematic, and will probably remain so, is how to define the relevant market that the plaintiff claims has been monopolized. The market definition must include both a product and a geographic dimension—for example, professional football entertainment in the United States; ticket sales for football entertainment (high school, college, and professional) in the New York metropolitan area; network television rights for all kinds of entertainment in the United States; television rights for all sports entertainment in New England; and so on. The possibilities are almost endless. The general rule for making this determination is that the proper market includes all the different brands and products sold within the appropriate geographical area that are economically competitive with one another—that is, those that serve approximately the same purpose for the average consumer so that consumers can switch from one to the other if price or quality materially changes.

Defining the proper relevant market is extraordinarily difficult. For example, how can one identify everything that meaningfully competes with NFL football in a single market description? What percentage of people who now buy tickets to New York Giants football games would, if the Giants' ticket prices increased by a certain amount, spend their entertainment dollars attending college football games? Would they attend Yankee baseball games or Broadway shows or watch cartoons on television? Adding in the geographic dimension, how far would disgruntled Giants fans be willing to travel to find a substitute activity? How many would choose gambling in Atlantic City or skiing in Vermont? Then again, what effect would the amount of the ticket price increase have on all these factors? No one can possibly know. Nonetheless, based on whatever information is available, a plaintiff must establish that some group of actual or potential product alternatives exists that is generally substitutable to a sufficient number of consumers within an identified geographic area so that they comprise a relevant market that the defendant has monopolized.

The market definition problem is not unique to sports cases. Defining a relevant market is a nightmare in almost all monopolization cases. Because of the complexity and conceptual difficulty (if not impossibility) of doing the necessary economic analysis, courts generally either have reached a knee-jerk conclusion (camouflaged by confusing rhetoric), or have ducked the issue by leaving the question to juries to do what they instinctively feel is just. But the fact that a defined relevant market is an essential element of a monopolization case always injects a great deal of unpredictability into these interleague cases.

This problem could be greatly reduced in cases between two leagues in the same sport, like the USFL and the NFL, simply by identifying the relevant market as the labor market in which the leagues employ their players instead of focusing on some market in which the leagues sell their entertainment products against one another. The labor market is undoubtedly the proper market for relevant concern. If the NFL wanted to drive the USFL out of business, by whatever method, it was not because it was seriously concerned about NFL ticket buyers or television networks switching over to the USFL. It wanted to stop the rapid escalation in player salaries caused by the USFL's competition in the market for hiring football players. If the NFL was trying to monopolize anything, it was this labor market. This market is easy to define, and a plaintiff could probably prove that an established league like the NFL or NBA has enormous market power in it.[4] By focusing on the player market in cases between two leagues in the same sport, plaintiffs would greatly increase their chance of success.

Ultimately, however, these types of cases will probably never be very significant in altering the shape of professional sports because of the great likelihood that in each sport no more than one established league will ever exist for more than a brief period. Since World War II, one hockey, two basketball, and four football leagues have sprung up to compete against the

NHL, NBA, and NFL, respectively, and not one has survived more than a few seasons. The public's demand for a single acknowledged "world champion," and the need over the long run to control player costs and competitive balance among teams (which cannot be done effectively in either league if two are competing in the same sport), make it quite likely that the established league in each sport will never face permanent competition or be supplanted by an upstart league. Thus no matter what legal doctrines are developed or what the outcome of any interleague monopolization cases may be, it is unlikely that these cases will ever be of long-term or structural significance.

The Intraleague Conspiracy Cases

The second type of sports antitrust case involves challenges to any league rule, decision, or action ("league conduct") by some dissatisfied person claiming that the conduct constituted a section 1 conspiracy of the league's member clubs to restrain competition among themselves. These cases are by far more frequent, more unpredictable, and doctrinally more problematic than the interleague monopolization cases.

Cases in this category have involved virtually every type of league conduct. For example, league rules barring players from the league for a variety of reasons[5] and rules assigning each player to a specific league member (like the player drafts and reserve rules)[6] have been attacked by individual players, player unions, and rival leagues. Persons disappointed with not being able to own a team have brought cases challenging league decisions not to expand the league membership[7] and not to approve the sale of a franchise.[8] Stadiums seeking league tenants and even league members have challenged league decisions not to allow teams to relocate their home games to a new city.[9] The Justice Department, fans, and television stations have sued over league broadcasting contracts and practices.[10] Equipment manufacturers and players have even challenged playing-field rules.[11] In each case, the allegation was that the league's action had involved a conspiracy of the individual league members to restrain competition among themselves in some commercial market.

Although the defendant leagues have won the overwhelming majority of these cases, a few widely publicized cases in which leagues lost have had an enormous impact on the structure and operation of professional sports. The most notable are the *John Mackey* and *Yazoo Smith* cases from the mid-1970s, which invalidated respectively the NFL's reserve system and college player draft as they were then structured, completely altering the shape of labor relations in professional sports. In the infamous *Los Angeles Memorial Coliseum* case the court found the NFL's efforts to require the then

Oakland Raiders to play its home games in Oakland (as it had contractually agreed to do) instead of in Los Angeles to be an unlawful conspiracy of the other NFL clubs. What was so significant about these decisions was not only the way they dramatically and directly changed the face of the game but how they were based on legal principles that were confusing, aberrational, and inconsistent both with other antitrust decisions and with antitrust doctrine generally. The legacy of these cases is that today there is virtually no conduct of any sports league (other than baseball) involving any matter that cannot conceivably be challenged successfully in the right court.

In order to understand why these conspiracy cases are so doctrinally confounding and troublesome for league operations, it is necessary first to understand what section 1's condemnation of conspiracies is all about. The basic theory of free enterprise is that the products consumers want will be produced in the greatest quantity, at the highest quality, and at the cheapest price if production decisions conform to the dictates of supply and demand forces. This equilibrium will be achieved when independent producers of the same or functionally interchangeable products compete with each other to attract customers. It is through competition and each firm's desire to attract the greatest number of customers that prices are kept to a minimum and quality maintained. It is for this reason that antitrust law seeks to maximize competition by outlawing both (a) one firm driving all competitors out of business (monopolization) and (b) groups of competitors getting together to agree on the price or quality of their otherwise competing products (conspiracies).

But section 1's condemnation of "every conspiracy in restraint of trade" is not as simple as it might seem. Obviously, totally independent companies like General Motors, Ford, and Chrysler cannot agree on the price or design of pick-up trucks without illegally conspiring, but what about the Chevrolet, Buick, and Cadillac divisions of GM agreeing on the price of their cars? Because these are merely different divisions of the same company, it is undisputed that they constitute a single legal person whose internal actions are not "conspiracies." This distinction underscores a critical aspect of antitrust doctrine that many courts have failed to appreciate in sports league cases—namely that every type and form of cooperative action between separate persons cannot possibly be illegal.

It thus becomes crucial for section 1 cases that the law define in some rational way which persons or entities are to be considered independent of each other—or, put another way, which persons or entities the law will require to be competitors of each other. When such independent persons or entities, who ought to be competitors of each other, reach agreements on how to conduct their business or sell their products, they may unlawfully conspire to restrain competition. But when persons or entities that are merely employees, partners, or divisions of a single business firm make agreements or joint decisions in an effort to operate the firm profitably, their actions are clearly ordinary lawful cooperation.

In most factual contexts, making this distinction has not been a significant problem for courts. Clearly, the different employees of a single corporation cannot illegally conspire with respect to carrying on the corporation's business. The partners in a recognized partnership (whether individual people, corporations, or other partnerships) never illegally conspire when making decisions about the partnership's business. Different divisions, and even different subsidiary corporations that are wholly owned by the same parent corporation (since the Supreme Court's *Copperweld v. Independence Tube* decision in 1984), can never illegally conspire.[12] There is only one type of business entity that continues to give the courts fits—the joint venture. Unfortunately, this category includes sports leagues.

It is curious that for virtually every other legal purpose, joint ventures and partnerships are treated identically. In fact, under standard business organization law principles, joint ventures are merely a kind of partnership different from more typical partnerships only in that joint ventures are created by their partners for a narrow specific purpose or for a limited period of time. Thus the special fiduciary obligations of partners to the business, the liability of partners for the business's debts, and the authority of partners to bind the business and the other partners are all exactly the same whether the business is a joint venture or a more typical partnership. For seemingly arbitrary reasons, federal antitrust courts have singled out joint ventures and generally treated the internal business agreements of their partners as conspiracies subject to condemnation if found to be "unreasonable," whereas agreements among traditional partners have never been held to be unlawful conspiracies.[13]

From the standpoint of antitrust policy (namely, the advancement of consumer welfare), the distinction between joint ventures (like sports leagues) and traditional partnerships and corporations is not justified. It is simply nonsense to allow judges or juries unfamiliar with the industry to second-guess the wisdom of business decisions made by persons whose business is affected. When the members of General Motors' corporate board of directors collectively decide where GM's factories will be located, or when the partners in a law, medical, or accounting firm collectively decide where to locate their offices, nobody in his right mind thinks the decision should be considered a conspiracy and tested for reasonableness by some judge or lay jury. But when the governing board of the NFL collectively decides that eight league games every year will be produced in Oakland instead of Los Angeles, the decision is treated as a conspiracy, which a Los Angeles judge and jury can render illegal if they believe it to be unreasonable (as happened in the *Los Angeles Coliseum/Raiders* case).

This distinction also has been made with respect to the hiring standards and employment practices of corporations, partnerships, and sports leagues. If IBM (corporation) or a major national accounting firm (partnership) decided not to hire anyone who had not completed college or insisted that employee John Doe would have to agree to work at the company's Kansas City Office if he wanted to be hired, nobody would question the policy as a potentially unlawful conspiracy. But when a sports league declines to employ players who have not completed their years of college training or requires quarterback John Doe to play for the team in Kansas City, courts condemn these decisions as unreasonable conspiracies (as in the *Denver Rockets, Mackey,* and *Smith* cases).[14]

The reason generally given by courts and plaintiffs for this distinction is that, unlike corporations and partnerships, sports leagues are not really single business firms; they are a group of separately owned teams with distinct legal identities that maintain their own separate books and have different profits and losses. While these points are superficially true, they are wholly irrelevant to antitrust policy because they overlook the fundamental nature of the business of a sports league and the relationship among a league's member teams. In fact, the antitrust policy of maximizing consumer welfare can be furthered only by treating league conduct in exactly the same way as the law treats corporate and partnership conduct. To understand why this is so, one must first recognize that the unique product a sports league produces is athletic (not economic) "competition," which requires separate teams as a necessary camouflage for the inherent partnership nature of a league.

Sports leagues produce a unique type of entertainment product—team athletic competition. At a bare minimum two different teams are always necessary to produce this product. Every game is the product of at least a two-team joint venture. Although game tickets and television broadcasts are often marketed as, for example, "Washington Redskins football," this single reference is quite misleading. The Redskins team alone is incapable of producing any football entertainment; the proper designation is "NFL football."

Furthermore, although a single NFL game may be a discrete entertainment event for some marketing purposes, it is not a separate product for any meaningful economic or antitrust purpose. The product is actually the league's annual series of 224 regular season games leading to a post-season tournament and a Super Bowl champion. It is only because each game is ultimately connected to the championship that it has substantial value. An isolated scrimmage game between two teams that did not count in any league standings or statistical rankings would be far less attractive to consumers, and it certainly could not command millions of dollars in television fees or twenty or more dollars a ticket from tens of thousands of fans.

A league's product is thus jointly produced, and no team produces anything by itself. Furthermore, no individual game is solely the product of even the two participating teams; the value of every game is largely generated by the trademark and imprimatur of the league and the cooperation and participation of all league members, each of which must recognize and accept the results of every game. Each individual team's fortunes, no matter how the league elects to divide total league revenues and expenses, are to a greater or lesser extent inherently affected by the success or failure of every single league game. Thus decisions affecting the structure of the league or the production or marketing of any league game affect the entire league, and every member has a stake and an inherent right to participate in those decisions, just as a partner in a law firm has a stake and a right to vote in his firm's business decisions. For example, although the location of the Raiders' home games will most greatly affect the Raiders (but only because of the league's pragmatic decision to give the majority of locally generated revenues to the home team), it also affects every other NFL member.[15] Without the acceptance, recognition, and occasional participation on the field of the other NFL members, those Raiders home games would be of very little economic value.

Accordingly, no individual sports team is capable of any production without the full cooperation of the other league members, and each team's economic existence, as well as its profits, depends entirely on its being an integral part of the league. It logically follows that these members are all inherent partners in the business of producing the league's wholly integrated entertainment product, and thus the teams are not and cannot be independent economic competitors of one another unless they voluntarily allow themselves to be for practical business reasons.[16] In short, it is the league, not the individual club, that is the relevant business firm for proper economic and legal analysis, and cooperation or agreements among the members should be indistinguishable from those among the members of any partnership or the directors of any corporation.

From this perspective, a Minnesota Vikings home game is not a Vikings product that the team is entitled unilaterally to produce and market any way it chooses; it is always the product of at least one other team, and, as part of the integrated NFL season, it is also the joint product of every member club. If one league member has a right to determine when, where, against whom, or under what rules it will play home games, logically the same set of rights should exist for each team regarding road games. But obviously, under such a disorganized regime no league product could be produced. Only when all the teams agree to some method for deciding these production issues can there be a league schedule and a valuable entertainment product. Clearly, there is no economic justification for legally requiring any of these decisions to be made by individual teams unilaterally.

Because every NFL game is necessarily the product of the entire league, the structural, production, and marketing decisions about every game are by definition league decisions. The league may elect for pragmatic reasons to have some of these decisions made by the individual teams (e.g., setting home game ticket prices or player salaries); by the hired commissioner (e.g., hiring game officials, drawing up the schedule of games, or negotiating network television contracts); or by some percentage vote of the member partners (e.g., determining the location of teams, setting the size of team rosters, or agreeing to collective bargaining agreements). But regardless of what decision-making methodology the league elects to use for any given matter, it is undeniable that the inherently joint nature of the league and its product makes every decision, expressly or tacitly, a decision of the collective league membership. For example, when the Raiders decided to play its home games in Los Angeles, it necessarily imposed a leaguewide decision on every NFL team to play extra road games there and to recognize and accept the results of the relocated games.

Despite the inherently joint or partnership nature of a sports league, many are skeptical. The reason is, as noted earlier, that in some ways leagues do not look like typical partnerships because each club has its own owner(s), maintains separate books, and earns its own profit or loss. In short, the teams look like independent and vigorous competitors. It is difficult for many to believe that the owners and employees of the various league teams, who often publicly insult and deride each other and threaten to commit mayhem on one another, are really business partners. But the economic reality is that they are and that these appearances are merely deceptive reflections of the unusual nature of the league product—athletic competition.

Because the league's product is athletic competition, it must ensure at least the appearance of honest and vigorous athletic rivalry among league members. Thus member teams are allowed to operate with a great deal of autonomy. It would look very suspicious to many fans and greatly diminish their enthusiasm if the clubs were largely controlled from league headquarters and seemed to lack financial incentive to perform well on the field and efficiently in the front office. But the fact that the league must create both the appearance and reality of intense athletic competition does not lead to the conclusion that the teams should be treated under the law like unrelated business competitors, which they clearly are not.

The economic competition that many mistakenly think exists between the teams because of their separate identities and limited operational autonomy is not unlike the internal rivalries within any company operating through semiautonomous profit centers. The only real difference is that leagues openly advertise and promote this internal rivalry because they want to heighten the appearance of vigorous athletic competition, whereas more typical businesses have no incentive to create a public appearance of "infighting." But the law should recognize that deliberately created athletic competition and internal rivalry in the league does not mean that the league members must treat each other like independent business competitors who are engaging in a conspiracy every time the league acts.

Furthermore, the fact that the individual teams make different profits or losses is not material to the antitrust issue: if all league revenues were put in a single common pot and all league expenses paid out of that pot, with the remainder being distributed evenly among the clubs, nobody would doubt that the league was a true partnership. The reason leagues do not operate in that fashion is that it would destroy any incentive for the clubs to field a top-quality team or keep costs down. To run the day-to-day operations of every team from central headquarters would be foolish from a management standpoint because it would destroy the necessary appearance (and perhaps the reality) of honest athletic competition.[17] It is clearly good business for each club to be responsible for its own expenses and the quality of its team.

The practice of having many decisions made and profits determined at a decentralized level certainly should not distinguish leagues from partnerships or corporations, many of which have the same profit-center type of management structure. In a law firm, an unequal profit-sharing arrangement or one that allows the lawyer members great latitude to develop their own practices is not grounds for treating every decision of the firm as an internal "conspiracy" subject to review by a jury for reasonableness. The decentralized sports league structure should be treated no differently.

It should be clear that treating every league rule, decision, or act as a conspiracy of the member teams is pure folly. It is, of course, true that a league may make bad business decisions from time to time, just as any business might. A league may even act irrationally or with improper motives. In short, league conduct may occasionally injure consumers or be unreasonable. But the business decisions of every corporation and partnership are sometimes foolish or injurious to consumers, yet that does not mean that antitrust policy is furthered by treating their every decision as a conspiracy. If every time a business acts it is an antitrust conspiracy of the people making the decision, then every rule, decision, or act can be challenged by any disgruntled person. Business entities that are truly single productive firms simply could not survive the cost and uncertainty of a system in which they had to defend the economic reasonableness of every company decision to a jury whenever an employee, customer, supplier, or competitor did not like that decision.

This is the very reason why there is no question that the decision of a corporation or a partnership to locate a branch office in Oakland instead of Los Angeles, to require employees to have a college degree, or to require employee John Doe to work in the company's Kansas City office does not constitute an illegal conspiracy of the company's partners or board members. It is also the reason why a sports league decision to have its franchises located in specific cities, to require players to have exhausted college eligibility requirements, or to force its players to play for designated teams should not be considered an illegal conspiracy of the teams. It is simply preposterous to presume that juries can generally make such league business decisions more wisely than can the very partners whose profits depend on acting wisely. It is for this reason that the legal doctrine allowing every league action to be reviewed by a court as a Sherman Act section 1 conspiracy of the league partners is irrational and contrary to antitrust policy and should be permanently scrapped.

Nevertheless, a few remaining policy concerns cause some to insist that courts should continue to use anticonspiracy law to review the business decisions of sports leagues. These concerns flow from the fact that in each sport there has always been, except for brief intermittent periods, only one league. For many purposes, this situation allows the league virtually to dictate terms to many with whom it deals. For example, a player excluded from the league, assigned to a team he strongly desires not to play for, or paid a salary he believes is unfair may have no alternative except not to play at all. A stadium, city, or equipment supplier with whom a league decides not to do business is often simply out of luck. Few corporations or traditional partnerships have that kind of power to impact the lives of its employees, customers, or suppliers so severely. Thus the notion persists that courts should exercise authority to review the decisions of leagues under section 1 in order to ensure that league power is exercised fairly.

This concern is certainly not frivolous. The problem, however, is that the underlying cause of the ability of leagues to wield such power is that for some purposes, leagues usually possess monopoly power—for example, in the labor market for players. Monopoly power in any industry is problematic from the standpoint of social and economic policy, which is precisely why Sherman Act section 2 proscribes monopolization and attempts to monopolize. But the law does not, and should never, make it unlawful for a business firm that has lawfully acquired monopoly power to operate, and it should never subject that firm's every business decision to a review on vague reasonableness grounds by a judge or jury. What is illegal is conduct designed to achieve or maintain monopoly power, not conduct that merely exercises it.

If a league has acted unlawfully to become or stay the only major league in its sport, it can and should be found in violation of section 2. That is what the interleague cases have all been about. However, if a league has not improperly become a monopoly or improperly remained one (perhaps because it is a natural monopoly), the antitrust laws should leave it alone. To try to correct a problem of monopoly power by allowing courts to review every league business rule or decision under irrelevant section 1 conspiracy doctrine, and to strike down on an ad hoc basis any decision with which the court disagrees or which it believes to be unfair, inevitably engenders chaos and inefficiency. The rash of NFL franchise moves and the frequent threats of moving by individual NFL owners that have followed the *Los Angeles Coliseum* case, after decades of total franchise stability in the NFL, is a dramatic example. Such cases essentially have created a prescription for turning the business of running leagues over to hundreds of federal judges with vastly different philosophies and abilities. In the long run nobody gains from such an unpredictable and irrational system.

If leagues do exercise their market power in ways that are unfair or otherwise contrary to public policy, perhaps Congress should consider legislative solutions. For example, if unreasonable player practices cannot be corrected through collective bargaining or under existing labor laws, they could be corrected in the same manner that various types of unfair discrimination in employment have been dealt with in civil rights legislation. But such a decision to regulate league conduct must come from Congress if the regulation is to achieve established policy goals and still be fair and consistent. The courts should apply existing law vigorously and creatively to correct evils that Congress has declared should be corrected; they should not manipulate a law condemning conspiracies to set themselves up as the arbitrator of every dispute between a league and its actual or potential employees, customers, or suppliers, based on wholly unpredictable ad hoc standards. No other business firm in the United States, monopoly or not, is so saddled with such constant judicial interference (unless Congress has specifically given the regulators the power to further specific policies and to follow specific standards and procedures). Neither should sports leagues be.

NOTES

1. These three decisions were *Flood v. Kuhn*, 407 U.S. 258 (1972); *Toolson v. New York Yankees*, 346 U.S. 356 (1953); and *Federal Baseball Club v. Ntl. League*

of Baseball Clubs, 259 U.S. 200 (1922). The scope of the "baseball exemption" is somewhat unclear. See *Henderson Broadcasting Corp. v. Houston Sports Ass'n*, 541 F. Supp. 263 (S.D. Tex. 1982); *Twin City Sportservice, Inc. v. Charles O. Finley & Co.*, 365 F. Supp. 235 (N.D. Cal. 1972), *rev'd on other grounds*, 512 F.2d 1264 (9th Cir. 1975) (both cases limiting the exemption to league structure and operations and player rules). Generally the scope of the exemption is thought to be quite broad, and it clearly covers all cases involving alleged conspiracies between the member clubs in a league.

2. One exception is a group of cases brought against the NFL teams that included both regular season and preseason game tickets in their season ticket package. Season ticket buyers in several cities alleged that this practice violated section 3 of the 1914 Clayton Act, which prohibits selling one product conditioned on the buyer's purchase of a second product. Although the courts have not been uniform in their reasoning, these cases have all been won by the defendant teams. See *Driskill v. Dallas Cowboys Football Club*, 498 F.2d 321 (5th Cir. 1974); *Coniglio v. Highwood Services, Inc.*, 495 F.2d 1286 (2d Cir. 1974); *Laing v. Minnesota Vikings Football Club*, 492 F.2d 1381 (8th Cir. 1974); *Pfeiffer v. New England Patriots*, 1973-1 Trade Cases ¶74,267 (D. Mass. 1972).

3. The NHL reserve system that emerged from this settlement is described in detail in a 1979 antitrust case brought by a player who was awarded to the Los Angeles Kings as "compensation" by an arbitrator after his old team, the Detroit Red Wings, signed the Kings' star goaltender. The NHL eventually won the case on the ground that the reserve system had been agreed to by the union in a collective bargaining agreement and was therefore exempt from antitrust attack. *McCourt v. California Sports, Inc.*, 600 F.2d 1193 (6th Cir. 1979).

4. When a defendant has enormous economic power in a market in which it purchases inputs used to produce its product, as opposed to one in which it sells its output, it is said to have a "monopsony." Although a monopsony is conceptually somewhat different than a monopoly and is relatively rare in antitrust cases, the economic evil of misallocated resources in either case is essentially the same, and section 2 of the Sherman Act probably applies equally to both.

5. Examples include *Neeld v. NHL*, 594 F.2d 1297 (9th Cir. 1979) (ban on one-eyed players found legal); *Denver Rockets v. All-Pro Management, Inc.*, 325 F. Supp. 1049 (C.D. Cal. 1971); *Linseman v. WHA*, 439 F. Supp. 1315 (D. Conn. 1977) and *Boris v. USFL*, 1984-1 CCH Trade Cases ¶66,012 (C.D. Cal. 1984) (minimum age or college eligibility requirements found unlawful); *Molinas v. NBA*, 190 F. Supp. 241 (S.D.N.Y. 1961) (suspension of player connected with gambling found lawful); *Bowman v. NFL*, 402 F. Supp. 754 (D. Minn. 1975) (ban on WFL players coming into the NFL past mid-season found unlawful).

6. For example, see *Mackey v. NFL*, 453 F.2d 606 (8th Cir. 1976), cert. dismissed, 434 U.S. 801 (1977) (commissioner-determined compensation for free agents found unlawful); *Smith v. Pro-Football Inc.*, 593 F.2d 1173 (D.C. Cir 1979) (NFL draft found unlawful); *Kapp v. NFL*, 390 F. Supp. 73 (N.D. Cal. 1974) (draft and reserve rules were found unlawful, but the NFL eventually won a jury verdict on the grounds of no injury); *Robertson v. NBA*, 389 F. Supp. 867 (S.D.N.Y. 1975) (NBA reserve system found probably unlawful).

7. In *Mid-South Grizzlies v. NFL,* 720 F.2d 772 (3d Cir. 1983), cert. denied, 467 U.S. 1215 (1984), the court found the NFL's decision not to give a former Memphis team in the WFL an NFL franchise lawful.

8. In *Levin v. NBA,* 385 F. Supp. 149 (S.D.N.Y. 1974), the court found the NBA's decision not to allow a sale of the Boston Celtics to plaintiffs lawful.

9. See *Los Angeles Memorial Coliseum Commission v. NFL,* 726 F.2d 1381 (9th Cir.), cert. denied, 469 U.S. 990 (1984) (NFL refusal to schedule Raiders game in Los Angeles found unlawful); *San Francisco Seals v. NHL,* 379 F. Supp. 966 (C.D. Cal. 1974) (NHL's refusal to schedule Seals game in Vancouver lawful). Also see *NBA v. SDC Basketball Club,* 815 F.2d 562 (9th Cir.), cert. dismissed, 108 S.Ct. 362 (1987) (NBA has a right to consider and vote on whether Clippers could move from San Diego to Los Angeles).

10. In *United States v. NFL,* 116 F. Supp. 319 (E.D. Pa. 1953), the court found NFL blackouts of one team's games in another team's city lawful when the other team is playing at home but unlawful when not playing at home. In both *WTWV, Inc. v. NFL,* 678 F.2d 142 (11th Cir. 1982) and *Blaich v. NFL,* 212 F. Supp. 319 (S.D.N.Y. 1962), the courts ruled that NFL blackouts of television signals within a 75-mile radius of a game is lawful.

11. For example, the court in *Carlock v. NFL,* an unpublished decision in case SA-79-CA-133 (S.D. Tex., Aug. 13, 1982), found the NFL decision not to use the plaintiff's laser gun to spot the ball after each play to be lawful. In *Smith v. Pro-Football Inc.,* an unpublished decision in case no. 1643-70 (D.D.C., June 27, 1973), *aff'd without opinion,* case no. 74-1958 (D.C. Cir., September 25, 1975), the court found the NFL rule requiring the team of an injured player to take a time-out if there is over a one-minute delay to be lawful.

12. Although no one disputes that the internal cooperation of corporations and partnerships is not illegal, the doctrinal basis for this conclusion is not necessarily the same in both cases. Corporate behavior is lawful clearly because a corporation is a single firm incapable of conspiring with itself, and its employees and directors are considered merely parts of the same legal person. See *Copperweld,* 467 U.S. 752 (1984). Partnership conduct, on the other hand, is more probably immunized by a different legal explanation—that although partners may be legally separate persons, their cooperation in running the partnership is always per se lawful. This position is referred to as the doctrine of ancillary restraints. See *Rothery Storage & Van Co. v. Atlas Van Lines, Inc.,* 792 F.2d 210 (D.D.C. 1986).

13. Although Sherman Act section 1 expressly prohibits "every" conspiracy in restraint of trade, since the Supreme Court's *Standard Oil* decision in 1911 the courts have read this language to proscribe only unreasonable restraints. Thus, if an agreement between two persons or entities is considered to be a conspiracy, it is then subject to the so-called Rule of Reason and condemned only if it is found to be unreasonable. Although for decades courts believed this rule allowed them to make subjective assessments about what they intuitively felt was fair and unfair, the U.S. Supreme Court has made it clear since the late 1970s that antitrust reasonableness is a term of art defined as being whatever is beneficial for consumer welfare. Thus conspiracies that benefit consumers are not illegal; conspiracies that injure consumers are.

14. In many of the cases involving restrictions on players, frequently an overriding issue has been present that obscured the underlying antitrust issues. Courts have held that when the players' union agrees to a league rule in collective bargaining, the rule is then immune from antitrust attack because of the so-called nonstatutory labor exemption. See *Powell v. NFL*, 888 F.2d 559 (8th Cir. 1989); *Wood v. NBA*, 809 F.2d 954 (2d Cir. 1987); *McCourt v. California Sports, Inc.*, 600 F.2d 1193 (6th Cir. 1979); *Zimmerman v. NFL*, 632 F. Supp. 398 (D.D.C. 1986). While the precise scope and application of the labor exemption is far from clear and is a fascinating issue of great importance to sports leagues today, it is well beyond the scope of the present discussion.

15. All sports leagues allow their member clubs to keep a majority or all of the revenues collected from the sale of tickets to home games, although most leagues also require that some of this revenue be shared with other league members. Giving the home team most of the locally generated revenue is done solely in order to create an incentive for each club to promote its home games vigorously and to develop an exciting winning team. But because each game requires the complete cooperation of the other league members, the league always has the inherent power to require that all gate revenues be divided equally (or any other way) among the members, just as the NFL divides the network television revenues from all NFL games equally. If any team refused, the other teams could simply refuse to play it or include it in the league standings. And if a league did require equal sharing of gate revenues, each member club would be indifferent as to which NFL game any fan attended since its share of the revenue would be the same either way. Any incentive the Raiders or any other team has to "compete" with other clubs or to move to a more lucrative market exists largely because the league allows home teams to keep most of their locally generated revenue.

16. This voluntary competition is not the type of competition required by the antitrust laws, and an entity's controlling such voluntary internal competition is not a "conspiracy" for section 1 purposes. This phenomenon is nothing more than internal firm rivalry similar to that encouraged by all companies between employees or divisions as an incentive for them to perform as efficiently as possible—for example, competition engendered by performance bonuses, sales awards, promises of promotion, and so on. But when internal rivalry between a company's employees or divisions becomes so cutthroat that it threatens to injure the company's profits, the company's efforts to control or eliminate the counterproductive behavior would never amount to illegal conspiracy.

17. Many decisions in any business are always better made at the local level, where people are best able to judge what is involved. For example, league executives in New York would be far less able than local executives to judge what an individual player is worth to a club, what rent is appropriate for each stadium, how best to market the local team, or how to cultivate good relationships with local political and business leaders.

Break Up the Sports League Monopolies

8

Stephen F. Ross

Our antitrust laws express a general economic policy that firms should compete in an open and free marketplace to supply consumers with the best possible product at the lowest possible price and to efficiently allocate society's resources. A judicial decree exempts major league baseball from the antitrust laws,[1] and the National Football League achieved monopoly status in 1966 after a statute specifically permitted it to merge with its one major rival, the American Football League.[2]

Policy decisions tolerating single leagues in each sport have led to predictable results. As lessees of stadia built and paid for by taxpayers, sports monopolists obtain favorable contract terms that require the public treasury to subsidize stadium operations. Monopoly sports leagues grant fewer franchises than would exist in a competitive market. To hold salary levels below the competitive level, monopoly leagues restrict the mobility of players, thereby limiting the ability of teams to improve themselves—the result is less exciting championship races. On the horizon, the existence of monopoly sports leagues risks a massive shift of sportcasts from free television to cable, forcing fans to pay for what they now receive for free. Finally, monopoly sports leagues tolerate inefficient and wasteful management practices by franchise owners that could not be tolerated by leagues facing the pressure of competition.

A competitive market can correct the harms inflicted on taxpayers and fans by the monopoly sports leagues. These harms would be substantially lessened if Congress were to enact legislation breaking major league baseball and the National Football League into separate, competing economic entities. Competing leagues would vie against each other for the right to play in public stadia, driving rents up and tax subsidies down. Leagues would be more eager to add new expansion markets, lest those markets fall into the hands of a rival league. Because the competing leagues would bid on players, salaries would more accurately reflect the players' fair market value. No league would have an incentive to unduly restrict the intraleague mobility of players, and teams would therefore have an easier time obtaining the right player for the right position. Leagues would be hesitant to move prime games to cable and risk losing their audience, as well as the loyalty of their fans, to a league whose games remained available on free television. Each league would feel the pressure of competition to maintain intelligent and efficient management.

Monopoly Sports Leagues Significantly Harm Taxpayers, Fans, and Players

In a variety of markets, the monopoly sports leagues or their member teams exercise monopoly power. Fans do not believe that a minor league professional baseball team, a major college football program, or a professional football team in a new league is a sufficient substitute for major league baseball or the National Football League, and local officials and civic groups eagerly beseech the existing leagues for expansion franchises. For fans, there are no acceptable alternatives to televised sporting events. Monopoly sports league members agree among themselves to limit competition for the services of players; for most professional athletes the next best available job is simply not a realistic option in lieu of professional sports.

Taxpayer Subsidies

To attract and retain sports teams in their communities, local governments find it necessary to provide franchises with substantial subsidies.[3] The typical tax subsidy takes the form of rent priced below the economic value of a facility or foregone taxes on stadium property.[4] Other types of subsidies include the development and construction of new stadia and improved highway and parking facilities.[5]

In a major study of this issue for the Brookings Institution, economist Benjamin Okner concluded that in 1971 stadium subsidies exceeded $8 million.[6] From the taxpayers' perspective, recent developments are even bleaker. A 1983 study reported that in 1981 and 1982 alone, at least thirteen of the forty-two localities hosting sports franchises saw demands for increased subsidies.[7] More recent examples abound.[8]

Team owners extract subsidies from local treasuries because of their significant advantage in bargaining power. For example, the number of cities desiring teams greatly exceeds the number of major league franchises. Incumbent owners use the threat of relocation to a city currently without a major league franchise to obtain concessions from local taxpayers.[9] In addition, leagues use franchise scarcity to wring concessions out of potential expansion cities.[10]

Economic theory suggests the existence of competing sports leagues would significantly reduce subsidies. An incumbent team, with its reservoir of good will and fan loyalty, would still obtain some subsidies to prevent it from moving. However, the city's ability to replace an existing franchise with a franchise from another league would limit the amount of the subsidy the city would willingly pay. Moreover, as demonstrated below, competing sports leagues can be expected to expand. The number of desirable cities without a major league team would dwindle, and a current team would be less able to set off a bidding war.

In modern times, only once did rival leagues battle for sole rights to an expansion metropolitan area. In 1960 both the NFL and the fledgling American Football League sought to establish a franchise in Houston. The owner of the Houston Oilers, Bud Adams, secured a five-year lease on an existing stadium with a promise to spend $150,000 of his own money to expand the seating capacity.[11] Twenty-seven years later, with a secure membership in the monopoly NFL, Adams threatened to relocate the Oilers to Jacksonville. He relented only after the Astrodome's operator agreed to add, at its own expense, an additional ten thousand seats and seventy-two sky boxes, as well as granting Adams a more favorable lease.[12]

Insufficient Expansion

In a free enterprise system, the market usually responds to increased consumer demand by spurring increased output. Monopoly sports leagues, in contrast, exercise their power to deliberately hold down their output—the number of available franchises. As a result, fans in cities with franchises are exploited by threats of relocation to the many "have-not" areas, and fans in cities without major league baseball or NFL franchises are deprived of the opportunity to have a team they can call their own.

Monopoly sports leagues have significant economic incentives to keep the number of franchises below the number that would exist in a free market. The fewer the franchises, the more likely the have-not cities will provide generous tax subsidies that induce an existing team to relocate. Even owners with no intention of relocating their own teams have powerful incentives to resist expansion. If a monopoly sports league has fewer teams, the resale value of each franchise rises. An increase in the number of team owners also means an increase in the number of people who share the revenues from the league's lucrative national television package. Expansion franchises pay huge sums of money to the existing owners when they buy entry into leagues; still, the smaller share of television revenue offsets the benefit of the one-time entry fee in just a few years.[13]

The one major policy argument against expansion is that there may not be "sufficient player talent to produce a proper caliber of play in expanded leagues."[14] Of course, any expansion reduces somewhat the average players' caliber. Even assuming this reduction in quality noticeably affects the fans' enjoyment of the game, any decreased satisfaction among fans in cities with teams will be outweighed by the dramatic increase in satisfaction in new expansion cities.[15] If enjoyment can be measured by gate attendance, expansion and the alleged dilution of player quality does not seem to have a negative impact on the fans' enjoyment of the game. For example, overall attendance increased in 1962, 1969, and 1977 after each major league baseball expansion.[16] Similarly, overall attendance at NFL games increased after each expansion.[17] Indeed, perhaps the ultimate test came when the National Hockey League expanded overnight from six to twelve teams in 1967. In spite of the significant decrease in player quality one would expect with such a rapid expansion, overall attendance at NHL games continued to increase.[18]

Economic theory suggests that competing leagues would have a greater incentive to expand to available markets. Each league would have a separate network television contract, valued by the number of fans viewing the league's games. Each league would eagerly tap new markets to attract viewers in those markets to its network package. For example, if the NFL had a contract with CBS and the AFL had a rival contract with NBC, CBS's ratings would most likely be higher in NFL cities, whereas NBC's would be higher in AFL towns. In markets distant from any current franchise, such as Memphis, ratings would probably be more equal. If the NFL expanded to Memphis, it could expect to see a favorable increase in its ratings, and NBC's AFL broadcasts would receive lower Memphis ratings because fans tend to watch the games of sports leagues that have franchises in their home cities. Thus, a league stands to profit by expansion or suffer through inaction while a rival league expands into a good market.[19]

Again, because rival leagues have seldom existed, only meager data are available about competitive expansion practices. Major league baseball did not expand for the first sixty years of this century, but when a rival Continental League threatened its monopoly, major league baseball quickly dispensed with its policy not to expand without unanimous approval and other expansion-discouraging rules.[20]

Inefficient Allocation of Players

Sports fans should prefer a system allocating players among teams that gives their own favorite team the opportunity to win the championship. But at the same time a league should provide for close, competitive games. To maximize fan attendance at games, revenues, and broadcast ratings, any league has an incentive to establish a player allocation system that creates the greatest fan interest. A monopoly league, however, has an additional anticonsumer incentive. When all teams in a single sport are members of one league, they can agree among themselves on rules that create a monopsony (a single buyer) in the acquisition of players. Monopoly leagues can create systems of allocating players that do not enhance the fans' enjoyment of the game but instead allow league owners to limit player salaries artificially. Although these restrictions have their most direct impact on players, the harm to fans seeking exciting pennant races is often overlooked.

The two player allocation systems that have sparked the most debate and litigation are the ones based on major league baseball's reserve clause and the National Football League's Rozelle Rule. The reserve clause, substantially modified in 1976 for veteran players, allocated the exclusive rights for the services of each player to one team. Unless those rights were waived, traded, sold, or otherwise assigned to another team, the player had to remain on the team with whom he signed his first contract.[21] In its original and modified form, the Rozelle Rule permits a player to sign with any NFL team at the expiration of a contract term. However, for all the top players, the player's new team must provide significant "compensation" to the player's former team to sign the player. (Currently, a team must give up one or two top draft choices to obtain most football players.) Moreover, the player's prior team may retain his services by matching any offer. The modified rules have virtually eliminated any free agency in football for all but marginal players.[22]

Competitive balance occurs where "there is relative parity among the member teams [and] each team has the opportunity of becoming a contender over a reasonable cycle of years and a reasonable chance of beating any other team on any given night."[23] By placing the outcome of any given game in doubt, competitive balance enhances a fan's enjoyment of a sport. Empirical studies by economists Roger G. Noll and Henry Demmert have demonstrated that attendance increases when championship races are closely contested.[24] Likewise, courts have recognized a sports league's "strong and unique interest" in maintaining competitive balance.[25] Although the current restrictive player allocation systems have been defended as necessary to promote competitive balance within the leagues, both economic theory and empirical evidence demonstrate the systems actually harm competitive balance, resulting in less exciting races for the league championships.

Many economists have argued that player restraints do not affect the allocation of players because teams can and do freely sell players for cash.[26]

This may well have been the case in major league baseball in the early and middle part of the twentieth century.[27] Recently, however, this premise has simply become inaccurate. National Football League regulations prohibit cash sales of players,[28] and, with the onset of free agency, the courts have sustained rulings by the Commissioner of Baseball that cash sales violate the best interests of the sport.[29] Even before this ruling, baseball owners may have been reluctant to sell top players for cash because of the negative press these sales receive and the negative reaction fans are likely to have to such transactions, since they so obviously weaken the team's playing strength solely for the owner's financial sake.[30] For example, the Yankees' dominance of the American League came to a halt shortly after the college and high school player draft began in 1966. If clubs could buy players as easily as trade for them, the Yankees would have attempted to reverse their downward trend by purchasing player contracts from other teams—yet the Yankees failed to do so.[31]

If teams actively bought and sold players for cash to the same degree that teams actively sign free agent contracts, the *Messersmith* decision, which led to free agency for veteran players, should not have affected the number of cash transactions.[32] Yet a comparison of trades and sales from 1969 to 1976 (pre-*Messersmith*) and trades, sales, and free agent signings from 1977 to 1981 disclosed a 9-percent increase in cash transactions after free agency.[33]

The reserve clause and the Rozelle Rule inefficiently allocate players among teams because of a simple economic principle: cash is superior to barter as a means of allocating goods in a market. Without cash transactions, any change in the current allocation of players is effectively limited to a direct transaction among two or, at most, three teams. Suppose, for example, that Team A has a surplus of outfielders, but needs relief pitchers. If Team B happens to have extra relievers but is weak in the outfield, the teams can arrange a trade. But suppose Team B can part with a reliever, but needs a power-hitting pinch hitter, and Team C has a power-hitting pinch hitter, but needs a utility infielder. In theory, some complex deal involving a number of teams might be arranged, but the transaction costs would be significant. Just as modern economies long ago shifted from a barter system as a means for allocating goods and services, it is more efficient for sports teams to use cash to allocate players. Team A would pay a premium for relief pitchers, but not for outfielders. Team B could acquire a free-agent pinch hitter. Team C could acquire the utility infielder it needs. Using cash as a medium of exchange, all the teams would improve their player talent, making their fans happier.

Relying on trades or other forms of noncash direct transactions is also inefficient and anticonsumer in situations where a team, perhaps due to bad luck or poor management decisions, finds itself with little player talent. In such cases, trades will rarely improve the team because it must give up quality players to obtain quality players. Intelligent drafting and development of young talent takes a long time; a draft limits poor teams to only one of the top rookies. In a free market, however, an owner seeking to increase attendance by improving a team could get immediate results by acquiring top players in the open market or by trying to sign several of the top players coming out of college.[34] It is ironic that the Rozelle Rule, the reserve clause, and the draft, which are supposedly designed to promote competitive balance, actually make it more difficult for poorer teams to improve themselves and thus promote competitive balance. Fans of teams with inferior talent suffer from these restrictions on player mobility.

Empirical evidence documenting the extent of major league baseball's competitive balance further demonstrates the reserve clause's harmful effects. By several measures, the level of competitive balance during the last seven years when the reserve clause was in effect (1969–75) was clearly inferior to seven comparable seasons following the *Messersmith* arbitration decision.[35] The number of teams that were "in the pennant race" (finishing within ten games of the leader) increased from thirty-four to forty-eight after free agency. Eleven baseball teams won divisions championships in the seven years before *Messersmith;* seventeen teams won them in the period studied after that decision. The Oakland A's, Pittsburgh Pirates, Cincinnati Reds, and Baltimore Orioles each won their respective division championships four times during the seven seasons immediately preceding *Messersmith.* In the seven seasons studied after the reserve clause system was disrupted, only the Kansas City Royals achieved that level of dominance. The goal of competitive balance has clearly failed when no team finishes within ten games behind the winner. There were eight such "blowout" races in the pre-*Messersmith* period; the seasons after *Messersmith* saw only three such races.

Owners in a monopoly league are willing to adopt inefficient player allocation schemes because their own profits from eliminating competition for players far exceeds any losses due to diminished fan interest in their sport. For example, total major league baseball attendance rose by approximately seven million from 1965 to 1975 (the last year of the reserve clause), but increased another seventeen million in the next decade, showing a strong increase in fan interest (57 percent) after the reserve clause was substantially eliminated.[36] After 1975 and the reserve clause's demise, salaries rose to a competitive level: the average player's salary increased from $44,676 to $371,157.[37] In constant dollars, this amounts to a 316 percent increase in costs.[38] Obviously, players and fans may profit from free agency for baseball veterans, but owners of monopoly sports leagues have strong incentive to eliminate competition for players and to artificially reduce player salaries so they can realize greater profits for themselves.[39]

In contrast, owners in competing sports leagues would take as a given that they must pay a competitive salary to a player; if not, the player will simply contract with a team from a rival league. Thus, the owners would have an incentive to restrict player mobility only if the restraints would promote competitive balance. If certain teams became dominant—because of location, winning tradition, or size of the market—the league could temporarily limit their ability to sign free agents, or inferior teams could draft players from the rosters of the more successful teams with minimal compensation paid to the dominant franchise. Although the empirical evidence does not support league officials' concerns that cities with franchises in larger markets would dominate their league,[40] any disparities that do exist could be addressed by some form of revenue sharing among franchises. Not only players but also fans would benefit by more balanced competition, retained incentives for individual team improvement, and more exciting play.

Preserving Opportunities to Watch Games on Free Television

Firms operating in a free market willingly lower the price of their goods and services to cost, even if many consumers would be willing to pay far in excess of that price.[41] Economists refer to the difference between the maximum amount consumers would pay and the actual price as "consumer surplus."[42] One of the principal functions of the antitrust laws prevents firms from engaging in tactics that shift wealth from consumers to producers by robbing consumers of this surplus.[43]

There are few markets in which consumers enjoy a greater amount of surplus than in the telecasting of major professional sports. The NFL broadcasts most of its games on free television.[44] Each major league baseball team broadcasts a large number of its games on free television as well.[45] All post-season playoff contests, the World Series, and the Super Bowl can be watched at no direct cost by any fan with a television set.

As technology makes it more feasible for monopoly sports leagues to capture consumer surplus, many observers predict that they will do so. Ted Turner, who owns the Atlanta Braves as well as the WTBS cable superstation, testified with characteristic bluntness: "There is going to be more and more movement from over the air, free telecasts to pay television for sports events." He predicted, "The only thing left to go on to pay television will be the World Series and the Super Bowl," and those games will remain on free television only because of congressional action.[46] In 1989 ESPN signed a four-year contract to televise baseball games.[47] Competing leagues would be unlikely, however, to shift to cable in cases where free television has a strong interest in obtaining broadcast rights. Each league would fear that cablecasts of its games would fare poorly against direct competition from free television broadcasts of a rival league's contests; general fan support, with a possible effect on live gate attendance, would also be jeopardized.

Inefficient Management

Another of the myriad benefits of competitive markets is their tendency to force firms to operate efficiently, providing the highest quality of goods and services to consumers at the lowest possible cost.[48] Firms that introduce innovations and quality control sell more (sometimes at premium prices) and gain higher profits; those firms that operate inefficiently lose business to rivals. Owners of teams in monopoly sports leagues, however, have substantial room to engage in inefficient behavior. They do not face the retribution of the marketplace for inefficient decisions about expansion, franchise relocation, player allocation systems, and many other matters.

In many cases, a monopoly sports league accepts intolerable inefficiencies because the owners do not wish to act against one of their own. If a competitive league entered the market with an efficient front-office management team, no incumbent league would permit the following examples of mismanagement: Baltimore (now Indianapolis) Colts owner Robert Irsay calling plays from his owners' box even though he had no experience in football;[49] the active management of the football franchise in the nation's second largest market by the former owner's wife, even though she had no experience and a reputation for incompetence;[50] the owner of the Philadelphia Eagles, Leonard Tose, trying to stay one step ahead of the creditors seeking repayment of his gambling debts.[51] When Commissioner Rozelle's office was questioned about Irsay's behavior, for example, a spokesman explained that "the League is not in a position to decide how an owner operates his team."[52] As with other abuses of monopoly power, consumers suffer the most from inefficient management. Loyal fans of local teams have little choice but to endure whatever management chooses; they have no marketplace alternative to which they can turn. Proud fans face the dilemma of suffering or else ceasing to patronize the teams.

Are Baseball and Football Natural Monopolies?

Thus far, I have argued that major league baseball and the National Football League should be separated into several leagues, competing as economic entities. As monopoly leagues, they impose significant costs upon taxpayers and fans, and a free marketplace featuring competing leagues would correct these economic deficiencies. Nevertheless, such a breakup would be ill-advised if each sport were a "natural monopoly," in which one firm can provide the product more efficiently than two or more firms competing with one another.

Sports leagues do not possess the critical characteristic of a natural monopoly—the ability of a single firm to enjoy such economies of scale that it can produce succeeding units of output at declining costs.[53] For example, one company can supply electricity to an entire city at less cost than two companies providing the same service. Once the first firm sets up its plant and wires the city, it is much cheaper for it to add additional homes than for a second firm to set up a completely separate plant and network. In contrast to industries characterized by very large fixed costs (for items such as plant and equipment), the annual fixed costs for a sports franchise have been estimated at less than $100,000.[54] There appears to be no reason why stadium rental, player salaries, and administrative costs should be any higher for a second league than for a monopoly league. Although any league needs a certain minimum number of teams to function, both baseball and football could easily restructure with three to four leagues in each sport, each with eight or more teams.

Nevertheless, because competition has never existed for any length of time, the argument persists that each sport is a natural monopoly. A brief review of the economic history of major league baseball and the NFL discloses alternative explanations for the absence of competitive leagues in each case.

Baseball

Major league baseball did not evolve naturally as a monopoly sports league. Rather, a 1902 agreement ending competition between the National and American leagues gave the owners in both leagues their monopoly. Throughout its history, major league baseball has responded to attempts to compete, either on the major league or the minor league level, by a series of boycotts, player blacklists, price wars, legal harassment, and deliberate scheduling of conflicting games.[55] The last effort to challenge the monopoly was led by baseball executive Branch Rickey, whose efforts to form a new Continental League foundered when the incumbent leagues announced their intention to expand to four new locales, including three sites targeted by the new Continental League.[56] Major league baseball has subsequently added six additional teams, further decreasing the markets available for a new entrant.

Football

Unlike the major leagues in baseball, the National Football League has faced several significant challenges to its monopoly position over the last few decades. Nevertheless, it has maintained its monopoly throughout this period. The circumstances surrounding the demise of economic competition in football do not, however, suggest that establishing rival football leagues is unworkable.

The All-American Football Conference (AAFC) played in the late 1940s but did not enjoy success as a rival league. Most observers attribute the league's failure to poor business judgment. The AAFC ignored the now-conventional wisdom that competitive balance among franchises is desirable, and the Cleveland Browns became the overwhelmingly dominant team. Games were not exciting, most teams had no chance for success in AAFC play, and attendance foundered.[57] Interleague rivalry in professional football returned in 1960 with the formation of the American Football League. At the time, the incumbent NFL had twelve franchises; a court subsequently found that thirty-one cities were capable of supporting professional football in 1960.[58] The AFL-NFL rivalry ended, however, with the merger between the two leagues in 1966.

Now that this congressionally sanctioned merger is in place, a new football entrant must face a giant incumbent, entrenched in all the major media markets and most of the largest markets in the country. The failures of the World and United States Football leagues may be explained by the inability of any league to compete with the behemoth NFL. Obtaining a network contract is essential if a league wants to compete successfully,[59] and a league's ability to locate franchises in at least some of the four or five largest metropolitan areas may be necessary to secure a national network contract. Disastrous managerial decisions by owners of the World Football League and United States Football League may also have significantly figured in their lack of success.[60]

The fact that recent entries into professional football have failed does not prove that football is a natural monopoly any more than unsuccessful attempts to enter the aluminum industry prior to the dissolution of Alcoa demonstrated the natural monopoly status of that industry.[61] A new league's experience in facing an entrenched incumbent provides no reliable indication of what the result would be if the NFL were divided into two or more competing entities, each with established franchises.

"Ruinous Competition"

Proponents of the natural monopoly theory argue that competing leagues will invariably engage in "ruinous competition" until one or both are bankrupt. This argument was made in connection with interleague rivalry in football and basketball.[62] Economic theory and some empirical evidence suggest, however, that league owners will generally not pay more in player salaries than they reasonably expect the players to produce in ticket sales and broadcast revenues.[63] The natural monopoly theorists have not explained why sports owners, unlike other business executives, would contract with a player knowing the club cannot possibly profit from that contract.

Two plausible alternate explanations belie the claims that bidding wars resulting in bankruptcy are inevitable. First, the figures showing that leagues are unable to maintain profitable operations during a bidding war for player contracts may be inaccurate. Franchises can take advantage of a host of accounting devices and tax breaks so as to appear unprofitable even though the franchises remain attractive as investments for their owners. The tax laws permit owners to deduct paper losses—such as the depreciation of player contracts—that do not affect the team's actual profitability. In addition, owners can use expenses other than player costs—such as administrative or front-office expenses—to realize profits in the form of salaries paid to themselves or their relatives. Moreover, in the case of an owner who has other investments, sports teams can appear to suffer losses yet actually generate profits for the owner—such as promoting higher ratings for an owner's superstation or promoting an owner's manufacturing product, for example, Anheuser-Busch beer.[64]

Second, even if a rival league, or even the incumbent league, is losing money, the losses may be due to the incumbent league's decision to engage in predatory behavior to rebuff the new entrant. To drive the new league out, teams in an incumbent league may spend more on player contracts than they possibly hope to realize in revenue. With competitors crushed, future monopoly profits would exceed these losses.

Although some dispute the likelihood of predation in a typical industry,[65] predation is much more plausible in sports. Unlike new competitors in most industries, an entrant in a sports market cannot succeed via price competition—by offering at a lower price what may be perceived as an inferior product. Most fans are likely to insist on the best talent.[66] Because a significant portion of revenue comes from broadcasting on free television, a new league cannot possibly convince fans to watch inferior games when for the same price (zero) they can watch the incumbent's superior product.

Predatory practices are unlikely when rival leagues compete. Imagine a world inhabited by three baseball entities—the National, American, and Continental Leagues. If a new league, the United States Baseball League (USBL), sought to enter the market, how would the three incumbent leagues respond? Assuming no collusion among them, would they raise their salaries to unprofitable levels? Of course not. There would be no reason for National League owners, for instance, to lose money in order to keep out the USBL, for even if they succeeded they would still have to compete with the other two leagues. Only the prospect of future monopoly profits gives league owners an incentive to engage in predatory conduct with short-run unprofitability. If the monopoly resulting from predation were clearly illegal, owners would not engage in predation. Competition would be the norm in baseball and football.

Monopoly Leagues, Rival Leagues, and the Antitrust Laws

Spokesmen for both major league baseball and the NFL have complained about the effect of the antitrust laws on their leagues. In a memorandum submitted to the House Judiciary Committee, major league baseball's legal counsel wrote that the rule of reason analysis used by courts in antitrust cases would not "provide meaningful protection for the basic practices of Baseball in the event the sport lost its existing antitrust immunity."[67] NFL Commissioner Pete Rozelle has commented that NFL owners are "damned in antitrust if they do, and damned in antitrust if they don't."[68]

The criticisms are not unfounded. The courts have not done a particularly good job analyzing antitrust challenges to the practices of monopoly sports leagues. Generally when courts discover monopolistic practices, they prefer to break up the monopoly, so that the market can correct itself; the market is likely to more accurately maximize consumers' welfare than a judge's well-meaning edicts. Antitrust policy thus prefers courts to establish rules fostering competition rather than to regulate monopolies. In contrast to these difficulties, in a world of competing leagues, existing antitrust doctrines could be sensibly applied to regulate competition.

Most reported antitrust cases against major sports leagues involve suits by players or other employees claiming that the leagues unreasonably restricted the market for their services.[69] How will courts evaluate restraints on players in a world of competing leagues? As long as players are able to receive truly competitive bids from different leagues, it will be difficult if not impossible for a player to prove that one particular league's rules have caused any harm. For example, if teams in the United States Football League and the American Football League had actively bid for the services of All-Pro tight end John Mackey in the 1970s, he could hardly have claimed significant injury because the National Football League allowed only the Baltimore Colts to bid on him.[70]

A second major source of antitrust litigation involves suits challenging franchise relocation, expansion, or other internal league decisions.[71] With competing sports leagues, the prospect of expansion or relocation by the other leagues makes it virtually impossible for a city or a maverick owner to prove the defendant league had harmed competition. If a market can support an additional team, rival leagues can be expected to fill the void. Thus competing leagues' individual decisions concerning franchise relocation should almost always survive antitrust challenges. Of course, collusion among rival leagues on these issues would be highly suspect.

The final major source of antitrust litigation has involved disputes by rival leagues alleging that the entrenched incumbent leagues unlawfully monopolized the market.[72] With several leagues that are, at least initially, roughly balanced, most conduct that is viewed with suspicion when practiced by a monopoly league will likely be viewed as vigorous competition if done by a single league in a competitive market. Practices that have been challenged in the past—such as enforcement of a uniform player contract binding players to their existing club for at least three years,[73] expansion into previously untapped markets,[74] or increasing the number of players permitted on each team's active roster and attempting to attract key players from rival leagues[75]—will likely pass antitrust muster. In sum, most of the major antitrust litigation brought against monopoly sports leagues has involved conduct that either would be unlikely to occur in a competitive market or would be sustained against antitrust attack because it had no anticompetitive effect.

Although most of the difficult and messy litigation against monopolists would disappear in a world of competing sports leagues, the courts would then face the new challenge of regulating collusion *by* the competing leagues. If judges properly apply recent antitrust law developments to interleague agreements, they will permit those arrangements that serve the interests of fans but reject agreements reducing competition and leading to the same harms now brought about by existing monopoly sports leagues.

The U.S. Supreme Court has made clear that the antitrust laws permit rival firms to act jointly when cooperation is essential to produce a new or distinct product.[76] Thus competing leagues could clearly agree to produce jointly such events as the World Series, the Super Bowl, and the All-Star Game. Any agreement necessary to produce these events would be considered "ancillary" to bringing about these games and would therefore be lawful as well.[77] The competing leagues could therefore grant exclusive telecasting rights, set ticket prices, and determine eligibility for these events.

Under the same theory, the antitrust laws would also permit interleague play, giving fans the opportunity to see contests and teams they would otherwise be unable to see. The leagues could agree on the terms essential to bring about such contests, including agreements governing the division of revenues and the sale of broadcast rights. However, agreements that went beyond those terms (dictating, for example, what each league did with its share of the revenue) would not be lawful.

Antitrust laws would be most effective in precluding agreements between leagues that do not involve necessary joint activities. Decisions that have the potential to most directly harm taxpayers and fans are not needed—such as decisions regarding the number and location of franchises, player restraints, broadcast policies, and other matters of internal operation. Each league would unilaterally decide these issues. The result would significantly reduce the ability of sports leagues to harm taxpayers and fans.

Implementing the Divestiture through Legislation

If the public interest would be served by breaking up the monopoly sports leagues, how should the divestiture be accomplished? One means would be a judicial decree upon a finding that the leagues had unlawfully monopolized in violation of the Sherman Act. Such a decree would be difficult to obtain, however. To break up major league baseball, the Supreme Court would have to overrule three prior opinions declaring baseball to be exempt from the antitrust laws.[78] To break up the NFL would require a trial court to find, contrary to previous trial courts, that since 1966 the NFL engaged in unlawful conduct to maintain its monopoly in professional football.[79]

A legislative solution would appear, then, to have the most promise of instituting free enterprise within baseball and football. Such legislation should:

1. Require major league baseball and the NFL each to submit a plan of divestiture into three or four leagues. A minimum of three leagues in each sport is probably necessary to gain the benefits of competition concerning expansion and franchise relocation for those areas that now have two franchises (Chicago, Los Angeles, New York, San Francisco). A divestiture resulting in a duopoly may create too high a risk of collusion between the two leagues. The business judgment of team owners could best determine whether existing alignments should be further subdivided (e.g., into the American League East and West and the National League East and West) or whether the leagues should be totally realigned (put all NFL West Coast teams in one league, for example). However, the plan should be subject to approval of the Justice Department or the Federal Trade Commission to ensure that the leagues begin the new era on equal terms. To allow a smooth transition, legislation should permit the leagues and a government antitrust enforcement agency to work out the timing of divestiture.

2. Specify permissible conduct. Although my reading of current antitrust doctrine will permit stable competition among competing leagues, not every judge may agree. Legislation should specify that the establishment of the World Series, Super Bowl, and other joint efforts is lawful.

3. Prohibit undesirable conduct. To ensure that the harms imposed by monopoly sports leagues are not imposed by agreements among competing leagues, the legislation should prohibit any interleague agreement concerning the number and location of franchises, rules for allocating players among teams, and (except for games involving teams from rival leagues) the sale of broadcast rights.

Conclusion

Baseball and football continue to arouse the passions of millions of fans. They are so enjoyable and are such a part of our culture that the social costs of allowing major league baseball and football to operate as monopolies are often overlooked. Monopoly sports league owners take advantage of their economic power to secure massive subsidies from local taxpayers, yet still deprive fans in many cities of expansion teams they could economically support and emotionally cherish. Owners conspire to limit player salaries by schemes that inefficiently allocate players among teams, denying individual franchises the opportunity to obtain the players they may need to develop winning or championship teams. Both major league baseball and football owe their current success and popularity to the broadcasting of their games over free television, yet the monopoly leagues are well positioned to force fans to pay millions of dollars to view these contests on cable television. Inefficient and incompetent sports executives, free from the rigors of economic competition, annually subject many fans to losing seasons for the fans' favorite franchises.

Although these harms are real, they are not inevitable. The existence of rival leagues would solve most of these economic problems. If cities had the option to seek a franchise from a rival league on more favorable terms, that possibility would limit a team's ability to extort tax subsidies. Competing leagues would seek out expansion cities to increase ticket and network revenues. No league would have an incentive to establish inefficient means of player allocation, because interleague competition would raise salaries to a competitive level; thus, each league's internal rules would be designed to produce the most exciting pennant and championship races. Leagues contemplating significant shifts to cable or pay-TV would hesitate to do so if their audiences could continue to watch rival league games for free. Finally, leagues could not afford to tolerate extreme mismanagement of individual franchises, for doing so would invite a direct head-on challenge from a competing league.

If baseball and football were characterized by competing leagues, the antitrust laws would serve as a workable means of regulating competition in the industry. Indeed, many of the troublesome issues now raised in antitrust sports litigation would disappear when the industry no longer featured a monopolistic structure. To carefully supervise the transition to a competitive environment and to avoid the need to overcome difficult judicial obstacles, Congress should act to benefit sports fans with the same free enterprise that we expect from other business endeavors.

NOTES

1. *Federal Baseball Club v. National League*, 259 U.S. 200 (1922).
2. Pub. L. No. 89-800, 80 Stat. 1515 (1966) (amending 15 U.S.C. secs. 1291–93 [1982]).
3. See Johnson, "Municipal Administration and the Sports Franchise Relocation Issue," *Public Administration Review* 43 (1983): 519.
4. See B. Okner, "Subsidies of Stadiums and Teams," in R. Noll, ed., *Government and the Sports Business* (Washington, D.C.: The Brookings Institution, 1974), 325.
5. Rosentraub, *Financial Incentives, Locational Decision-Making and Professional Sports: The Case of the Texas Ranger Baseball Network and the City of Arlington, Texas,* repr. in *Inquiry into Professional Sports: Final Report of the House Select Committee on Professional Sports*, H.R. Rept. No. 1786, 94th Cong., 2d Sess., 202 (1977) (hereafter cited as *Sisk Report*).
6. Okner, "Subsidies of Stadiums and Teams," 341.
7. Johnson, "Municipal Administration," 520.
8. See, for example, R. Baade, "Is There an Economic Rationale for Subsidizing Sports Stadiums?" Heartland Institute Policy Study Paper, February 23, 1987, 9; Johnson, "Municipal Administration," 521–22; Rosentraub, "Financial Incentives," 201–15.
9. See D. Harris, *The League: The Rise and Decline of the NFL* (New York: Bantam, 1986), 614–15, 642.
10. See *Los Angeles Memorial Coliseum Comm'n v. National Football League*, 726 F.2d 1381, 1394 (9th Cir.), cert. denied, 469 U.S. 990 (1984) (hereafter cited as *Raiders*). The evidence showed that the NFL "remained expressly noncommitted on the question of team movement" in order "to give owners a bargaining edge when they were renegotiating leases with their respective stadia." See also Harris, *The League,* 176–77.
11. *Houston Post*, October 29, 1959, 1.
12. Deford, "This Bud's Not For You," *Sports Illustrated*, November 2, 1987, 70.
13. See *Professional Sports Community Protection Act: Hearings on S.259 and S.287 before the Senate Committee on Commerce, Science, and Transportation,* 99th Cong., 1st Sess. (1985), 62–63 (hereafter cited as *Danforth '85 Hearings*) for the testimony of NFL Commissioner Pete Rozelle.
14. See *Inquiry into Professional Sports: Hearings before the House Select Comm. on Professional Sports*, 94th Cong., 2d Sess. (1976), 1:64 (hereafter cited as *Sisk Hearings*) for the testimony of Cincinnati Reds official Robert Howsam. But see B. James, *Baseball Abstract* (1988), 21 (talent sufficient for major league baseball to expand to sixty teams).
15. Canes, "The Social Benefits of Team Quality," in *Government and the Sports Business,* 96–97. Attendance rose during World War II in cities whose

teams' records had improved, although overall league attendance declined because of the lower quality of teams spurred by the loss of many players to military service.

16. See H. Turkin and S. Thompson, *The Official Encyclopedia of Baseball* (1979), 71.

17. See *The Sporting News Pro Football Guide* (1987), 391.

18. See *National Hockey League, Official Guide and Record Book, 1987–88*, 130.

19. For example, in 1983 the Colts were in Baltimore; in 1984 they moved to Indianapolis. According to Arbitron ratings, NFL football on NBC's Indianapolis affiliate (which shows AFC contests) went up from a 10 rating (29-percent market share) to a 17 rating (41-percent market share). During the Colts' last year in Baltimore, the Baltimore NBC affiliate enjoyed a 19 to 10 rating edge (47- to 27-percent market share); when the Colts left, the margin decisively narrowed (NBC: 15 rating / 34-percent market share; CBS: 13 rating / 31-percent market share). Just for comparison, in Phoenix the ratings were both lower and closer. (NBC: 13 rating / 39-percent market share; CBS: 11 rating / 32-percent market share).

20. Davis, "Self-Regulation in Baseball," in *Government and the Sports Business*, 371–72.

21. See *Flood v. Kuhn*, 316 F. Supp. 271, 273–75 (S.D.N.Y.), aff'd, 443 F.2d 264 (2d Cir. 1971), aff'd, 407 U.S. 258 (1972).

22. See *Powell v. National Football League*, 678 F. Supp. 777, 779–80, and note 2 (D. Minn. 1988).

23. *Philadelphia World Hockey Club v. Philadelphia Hockey Club*, 351 F. Supp. 462, 486 (E.D. Pa. 1972).

24. H. Demmert, *The Economics of Professional Team Sports* (Lexington, Mass.: Lexington Books, 1973); Noll, "Attendance and Price Setting," in *Government and the Sports Business*, 119.

25. *Mackey v. National Football League*, 543 F.2d 606, 621 (8th Cir. 1976). See also *National Collegiate Athletic Ass'n v. Board of Regents of Univ. of Oklahoma*, 468 U.S. 85, 117 (1984).

26. See, for example, *Sisk Report* (teams "have almost complete freedom to purchase contracts from other teams"); Demmert, *The Economics of Professional Team Sports*, 36 (if a player is more highly valued by another team, current club will sell rights to player); Canes, "The Social Benefits of Team Quality," 84 (describing reserve system with assumption that reserve clause rights can be sold); Quirk and el Hodiri, "The Economic Theory of a Sports League," in *Government and the Sports Business*, 39–40 (contrasting effect of draft if sale of player contracts were prohibited with present structure); Rottenberg, book review of *Government and the Sports Business, Journal of Economic Literature* 18 (1975): 87, 88 (assuming that "the purchase and sale by teams of rights to players' services is permitted").

27. See Quirk and el Hodiri, "The Economic Theory of a Sports League," 33.

28. Letter of Jeffrey Pash, Esq., counsel to National Football League, to author, July 27, 1988.

29. *Charles O. Finley Co. v. Kuhn*, 569 F.2d 537 (7th Cir. 1978).

30. See, for example, Hunt and Lewis, "Dominance, Recontracting and the Reserve Clause: Major League Baseball," *American Economic Review* 66 (1976): 936.

31. Daly and Moore, "Externalities, Property Rights and the Allocation of Resources in Major League Baseball," *Economic Inquiry* 19 (1977):77.

32. *Twelve Clubs Comprising Nat'l League of Professional Baseball Clubs and Twelve Clubs Comprising Amer. League of Professional Baseball Clubs v. Major League Baseball Players Ass'n,* 66 L.A. 101 (December 23, 1975) (Seitz, Arb.) (hereafter cited as *Messersmith*).

33. The data are provided in J. Reichler, ed., *The Baseball Encyclopedia* (1985), 2145–2575.

34. See, for example, Demmert, *The Economics of Professional Team Sports,* 66 (a baseball club finishing five games behind will draw 253,000 more fans than a similar club finishing fifteen games behind); R. Lucke, "Antitrust Policy and the Professional Sports Industry," honors thesis, University of California, 1977, 18 (one additional victory will generate 18,798 more fans).

35. The pre-*Messersmith* period consists of the 1969–75 seasons. Prior to 1969, major league baseball did not use divisional play; hence comparisons involving team standing or games behind a leader became difficult for seasons prior to 1969. I then sought to find a comparable seven-year period after *Messersmith*. The 1981 strike season, which involved fewer games and playoff contenders that were selected based on their performance in two different halves of the season, was eliminated. I also eliminated the 1986 and 1987 seasons. The Major League Baseball Players Association has alleged that owners conspired not to bid on free agents during these seasons. An arbitrator has sustained these contentions as to the 1986 season in *Major League Baseball Players Association v. The Twenty-Six Major League Baseball Clubs,* Grievance No. 86-2 (September 21, 1987) (Roberts, Arb.) (hereafter cited as *Collusion I*); ibid., Grievance No. 87–3 (August 31, 1988) (Nicolau, Arb.) This left nine seasons during which there were no significant limits on player mobility (1976–80, 1982–85). I eliminated the first two seasons of free agency (1976 and 1977) because the effects of free agency would not be as pronounced in the period immediately following a half-century of total monopsony in the major league baseball player market.

The data were compiled from standings listed in *The Baseball Encyclopedia,* 478–574, and *The Sporting News, 1986 Baseball Yearbook,* 139, 147.

36. Total major league baseball attendance in 1965 was 22,441,900, according to *The Sporting News Official Baseball Guide* (St. Louis: The Sporting News, 1966), 227. In 1975 it totaled 29,789,923, as reported in Turkin and Thompson, *The Official Encyclopedia of Baseball,* 71. In 1985 it totaled 46,824,379, as recorded in *The Sporting News Official Baseball Guide* (1986), 287.

37. Major League Baseball Players Association, *Average Salaries in Major League Baseball 1967–1987,* 3 (filed as exhibit in *Collusion I*).

38. The Consumer Price Index rose from 161.2 in 1975 to 322.2 in 1985. U.S. Bureau of the Census, *Statistical Abstract of the United States* (1986), 478 and (1987), 463. Had average player salaries risen only with inflation, the 1985 average would have been $89,296.57—less than one-third of the actual 1985 average.

39. See Daly and Moore, "Externalities, Property Rights, and Baseball," 81, and note 3; Medoff, "On Monopsonistic Exploitation in Professional Baseball," *Quarterly Review of Economics and Business* 16 (1976): 113 (1972–74 data show

players receive between 30 and 50 percent of worth); Scully, "Pay and Performance in Major League Baseball," *American Economic Review* 64 (1974): 915 (1967–68 data show players receive 11 percent of economic worth).

40. See, for example, *Sisk Hearings*, 1: 215–16 (testimony of football union director Edward Garvey) (players did not move to wealthy franchises in large, warmweather cities during one-year "window" of free agency in 1976); Besanko and Simon, "Resource Allocation in the Baseball Players' Labor Market: An Empirical Investigation," *Review of Business and Economic Research* 21 (1985): 71, 83 (free agents tend to move from good teams to poorer teams).

41. E. Mansfield, *Microeconomics: Theory and Applications*, 4th ed. (New York: Norton, 1982), 15.

42. Ibid.

43. See generally Lande, "Wealth Transfers as the Original and Primary Concern of Antitrust: The Efficiency Interpretation Challenged," *Hastings Law Journal* 34 (1982): 65.

44. *Statement of Pete Rozelle: Testimony before the Subcommittee on Antitrust, Monopolies and Business Rights of the Senate Committee on the Judiciary*, 100th Cong., 2d Sess. (October 6, 1987), 5–6 (unofficial statement).

45. See "Baseball Bags Almost $370 Million in Rights," *Broadcasting*, March 7, 1988, 54–63.

46. *Antitrust Policy and Professional Sports: Oversight Hearings before the House Subcomm. on Monopolies and Commercial Law of the Committee on the Judiciary on H.R. 823, H.R. 3287, and H.R. 6467*, 97th Cong., 1st and 2d Sess. (1982), 97 (hereafter cited as *Rodino '82 Hearings*) See also ibid., 147, 159 (testimony of sports journalist Howard Cosell and NBA union director Lawrence Fleisher).

47. I have elsewhere discussed why this particular cable contract does not harm customers. See Ross, "An Antitrust Analysis of Sports League Contracts with Cable Networks," *Emory Law Journal* 39 (1990): 463, 480.

48. F. Scherer, *Industrial Market Structure and Economic Performance*, 2d ed. (Boston: Houghton Mifflin, 1980), 13.

49. Harris, *The League*, 478.

50. Ibid., 465–66, 572 (describing Los Angeles Rams owner Georgia Frontiere).

51. Ibid., 111–21, 292–98, 556–62.

52. Ibid., 190.

53. A. Kahn, *The Economics of Regulation: Principles and Institutions* (1971), 2:173.

54. Noll, "Major League Team Sports," in W. Adams, ed., *The Structure of American Industry*, 5th ed. (New York: Macmillan, 1977), 395.

55. Note, "Monopsony in Manpower: Organized Baseball Meets the Antitrust Laws," *Yale Law Journal* 62 (1953): 576, 604, and note 150, citing H.R. Rept. 2002, 82d Cong., 2d Sess. (1952).

56. Prell, "Delay Action Until C.L. is Counted Out," *The Sporting News*, July 20, 1960, p. 1, col. 4.

57. See H. Claassen, *Encyclopedia of Football*, 3d ed. (New York: Ronald Press Co., 1963), 1–27.

58. *American Football League v. National Football League,* 323 F.2d 124, 128 (4th Cir. 1963).

59. *United States Football League v. National Football League,* 842 F.2d 1335, 1353 (2d Cir. 1988).

60. See ibid., 1345 (World Football League underfinanced and located franchises in mostly smaller markets); ibid., 1351–52 (extensive evidence that the USFL's downfall was caused by strategy of moving from spring to fall, escalating salary bids, and relocating franchises to markets without NFL teams in hopes of achieving merger with NFL).

61. See generally *United States v. Aluminum Co. of America,* 148 F.2d 416 (2d Cir. 1945).

62. See, for example, *Professional Basketball: Hearing before the Subcomm. on Antitrust and Monopoly of the Senate Comm. on the Judiciary on S. 2373,* 92nd Cong., 2d Sess. (1972), 93, 665 (testimony of Senator Kuchel and NBA Commissioner Walter Kennedy); *Professional Football League Merger: Hearing before Antitrust Subcomm. of the House Comm. on the Judiciary on S. 3817 and Similar Bills,* 89th Cong., 2d Sess. (1966), 35 (testimony of NFL Commissioner Pete Rozelle).

63. See Demmert, *The Economics of Professional Team Sports,* 25 (most observers consider clubs to function as profit maximizers); L. Koppett, *A Thinking Man's Guide to Baseball* (1967), 217 ("when a clear-cut choice arises between more victories and more profit, the path toward more profit is chosen); Jones, "The Economics of the National Hockey League," *Canadian Journal of Economics* 2 (1969): 1 (behavior of NHL franchises explained by model of profit maximization); Noll, "Major League Team Sports," 388 (St. Louis Browns and Brooklyn Dodgers continued to sell players for cash in 1930s, despite mediocre record, thus preferring profit to victories).

64. See Noll, "Economics of Sports Leagues," in Jerry Uberstine, ed., *Law of Professional and Amateur Sports* (New York: Clark Boardman, 1988), 17-7 to 17-9.

65. See *Matsushita Elec. Indus. Co., Ltd. v. Zenith Radio Corp.,* 475 U.S. 574, 588–91 (1986).

66. See *Sisk Hearings,* 1:486 (testimony of WHA Cleveland owner Jay P. Moore) (could not compete against NHL on price; tried cutting ticket prices, but attendance did not increase).

67. *Rodino '82 Hearings,* 445 (memorandum of Arnold and Porter).

68. Ibid., 185.

69. Football cases: *Smith v. Pro-Football, Inc.,* 593 F.2d 1173 (D.C. Cir. 1978); *Reynolds v. National Football League,* 584 F.2d 280 (8th Cir. 1978); *Mackey v. National Football League,* 543 F.2d 606 (8th Cir. 1976); *Powell v. National Football League,* 888 F.2d 559 (8th Cir. 1989); *Zimmerman v. National Football League,* 632 F. Supp. 398 (D. D.C. 1986); *Boris v. United States Football League,* 1984-1 Trade Cas. (CCH) par. 66,012 (C.D. Cal. 1984); *Hayes v. National Football League,* 469 F. Supp. 247 (C.D. Cal. 1979); *Alexander v. National Football League,* 1977-2 Trade Cas. (CCH) par. 61,730 (D. Minn. 1977); *Bowman v. National Football League,* 402 F. Supp. 754 (D. Minn. 1975); *Kapp v. National Football League,* 390 F. Supp. 73 (N.D. Cal. 1974); *Beach v. National Football League,* 331 F. Supp. 249 (S.D.N.Y. 1971).

Baseball Cases: *Flood v. Kuhn*, 407 U.S. 258 (1972); *Salerno v. American League*, 429 F.2d 1003 (2d Cir. 1970), cert. denied, 400 U.S. 1001 (1971); *Tepler v. Frick*, 204 F.2d 506 (2d Cir. 1953); *Kowalski v. Chandler*, 202 F.2d 413 (6th Cir. 1953); *Martin v. National League*, 174 F.2d 917 (2d Cir. 1949).

Basketball cases: *Haywood v. National Basketball Association*, 401 U.S. 1204 (1971); *Wood v. National Basketball Association*, 809 F. 2d 954 (2d. Cir. 1987); *Bridgeman v. National Basketball Association*, 675 F. Supp. 960 (D. N.J. 1987); *Robertson v. National Basketball Association*, 389 F. Supp. 867 (S.D.N.Y. 1975); *Saunders v. National Basketball Association*, 348 F. Supp. 649 (N.D. Ill. 1972); *Hawkins v. National Basketball Association*, 288 F. Supp. 614 (W.D. Pa. 1968); *Molinas v. National Basketball Association*, 190 F. Supp. 241 (S.D.N.Y. 1961).

Hockey Cases: *McCourt v. California Sports, Inc.*, 600 F.2d 1193 (6th Cir. 1979); *Neeld v. National Hockey League*, 594 F.2d 1297 (9th Cir. 1979); *Boston Professional Hockey Ass'n, Inc. v. Cheevers*, 472 F.2d 127 (1st Cir. 1972); *Linseman v. World Hockey Ass'n*, 439 F. Supp. 1315 (D. Conn. 1977).

70. Cf. *Mackey v. National Football League*, 543 F.2d 606 (8th Cir. 1976).

71. See, for example, *National Basketball Association v. SDC Basketball Club, Inc.*, 815 F.2d 562 (9th Cir. 1987) (declaratory judgment in favor of NBA effort to determine initially proposed relocation of Clippers from San Diego to Los Angeles); *Oakland Raiders v. National Football League*, 726 F.2d 1381 (9th Cir.), cert. denied, 469 U.S. 990 (1984) (league denial of permission for Raiders to move from Oakland to Los Angeles); *Washington v. American League*, 460 F.2d 654 (9th Cir. 1972) (league approval for relocation of Seattle Pilots to Milwaukee and refusal to grant expansion franchise for Seattle); *Buffalo v. Atlanta Hawks Basketball, Inc.*, Civ. No. 76-0261 (W.D.N.Y. June 15, 1976) (league approval of planned relocation of Buffalo franchise to Florida), cited in J. Weistart and C. Lowell, *The Law of Sports* (1979) 716–19. *Wisconsin v. Milwaukee Braves, Inc.*, 1966 Trade Cas. (CCH) par. 71,738 (Cir. Ct. Milw. Co.) (league approval for relocation of Braves to Atlanta and refusal to grant expansion franchise for Milwaukee), rev'd on other grounds, 1972 Trade Cas. (CCH) par. 73,933 (Wisc.).

72. *United States Football League v. National Football League*, 842 F.2d 1335 (2d Cir. 1988); *World Hockey Ass'n v. National Hockey League*, 531 F.2d 1188 (3d Cir. 1976); *American Football League v. National Football League*, 323 F.2d 124 (4th Cir. 1963); *American Basketball Ass'n Players Ass'n v. National Basketball Association*, 72 F.R.D. 594 (S.D.N.Y. 1976); *Philadelphia World Hockey Club, Inc. v. Philadelphia Hockey Club, Inc.*, 351 F. Supp. 462 (E.D. Pa. 1972).

73. *Philadelphia World Hockey Club, Inc. v. Philadelphia Hockey Club, Inc.*, 351 F. Supp. 462, 511 (E.D. Pa. 1972).

74. *Amercian Football League v. National Football League*, 323 F.2d 124 (4th Cir. 1963).

75. *United States Football League v. National Football League*, 842 F.2d at 1343.

76. *National Collegiate Athletic Ass'n*, 468 U.S. 85 (1983); *Broadcast Music, Inc. v. Columbia Broadcasting System, Inc.*, 441 U.S. 1 (1979)

77. See *Broadcast Music*, 441 U.S. 1; *United States v. Addyston Pipe & Steel Co.*, 85 F.2d 271 (6th Cir. 1898), aff'd, 175 U.S. 211 (1899).

78. *Flood v. Kuhn*, 407 U.S. 258 (1972); *Toolson v. New York Yankees*, 346 U.S. 356 (1953); *Federal Baseball Club of Baltimore, Inc.*, 259 U.S. 200 (1922).

79. See, for example, *United States Football League v. National Football League*, 842 F.2d at 1357 (NFL conduct did not cause USFL's demise).

The Blue Line and the Bottom Line: Entrepreneurs and the Business of Hockey in Canada, 1927–90 9

David Mills

Since the formation of the National Hockey League in 1917, the business of hockey has grown spectacularly. The NHL began with franchises in Toronto, Ottawa, Montreal, and Quebec, and, like earlier professional leagues, it attracted promoters and fast-buck artists, local "athletic facility" owners, and businessmen. These entrepreneurs argued among themselves over players, gate receipts, rink sizes, and franchise rights. Because of money woes only three teams finished the first season. From this halting beginning, the NHL has developed into a major professional sport league with twenty-one teams in twenty cities throughout North America. In the process, it has become a big-league enterprise that has attracted major corporate owners such as Molson Companies, Ltd. in Montreal and Paramount Communications, Inc. in New York. The NHL has acquired a corporate orientation that emphasizes the necessity of achieving cooperation among the owners in order to maintain league control over both the game and its players and maximize profits.[1]

In spite of this corporate orientation, the ownership of hockey teams continues to attract individual entrepreneurs as readily today as it did over seventy years ago. It is the pattern of entrepreneurship that has changed. By exploring the sports-business activities of owners such as Conn Smythe in Toronto and Peter Pocklington in Edmonton, I assess in this chapter the nature of this change in entrepreneurship in the NHL.

What have been the strategies for success in the NHL? Can a team both win games and maximize profits? Does a franchise have a clearly defined decision-making process, or is it subject to the whims of the owner? In seeking the answer to these questions I primarily examine the Toronto Maple Leafs and the Edmonton Oilers, analyzing them within the context of the business of hockey in the NHL and as they relate to the other enterprises controlled by their respective owners, Conn Smythe and Peter Pocklington.

Smythe and Pocklington were active in different eras—Smythe from 1927 to 1961 and Pocklington from 1977 to the present—and their activities suggest different management approaches. Conn Smythe was a "hockey man" who expanded his concerns from the arena to the larger business world; his team and his sand and gravel business were conducted as family concerns. Peter Pocklington, while relishing the nickname "Peter Puck," is not consumed by hockey: he is an entrepreneur and businessman with a "bottom-line" orientation. An NHL franchise offers opportunities to gain large profits, and the Edmonton Oilers have become an important component in Pocklington's financial empire. As professional hockey has become a bigger business, owning a team has come to be seen as just one component in the business activities of the entrepreneur rather than as a sole means to achieve economic success.

The growth of the business of hockey can also be linked to the emergence of the mass audience for professional sports. Hockey is promoted as a benefit to the community, and even the nation. Smythe, for example, revitalized the Toronto franchise when he took over the team in 1927. As a result of radio, the Maple Leafs became a national institution during a period when it appeared that the massive influx of U.S. capital into the NHL might overwhelm Canadian hockey. Similarly, Pocklington brought major league hockey to Edmonton when the NHL absorbed four World Hockey Association teams in 1979; in the wake of five Stanley Cup championships in the 1980s, Edmonton now proudly styles itself as the "City of Champions." This "social purpose" should not disguise the fact that the primary concern of hockey promoters is to make a profit. The ownership of hockey teams allowed Smythe and Pocklington to promote their own economic interests and fulfill their desire for personal success.

Both men are considered independent operators in the hockey world, although, to some extent, their individualism had to be checked when they worked in concert with the other owners to ensure the success of the league. Moreover, flamboyant personalities like Smythe and Pocklington became important public figures because they owned hockey franchises; their teams did not simply promote their economic interests but provided them with celebrity status in their own communities.

Analytical Models

Much of what we know about the business of hockey is drawn from popular literature and sports journalism, which, with few exceptions,[2] tend to portray team owners as folk heroes.[3] But serious academic works by sports economists, historians, and sociologists often evoke an equally simple image—the team owner as robber baron. Sport becomes a microcosm of the larger society and, in its most extreme interpretation, is analyzed under Marxist theory.[4] Capitalists control the game, much as they dominate the rest of society. J. C. H. Jones, for example, has argued that the economics of the NHL were shaped by the desire of the owners to maximize personal profits. This was accomplished by the formation of a cartel to increase league profits by such devices as redistributing broadcast revenues and establishing a draft to divide the talent pool of players to maintain competitive balance on the ice. As a result, the owners were able to maintain their monopoly over the product and its markets and yet ensure sufficient interdependence to keep both personal and league profits high.[5]

Throughout the 1970s and 1980s a number of scholarly works focused upon the development of models to explain how individual teams and professional leagues pursued strategies for success. Studies of player relations and public policy, for example, illustrated these strategies. Paul D. Staudohar has suggested that

> management, operating through league structures and team ownership, provides for the planning, supervision, and control of corporate enterprise decisions. The leagues have responsibility for such functions as negotiating collective bargaining agreements, setting rules for drafting players, determining policies for the enforcement of management rights, and negotiating national television agreements. Owners of clubs give much of their authority to the league offices but retain decision-making authority in areas such as negotiating individual player contracts, movement of players to other teams . . . , hiring coaches and front-office personnel, and entering into local television contracts.[6]

Yet even with the development of general models and the wealth of information concerning sports' commercial dynamic, the literature does not take us much further than the conclusions that were presented almost a generation ago. In his recent study of the political economy of sport, Rob Beamish defines sports as "a commodity which could be bought and sold." The capitalists who control sport seek to maximize their profits by creating a cartel to eliminate competition and ensure greater economic stability by allocating and controlling production and markets. They act as a monopsony (or one-buyer market) to stop the practice of competitive bidding for players because it drives up salary costs. The professional sports league itself guarantees the owners exclusive selling rights throughout their respective markets, plus a monopoly over the revenue generated through radio and television rights. In addition, the owners "have the power to determine membership in this exclusive league. Competition for facilities such as stadiums, parking, and food concessions is also reduced. Owners have sole access to live and televised spectator markets and they can work out various revenue-sharing schemes to maintain the stability of the league."[7]

The construction of theoretical models of behavior and the pursuit of ideology often overshadows the empirical base necessary to support these interpretations. Consequently, sports owners have been studied in moral rather than analytical terms. But also important is the study of the business side of sports ownership. The economic historian Alfred D. Chandler, in his examination of the development of corporate capitalism in the twentieth century, argues that the "visible hand of management" has replaced market mechanisms in coordinating economic activity and allocating economic resources. The result has been the development of business policies favoring long-term stability and growth.[8]

The Montreal Canadiens franchise provides the best example in the NHL of the pattern of corporate capitalism described by Chandler. Le Club de Hockey Canadien is the most successful team in the league; since its formation in 1909 it has won twenty-three Stanley Cups, including seventeen since 1944. The franchise's long-term commitment is to present a team that is both exciting and performing well.[9] The operation is also a big business; in 1978 it was purchased by Molson Companies, Ltd. from the Bronfmans' Carena Bancorp Holdings, Ltd. for $20.05 million. With an average gate of about 283,140 over forty home games, plus concessions, broadcasting revenues, souvenirs, and playoffs, the team generates about $20 million a year.

The Montreal Canadiens must be run as a business as well as a hockey franchise. Sam Pollock, former general manager and vice president of hockey operations, explained: "When I started, front office management might have been 50 percent hockey acumen and 50 percent business skills. . . . Now, I think it is 15 percent hockey sense and 85 percent business skills. If you want to be successful in this business, you have to follow sound business principles. That means keeping expenses low and profits high."[10] The team is also expensive to operate; the Molson family "likes to see the franchise well run." Therefore, according to Jean Beliveau, former team captain and now senior vice president of corporate affairs, "the players are well-paid and marketing may be a little high";[11] Moreover, the team employs a permanent staff of 200, and its part-time employees number about 450. The farm system and scouting cost about $1 million annually. As a consequence, the Canadiens have generated "a little profit" recently, but "for many years we lost money."[12]

While the Montreal Canadiens might be a large hockey operation, the franchise remains a tiny part of the huge Molson conglomerate. In 1988 Molson Companies, Ltd. generated revenues of $1.383 billion and turned a profit of $78 million. The team is attached to the most profitable division of the company for tax purposes; it was first purchased by the brewing division and is now part of the Retail Merchandising Group, which includes Beaver Lumber and Molstar Productions, the producer of Hockey Night in Canada.

Although a "corporate orientation" dominates the business of hockey, there is plenty of room for the entrepreneur in the world of professional sports. It is the personal nature of sports enterprises that is most important; satisfaction is gained from "the joys of ownership—the sense of having created an on-going organization, of having built something useful, of having been one's own boss."[13] Chandler observes that entrepreneurs maintain "a close personal relationship with their managers, and they [retain] a say in top management decisions, particularly those concerning financial policies, allocation of resources, and the selection of senior managers."[14] It is this model rather than a Marxian one that more readily contributes to our understanding of the nature of the business of hockey.

It is difficult to draw a detailed financial picture of the hockey business because most clubs are privately owned and therefore do not reveal their financial affairs to the public. Fortunately, information on Maple Leaf Gardens, Ltd. is available because it is a publicly traded corporation. In addition, the Conn Smythe Papers, which contain a wealth of information about Smythe's hockey and business activities, are publicly available. Material about Peter Pocklington's enterprises, however, must be pieced together from newspapers, the corporate registry, and interviews. It must also be noted, as Markham and Teplitz point out, that "interest in clubs' finances has probably been heightened by the fact that practically all the clubs are privately held. . . . The mystery and secrecy surrounding the game and its personalities contribute in part to its glamour and excitement."[15]

According to Staudohar, "Hockey owners have been relatively aloof in the past." He describes today's owners as "flamboyant entrepreneurs" who are "taking a more businesslike approach to running the franchises, which often includes entertainment hype to stir interest among the fans and media. . . . Players are more openly criticized, coaches are fired more often, and team strategy is dictated from the front office. . . . The owners reason that since they pay the bills, they have the right to operate the team as they see fit. Sports ownership has never been a totally benign business, but modern owners are far more cutthroat and egotistic. They figure they have to be tougher because competition is keener."[16] While this description applies to Peter Pocklington, it also accurately portrays the career of one of the early builders of the NHL—Conn Smythe.

The Smythe Era

Constantine Falkland Karrys Smythe was born in Toronto on February 1, 1895. His father, Albert Ernest Stafford Smythe, was a journalist who edited a magazine for the Theosophical Society and wrote for the Toronto *World*; his mother, Mary Adelaide Constantine, died when he was eight. Late in life, Conn recollected that the family scraped by during his childhood and that once his father was not paid for sixteen weeks: "He couldn't have cared less but that's when I made up my mind I wanted to have money."[17] He attended Upper Canada College, the school favored by the Toronto elite, and went on to the University of Toronto. His studies were interrupted by military service during World War I, but he graduated with a degree in civil engineering. Smythe's real love was sports, not education, and although he was small, he poured his energies into football and especially hockey; he was captain of the Varsity Juniors, which won the Ontario Hockey Association (OHA) junior championship in 1915. After joining the army, he was stationed in Toronto and became playing-manager of the 40th Battery hockey team, which played in the OHA senior league before shipping out to Europe.

When Smythe returned to Toronto in 1919 he first went to work with the Toronto Department of Public Works and then went to a small contracting company, in which he quickly became a partner. In 1920 he went out on his own, supplying sand and gravel to the city. Eventually he was able to buy his own sand pit and expand his fleet of equipment.

Although his business grew, he continued to be involved in hockey. As Smythe said: "In hockey everything I said or did seemed to become headlines. Maybe it was inevitable that my really solid source of income, the one that would have supported my family even if I'd never stepped inside a hockey rink, didn't get much publicity. There were no headlines saying, SMYTHE ADDS FOUR SECONDHAND TRUCKS TO GROWING GRAVEL FLEET."[18] From the outset, then, his motivation was more than just the bottom line. He became manager-coach of the University of Toronto club, which later won the 1927 Allan Cup and the 1928 Olympics. By that time, though, Smythe had attracted the attention of Col. John Hammond, who hired him to assemble and coach the New York Rangers franchise, established in 1926. But Smythe was fired by Hammond before the 1926–27 season began because Lester Patrick became available. After his $10,000 contract was paid off, he returned to Toronto and offered to run the St. Pats. He was turned down.

Hockey was just becoming a big business in the 1920s. Mass audiences were attracted to professional sports, and newspapers sought to increase circulation by covering sports. Moreover, some small-time entrepreneurs saw the ownership of teams as a means to earn profits. But the Toronto St. Pats, like many other Canadian clubs, were in financial trouble. The Quebec Bulldogs had dropped out of the NHL in 1920, and the rival Pacific Coast Hockey Association and the Western Canadian Hockey League had both folded by 1926. The solution for NHL owners was simple—expansion to the United States. Boston was granted a franchise for $5,000 in 1924; the Hamilton Tigers were purchased for $75,000 in 1925 and transferred to

New York, where they became the Americans; and the Pittsburgh Pirates were admitted to the NHL in 1925. The following year the Rangers, the Chicago Black Hawks, and the Detroit Cougars were established, and the entry fee had jumped to $15,000. These developments prompted one Toronto journalist to lament: "Will U.S. cash cripple hockey? How long will Canada be able to hold its teams? Our neighbours to the South possess more of that useful commodity, variously known as "jack" or "dough" or "mazuma," than we do [and] the longest purse is bound to win.[19]

Then in 1927 a group from Philadelphia offered to buy the Toronto St. Pats for $200,000, and Smythe saw his opportunity. Through a couple of parlayed bets he raised $10,000, and then he approached two Toronto businessmen to join his venture. Smythe appealed to the civic pride of the owners and bought the team for $160,000, although one of the St. Pats' directors, J. P. Bickell, a millionaire gold mine promoter, kept his $40,000 investment in the new team. The club was renamed the Maple Leafs and adopted the now-familiar blue-and-white uniforms with the Maple Leaf crest. But the Toronto franchise continued to lose money. Its Mutual Street arena held only nine thousand spectators, and if every game had been a sell-out, Smythe estimated that the team might have taken in $200,000 for the season. As it was, Toronto finished fourth in the NHL's Canadian division and lost $40,000 in the first year. By way of comparison, the Chicago Black Hawks—a team that had cost the new owner, Frederick McLaughlin, $100,000 and had finished last in the American division—showed a profit of $5,344.52 on revenues of $112,320.

Smythe was determined to turn the Maple Leafs into winners—both on the ice and at the box office. As managing director of the team, he hired such excellent staff persons as Frank Selke, named assistant manager in 1929, and Dick Irvin, who became coach in 1931. He also actively bought and sold players; for instance, in spite of his reputation as a tight-fisted businessman, he made a deal for star defenseman Francis "King" Clancy that cost the team $35,000 and two players. Yet the franchise still could not compete with the U.S. division teams; therefore Smythe was determined to build a new arena. He put together a consortium, Maple Leaf Gardens, Ltd., which included J. P. Bickell; Alf Rogers, president of St. Mary's Cement and owner of a radio station; and J. J. Vaughan of T. Eaton Company, one of Canada's largest department stores. This group bought most of the new company's 100,000 preferred shares, which were issued at $10; there were also 50,000 common shares, which had no par value.

Although money was tight because of the Great Depression, Smythe bought land in downtown Toronto for $350,000 from the T. Eaton Company (which took a second mortgage of $300,000 and $25,000 worth of stock). In order to build an arena, Smythe borrowed $900,000 from the Sun Life

Assurance Company, which held the first mortgage, and another $900,000 from the Bank of Commerce; both institutions had their own men on the board of directors of Smythe's company. They not only provided capital for the creation of Maple Leaf Gardens, Ltd., they participated in the financial decision making of the company. Maple Leaf Gardens opened on November 12, 1931, with a standing-room-only crowd of 13,542. Moreover, Smythe's company had been able to overcome a financial crisis that had left it short of funds; the construction unions in the Toronto Labour Council had finally agreed to take 20 percent of their wages in common stock. C. Smythe, Ltd. also provided the sand for construction of the Gardens.

The Maple Leafs won the Stanley Cup in 1932, and although the team would not win another championship until 1942, Maple Leaf Gardens prospered during the 1930s, even as franchises like Chicago and Detroit suffered. The company made a net profit of $40,535 in its first year, and by 1938 profits had more than doubled, rising to $87,720. Smythe attributed this financial success to the Leafs—"we were winning and we were exciting."[20]

Smythe remained as general manager of the Maple Leafs and managing director of Maple Leaf Gardens, Ltd., until he reenlisted during World War II. His initial salary was $2,500, but this was increased to $12,500 at the beginning of the 1932–33 season; from 1937 to 1941 he earned $15,000 annually.[21] Smythe hired scouts and established a farm system to supply the big-league club with trained players, kept charts and player statistics to aid the coach, and even sent messages during games to the bench. He also controlled expenditures, kept an eye on Maple Leaf Gardens' employees (including their working hours and whether they smoked), looked after ticket sales, did some accounting, and even helped with cleaning the arena and manning the phones. Smythe was also able to exploit the media to publicize his team and the Gardens. He told a sports writer for the Toronto *Star* that he wanted a place with class: "a place to go all dressed up; we don't compete with the comfort of theatres and other places where people can spend their money. We need a place where people can go in evening clothes, if they want to come there from a party or dinner." Smythe himself wore a tuxedo to the rink on one occasion.[22] More important, he recognized the potential of radio; during the 1930s the Leafs became English-Canada's team as their games were broadcast coast-to-coast every Saturday night.

With the outbreak of World War II, the 45-year-old Smythe reenlisted in the Canadian army, where he attained the rank of major. He put his affairs in order by selling his racing stable and leaving "Hap" Day, who was also coach of the Leafs, in charge of the sand and gravel business. A committee, composed of E. W. Bickle, William MacBrien (two of Smythe's original partners), and Frank Selke, was created to run Maple Leaf Gardens, Ltd. While in France, Smythe was seriously wounded and returned to Canada as a decorated war hero. He also generated some controversy when he attacked the failure of the Canadian government to introduce the conscription of men for overseas service. He chafed at his exclusion from the decision-making process at Maple Leaf Gardens. Therefore, after the war, he was determined to regain control, only this time as president. He owned 6,000 shares of common stock and purchased an additional 30,000 shares from Percy Gardiner for $300,000. With the support of J. P. Bickell, Smythe became president of Maple Leaf Gardens in November 1947.

By this time, Maple Leaf Gardens, Ltd. was a healthy company; in 1944 the mortgage had been paid off, and in 1946 $800,000 worth of preferred stock was redeemed. Common stock prices reached $100 per share (as compared to $10 in 1940) before it experienced a 4–1 split. Profits, which had averaged about $85,000 during the war, jumped to over $190,000 in both 1947 and 1948, years when the Maple Leafs won the Stanley Cup. Higher profits were largely the result of the increased number of attractions, and thus increased attendance, at Maple Leaf Gardens. The Maple Leafs began to sell out for every home game, even when attendance was down in other cities.

Smythe poured his energies into the Maple Leafs: "I continued to go by the axiom that if you win you sell tickets, so the job was to keep on winning."[23] Led by players like Max Bentley and Ted Kennedy, the team won four more Stanley Cups, including three in a row from 1947 to 1949. But Smythe was becoming increasingly authoritarian. In a series of memos to his coach, Joe Primeau, Smythe dictated lineups for games and drills for practice sessions; he even compiled a list of ten commandments for the coach to follow. He expected his employees to follow orders; when player Johnny McCormack was married during the hockey season, against Smythe's wishes, he was sent to the minors and then traded. When the players tried to form an association in 1957, Smythe traded the team's representative, Jim Thomson, even though he was the captain of the Maple Leafs. After the 1956–57 season, when the Leafs finished out of the playoffs for only the third time since Maple Leaf Gardens had opened, Conn Smythe asked the team's coach, Howie Meeker, to outline his views on the roles of the coach and the general manager (Smythe). In a three-page letter Meeker proposed that "the coach should have 90% of the choice in picking the team. . . . He should have at his disposal on the NHL team the strongest players in the organization at the time he is expected to win. Regardless of the player's age, ability or personality." Smythe's philosophy was different: "A coach shall coach his players individually and collectively so they play pleasing and winning hockey. A manager shall supply economically, the players necessary to produce a winning team." On Meeker's letter he penciled the following comment: "The manager should pick the team & you cannot wreck the whole organization for the coach." Meeker was fired.[24]

The continued success of the hockey team on the ice was one important factor behind the growing profits for Maple Leaf Gardens, Ltd. in the 1950s. Consequently, the company began to attract the attention of the business community. In 1951 *Canadian Business* called Maple Leaf Gardens "A Blue Chip off the Hockey Block." Smythe was aware that profits were increasing, even though total attendance at the Gardens was declining and expenses, especially players' salaries, were increasing. In comparison with totals in 1946, he noted that in 1958 there were sixty less attractions, drawing 511,360 fewer people, yet profits were $92,000 higher. The reason was television—in 1955, for example, television revenues were $141,775 (an increase of $32,425 over the previous year). These revenues were higher than those for the concessions that year, $99,445, and radio, $33,233; revenues from hockey totaled $943,347, and from other attractions, $217,224. As the time went on, television revenues became increasingly important. In 1958, a three-year contract was signed for $1 million, and in 1961 Maple Leaf Gardens, Ltd. signed a five-year contract with MacLaren Advertising Company for $2.25 million.

Not all observers approved of Smythe's approach. Charlie Conacher, a member of Toronto's "Kid Line" in the 1930s, believed that Smythe had turned hockey into a business and that this trend was spoiling the game. A Detroit sports writer commented: "Smythe is an ivory tower dweller who looks out upon all Canada as his private domain, and upon all hockey as his personal vehicle to immortality. His egoism is as excessive as his "flamboyancy," a trait prompting belief that his objective is to further Toronto hockey no less than his own status."[25]

Smythe did want to bring winning and entertaining hockey to the Toronto fans and increase profits for his company. But he was also concerned about the welfare of the NHL as a whole because he knew that the league's welfare affected his team. In the 1950s the six-team NHL was known as the Norris House League because the wealthy James D. Norris family controlled the Detroit and Chicago franchises and owned Madison Square Gardens, which gave them control over the New York Rangers. But Smythe was the chairman of the owners' committee. When the Chicago franchise was in financial difficulty, he made sure that players were traded to the Black Hawks to equalize league strength and that the NHL guaranteed the team's income. As Smythe put it: "It wasn't charity. We needed them, too, or we wouldn't fill our rinks. It was a good hockey deal."[26] It was also apparent that Smythe did not maximize profits at Maple Leaf Gardens in this period. Among the six teams, Toronto's gross hockey revenues and paid attendance were second to those of Montreal throughout the 1950s, yet ticket prices at Maple Leaf Gardens were the lowest in the league. For Smythe it was as important to win games and fill the Gardens as it was to maximize profits.

Smythe was so busy with his businesses, horse racing, and philanthropy in the mid-1950s that he stepped down as general manager of the Maple Leafs on February 1, 1955—his sixtieth birthday. He admitted, "What really made up my mind was that my powers as a hockey man were failing."[27] Smythe remained as president of the team and of Maple Leaf Gardens, Ltd. at an annual salary of $25,000, which was later raised to $35,000 in 1957. He also owned 23,001 shares of stock, which traded for as much as $22.50 in 1957.

By 1961, Conn Smythe had had enough. He sold majority control of Maple Leaf Gardens to his son Stafford, Harold Ballard, and John Bassett, owner of the Toronto *Telegram*, for $2 million. He remained as chairman of the board until 1966, when he resigned because of plans to stage a fight featuring Muhammad Ali. In Smythe's opinion, the owners were putting "cash ahead of class."

Conn Smythe represented the entrepreneurial capitalism that shaped the early business of hockey. Although fundamentally a hockey man, he was able to turn the Toronto franchise into a profitable business—he saw winning Stanley Cups and making money as equally important goals. But he was not a pure profit maximizer. As he said shortly before his death at the age of eighty-five in November 1980: "Hockey gave me my biggest push financially at first, but building great teams was the real kick I got out of it. Of course, if you win games you sell tickets."[28] Smythe dominated the management of Maple Leaf Gardens from 1927 to 1961; he made financial policies, selected coaches and managers, and handled the players; after 1947, he was the majority owner of the company. He was able to succeed as an individual entrepreneur within the corporate structure of professional sports.

It is interesting to note that Maple Leaf Gardens, Ltd. made more money after Smythe stepped down as president in 1961. The era of the hockey man had given way to a new emphasis on making money rather than building winning teams. Maple Leaf Gardens was to be run as a business, designed to maximize profits. Seating in the arena was enlarged from 12,737 to 16,700, and ticket prices were increased, prompting Smythe to say of the new seats, "You need to be a skinny, little, underfed kid to fit into them and a fat old banker to afford them."[29] The number of non-hockey attractions at the arena also increased; Maple Leaf Gardens, Ltd. was in the entertainment business.

Conn Smythe continued to believe that the individual entrepreneur was essential to the success of the NHL. In an interview he asserted that "beer companies and the rest" knew "Sweet Fanny Adams about runnin' a club. They take the attitude that they're opening a branch plant, . . . and if it doesn't work out in two years, then they'll move it someplace else. You can't go at hockey like that. What ya need for a new owner is a millionaire who can stand the gaff. You need a fella who's got the patience to lose a few dollars, a fella who's gonna put everything into the club personally, his heart and his head and his money."[30] Smythe could have been describing the new owner of the Edmonton Oilers, Peter H. Pocklington. Pocklington was not from the corporate business world but from the entrepreneurial sector, notably real estate. He became wealthy through his own salesmanship and enterprise; he is a successful wheeler-dealer who operates in the rapid-growth entrepreneurial sector of the economy.

Pocklington and the Oilers

Peter Pocklington was born on November 18, 1941, and grew up in London, Ontario. His father was a successful insurance agent. After leaving school at seventeen Pocklington eventually went into the auto business and came to Alberta in 1971 when he acquired a car dealership in Edmonton. By the age of twenty-seven he had made his first million in car sales.

Alberta's prosperity in the 1970s was fueled by an oil boom there that stimulated rapid growth in real estate and property development. This growth was fueled as well by the Canadian government's creation of special tax shelters to encourage the construction of multiple-unit residential buildings (MURBs) in 1974. Investments in MURBs could be turned over quickly for large profits and thus attracted the attention of western Canadian entrepreneurs like Dr. Charles Allard, Nelson Skalbania, and Peter Pocklington. Pocklington utilized the cash flow from his auto dealership to finance real estate investments; in 1978, for example, he and Skalbania swung a $51 million deal for some apartment buildings in Toronto that resulted in a joint profit of about $20 million. With his share, Pocklington, through his Patrician Land Corporation, bought Gainers, a pork-packing company with annual sales of $70 to 80 million, mostly in markets across western Canada.

It was reported that Pocklington bought Gainers for about $7.5 million in Alberta mortgages and real estate. Access to mortgage money was essential to finance such deals, and entrepreneurs were often able to short-cut the normal arm's length borrowing from established financial institutions. They would buy their own money suppliers, often trust companies that had broad deposit-taking and lending powers. (Canadian tax laws allowed trust companies to invest 10 percent of their assets in real estate subsidiaries.) Allard bought North West Trust, and in 1979 Pocklington bought a controlling interest in Fidelity Trust, Canada's twelfth largest trust company, with assets of $1.6 billion, for $15 million ($6.9 million in cash and $8 million in preferred stock). He then bought the balance of the company for a reported $10 million and folded his real estate company, Patrician Land Corporation, into it.[31]

Pocklington's goal was to be rich: "You become what you think about becoming. I wanted to become wealthy. So I did."[32] He was a vocal exponent of entrepreneurial capitalism. Pocklington also believed in holding a 100-percent interest in his investments: "I prefer to own what I'm doing instead of getting the world in bed with me. Entrepreneurs are the salvation of business. Many companies are dying because they're looked after by caretakers who behave like bureaucrats."[33] In addition, his financial empire was built on borrowed capital. As Pocklington said, "To create wealth you must utilize other people's money and other people's labour." A federal tax judge was more succinct in his assessment of the deal maker: Pocklington "was ready to sell anything, except his wife."[34]

It was in the late 1970s, as Pocklington was expanding his business holdings, that he began to acquire an interest in the Edmonton Oilers, then just another money-losing franchise in the World Hockey Association. "Wild Bill" Hunter, an amateur hockey promoter, had acquired the franchise when the WHA was incorporated in 1971, and he was chiefly bankrolled by Dr. Charles Allard. The Oilers were not very successful on the ice, and their financial losses approached $3 million by 1976 in spite of the fact that they had moved into the new city-built Northlands Coliseum, where the average attendance jumped from 4,423 to 10,722—the highest total in the WHA. Allard wanted out and sold 80 percent of the team to Nelson Skalbania, a Vancouver real estate promoter whose hobby became buying and selling sports franchises.

In March 1977 Skalbania sold a 40-percent interest in the Oilers (a controlling interest) to his friend Peter Pocklington in exchange for Pocklington's assumption of half the debt Skalbania incurred when he bought the team and also, it is reported, for a 1928 Rolls Royce, two oil paintings, a diamond ring, and a mortgage note for $500,000 worth of real estate. This change in ownership marked the beginnings of a turnaround for the Oilers, both on the ice and on the books. Pocklington appointed Glen Sather, then a player with the club, as coach and later put him in charge of all hockey operations. The Oilers made the playoffs after the 1977–78 season and finished first in 1979, losing the Avco Cup to the Winnipeg Jets. Pocklington was not a "meddler in the day-to-day operation but [was] always available for consultation," according to the public relations director then, John

Short. It was Pocklington's friendship with Nelson Skalbania, though, that allowed him to acquire the teenage phenomenon, Wayne Gretzky, from the Indianapolis Racers in November 1978.

Pocklington had a long-term strategy when he purchased the Oilers: it was the first step toward gaining an NHL franchise. In the short term the WHA team continued to lose money. Revenues of about $2.8 million were generated for the 1977–78 season, but expenses ran to about $3.8 million, of which just under 50 percent went for salaries and 10 percent went for rent to the Edmonton Exhibition Association, which also collected funds from concessions, parking, and in-arena advertising. Then in June 1978 Pocklington and three other WHA owners applied to join the NHL but were rejected. When Pocklington then tried to buy the NHL team the Colorado Rockies, he was dissuaded by the high price tag and opposition from owners in both leagues. Finally, in 1979 the NHL merged with the WHA to expand into Quebec, Hartford, Winnipeg, and Edmonton.

The Oilers faced a stiff initiation. The NHL entry fee was $6 million (with about $4.6 million to be paid immediately and the remainder to be covered by a letter of credit), and another $1.7 million had to be set aside to meet possible legal challenges from the WHA teams left out of the expansion. The hockey team also cost considerably more to run now. Estimates for expenses during the 1979–80 season were as follows: salaries, $2.5 million; travel, $500,000; training, $100,000; supplies, $75,000; hospital and medical, $525,000; and rent, $920,000. Moreover, the team could not expect to share national television revenue for five years. But Edmonton fans were eager to see big-league hockey. The Oilers sold 14,000 season tickets for 1979–80 and thus generated gross gate revenues of about $6.14 million. In addition, Pocklington was able to negotiate a local television deal with Molson Breweries, in which the team received $2 million up front and $75,000 annually for five years and gave Molson exclusive advertising and promotional rights for this period. As a result, the Oilers were able to generate large profits in their first year of operation in the NHL. Estimated profits of about $1.4 million were used to offset the NHL entry fee and legal costs while the promotional funds covered the losses carried over from the team's WHA days.

Pocklington did not restrict his sports-business activities to hockey—he sought to create an empire of sports franchises to match that of his other businesses. These ventures did not prove to be nearly as successful, though. In February 1979 he bought the Oakland Stompers of the North American Soccer League and transferred the franchise to Edmonton as the Drillers. He also purchased the Ogden baseball club, a member of the Pacific Coast League, in October 1980, which then became the Edmonton Trappers. Neither franchise was to prove as profitable as the Oilers.

By 1981 the Oilers had become one of the most exciting teams in the NHL. Edmonton even knocked the Montreal Canadiens out of the playoffs before losing to the eventual Stanley Cup winners, the New York Islanders. The club generated revenues of about $10 million and earned profits of perhaps $1.6 million. The success of the Oilers gave rise to a proposal in 1981 to sell 49.9 percent of the interest in Pocklington's teams under the umbrella of Professional Sports Investments, Ltd. Originally, units were to sell for $100,000, although later the price was dropped to $25,000 for each of 760 limited partnerships. The offering was intended to raise $19 million. Not only would Pocklington get the money, he would retain majority control of the team (his stated preference for 100 percent ownership of all ventures would of course be violated). In addition, his Pocklington Financial Corporation (PFC) was to retain a management contract with the Oilers that would earn $200,000 annually, or 9 percent of profits, whichever was larger. The prospectus stated: "The selection and development of skilled players on a cost-effective basis is important to the establishment and maintenance of a competitive team. . . . PFC's experience as a manager will be an important factor in the successful operation."[35] Although this proposal did not fly, Pocklington continued to expand his business empire. His desire to enter the oil business, which he saw as a growth industry, prompted him to buy Capri Drilling Canada, Ltd. in July 1981 for $17 million.

Ownership of the Edmonton franchise also raised Pocklington's public profile. In his words: "Hockey is like motherhood and nickel cigars. It's a ticket to an almost crazy place in the sun. It certainly allows me to talk on things I like to speak out about, and to be recognized."[36] This "Oiler effect" was a factor in his decision to contest the leadership of the Progressive Conservative Party of Canada even though he was an outsider in politics. "The Oilers are the rising star," he commented, "and I don't mind hitching myself to that star. The Oilers will mean a lot to the campaign. For starters, there's increased visibility. And name me a better marketing vehicle in this country than Gretzky and this hockey club."[37] Pocklington was the voice of the "new right" in Canada, advocating deep cuts in government spending, deregulation, and privatization of government-owned corporations. His prescriptions were based on Ayn Rand's idea of creative selfishness, "the belief that collective well-being can only be maximized if each individual is encouraged to pursue self-enrichment."[38] Pocklington finished well back in the race, which was won by Brian Mulroney, who went on to become prime minister in 1984.

At the same time that his political aspirations were dashed, his business empire began to crumble. Pocklington had borrowed heavily to campaign and had even proposed to sell his companies to concentrate on politics. But events overtook him: the collapse of the Alberta economy in the early

1980s hit oil and real estate especially hard. Capri Drilling lost $8 to 10 million before it went into receivership in April 1983; between March and August of the same year the eastern divisions of Gainers were sold off, reducing a national company to one based almost exclusively in Alberta. Real estate was sold off and the assets of Patrician Land Corporation were written down. As a consequence, Fidelity Trust collapsed after running up losses of $17.7 million by early 1983.[39]

Pocklington was unwilling to sell the Oilers: "the hockey team is sacred to me." Three days later he expanded on this theme, declaring, "You don't own a professional sports franchise. You hold it in trust for the community."[40] Hyperbole aside, the Oilers were to provide the foundation for Pocklington's economic recovery: using the franchise and the players' contracts as security, he was able to borrow $31 million from the banks to finance new business deals. Through Gainers, Pocklington was able to reconstruct a North American meat-packing and food empire that included Magic Pantry, Z & W Foods, Marybank Foods, three American meat processing plants (with annual sales of $500 million), Palm Dairies (purchased for $52.5 million in April 1987), and Canbra Foods Ltd., which produced edible oils for food processing to supply Gainers and Palm Dairies, for $13.5 million. Gainers became the second largest food-processing company in Canada. It also acquired title to Cromwell Resources Inc., an oil and gas company that Pocklington had purchased in August 1984.

At the same time that he was resurrecting his financial empire, Pocklington continued to make money on the Oilers. After the team won its first Stanley Cup, ticket prices were raised to offset higher player contracts and rent; as a result, Oiler tickets were among the highest in the league. It was also reported that distributions to the owner had increased; from December 15, 1984, to August 31, 1985, Pocklington received $5.7 million. Profits in fiscal 1986 amounted to another $3.2 million.

Pocklington continued to look for ways to maximize profits. After the Oilers had won their third Stanley Cup in four years, he said that he could put "$40–50 million in my jeans" by going public with the Oilers.[41] He was prepared to sell off 60 percent of the team for $60 million; after brokers' fees, he would be left with $54 million in cash and 40 percent of the club, and he would get a $250,000 annual management fee and 1 percent of cash earnings.

The profit picture of the Edmonton Oilers for 1986 (Table 9.1) appears brighter than that of Maple Leaf Gardens, which earned $2,055,000 on revenues of $33,913,000 in the same fiscal year. And the Gardens is called "a jewel" by an investment analyst; it reported a very high return on capital of 79.56 percent over a five-year period.[42] Yet it was generally believed that Maple Leaf Gardens was poorly run; Harold Ballard, who became ma-

Table 9.1 Operations of the Edmonton Oilers Hockey Club, 1986 (Thousands of Dollars)

Revenues		17,701
Admissions	13,116	
Broadcasting	2,292	
Other	2,293	
Operating Expenses		14,169
Team costs	6,618	
Other hockey costs	3,299	
Marketing and novelties	1,082	
Minor league team	976	
General and admin.	2,194	
Income		3,532
Revenue from playoffs		2,234
		4,766
Amortization of NHL franchise		(1,109)
Provision for WHA settlement		(120)
Income before taxes		3,537[a]

[a]This figure is based on unaudited pro forma financial statements presented to the National Hockey League, March 11, 1987.

jority owner of Maple Leaf Gardens in 1971 and owned 79 percent of the stock, ran the show. He paid the bills, so authority rested with him. There were no layers of management—the general manager and the treasurer reported directly to Ballard. He not only made financial decisions but could force player trades or cancel deals. When asked about the dismal performance of the hockey team in a seventeen-minute annual meeting in 1985, he replied, "Our stocks are all right and we're making money, so what the hell do we care?" Ballard himself netted more than $1 million annually from Maple Leaf Gardens, Ltd.

The Maple Leaf Gardens arena is profitable because it sits on prime downtown property in Toronto, draws on a large market in southern Ontario, and is in the general entertainment business. For Peter Pocklington "the team means all," especially in a small market like Edmonton. His view is that running a hockey team is like running a business; the emphasis is on "quality in what you sell. Sell it properly, present it properly, price it properly."[43] Like Conn Smythe, Pocklington believes that the business of hockey is "simple, as long as you're winning and creating excitement. A winning team can make a lot of money."[44]

Although Pocklington stated that in the running of the hockey team, "I don't interfere at all," he is consulted on management decisions by the president and general manager of the Oilers, Glen Sather. He also admitted that when players seek contracts over $300,000 (like Paul Coffey did before he was traded in October 1987) or when they seek to renegotiate their contracts (like Mark Messier did in September 1987), they "deal with me."[45]

When asked to elaborate on the reasons for the success of the Oilers, Pocklington replied, "If I run the team like a business and don't get emotionally involved, it's very easy to run." This was the reason why he became personally involved in the trade of perhaps the greatest player in hockey, Wayne Gretzky, to the Los Angeles Kings in August 1988 for two players, three draft choices, and a reported $15 million in cash. In spite of the huge uproar in Edmonton, which prompted several local businesses to boycott products from Gainers and Palm Dairies and even made Pocklington a target on the cartoon page, the owner insisted that there were valid reasons for the transaction—it made both business and hockey sense. Gretzky would become a free agent without compensation in 1992; he was "an asset worth zero in four years." (There were also tax advantages in shedding a large contract that could no longer be depreciated for two smaller ones that could.) In addition, Pocklington asserted that "my first love is to the team, not Wayne Gretzky."[46] Pocklington also maintained that he was concerned with the future of the team, whose stars were getting older; younger players would provide the nucleus for "a competitive club that can win more Stanley Cups. . . . We're not going to be in last place in a couple of years."[47]

Although the Oilers had a disappointing season on the ice in 1988–89, being knocked out of the playoffs in the first round by the Gretzky-led Kings, the franchise continues to make money for Pocklington. Even though average paid attendance at home games declined to 16,780 from 16,957 in the wake of the Gretzky trade, projected ticket sales yielded about $14.52 million. In addition, broadcasting revenues were over $3 million. With total expenses of about $13.7 million, Pocklington admitted that "our bottom line will be almost identical to last year" (a profit of about $3 to $4 million).[48]

Pocklington also envisions long-term profits from the Oilers. In an effort to cut down on the no-shows at home games, he intends to reduce the number of games shown free on television. Instead, games will be on pay-TV. "There are 350,000 homes in our viewing area, and I'm hoping for a 10 percent audience at $4 per game." He hopes to generate a profit of $100,000 per game over an eighty-game schedule.[49]

Revenues from the Oilers continue to support Pocklington's other business ventures; the team is his cash cow. After the Gretzky trade, Pocklington reorganized his empire, amalgamating Cromwell Resources, Inc. and Edmonton Oilers Hockey, Ltd. with his holding company, PFC Financial, Ltd. The new company was to be the vehicle to organize his cash flow and business dealings. When asked if he needed the money from the Gretzky trade, Pocklington replied, ''I made a billion and a half in food sales. I have over 7,000 people working for me, and all my companies are very healthy financially.''[50] In 1989 Pocklington defaulted on a loan payment to the government of Alberta's treasury branch. This default caused the government to have to take over Gainers, and it will cost the provincial taxpayers about $100 million.

Peter Pocklington's sports-business dealings reveal his desire to maximize profits and reflect his ''bottom-line'' philosophy. The Oilers are closely integrated within Pocklington's larger financial empire, and profits from the hockey team are important to his other ventures. But in order to increase profits, the Edmonton Oilers must win, and a successful franchise generates higher operating costs. This situation is not lost on Pocklington, and it would seem that his true payoff may be related to his desire for prestige. Owning a hockey team promotes his economic interests, but it has also made Pocklington a public figure—it has become a power symbol. It is this aspect of team ownership that was reflected most clearly in the career of Conn Smythe, as well.

Concluding Remarks

The business of hockey was far larger and far more complex in the 1980s than it was in the era of the six-team NHL. An owner like Smythe could be a hockey man first and foremost. He believed that building a winning team and making profits were equally important goals. Although Maple Leaf Gardens, Ltd. made money throughout the Smythe era and continues to prosper, it has always been dependent on a variety of attractions, not just hockey, to draw revenues. The fiscal success of the company has more to do with the location of its arena in Toronto than on the fortunes of its hockey team.

The profitability of the Edmonton Oilers, on the other hand, is directly linked to a number of factors. The first factor is Pocklington's prowess as a businessman, because the team is closely integrated within his larger financial empire. It is clear, though, that the management style of the Oilers' owner has changed. When the Oilers entered the NHL, Pocklington was concerned with creating a profitable franchise; he selected his managers and made financial decisions rather than hockey decisions. The success of the team has been accompanied by a growing tendency for its owner to become involved in the hockey side of the business. In a small market like Edmonton, the profit picture for an NHL franchise is directly related to the team's ability to win games; the bottom line is shaped by the revenues generated through high ticket prices and television contracts. Therefore, in the

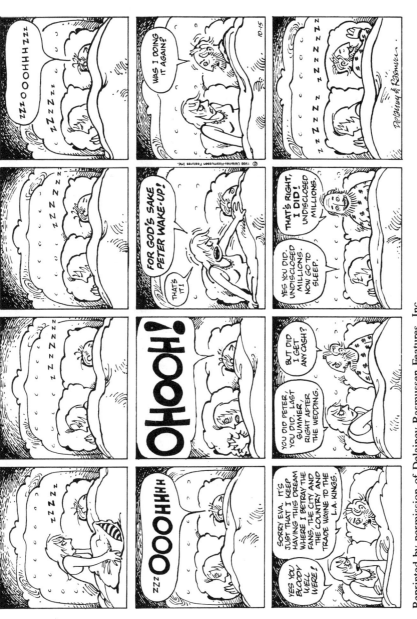

Reprinted by permission of Delainey-Rasmussen Features, Inc.

final analysis, Pocklington's strategy for success remains the same as that of Conn Smythe—the team must win if profits are to be increased.

It is interesting to note that Smythe and Pocklington reveal just two patterns of ownership among the Canadian teams in the NHL. Although Chandler's metaphor of the "visible hand of management" aptly applies to the activities of entrepreneurial owners, NHL owners do not necessarily represent the pure profit maximizers described in the literature. There remains a strong element of what Wray Vamplew has labeled "utility maximization" (winning is more important than profits),[51] in the activities of NHL owners in Canada. Profits were not the sole motivation for self-made men like Smythe and Pocklington; these owners also found status and power in the sports arena. But the pattern of ownership is different for each franchise. Harold Ballard's disdain for winning hockey in Toronto, so long as Maple Leaf Gardens continues to make money, more readily fit the model of the pure profit maximizer. Yet even the long-suffering Toronto fans became disenchanted with the meddling of the Leafs' owner, and revenues from hockey began to decline from their highs in the mid-1980s. Ballard's death in 1990 may change the way the franchise is operated.

The Calgary NHL franchise, on the other hand, is clearly run as a utility maximizer. The owners of the Flames (Daryl K. Seaman, Byron Seaman, Harley N. Hotchkiss, Sonia Scurfield, and Norman L. Kwong) keep a low public profile and separate their outside business activities from the operations of the team. More important, they do not exploit the franchise in order to maximize personal profits; instead much of the profit is put back into amateur sports such as the Canadian Olympics and local youth hockey teams. In addition, the NHL team is intended to raise the profile of the city of Calgary; the owners of the Flames are boosters, a group long associated with the urban and economic development of Alberta. (The Montreal Canadiens, owned by the corporate giant Molson Companies, Ltd., follows the same pattern of utility, rather than profit, maximization.) Moreover, the success of these franchises is directed by the "visible hand" of management rather than ownership. The pattern of the business of hockey in the 1980s more closely reflects that of North American business as a whole.

Much is made of the growing corporate orientation of professional sports since they have become big businesses. The leagues themselves are cartels in which owners must cooperate to set policy, maintain competitive balance, and maximize joint profits. The cartel does not limit the profit potential of individual franchises and for that reason will continue to attract individual entrepreneurs. Sports teams can be good investments, but most owners also want to win. They are competitors and act like nineteenth-century capitalists; but then hockey is a nineteenth-century game, and the people in it—owners, managers, and players—are strongly individualistic rather than corporate-oriented. They play by the same rules. Even Alan Eagleson, director of the NHL Players Association, believes that although professional sports is a business, "sport is unique, and . . . had to develop its own system. The commodity it sells is entertainment, and the vehicle it uses to promote that commodity is competition."[52]

Thus individual entrepreneurs continue to exist, and prosper, in this age of corporate capitalism—Conn Smythe and Peter Pocklington give testimony to the enduring strength of entrepreneurship. The pattern of ownership has changed, though, since the 1920s; franchises can still be run as personal enterprises, but there is no longer room for a hockey man like Smythe. Owners are now primarily businessmen and run their teams primarily as a business. Although some owners, like Pocklington, cannot resist the temptation to meddle in the hockey operations of their teams, it is increasingly apparent that successful franchises are directed by the "visible hand of management." As Pocklington himself has concluded, "Sports is too much of a business to be a sport."[53]

NOTES

I would like to thank the following people for their assistance in the preparation of this article: Peter Pocklington, owner of Edmonton Oilers Hockey Club; Bob Stellick, publicity director of the Toronto Maple Leafs Hockey Club; Timothy Godfrey of Scotia McLeod in Toronto; Neil Waugh of the *Edmonton Sun*; Duncan McDowall at Carleton University; Barry Ferguson at the University of Manitoba; Denise Richman at Simon Fraser University; and my colleagues at the University of Alberta, Rod Macleod, Doug Owram, and Paul Voisey.

1. Richard S. Gruneau, "Elites, Class and Corporate Power in Canadian Sport: Some Preliminary Findings," in John W. Loy, Gerald S. Kenyon, and Barry D. McPherson, eds., *Sport, Culture and Society: A Reader on the Sociology of Sport* (Philadelphia: Lea and Febiger, 1981), 361–62.

2. See, for example, Bruce Kidd and John Macfarlane, *The Death of Hockey* (Toronto: New Press, 1972); also Joseph Durso, *The All-American Dollar: The Big Business of Sports* (Boston: Houghton Mifflin, 1971); Paul Hoch, *Rip Off the Big Game: The Exploitation of Sports by the Power Elite* (Garden City, N.Y.: Anchor Books, 1972); and Leonard Koppett, *Sports Illusion, Sports Reality* (Boston: Houghton Mifflin, 1981), 38–50.

3. See Jack Batten, *Hockey Dynasty: The Inside Story of Conn Smythe's Hockey Dynasty* (Toronto: Pagurian Press, 1969); William F. Dowbiggin, ed., *Positive Power: The Story of the Edmonton Oilers* (Edmonton: Executive Sport Publications, 1982); Peter Gzowski, *The Game of Our Lives* (Toronto: McClelland & Stewart,

1981); William Houston, *Ballard: A Portrait of Canada's Most Controversial Sports Figure* (Toronto: Summerhill Press, 1984); Peter C. Newman, *The Acquisitors: The Canadian Establishment*, vol. 2 (Toronto: McClelland & Stewart, 1981); and Scott Young, ed., *If You Can't Beat 'Em in the Alley: The Memoirs of the Late Conn Smythe* (Toronto: McClelland & Stewart, 1981).

4. Examples include Richard S. Gruneau, "Sport, Social Differentiation and Social Inequality," in D. W. Ball and J. W. Loy, eds., *Sport and Social Order: Contributions to the Sociology of Sport* (Reading, Pa.: Addison-Wesley Publishing Co., 1975), 121–84; and Rob Beamish, "Sport and the Logic of Capitalism," in Hart Cantelon and Richard Gruneau, eds., *Sport, Culture and the Modern State* (Toronto: University of Toronto Press, 1982), 141–97.

5. J. C. H. Jones, "The Economics of the National Hockey League," in Richard S. Gruneau and John G. Albinson, eds., *Canadian Sport: Sociological Perspectives* (Don Mills: Addison-Wesley (Canada), 1976), 225–48.

6. Paul D. Staudohar, *The Sports Industry and Collective Bargaining* (Ithaca, N.Y.: ILR Press, Cornell University, 1986), 9. See also Henry G. Demmert, *The Economics of Professional Team Sports* (Lexington, Mass.: Lexington Books, 1973); Roger G. Noll, ed., *Government and the Sports Business* (Washington, D.C.: The Brookings Institution, 1974); Jesse W. Markham and Paul V. Teplitz, *Baseball Economics and Public Policy* (Lexington, Mass.: Lexington Books, 1981); and Robert C. Berry, William B. Gould, and Paul D. Staudohar, *Labor Relations in Professional Sports* (Dover, Mass.: Auburn House Publishing Company, 1986).

7. Rob Beamish, "The Political Economy of Professional Sport," in Jean Harvey and Hart Cantelon, eds., *Not Just a Game: Essays in Canadian Sport Sociology* (Ottawa: Ottawa University Press, 1988), 141–43.

8. Alfred D. Chandler, *The Visible Hand: The Managerial Revolution in American Business* (Cambridge, Mass.: Harvard University Press, 1977), 1, 10.

9. Interview by the author with Jean Beliveau, senior vice president for corporate affairs, January 30, 1989.

10. Quoted in Chrys Goyens and Allan Turowetz, *Lions in Winter* (Scarborough, Ont.: Prentice-Hall Canada, 1986), 171.

11. Beliveau interview, January 30, 1989.

12. Ibid.

13. Michael Bliss, *Northern Enterprise: Five Centuries of Canadian Business* (Toronto: McClelland & Stewart, 1987), 569.

14. Chandler, *The Visible Hand*, 9.

15. Markham and Teplitz, *Baseball Economics and Public Policy*, 77.

16. Staudohar, *The Sports Industry and Collective Bargaining*, 127.

17. *Toronto Globe and Mail*, May 3, 1968.

18. Young, *The Memoirs of Conn Smythe*, 89.

19. *Macleans Magazine*, March 1, 1925.

20. Young, *The Memoirs of Conn Smythe*, 120. The team had players like future Hall-of-Famers Syl Apps; "Turk" Broda; "Hap" Day; the "Kid Line" of Charlie Conacher, Joe Primeau, and Harvey Jackson; and "King" Clancy, "Red" Horner, and "Sweeny" Schriner.

21. Conn Smythe Papers, MU 5669, Series C, Box 34, Provincial Archives of

Ontario (hereafter cited as PAO). Smythe also controlled 3,880 shares of Maple Leaf Gardens.

22. Young, *The Memoirs of Conn Smythe*, 102–3.

23. Ibid., 180.

24. Conn Smythe Papers, MU 5967, Series C, Box 32, Hockey Files 1932–78, PAO; material dated April 27, 1957.

25. Stan Helleur, "Charlie Conacher Reveals: Big Business Is Spoiling Canadian Hockey," *Liberty*, December 1955, 22; *Saturday Night*, December 1951.

26. Young, *The Memoirs of Conn Smythe*, 197; see also Conn Smythe Papers, MU 5967, Series C, Box 32, PAO.

27. Young, *The Memoirs of Conn Smythe*, 198.

28. Ibid., 246.

29. *The Hockey News*, December 5, 1980.

30. Jack Batten, "King Conn," *The Canadian*, October 8, 1977, 10.

31. *Edmonton Sun*, April 18, 1982.

32. *Edmonton Sun*, September 10, 1978.

33. Newman, *The Acquisitors*, 292.

34. *Edmonton Sun*, April 1, 1979.

35. *Edmonton Journal*, August 18, 1988.

36. Newman, *The Acquisitors*, 294.

37. *Edmonton Sun*, May 6, 1983.

38. Patrick Martin, Allan Gregg, and George Perlin, *Contenders: The Tory Quest for Power* (Scarborough, Ont.: Prentice-Hall Canada, 1983), 147. The ownership of the hockey team had become a power symbol. In a world in which the "free enterpriser" feels constantly tormented by competition and regulation, the team provided an escape into a world unfettered by other controls.

39. *Toronto Globe and Mail*, April 19, 1983.

40. *Edmonton Sun*, July 28 and 31, 1983.

41. Ibid., June 2, 1987.

42. *Toronto Globe and Mail*, November 5, 1986, and June 11, 1987.

43. Interview by the author with Peter Pocklington, owner, Edmonton Oilers, October 11, 1988. Even though the Oilers won their fourth Stanley Cup in five years in May 1988, ticket prices fell below those of seven other teams for the 1988–89 season. *The Hockey News*, October 28, 1988.

44. Pocklington interview, October 11, 1988.

45. Ibid.

46. Ibid.; *Edmonton Sun*, August 11, 1988.

47. *Edmonton Sun*, January 27, 1989.

48. Ibid., February 28, 1989; *Toronto Globe and Mail*, March 3, 1989.

49. Pocklington interview, October 11, 1988; *Edmonton Sun*, February 28, 1989.

50. *Edmonton Journal*, August 11, 1988.

51. Wray Vamplew, "The Economics of a Sports Industry: Scottish Gate-Money Football, 1890–1914," *The Economic History Review* 35 (November 1982): 549–67.

52. Deidre Clayton, *Eagle: The Life and Times of R. Alan Eagleson* (Toronto: Lester & Orpen Dennys, 1982), 137.

53. *Edmonton Journal*, August 10, 1988.

The Impact of Corporate Ownership on Labor-Management Relations in Hockey 10

Rob B. Beamish

Looking back over the last twenty-five years of labor relations in professional sport, two points stand out. First, the formation of players' associations has, ironically, allowed the owners to continue certain labor relations practices that are not in the best interests of the players. The owners could not have continued these practices without the presence of the unions and the institutionalization of collective bargaining. The most celebrated case in point is the Rozelle Rule—although the same might be said of all clauses in standard players' contracts and collective agreements that restrict player movement (see Beamish 1988; Staudohar 1986). The second point is that despite the fact that the players have united into collective bargaining units in order to negotiate more equitably for the revenues they produce through their labor, the balance of power still weighs heavily on the side of the owners. To many observers this is a perplexing issue. Why is it that the operation of player unions has not fully corrected the balance of power that existed between owners and players in the pre-union era of sport?

In this chapter I use the example of the ownership patterns among the seven Canadian teams in the National Hockey League to indicate one of the fundamental reasons why the National Hockey League Players Association (NHLPA), and professional athletes in general, have not enjoyed the dramatic increase in negotiating power that many associate with unionization.[1] The explanation lies in the corporate nature of ownership that characterizes professional sport.

Ownership Patterns among the Seven Canadian NHL Teams

The following analysis of corporate ownership and control examines four factors: the type of ownership; the share distribution among corporate directors and advisors controlling the corporation; the backgrounds of the corporate directors; and the corporate interlocks among the directors to various other companies. The first two factors are easily the most significant.[2] The type of corporate control found among the NHL teams is based on the distribution of the voting shares for each team/corporation. According to this criterion, three ownership patterns exist in the NHL—individual (or small group), family, and conglomerate.

Niosi (1978) argues that the researcher, in addition to noting where the majority of voting shares is concentrated, must pay attention to the level of control afforded by share distribution. Niosi has established four levels of control—virtually absolute (80 to 100 percent), majority (50 to 79 percent), minority (5 to 49 percent), and internal (0 to 5 percent). I will also draw attention to the type of control that exists within each team.

Individual or Small Group Control

Despite popular notions to the contrary, the ownership and control of large corporations still often rests with single individuals or small groups, and the case of the NHL is no exception. In fact, more than half of the seven Canadian NHL franchises—the Toronto Maple Leafs, Edmonton Oilers, Calgary Flames, and Winnipeg Jets—all fall within this category of ownership.

The Toronto hockey club was among the NHL's original teams when the league was founded in 1917 (Spencer 1978). Conn Smythe and a group of investors purchased the Toronto St. Patrick franchise in 1927 for $160,000 and in 1931 changed the name to the Maple Leafs. From then until 1961, when he sold his majority interest to a group of investors headed by his son, C. Stafford Smythe, Conn Smythe remained the majority shareholder. The 1961 ownership group also included Larkin Maloney, John Bassett, and Harold Ballard. Between 1961 and 1971 Bassett tried, unsuccessfully, to gain majority control of the Leafs and Maple Leaf Gardens. Continually outvoted, he sold his shares to Smythe and Ballard in 1971. This move was the first step toward the consolidation of ownership under Ballard.

Following Stafford Smythe's death in October 1971, Ballard, as the executor of Smythe's will, used his own corporation, Harold E. Ballard, Ltd. (HEBL), to purchase Smythe's shares at market value. This move gave HEBL outright control of the Maple Leafs and the Gardens (see Houston 1985, 101–5). As of 1988, through HEBL Harold Ballard owned 70.75 percent of the outstanding common shares in Maple Leaf Gardens, Ltd. (MLGL).

MLGL owns and operates the Maple Leaf Hockey Club, the Maple Leaf Gardens Sports Arena, the Hamilton Tiger-Cat Football Club of the Canadian Football League (CFL), the former St. Catherines Saints (now the New Market Saints) of the American Hockey League, and a Tier I Ontario

Hockey League junior hockey franchise, the Toronto Marlboros.[3] In addition to its sports operations, MLGL, through a wholly owned subsidiary, owns a printing company that has exclusive control over all of MLGL's publishing activities, which range from tickets and souvenir programs to flyers that advertise coming attractions to Maple Leaf Gardens (see Figure 10.1).

In 1988, Ballard technically enjoyed only majority control according to Niosi's criteria, although the remaining shares were so widely dispersed that Ballard had, in fact, virtually absolute control of the corporation and, consequently, all its subsidiaries. Under his control, HEBL expanded its operations beyond hockey. In 1978 the company purchased all the issued and outstanding shares of the Hamilton Tiger-Cat Football Club, Limited, for a total of $1,300,000. In the same year HEBL acquired a 50-percent interest in the American Hockey League team in Moncton, New Brunswick. In 1980 HEBL reorganized its financial portfolio so that its sport holdings were amalgamated under MLGL. In the following year, MLGL acquired Davis Printing and secured full ownership of the American Hockey League team in Moncton. As MLGL grew, so did its income (see Table 10.1).[4]

The Edmonton Oilers Hockey Club is also owned and controlled by a single individual. According to Niosi's classification, Peter Pocklington's ownership of Pocklington Financial Corporation (PFC) gives him virtually absolute control of the parent corporation and, therefore, of the Oilers.[5] PFC represents a collection of diverse investments in food processing, professional sports, office furniture manufacturing, oil and gas production, and real estate. Pocklington's past investments also included the ownership of

Figure 10.1 Portfolio of Harold E. Ballard, Ltd. (Toronto Maple Leafs)

		Harold E. Ballard, Ltd.			
		Maple Leaf Gardens, Ltd.			
		Sports			Other
Maple Leaf Gardens, Ltd.	Toronto Maple Leaf Hockey Club (NHL)	St. Catherines Saints (AHL) (now New Market Saints)	Toronto Marlboros Hockey Club (Jr.)	Hamilton Tiger-Cat Football Club (CFL)	Davis Printing

Table 10.1 Limited Financial Records of Maple Leaf Gardens, Ltd. (Millions of Dollars)

Fiscal Year	Total Assets	Total Revenue
1966	5.0	6.5
1970	5.7	6.8
1974	7.4	10.5
1978	6.7	12.8
1982	7.8	22.8
1984	11.3	27.5
1985	13.1	30.6

Sources: Financial Post Corporation Service (1984); *Maple Leaf Gardens, Limited, Annual Report* (1985).

almost 80 percent of the Winnipeg-based Fidelity Trust Company, the North American Soccer League team the Edmonton Drillers, and, between 1979 and 1983, Toronto's largest Ford car dealership.[6]

Peter Pocklington's financial portfolio represents a well-diversified set of successful investments. For example, Gainers is one of Canada's three largest meat processing companies. Employing over 1,500 workers, Gainers had sales of more than $400 million in 1984. Hartford Properties, a wholly owned subsidiary of PFC, operates the real estate activities of Pocklington's organization. Centered mainly in the province of Alberta, Hartford Properties administers and develops commercial as well as residential properties. PFC became involved in oil and gas exploration and development in 1984 with the development of Cromwell Resources Incorporated, which also centers its activities in western Canada. PFC diversified further by be-

Figure 10.2 Portfolio of Pocklington Financial Corporation, Inc. (Edmonton Oilers)

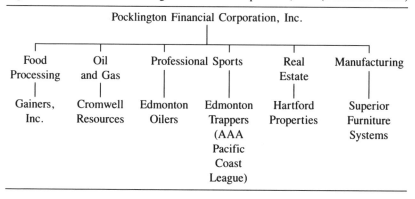

coming a major shareholder in Superior Furniture Systems. Based in Edmonton, this company is involved in the manufacturing of office furniture, which it supplies to Canadian and U.S. markets.[7]

In the case of both the Oilers and the Maple Leafs, the individual team owners who control the team preside on the team's board of directors and are extremely active in the team's operation. Pocklington's sale of Wayne Gretzky, the Oilers' most valuable asset, to the Los Angeles Kings in 1988 for $15 million indicates the role he plays in his team's operations. Ballard's involvement with the Maple Leafs was legendary, and with every report of his ill health, the stock in MLGL rose in value. This behavior by investors was partly due to the belief that the Maple Leaf hockey team would perform better under new ownership, but the main reason for it was the hope that Ballard's heirs would sell Maple Leaf Gardens because of the large amount of money its sale would generate as a valuable real estate site in downtown Toronto. (Ballard died in 1990.) Both Pocklington and Ballard also sat on the NHL's Board of Governors and thus exerted direct influence on the operations of the league.

The Calgary Flames and the Winnipeg Jets fall under the category of group control. The Calgary club has had a history of individual or small group ownership. The Flames entered the NHL through expansion in 1974 and were based in Atlanta and owned by Georgia businessman Tom Cousins, whose economic portfolio centered mainly in real estate development. Following eight years of the team's lackluster performance on and off the ice, Cousins sold the franchise in 1982 for an estimated $16 million to a group of businessmen that included Calgary's flamboyant entrepreneur Nelson Skalbania (Newman 1981, 139).

In that same year Skalbania acquired the ownership of six other sports franchises—two junior hockey teams, the Calgary Wranglers and the New Westminister Bruins; the Memphis Rogues of the North American Soccer league, which he moved to Calgary; the Vancouver Canadians of baseball's Triple 'A' Pacific Coast league; and the Montreal Alouette football team of the CFL. Sixteen months later Skalbania sold his interest in these sports franchises.[8]

As of 1988, the Flames are owned by six Calgary investors—Norman N. Green, Harley Hotchkiss, Norman Kwong, Byron Seaman, Daryl Seaman, and Mrs. Ralph Scurfield. Norman Green is the chairman of the board of Steward, Green Properties, Ltd., which is an integrated group of privately owned investment companies that specialize in the development, management, and ownership of shopping centers in Canada and the United States. Harley N. Hotchkiss has business interests in oil, gas, real estate, and agricultural enterprises, and he holds board positions with Conwest Exploration Company, Ltd., Mesa Petroleum Company, and the Alberta corporation Nova. Norman L. Kwong is a former CFL all-star with the Edmonton Eskimos who now serves as president and manager of Norman Holdings, Ltd., which is primarily involved in the Calgary real estate market. Byron J. Seaman is the chairman of the board and chief executive officer of Bow Valley Resource Services, Ltd. Daryl K. Seaman is the chairman of the board of Bow Valley Industries, Ltd., and sits on the boards of several other resource companies, including Nova and Pan-Alberta Gas, Ltd. Mrs. Ralph Scurfield is the widow of the late Ralph Scurfield, who was involved in several resource companies.[9] The six shareholders constitute the board of directors for the club, although the daily operation of the franchise is left to individuals who are not part of the ownership unit. The team is represented by a team employee at the NHL's Board of Governors meetings.

If little is known about the ownership of the Flames, then even less is publicly available concerning the Winnipeg Jets. Formerly a member of the World Hockey Association, the Jets were among the four teams that joined the NHL through league expansion in 1979.[10] Among the owners of the Jets since their entry into the NHL is Moffat Communications, Limited, which acquired 10.8 percent of the club in 1982.[11] Michael Gobuty, president of the Jets until 1983, was once the majority shareholder of the club (he is no longer involved with the team). With ownership currently held largely in private hands so it cannot be easily traced, the club is run by a board of directors.[12] The 1987 board consisted of Barry Shenkarow, Jim Ernst, Harvey Sector, Jerry Kruk, Don Henderson, Michael Dennehy, Bill Davis, and Marvin Shenkarow. Barry Shenkarow, a real estate investor, was the club's president.

Family Control

Niosi (1978, 90) notes that a company is under "family control if the principal group of shareholders—the group with 5% or more of the voting shares—comes from one family, whether or not members of the family sit on the company's board of directors." The NHL actually has a long history of family ownership. The most celebrated example is the Norris family. James Norris was the head of a family that at one time owned the Chicago Black Hawks and controlled Madison Square Gardens Corp., which concurrently owned the New York Rangers. Norris's sisters and brother owned the Detroit Red Wings during that same period. As a result, the Norris family controlled half of the teams in the then six-team NHL. Among the seven Canadian franchises today, the Montreal Canadiens and the Vancouver Canucks are controlled by families.

Le Club de Hockey Canadien de Montréal, or the Montreal Canadiens, was founded in 1909 by northern Ontario railway heir Ambrose O'Brien. Throughout most of its history, however, the team has been closely associated with the Molson family. The association began in 1924 when brothers Col. Herbert, Kenneth, and Walter Molson and cousins Fred W. and Bart Molson purchased shares, for $100 each, in the original issue of the Canadian Arena Corporation (CAC). The CAC, in turn, controlled the majority interest of the Canadiens (Woods 1983, 296). Thirty-three years later, when Senator Donat Raymond, the aging president of the CAC, decided to sell his interest, he arranged for a private sale to Senator Hartland Molson (who was appointed to the Canadian Senate in 1955) and his brother Tom, both sons of Col. Herbert. The shares sold for almost $2 million.

Nine years later Hartland and Tom's cousin, David Molson, who was also the president of the Canadiens at the time, proposed that he and his two brothers—Billy and Peter—would purchase the Molson shares in CAC for 25 percent more than Hartland and Tom had originally paid. Because Hartland and Tom Molson were in the midst of massive renovations to the Montreal Forum, where the Canadiens play, they delayed the sale of their shares to their cousins David, Billy, and Peter until 1968 (Woods 1983, 315–16). In view of the money that Hartland and Tom had invested in the Canadiens and the Forum as well as the other interests that the CAC owned, the sales price of $3 million was essentially a multimillion-dollar gift. The largesse was partly due to the fact that the Molson brothers were happy to keep the Canadiens in the family and partly because they wanted to concentrate on other divisions within the Molson economic portfolio. Keeping the Canadiens in the family, however, proved to be far more problematic than Hartland and Tom had ever imagined.

Just three years after purchasing the controlling interest in CAC, David, Billy, and Peter Molson sold their shares to Placement La Rondelle, Limitée, which was controlled by two brothers from another Quebec family that ranks among Canada's corporate elite, Edward and Peter Bronfman.[13] This time the sales price was $13.1 million and David, Peter, and Billy Molson completed the deal just two days before a capital gains tax was introduced into Canada. For the Molson family associated with Molson Breweries—Hartland and Tom Molson—the sale was a tragedy, partly because it meant the family had lost control of the Canadiens but also because it meant that the family's brewing interests now had to pay full market prices for its association with the hockey club.

In 1978 the Bronfmans made some economically based decisions concerning the continued growth and development of their conglomerate Brascan that included selling off their interest in the CAC. The Molsons were not particularly enthusiastic about repurchasing the Canadiens until they learned that Labatt's Breweries, one of their major competitors, was in pursuit of the franchise. Within a matter of months of the first informal contacts, Hartland and Tom Molson paid over $20 million for the Bronfmans' shares in CAC.

The key to family ownership on the part of the Molsons is its corporate involvement in Molson Breweries and a variety of other corporate endeavors (see Figure 10.3). Molson Companies, Ltd. (MCL), was a privately held corporation owned and operated exclusively by the Molson family until 1945. Through the sale of public shares, the Molson family has enjoyed tremendous income while maintaining minority control of the corporation. In addition to minority stock control, the Molsons exercise some direct control through two of their family members who sit on MCL's board of directors. As of 1988, Eric Molson—a nephew of Senator Hartland Molson and the great-great-great-grandson of John Molson, who founded the family's brewing interests in 1876—was the deputy chairman of the board. In 1988, directly or indirectly, Eric controlled 23.77 percent of MCL's shares, and his uncle Senator Hartland Molson was also on the board. More important, both Eric and Senator Molson sat on the seven-man executive committee of MCL and thus exercised decisive control over the company's major decisions (see Woods 1983, 339–40).

Even though Le club de hockey Canadien is a subsidiary of Molson Breweries of Canada, which is owned and operated through the CAC, the club maintains a separate board of directors. This board oversees the entire operation of the NHL franchise and largely controls the activities of the other sport franchises owned by MCL through the CAC and Molson Brew-

Figure 10.3 The Portfolio of Molson Companies, Ltd. (Montreal Canadiens)

	The Molson Companies, Ltd.		
Brewing	Chemical	Retail Merchandising	Other
Molson Breweries of Canada, Ltd. Canadian Arena Corp.	Diversey Corp.	Beaver Lumber	Grayrock Capital, Ltd.
Montreal Canadiens (NHL) Nova Scotia Voyageurs (AHL)	Vancouver Canadiens (Pacific Coast League)		

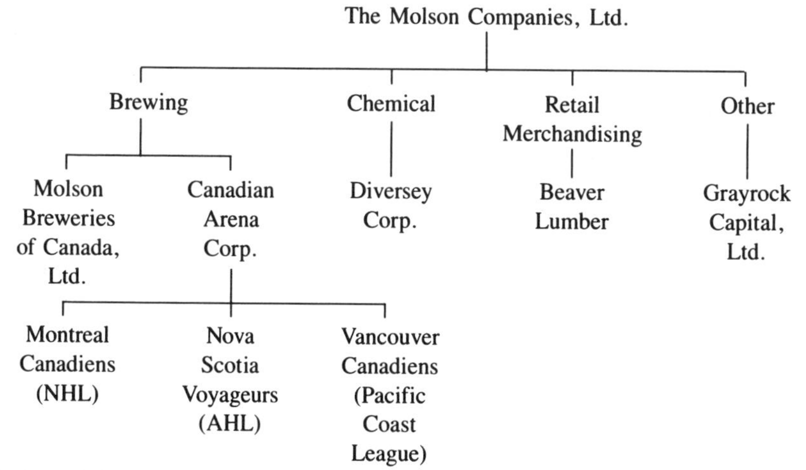

eries. The board of directors of the hockey franchise has, of course, a representative from MCL's board of directors. Interestingly enough, it is Jean Beliveau, a former all-star performer with the Canadiens who is now a member of the board of MCL and the club's senior vice president of corporate affairs.

MCL's operations fall into three main categories—brewing, retail merchandising, and speciality chemical sales. Revenues have grown steadily for MCL (Table 10.2). In 1985 MCL had sales of $1.87 billion with net earnings of $45.2 million. This financial picture broke down roughly as follows. Diversey Corporation, a world leader in specialty chemicals that was purchased by MCL in 1978, had sales of $.51 billion in 1985 and generated $36.2 million in profits.[14] Beaver Lumber, purchased in 1972, contributed an additional $.5 billion in sales.[15]

The bulk of the remainder came through MCL's most important outlet—Molson Breweries of Canada, Ltd. Founded in 1876, Molson Breweries is North America's oldest brewery. In 1985 its brewing operations had sales of $1.06 billion and generated profits of $30 million. This profit figure is particularly significant when one considers that the sports franchises, not all of which show a profit in the firm's accounting records, are part of the brewing operations.

While the ownership of the Canadiens is clearly in the hands of the Molson family, the case of the Vancouver Canucks provides a good example of how control of a franchise can remain with a family and yet appear to lie elsewhere. The Griffiths, through their majority control of Western Broadcasting Company, Ltd. (WBCL), essentially control the Vancouver Canucks (see Figure 10.4). Frank A. Griffiths and his wife, Emily, through various agreements and holding companies, own a majority of voting shares in WBCL, and Arthur R. Griffiths, Frank's brother, also holds voting shares in companies involved with WBCL. WBCL holds 77 percent of the shares in Northwest Sports Enterprises, Ltd. (NSEL) (see Table 10.3), which owns

Table 10.2 Limited Financial Records of Molson Companies, Ltd.
(Millions of Dollars)

Fiscal Year	Total Assets	Total Revenue	Net Earnings
1976	421.3	812.0	23.6
1978	462.4	952.8	33.0
1980	706.1	1,392.2	50.9
1982	855.9	1,651.1	54.6
1984	986.7	1,800.2	51.3
1985	1,033.9	1,871.8	45.2

Source: The Molson Companies, Limited, Annual Report (1985).

Figure 10.4 Portfolio of the Griffiths (Vancouver Canucks)

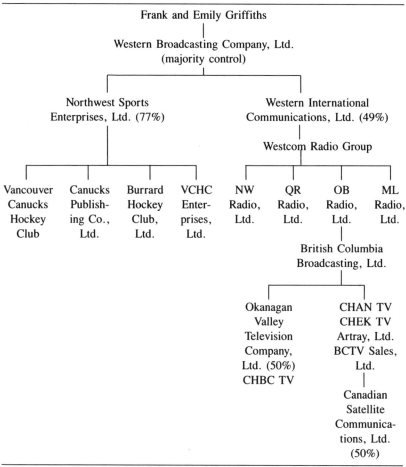

and controls the majority of shares in the Vancouver Canucks and its affiliated companies. In addition, WBCL is a part owner of the Fredericton Express of the American Hockey League.[16] WBCL also owns 49 percent of Western International Communications, Ltd., which is engaged in radio, television, and related services in British Columbia, Alberta, Manitoba, and Ontario.[17] The board of directors of the Canucks has members from the boards of directors of both NSEL and the parent company, WBCL. Frank Griffiths, the majority shareholder of WBCL, represents the Canucks on the Board of Governors of the NHL and was vice president of the NHL's Board of Governors in 1985.

Table 10.3 Financial Record of Northwest Sports Enterprises, Ltd.
(Millions of Dollars)

Fiscal Year	Total Assets	Total Revenue	Net Earnings
1970	8.8	1.6	1.44
1975	14.1	5.9	.71
1980	14.4	8.8	6.37
1984	21.7	13.3	3.15
1985	16.0	13.3	2.26

Source: The Financial Post Corporation Service (1985).

Conglomerates

The final form of control found among the Canadian NHL teams is ownership through financial conglomerates. A conglomerate, Clement (1977, 134) notes, refers to "a heterogeneous company, the product of either mergers or acquisitions, engaged in a variety of unrelated activities." Through the development of a conglomerate, investors can enjoy expanded power through the practice of "pyramiding." Pyramiding is an investment procedure through which one company gains effective control of another company so that it can wield economic influence in excess of the capital which it actually invests within the parent company (ibid., 36).

The Quebec Nordiques are the only Canadian NHL team that is part of a conglomerate, and this conglomerate's structure, of which the Nordiques are just one small part, demonstrates clearly what conglomerate ownership means to professional sport (see Figure 10.5).[18] At the top were two major owners—Philip Morris, Inc., and the Rupert Foundation. Of the two, Philip Morris, which owns 24.9 percent of Rothmans International, is the most interesting and powerful in terms of its multinational economic activity.

Philip Morris is the second largest cigarette company in the world, but it also has a diverse economic portfolio. Among its other operations, it fully controls the Miller Brewing Co., the second largest brewery in the U.S.; owns the Seven-Up Co., the third largest soft drink manufacturer in the world; and holds diversified interests involved in the manufacture of specialty papers, tissues, and packaging materials, and in community development. Through its subsidiaries, it operates in over 170 countries, and it enjoys sales of $1.1 billion just from its export sales alone, which include cigarettes, tobacco, beer, soft drinks, and other products. In 1984 Philip Morris had a total net revenue of $13.8 billion and a net income of $888.5 million.

The Philip Morris subsidiary of interest for this discussion is Rothmans International of London, England. It is primarily engaged in the light con-

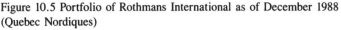

Figure 10.5 Portfolio of Rothmans International as of December 1988
(Quebec Nordiques)

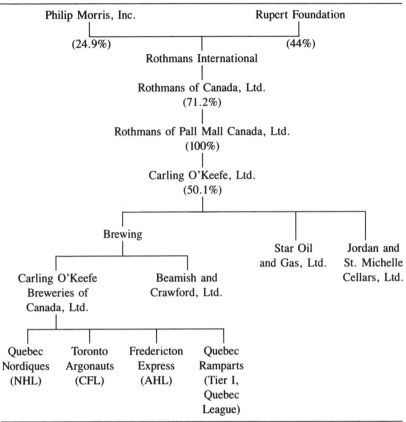

sumer goods market with interests in tobacco, brewing, and luxury consumer goods. It owns 71 percent of the stock in Rothmans of Canada, Ltd.,
while the other 29 percent is dispersed among public buyers. Rothmans of
Canada, in turn, owns 100 percent of Rothmans Pall Mall of Canada, which
controls just over 50 percent of the stock in Carling O'Keefe, Ltd. Pall Mall
began with an 11 percent purchase of Carling O'Keefe in 1968 and in 1969
added an additional 38.5 percent at a cost of $108.9 million (*Moody's In-
dustrial Manual* 1984).

Rothmans Pall Mall of Canada and its subsidiaries are primarily engaged
in the production and sale of tobacco products in Canada. In fact, it ranks
as Canada's second largest manufacturer and distributor of cigarettes. Carling O'Keefe itself is a diversified corporation with interests in brewing,

wine, and oil and gas. Star Oil and Gas, Ltd., wholly owned by Carling O'Keefe, had $23.4 million in sales in 1984, and Jordan and St. Michelle Cellars, Ltd., had wine sales of $57.7 million the same year (*Carling O'Keefe, Limited, Annual Report* 1985). It is the brewing operations, however, that are most important to the corporation.

Carling O'Keefe Breweries operates seven breweries in Canada and one in Ireland—Beamish and Crawford—and owns and controls all of them. Its Canadian operations make Carling O'Keefe one of Canada's three major brewers, which together account for 96 percent of all Canadian beer sales. John Labatt, Ltd., which has a majority interest in the Toronto Blue Jays of the American Baseball League, has approximately 41 percent of the market; the Molson Companies, Ltd., have 31 percent of the market; and Carling O'Keefe holds 24 percent of the Canadian market. During 1984 Carling O'Keefe had $800 million in sales (*Carling O'Keefe, Limited, Annual Report* 1985).

Finally, Carling O'Keefe was the sole owner of the Quebec Nordique hockey club. It purchased 91.5 percent of the club shares in 1976 and bought the rest of the club's shares in 1979. The primary reason for the purchase of the club, and the other sport franchises in its economic portfolio, was to increase its visibility among those who were most likely to consume beer—males between the ages of eighteen and forty-five—which is the group most apt to follow professional sport. In 1988 the Nordiques were involved in a series of transactions that resulted in the sale of the majority ownership of the club by Carling O'Keefe—a major change in the ownership of a Canadian team. But little has changed regarding the patterns of ownership in the NHL.

The ultimate sale of the majority interest in the Nordiques to a business group headed by Marcel Aubut, the president of the Nordiques, actually began in April 1987 and had nothing to do with hockey and everything to do with capital investment, profits, and beer. In April 1987, Elders IXL, an Australian conglomerate with a decided interest in brewing, purchased the majority interest in Carling O'Keefe of Canada for about $400 million (*Toronto Globe and Mail* 1988a). This purchase was motivated by two factors. First, the Australian firm wanted to aggressively market its products, particularly Foster's beer, in North America. The purchase of Carling O'Keefe gave Elders both expertise in beer sales within North America (since the existing management team at Carlings remained in place) as well as facilities for brewing Foster's and other beers at less expense than exporting them from Australia. Second, and probably equally important, Canada and the United States were in the process of negotiating a free trade agreement. By owning a majority share in Carling O'Keefe, Elders positioned itself to gain access to the lucrative U.S. beer market without worrying about tariff barriers that it would otherwise face as an Australian brewery.

Once Elders purchased Carling O'Keefe, however, the "need" to own the Nordiques came under review. Given a different corporate philosophy at Elders concerning how one obtains the best value for one's marketing dollar, the Australian conglomerate decided to divest itself of the majority ownership it held with the Nordiques and totally divest itself of the Toronto Argonauts. At the time, Elders saw this as a simple, straightforward business transaction (*Toronto Globe and Mail*, 1988b). But it was not that simple.

The Nordiques, one must understand, are more than just another hockey team to the majority francophone population of Quebec. It is the only hockey team in North America that operates exclusively in French, and the fleur-de-lis on the team sweater symbolizes to the entire world the strong nationalist sentiments that still exist among many francophones in Quebec. Furthermore, in the centuries-old rivalry between Montreal and Quebec, the Nordiques are the antithesis of the Canadiens and thus a rallying point for many francophone Quebecers. The management structure of the Nordiques is completely French, its supporters are individual Quebecers and not large multinational corporations, and the Nordiques are the most important cultural symbol in the city—a source of national and local pride that attests on a daily basis to the entrepreneurial skills of francophone businessmen. As a result, the potential sale of the Nordiques to a group backed by anglophone finance capital created a tremendous emotional reaction within Quebec since the sale would not guarantee that the club would remain in Quebec city. With a number of lucrative sites elsewhere—Hamilton, Milwaukee, and a few California cities were cited as possible new locations for the franchise (*Toronto Globe and Mail* 1988b, A13)—there was genuine concern that new owners would quickly move the club to a market where television revenue would be significantly higher than in Quebec.

In the end, by exercising an "option to purchase" clause in his contract as president of the Nordiques, Marcel Aubut was able to bring together enough French business interests—along with some investment capital from a local Quebec subsidiary of the Japanese firm Daishowa Paper Manufacturing Co., which purchased 18 percent of the Nordiques (*Sports Illustrated* 1989, 54)—to meet the $20 million selling price that Elders was seeking. At the same time, Carling O'Keefe maintained a 10-percent share in the hockey club and has apparently kept its exclusive promotion and television advertising rights with the club.

The Implications Ownership Patterns Have for Labor Relations in Professional Hockey

At the outset of this chapter it was noted that the nature of corporate ownership that characterizes the NHL in particular, and professional sport in general, is one of the most important factors in determining the balance of power in labor relations in professional sport. First, despite the apparent diversity in ownership, there are more commonalities among the owners with respect to issues that affect players in the negotiation process than there are differences. The most important common feature is the fact that team "owners" are not individuals at all. Each owner—even Harold Ballard and Peter Pocklington—is a large corporate entity with a diverse economic portfolio. The portfolios may differ in size and the importance of the hockey investment within each portfolio may vary, but the corporate nature of team ownership is clear and decisive.

Second, in view of the corporate nature of NHL team ownership, the players require enormous economic resources to even begin to balance the capital behind the owners. Despite the salaries that players earn, there is no common pool of resources upon which they can draw to match that which lies behind the owners. This fact has a number of implications, of course, but it ultimately boils down to the question of which side can best afford to "take a strike." As the most recent strikes in baseball and football have indicated, a strike may be costly to the owners, but it has not driven any of them out of business—in sport or in their other interests. For the players, the costs must be borne by the individual, and these costs become unbearably high when players begin to calculate their losses in terms of potential career earnings.[19]

Third, as a result of the diverse corporate involvement that characterizes NHL ownership patterns, the owners are part of a relatively tightly knit economic elite, especially in Canada. As a result, no "owner" or management team operates in a vacuum. The owners as entrepreneurs of teams and as part of a league draw upon the economic expertise of a vast pool of resources throughout the Canadian and U.S. economies. This vast pool of expertise, advice, and personal networks is overlooked too often and underestimated in terms of its impact upon owners' strategies in a wide array of labor relations issues. These issues can range from advice on how to best handle an upcoming set of negotiations over the league's collective agreement with the players to how the league can influence the legislature's attitudes toward professional sport as a business with a special status. In these instances, personal networks often bring in more valuable help and information than money could ever buy.

Fourth, in view of the above membership in the Canadian and U.S. corporate elite, the NHL owners all operate their businesses and their labor negotiations with the players within the context of strongly market-oriented liberal ideology. Thus when players' unions negotiate with the owners they not only confront a massive concentration of capital, which is buttressed by personal links among the corporate elite of the country, they are also operating in a social context that tends to treat collective action by workers as abnormal, unnatural, and, indeed, pathological. This shared common sentiment among owners creates a degree of solidarity among the owners during contract negotiations that is impossible to achieve among the players, who hold such diverse and competing ideologies about the nature of unionization, labor negotiations, and the role of the strike in the economic advancement of the players. As much as the gap that exists between the players and the owners in terms of economic resources, the gap in ideological solidarity between the owners and the players tips the scales of power decisively in favor of the owners.

Finally, the recent sale of the Nordiques highlights yet another factor in the balance of power in labor relations in professional sport. The sale of the Nordiques by Elders IXL was purely an economically motivated decision. A new corporate owner chose to pursue a different corporate strategy than the previous owner. The response touched off a decidedly noneconomic response. Due to particular nationalist sentiments and the relatively unique cultural role that the Nordiques play in Quebec, a variety of social forces coalesced and exerted considerable influence on this original economically calculated decision to sell. Despite the presence of these powerful social forces, however, the economics of the transaction were only moderately influenced by the pressures of politics—the Nordiques were sold to a Quebec-based business group, but the group was a business group nonetheless. This example underscores what many sociologists term the "primacy" of the economic moment. While it is true that all economic decisions are overlaid with social, political, and cultural influences, in a market society—in the world of business—the economic moment assumes primacy, and all other factors are only accommodated insofar as they must be taken into account. Sport owners, in this regard, are businessmen first, and the bottom line of their economic portfolios determines more than anything else what moves they will make in the marketplace.

This primacy of the economic moment has another implication. Just as an economically sound corporation that is undervalued on the stock market is always ripe for a hostile takeover, sport franchises are continually monitored as investment and marketing possibilities by a number of corporate entities. What this means in the short run, at least as long as sport is viewed as a cost-effective means of reaching particular segments of the consumer market, is that the value of franchises will continue to increase as large corporate consumers purchase franchises. This will mean that team owners will be progressively drawn from more powerful interests in the economy as a whole. The end result here, of course, is that the nature of corporate ownership that players will confront will not only become larger and more powerful, it will also view its relationship to the players and the business of professional sport in more and more narrowly defined economic terms. The possible expansion of larger corporate owners will be motivated by concerns with the bottom line—whether the investment is paying for itself the way it should—and, accordingly, the attitude of owners to players will become progressively more profit-oriented.

Concluding Comments

It is clear from the case study data on the seven Canadian teams in the NHL that professional sport owners are not individuals, even though it is the personalities of Harold Ballard and Peter Pocklington that the news media focus upon. Instead, it is corporate capital—Harold E. Ballard, Ltd., and Maple Leaf Gardens, Ltd., the Pocklington Financial Corporation, the Molson Companies, Ltd., or Western Broadcasting Company, Ltd.—that really owns and controls NHL franchises. This point has a number of far-reaching implications concerning the balance of power in labor relations in professional sport.

It is clear that professional sport is only one part of a corporation's total investment portfolio. The owners have a tremendous pool of capital resources behind them, and they share a number of valuable personal linkages and networks with other areas of the corporate and state elite in Canada and the United States. The owners as a whole are able to draw upon a widely held ideological perspective in the conduct of their business affairs in the market in general and in the player market in particular. Other factors affect the balance of power between the owners and the players as well, but they operate within an environment dominated by the economic structure of ownership in professional sport. Players' associations, collective bargaining, and government intervention have modified the disparity of power between labor and management, but the vast capital resources of franchise owners keep them masters of the game.

NOTES

1. The data presented on ownership patterns among the Canadian NHL teams are the result of work that John Villemaire and I conducted in 1985 and 1986. I would like to gratefully acknowledge John Villemaire's contribution to this research work. For a chart of the major owners for all the NHL teams, see Staudohar (1986, 128).

2. See Beamish and Villemaire (1989a, 1989b) for a full discussion of all four factors.

3. Toronto and Montreal play in arenas that are owned wholly or in part by their majority shareholders.

4. As of 1985 Harold Ballard owned 520,424 shares of Maple Leaf Gardens, Ltd.; thus a dividend of $3.71 represented an income of $1,930,784.00 for 1985. This dividend income was over and above the salaries he drew for his board positions on any of the companies in his economic portfolio. Houston (1985, 323) estimates that between 1977 and 1984, MLGL paid out almost 73 percent of its operating profits in dividends to shareholders. This exceptionally generous policy—contrasted to the 20 to 25 percent characteristic of most corporations—clearly rewarded Harold Ballard handsomely. For information on the operations of MLGL, see Financial Post Corporation Service (1985).

5. Pocklington, who acquired the Oilers in 1976, is the sole owner, as well as director and chief officer, of the Edmonton Oilers Hockey Club (based on information received through correspondence with Pocklington Financial Corporation, January 1986).

6. See the *Kingston Whig-Standard Magazine*, January 4, 1986.

7. The information presented here on the operations and subsidiaries of Pocklington Financial Corporation comes from the company's 1985 annual report.

8. For a more detailed discussion of Skalbania's short-lived venture into professional sport, see Newman (1981, 139–43).

9. All information about who currently owns the Flames was supplied by the Calgary Flames Hockey Club through correspondence in January 1986. Because the club is a privately held corporation, little public information exists about it.

10. Although the NHL termed the inclusion of four World Hockey Association teams in the NHL as "expansion," the move was really little more than a merger that reestabilized professional hockey in North America into its traditional monopoly pattern at its highest level (see Beamish 1988, 145–46).

11. Moffat Communications operates radio and television stations in western Canada and cable television systems in Winnipeg, Houston, Texas, and Florida (Financial Post Corporation Service 1985).

12. According to the 1985 *Moffat Communications Annual Report*, the company held a 10.67-percent interest in the Jets. Attempts to secure further ownership information through correspondence with the club and the use of a variety of financial directories did not yield any results.

13. Edward and Peter Bronfman owned 58.8 percent of Placement La Rondelle, Limitée; John Bassett, through Baton Broadcasting, owned 11.8 percent; and the Bank of Nova Scotia owned the remaining 29.4 percent of the company.

14. Diversey markets over three thousand chemical products to more than one hundred countries around the world.

15. Beaver Lumber Company, Ltd., was founded in 1906. With more than 160 retail outlets from Quebec to British Columbia, it is a major lumber, building materials, and related hardware goods dealer in Canada.

16. This information on the ownership and control of Northwest Sports Enterprises, Ltd. and Western Broadcasting Company, Ltd., is stated in the 1985 *Information Circular* of Northwest Sports Enterprises, Ltd.

17. In 1984 Western Broadcasting Company, Ltd., had revenues of $77 million and generated a profit of $17.5 million (*Western Broadcasting Corporation Annual*

Report, 1985). Originally a public corporation, Western Broadcasting was sold to private share holders in 1981. The corporation's holdings were reorganized, and the communications-related businesses, assets, and investments were acquired directly or through subsidiaries by the company for $87.3 million (Financial Post Corporation Service 1985).

18. As will become clear in the discussion to follow, the sale of the Nordiques has only changed the majority owner of the club and moved it under the influence of a different conglomerate. The nature of the ownership of the Nordiques still remains conglomerate in nature, although it will take a bit more time before one can trace out the entire ownership structure of the Nordiques under this new set of arrangements.

19. To get an idea of how much players can lose financially in a strike, the 57-day NFL strike in 1982 cost the players 10 percent of their career earnings.

BIBLIOGRAPHY

Beamish, Rob. 1988. "The Political Economy of Professional Sport." In J. Harvey and Hart Cantelon, eds., *Not Just a Game: Essays in the Sociology of Sport*, 141–58. Ottawa: University of Ottawa Press.

Beamish, Rob, and John Villemaire. 1989a. "Who Owns the Canadian Teams in the NHL? Demystifying the Popular Image." Submitted to *The Sociology of Sport Journal*.

———. 1989b. "Corporate Interlocks and Corporate Management of the Canadian Teams in the NHL: A Test of the Managerial Revolution Thesis." Submitted to *The Sociology of Sport Journal*.

Brower, Jonathan J. 1977. "Professional Sports Team Ownership: Fun, Profit and the Ideology of the Power Elite," *International Review of Sport Sociology* 4 (12): 79–98.

Carling O'Keefe, Limited, Annual Report. 1985. Toronto: Carling O'Keefe, Ltd.

Clement, Wallace. 1977. *The Canadian Corporate Elite*. Toronto: McClelland and Stewart.

Conference Board of Canada. 1977. *Canadian Directorship Practices: A Profile*. Ottawa.

Eitzen, D. Stanley. 1979. "The Business of Team Ownership." In S. Eitzen, ed., *Sport in Contemporary Society*, 325–30. New York: St. Martin's Press.

Financial Post Corporation Service. 1978, 1984, 1985. *Financial Post Directory of Directors*. Toronto: Maclean-Hunter.

Gruneau, Richard. 1981. "Elites, Class and Corporate Power in Canadian Sport: Some Preliminary Findings." In John W. Loy, Gerald S. Kenyon, and Barry D. McPherson, eds., *Sport, Culture and Society*, 348–71. Philadelphia: Lea and Febiger.

Houston, William. 1985. *Ballard: A Portrait of Canada's Most Controversial Sports Figure*. Toronto: Seal Books.

"Japan Coming on Strong," *Sports Illustrated*, August 21, 1989, 54.

Maple Leaf Gardens, Limited, Annual Reports. 1966–85. Toronto: Maple Leaf Gardens.

Moffat Communications Annual Report. 1985. Toronto: Moffat Communications, Ltd., 1985.

Molson Companies, Limited, Annual Reports. 1976–85. Montreal: Molson Companies, Ltd.

Moody's Industrial Manual. 1984. New York: Moody's Investors' Service.

Moody's International Manual. 1976. New York: Moody's Investors' Service.

Newman, Peter. 1981. *The Acquisitors.* Toronto: McClelland and Stewart.

Niosi, Jorge. 1978. *The Economy of Canada: A Study of Ownership and Control.* Montreal: Black Rose Books.

Northwest Sports Enterprises Financial Reports. 1970–85. Vancouver: Northwest Sports, Ltd.

Pocklington Financial Corporation Annual Reports. 1985–86. Edmonton: Pocklington Financial Corporation, Ltd.

Spencer, David. 1978. *The New Professional Hockey Almanac.* Toronto: Pagurian Press Limited.

Staudohar, Paul D. 1986. *The Sports Industry and Collective Bargaining.* Ithaca, N.Y.: ILR Press, Cornell University.

Styer, Robert A. 1970. *The Encyclopedia of Hockey.* New York: A. S. Barnes and Company.

Toronto Globe and Mail. 1988a. "Nordique President Vows to Fight Loss of Team," November 1, A14.

Toronto Globe and Mail, 1988b. "Nords Not Planning to Leave, Carling Head Says," November 2, A13.

Who's Who in Canada. 1985–86. Toronto: International Press.

Who's Who in Canadian Business. 1985–86. Toronto: International Press.

Woods, Shirley. 1983. *The Molson Saga: 1763–1983.* Scarborough, Ontario: Avon Books of Canada.

A Social Profile of the Professional Football Player, 1920–82

Steven A. Riess

Despite the enormous popularity of professional football, its extensive press coverage, and the current academic interest in sports studies, very little is known about the thousands of men who have played professional football. We actually know a great deal more about professional boxers and major league baseball players, who have been the subjects of a number of major studies.[1] The conventional wisdom is that a career in the National Football League provided an important source of social mobility for athletically talented young men, especially for second-generation eastern Europeans whose fathers were coal miners or industrial workers in western Pennsylvania and the Ohio Valley, for struggling small-town Texans, and more recently, for indigent rural southern blacks. But what actually are the social characteristics of the men who played in the NFL?

Today NFL players are lionized, well-paid heroes who earn six-figure salaries during their very brief athletic careers. The situation was far different in the sport's early days when it did not yet rival baseball for recognition as the national pastime or dominate fall Sunday afternoons. I will examine the class, ethnic, and geographic origins of NFL players active in the 1930s, the 1950s, and 1982, as well as their levels of education, wages, tenure, and subsequent job history, to develop a collective portrait of NFL athletes in three distinct eras, examine what changes, if any, have occurred in recruitment patterns, and evaluate the sport's value as a vehicle of social mobility.

The Wages of the Professional Football Player

The first professional football player was Pudge Heffelfinger, a former Yale All-American, who was paid $500 in 1893 to play for the Allegheny Athletic Association against local rivals, the Pittsburgh Athletic Club. One year later the AAA paid three men each $50 a game, and by 1895 all its players were compensated. Pittsburgh became the principal locus of professional football, with most elevens sponsored by local steel magnates. Among the leading teams were the Braddock Carnegies, mainly steelworkers who received bonuses to play and were excused from millwork during the season, and the Homestead Library and Athletic Club, primarily comprised of former college All-Americans. By 1903 the professional game had shifted west to small Ohio industrial cities like Canton and Massillon. They recruited either former collegians or active collegians, who played under pseudonyms to protect their eligibility, and paid them $50 a game plus expenses. Other early teams were completely made up of blue-collar workers. The Columbus Panhandles, for instance, were Pennsylvania Railroad mechanics who put in a full six-day week at the factory, leaving on Saturday at 4 P.M. to catch a train for an out-of-town game, who then returned home in time for work on Monday morning.[2]

The rise of the first professional league, the American Professional Football Association in 1920 (renamed the NFL in 1922) did not immediately change the low status and modest wages of the occupation. Interest in professional football lagged far behind the college game, and most of the early teams were former semiprofessional clubs like the Decatur Staleys (the future Chicago Bears), who were sponsored by local boosters or industrialists as part of their welfare capitalism programs. Nearly all the franchises were located in the Midwest and included such cities as Hammond, Akron, and Canton. New York City did not join until 1925. The average player made about $75 to $100 a game at a time when the typical major league ballplayer earned about $5,000 a year. In 1925 the owner of the Bears, George Halas, took a bold step toward improving public interest and respect by signing Red Grange of Illinois, the greatest college player of the 1920s, to an extraordinary contract. Grange's income was tied to gate receipts, and he was such a great attraction (38,000 spectators turned out for his first professional game) that he earned about $250,000 in one year, mostly from two whirlwind postseason exhibition tours. Yet while Grange's presence generated a lot of favorable publicity for professional football and helped place the NFL on a firmer financial base, it had less of an impact on average wages. Throughout the 1920s professional football was mainly a weekend job to supplement one's primary job. Occasionally, as in the case of Paul Robeson, it was a means of financing one's postgraduate education.[3] In 1928 University of Nebraska All-American tailback Glenn Presnell turned down an offer of $150 to $175 per game to play with the New York Giants for three months and instead signed with the semiprofessional Ironton (W.Va.) Tanks. Presnell explained, "The Tanks offered almost as much per game as the Giants, plus they offered me a job teaching at Ironton High School at $1,600 for nine months. That really appealed to me because I had my degree in physical education and science and knew I wanted to be a teacher in the future."[4]

In the 1930s professional football became a much more stable enterprise than it had previously been. By 1934 all the small-town franchises except Green Bay had been replaced by teams in major metropolitan areas, where they were able to draw larger crowds. Playing professional football had become a respectable, if not prestigious, job, and it attracted nearly all the top college stars, except Jay Berwanger of the University of Chicago. In 1936 Berwanger had become the first Heisman Trophy winner, but he sought more lucrative opportunities in the private sector. The best-paid player was Rhodes Scholar Byron "Whizzer" White of the University of Colorado, a future U.S. Supreme Court justice, who earned $15,000 as a rookie in 1938. Salaries fluctuated during the Depression, with the top players earning from $3,600 to $6,000. The overall level of compensation rose together with the winner's share of the league championship game, which increased from $210 in 1933 to $900 in 1938.[5]

Professional football struggled to survive during World War II but enjoyed quite a boom after the war. The emergence of a rival league, the All-America Conference, pushed the average NFL salary up to $8,000 in 1949. In the 1950s the NFL achieved a high level of stability with attendance averaging 25,000 per game, the introduction of television boosting public interest, and franchise shifts ceasing after 1953. Yet salaries rose only modestly, to $9,200 by the mid-1950s, and did not keep pace with the rate of inflation. However, the rise of the American Football League in 1960 significantly changed salary patterns, with the competition for players pushing wages up to $25,000 in 1967, nearly one-fourth more than those of major league ballplayers. Following merger, football salaries, which reached $42,000 in 1975, began to lag behind baseball and basketball, which had free agency. Still the average NFL player was paid $69,000 in 1980. By 1988 the mean had skyrocketed to $245,000.[6]

The Geographic Origins of Professional Football Players

The patterns of recruitment in professional football have always been connected to geographic variables. Semiprofessionals in the pre-NFL era were drawn from the Pennsylvania-Ohio football belt from nearby steel mills, sandlots, and college gridirons. Early NFL teams also recruited heavily from their general locality because they lacked the resources to attract players from distant towns and depended on local heroes to bring in the crowds. Hence the Green Bay Packers relied heavily on Wisconsin-area athletes; the Bears on lads from metropolitan Chicago; and the Providence Steamrollers on New Englanders. Overall, though, the Pennsylvania-Ohio nexus still dominated.

In the 1930s and 1940s the sources of recruitment expanded, reflecting the nationwide popularity of interscholastic and intercollegiate football. Texas in particular developed into a new source of football talent and joined the football belt. In 1949 seven out of ten players came from three geographic regions: the Midwest (27 percent), the Mid-Atlantic (25 percent), and the Southwest (18 percent). The leading individual states were Pennsylvania (47 players) and Texas (37), followed by Ohio, Illinois, and California (which was becoming an all-around center for sports because of its climate). This basic pattern persisted into the 1960s, with Texas becoming the most productive state, followed by Pennsylvania, Ohio, and Illinois. In 1982 California was in the lead, with about 12.6 percent of the total number of players, followed by Texas, a distant second, and then Michigan, Ohio, and Pennsylvania. These states dominate because of local sporting traditions, unequal income distributions, and regional variations in parental, peer, and community support of football.[7]

Professional football players have typically been less urban in origin than either boxers or basketball players and about as urban in origin as major league ballplayers. Slightly more than half (54.2 percent) of NFL players active in the 1930s were born in cities, a figure about equal to the national urban population in 1930 (56.2 percent). But it is noteworthy that a majority (52.1 percent) came from sites with 5,000 or fewer residents (see Table 11.1), yet it was also true that players were more likely to come from large cities with over 100,000 inhabitants (27.1 percent) compared to the national population (22 percent). The rural background of NFL players in the 1930s is actually overstated by birthplace data because the players' families were geographically mobile. Although 52.1 percent of the players in this cohort were born in rural areas or very small towns, just one-third were still residing there by the time they were in high school. Small schools were generally unable to provide a sufficient level of interscholastic competition to prepare their athletes for big-time sports or secure star players sufficient exposure to warrant a college scholarship.[8]

NFL players active in the 1950s were only about half as likely as their predecessors to have been born in rural areas and very small towns (23.1 percent) or to have attended high school there (12.8 percent). They were just as likely to have been born in big cities with over 100,000 residents, but they were far more likely to have been raised in either a small town (5,000–10,000) or a small-to-midsized city (20,000–100,000). The best per capita producers were small working-class towns and cities in the football belt, where the sport controlled the tempo of life: residents did not have much else to do on Friday nights in the fall other than attend local high-

Table 11.1 Geographic Origins of American-Born Professional Football Players, 1930s–82

Size of Site	1930s		1950s		1982	
	Home Town	High School Locale	Home Town	High School Locale	Home Town	High School Locale
	(n = 48)		(n = 116)		(n = 454)	
Rural (under 2,500)	45.8%	22.9%	23.1%	12.8%	11.2%	19.9%
2,500–5,000	6.3	10.4	12.0	8.5	5.4	6.9
5,000–10,000	4.2	4.2	5.1	9.4	9.1	10.0
10,000–20,000	10.4	10.4	11.1	7.7	8.6	9.7
20,000–50,000	4.2	6.3	9.4	12.2	14.0	11.9
50,000–100,000	2.1	8.3	12.0	17.9	11.4	9.1
100,000–500,000	8.3	14.6	12.8	14.5	20.7	17.5
500,000 +	18.8	22.9	14.5	17.1	19.6	15.1
Total	100.1[a]	100.0	100.0	100.1[a]	100.0	100.1[a]

Sources: Study data; computed from sample from The Sporting News Football Register, 1982 (St. Louis: The Sporting News, 1982).
[a]Error due to rounding off.

school games. The coaches were leading figures in the community; there was a lot of pressure to win; and the fierce competition and high level of play produced many future college and professional players.[9]

By 1982 virtually 90 percent of the players were urban-born. They were roughly only half as likely as players from the 1950s to come from localities with 5,000 or fewer residents, and about one-half more likely to have been born in cities with over 100,000 residents. Yet members of the 1982 cohort were more likely to have grown up in a rural area (as shown by high school attendance), and just as likely to have gone to high school in a large city. I suspect that the large proportion of NFL players who lived in rural areas when they attended high school is largely due to the increased presence of southern rural blacks on NFL rosters. On the other hand, the productivity of big-city high schools diminished throughout the 1930–82 period. Professional players from big cities were proportionately overrepresented in the 1930s but have been underrepresented ever since then. In 1982, for instance, the proportion of NFL players coming from high schools in metropolitan centers with over one million residents was just half its expected percentage share. The big-city decline was caused by such problems as inadequate playing space, insufficient community support (caused in part by the availability of alternate sports and recreations), and the high cost of outfitting interscholastic elevens. Underfinanced urban public schools have been much more successful with cheap team sports, like basketball, that do not require much space. In the 1960s New York City produced only 13 percent of its expected share of Division I football players at a time when its suburbs were producing their proportionate share. Detroit, Boston, St. Louis, San Francisco, Philadelphia, and Milwaukee were among major cities producing less than 60 percent of their proportionate share.[10]

Historically, Cleveland and Pittsburgh—both in the heart of the traditional football belt—and Chicago, just on the fringe, have been leading producers of excellent football players. In the 1960s, for instance, Cleveland produced 1.83 and Pittsburgh 2.56 times their expected numbers of football players. Chicago, like those two cities, has had a long tradition of high-school football, and by the early 1900s top games were receiving a lot of press coverage. High-school football was a popular cheap entertainment during the Depression in Chicago, and in 1937 an estimated 120,000 spectators attended the city championship game between Austin and St. Leo's at Soldier Field. In more recent times the public schools have had a hard time supporting the game, but it is still well backed by Chicago's large Catholic parochial school system.[11]

Most of the other major cities that are very productive sources of Division I football players are also in the football belt, including Cincinnati, Dallas, San Antonio, Houston, and Toledo. Outside the football belt, Atlanta, San Jose, and Los Angeles are very productive. Los Angeles County was the leading producer of Division I football players in the early 1960s, not because of the single-minded devotion that characterizes much of the football belt, but because its sports-minded public has taken advantage of its climatic conditions to promote year-round, high-quality athletic programs.[12]

The Ethnic Backgrounds of Professional Football Players

In the 1920s the NFL was mainly comprised of WASPs, German-Americans, and Irish-Americans, but it was open to all ethnic and minority groups, including blacks, until 1934—a situation connected to the league's low prestige. There was even an all-Indian team, the Oorong Indians, a touring team based in Marion, Ohio, from 1922 to 1924. Only a small proportion of players in this period were sons of new immigrants from eastern and southern Europe (3.5 percent Slavic and 2.1 percent Italian). This fact reflected their impoverishment, limited leisure time, lack of higher education, and the limited extent of their assimilation. By the 1920s Russian Jews and Italians had achieved considerable renown in prizefighting and basketball but much less in either football or baseball, sports that were far less congruent with life in urban slums.[13]

The visibility of eastern and southern Europeans in the NFL increased markedly in the period 1933–45 as they became more fully acculturated and were able to earn football scholarships to college. In this era one-fifth of team rosters were comprised of either Slavic-Americans (13.5 percent) or Italian-Americans (6.5 percent). These ethnic groups were making their mark in football at about the same time that they were breaking into baseball. There was no Polish batting champion until Al Simmons in 1930, and no Italian until Ernie Lombardi in 1938. These groups' meager representation in the major leagues changed in the late 1930s, and by 1941 9.3 percent of big leaguers were Slavic and 8 percent were Italian, similar to their share of NFL rosters and about double their proportion of the national white population. Since most first-generation Poles and Italians were unskilled laborers, the second-generation Poles and Italians in the NFL were presumably from poor families. But more research is needed to confirm that inference.[14]

Eastern and southern European representation in the NFL peaked after World War II. In 1949 when one-third of all football players were sons of immigrants, one-fourth were either of eastern European (15 percent) or Italian (9 percent) extraction. But by the 1950s the ratio of new immigrant players declined to about one out of six; 9.8 percent were Slavic and 6 percent were Italian. In 1982 the proportion of Slavic players was down to 6.8 percent, and Italians to 2.2 percent.[15]

Another important postwar development was the reintegration of the NFL. A few blacks had played on NFL teams in the 1920s and early 1930s until 1934, when, by a general understanding among owners, no more blacks were hired. The admission of blacks into the NFL started out as a trickle, and as late as 1956 they comprised just 6 percent of league rosters. It was not until 1962 that the last holdout, the Washington Redskins, hired a black player. By the mid-1960s, one-fourth of the players were black, including many from black colleges who had been previously overlooked. By 1982 blacks constituted a majority (52 percent) of NFL players.[16]

The Social Backgrounds of Professional Football Players

The conventional wisdom has long been that professional football was an important alternate source of social mobility for athletically talented youth who came from the industrial or mining regions of the football belt, but the reality was somewhat different. Players active in the 1930s came from families that were economically and socially distinctly middle class. Nearly three out of five (57.8 percent) had white-collar fathers, and just one out of three (33.3 percent) had blue-collar fathers (see Table 11.2). (By comparison, in 1930, 25.8 percent of the national male work force was white-collar, and 51.4 percent was blue-collar). The results of this study of 1930s players is almost identical to that from a sample consisting of the fathers of star players active from the 1920s through the 1940s (53 percent white-collar and 33.3 percent blue-collar). Also quite notable was the finding that

Table 11.2 Occupations of Fathers of NFL Players Active 1920–80s

Occupational Category	1920s–40s[a]*** (n = 66) (%)	1930s[b]** (n = 45) (%)	1949[c]*** (n = 300) (%)	1950s[b]*** (n = 111) (%)	1950s–80s[a]*** (n = 124) (%)
White-collar	53.0	57.8	46.6[d]	40.5	40.3
Blue-collar	33.3	33.3	45.5[d]	52.3	53.2
Farm	13.6	8.9	7.9[d]	7.2	6.5
Total	99.9[e]	100.0	100.0	100.0	100.0

Sources: Computed from data in [a]David L. Porter, ed., *Biographical Dictionary of American Sports*, vol. 2, *Football* (Westport, Conn.: Greenwood Press, 1987); [b]author's study data; [c]Paul Governali, "The Professional Football Player: His Vocational Status" (M.A. thesis, Teachers' College, Columbia University, 1951), 49. [d]Adjusted to account for no data responses. [e]Error due to rounding off.
**p < .01.
***p < .001.

just 8.9 percent of the 1930s cohort were sons of farmers even though nearly half the players active in the 1930s were of rural origins. Another important point was that most fathers in this cohort were either high-level white-collar or blue-collar aristocrats. Fathers in nonmanual occupations included builders, an attorney, and a contractor, while artisans comprised approximately two-thirds (64.3 percent) of the fathers in manual occupations. Merely 6.3 percent of all the fathers were miners, a fact that flies in the face of conventional beliefs.[17]

The middle-class dominance of professional football declined and then ended in the 1940s as the occupation attracted upwardly mobile athletes who used their prowess to secure college scholarships and then continued on to the professional ranks. Paul Governali found in his study of NFL players active in 1949 that white-collar sons no longer made up a majority of team rosters and barely outnumbered blue-collar players (46.6 percent to 45.5 percent). The white-collar fathers were still predominantly high-level individuals (61 percent), but the labor aristocracy no longer dominated the blue-collar ranks. In fact the proportion of fathers who were unskilled workers (42.5 percent) surpassed that for artisans (40 percent), indicating that more players were coming from lower socioeconomic levels. In the 1950s blue-collar players comprised the majority (see Table 11.2), a pattern that has persisted (at least for star athletes) through the 1980s. In the 1950s most blue-collar fathers were semiskilled, and just one-third were artisans. The bulk of the manual workers were factory operatives (57.6 percent). Yet there were only a handful of miners (5.4 percent) in the sample. The proportion of NFL players in the 1950s whose fathers were blue-collar (52.3 percent) was virtually identical to the national distribution of male workers in 1950 (54.4 percent). The main difference was that the athletes' fathers were more likely to be white-collar (40.5 percent) than the national norm (30.6 percent) and half as likely to be farmers (7.2 percent versus 15 percent).[18]

The social class backgrounds of players active in the 1950s is very similar to that of long-term journeymen players active in the 1970s and almost identical to that of the football stars who played in the period from the 1950s to the early 1980s. In the 1950s, 1960s, and 1970s, most of the stars came from blue-collar backgrounds. In the 1970s, for instance, nearly two-fifths of the stars (37.1 percent) were white-collar in origin, more than half (57.2 percent) were blue-collar, and the rest (5.7 percent) were sons of farmers. The star players were sharply differentiated by race. White players were almost evenly divided up between those with fathers in nonmanual occupations (44.4 percent) and those with fathers in manual occupations (48.8 percent), but the black stars were overwhelmingly blue-collar in origin (64.7 percent), with a small minority (29.4 percent) from households headed by white-collar fathers. Furthermore, black white-collar fathers usually held lower-level nonmanual jobs, and black blue-collar fathers were usually in unskilled or semiskilled occupations. The job of professional athlete was a distinct move up for black football players, and it was a step up for about half of their white colleagues. This was a dramatic change in comparison to the prewar NFL players, who had come from very middle-class families.[19]

The Education of NFL Players

Despite the negative stereotype of professional football players as "dumb jocks," they were historically far better educated than most U.S. citizens. Even in football's semiprofessional era and the early days of the NFL, when many players lacked college experience, the professionals had an educational level much higher than the national norm. Nearly one-fifth of players active in the period 1920–32 (18.7 percent) had not attended college, and over four-fifths (81.3 percent) had (see Table 11.3). By comparison, just one-fourth of major leaguers in the 1920s were college men. In 1910 merely 5 percent of college-age men were in school.[20]

The noncollege men active in the early years of the NFL (1920–32) were heavily concentrated in the period before 1926 (81.3 percent) when the league was struggling to survive and was having a hard time recruiting intercollegiate stars. But thereafter the NFL overcame its initial recruitment problems; about 98 percent of its players active between 1933 and 1946 had attended college. The college gridiron became the training ground for future professional football players just as baseball's minor leagues provided the seasoning for future major leaguers.

Franchise owners sought college men in the 1920s because of their intelligence, their experience playing high-quality competitive football, and their marquee value, which would help attract crowds and lend respectability to the professional game. In the early part of the 1920s college stars avoided the NFL because of the meager pay, low status, and the feeling that they were stepping down to a lower level of competition. Thereafter professional football shed much of its negative image as stars like Benny Friedman of the University of Michigan signed lucrative contracts. Though most of the other players could not expect to sign for several thousand dollars, the professional game did have certain attractions. It provided a means to continue playing an enjoyable, manly game, a chance to arrest adulthood and its pressures for a few years, possible off-season job opportunities through the team's owner or because of one's fame, and a way to improve one's future occupational prospects by making good connections, gaining experience for an eventual coaching career, or earning money to pay for

Table 11.3 Education of NFL Players Active 1920–82

Education	1920–32[a] n = 1784 (%)	1930s[b] n = 48 (%)	1933–45[a] n = 1647 (%)	1949[c] n = 300 (%)	1946–59[a] n = 1936 (%)	1950s[b] n = 117 (%)	1982[d] n = 454 (%)
No college	18.7[e]	2.1	1.2	2.0	1.6	0.9	0.2
Some college	81.3	12.5	98.8	30.0	98.4	9.8	68.3
College degree	n.d.	54.2	n.d.	66.0	n.d.	59.8	31.5
Postgrad. degree	n.d.	31.3	n.d.	2.0	n.d.	29.5	n.d.
Total	100.0	100.1[f]	100.0	100.0	100.0	100.0	100.0

Sources: Computed from [a]David S. Neft, Richard M. Cohen, and Jordan A. Deutsch, *Pro Football: The Early Years: An Encyclopedic History 1895–1959* (Ridgefield, Conn.: Sports Products, 1978); [b]author's study data; [c]Paul Governali, "The Professional Football Player: His Vocational Status" (M.A. thesis, Teachers' College, Columbia University, 1951), 69; [d]computed from sample drawn from *The Sporting News Football Register, 1982* (St. Louis: *The Sporting News*, 1982). [e]Two-fifths (40.5 percent) of the noncollege men in my source were listed as "no college." There were no educational data for the other players identified here as "no college," and they were presumed to have not attended college. Consequently, the noncollege cohort may have been somewhat overstated. [f]Error due to rounding off.

further education. Finally, salaries did increase, and during the hard times of the Depression, playing football provided a good paycheck for men whose classmates were out of work.[21]

NFL players active in the 1930s were among the best-educated men in the United States. Not only had virtually all of them attended college, but 85.5 percent had graduated, and more than three out of ten (31.3 percent) had earned advanced degrees (Table 11.3). They were not tramp-athletes like so many college stars of the early 1900s, but true scholar-athletes. They were much more likely to have attended college compared to other professional athletes like major league baseball players (29 percent in 1941), or the pioneer professional basketball players active before 1940 (74.4 percent).[22]

Professional players in the the postwar era were also extremely well educated. In 1949, for example, when one-fifth (20.1 percent) of college-age men (18–24) were in school, 98 percent of the players had attended college, and over two-thirds (68 percent) were college graduates. Virtually all of the professional players active in the 1950s were college men (99.1 percent), and a remarkable 89.3 percent received degrees, either before, during, or after their NFL years. Players in this era were future-oriented with aspirations that extended well beyond their gridiron careers.[23]

Although the educational achievements of players active in the 1930s and 1950s were similar, the college men in the former cohort were mainly middle class, while the men in the latter group came from more modest origins. During the 1920s and the 1930s it was very difficult for working-class youth to attend college even if they could qualify for an athletic scholarship because their families needed their wages to make ends meet. Consequently many gifted working-class athletes took whatever jobs they could get, or else they went into professional baseball instead of football because it did not require a lengthy amateur apprenticeship. By the 1940s second-generation immigrants had become more aware of the value of higher education, and many opportunities became available through academic scholarships, G.I. benefits, or athletic grants-in-aid, and the latter assistance was invaluable to highly skilled high-school football stars. At Notre Dame, for instance, one-half of its football alumni who graduated between 1946 and 1965 were of lower-class origins, double the same proportion for the total student body. Football provided a ticket out of poverty because it paid for an education rather than an apprenticeship for professional ball.[24]

The graduation rate of players has sharply declined from the 1950s rate of about 90 percent to merely 31.5 percent in 1982 and 41 percent in 1985. The graduation rate was strongly tied to race. In the 1982 sample only one-fifth (20.1 percent) of the blacks had a degree compared to two-fifths

(38.2 percent) of the whites. In 1985 it was one-third of the blacks and nearly half of the whites. A Dallas *Times-Herald* analysis of the 1985 data found that NFL graduation rates were 10 to 30 percentage points below national rates of graduation for all students (20 to 40 percent below for black NFL players). Furthermore, according to Dallas Cowboys president Tex Schramm, few players would ever return to school. This poor academic record reflected inadequate scholastic preparation, lack of interest, or limited aptitude on the part of many football scholarship holders. Some enrolled in college simply to study football, enjoy their fame, and complete their eligibility with a lucrative NFL contract.[25]

The Major College Producers of NFL Players

During the history of the NFL the prime feeders of the league have considerably varied over time (see Table 11.4). Only Notre Dame and Ohio State were continuously among the top ten producers in the league's first forty years (for the periods 1920–32, 1933–45, 1946–59), and only Ohio State was in the elite ten in 1982. None of the leading producers in the first era were located south of the Mason-Dixon line or west of Iowa, which reflected the conventional wisdom then that the quality of play was best in the East and Midwest. It also reflected the low wages paid by poorly financed teams in what was mainly a regional sport during the 1920s. NFL franchises recruited heavily from nearby sandlots and colleges and seldom could offer sufficient compensation to attract collegiate stars from outside the team's general vicinity. Thus the Providence Steamrollers relied heavily on Brown University alumni. In 1924 nine of the team's twenty-two-man roster were Brown men.

The top five producers in the NFL's early days, four of which were midwestern institutions, are long-standing football powers, but such was not the case for the second five in the period 1920–32. Washington and Jefferson, a small western Pennsylvania liberal arts college located in the football belt, had a brief but glorious era of athletic prominence when it competed successfully with the sport's major powers, as did such institutions as Carlisle and Centre College. Brown was never a major factor in the sport compared to other elite eastern colleges. Georgetown, Detroit, and Marquette were all urban Catholic institutions that provided important opportunities for local working-class second-generation Catholic youth who were the first in their families to attend college. The top ten schools together accounted for 26 percent of the college-trained football players active in the period 1920–32, the highest degree of concentration of any of the four periods under examination.[26]

Significant changes in recruitment patterns occurred in the second era, 1933–45, when schools from all sections of the country were for the first

Table 11.4 Leading College Producers of NFL Players Active 1920–82

College	Number of Players	College	Number of Players
1920–32		1933–45	
Notre Dame	65	Pittsburgh	34
Syracuse	47	Duquesne	33
Illinois	39	Notre Dame	31
Iowa	35	Minnesota	26
Ohio State	35	Oklahoma	26
Washington		Ohio State	24
and Jefferson	33	Southern Cal	23
Brown	32	Purdue	22
Georgetown	31	Alabama	21
Detroit	30	Nebraska	20
Marquette	30	Fordham	20
1946–59		1982	
Notre Dame	95	Southern Cal	41
Ohio State	48	Penn State	38
Southern Cal	41	Colorado	36
Tennessee	41	Ohio State	35
Alabama	38	UCLA	35
Georgia	37	Oklahoma	34
Wisconsin	34	Nebraska	29
Illinois	33	Pittsburgh	29
Purdue	33	Michigan	27
Miami	31	UC, Berkeley	26

Sources: Computed from data in Neft, Cohen, and Deutsch, *Pro Football; The Sporting News Football Register, 1982*.

time represented among the leading producers of NFL players. The broadening recruitment net was reflected in the deconcentration of players among the top ten producers to one in six (16 percent) compared to one in four in the prior era. Other important changes were the absence of any elite eastern college and the presence of just one school (Fordham) from the Atlantic seaboard. The two top producers (the University of Pittsburgh and Duquesne) were both from the city of Pittsburgh, located in the heart of the football belt. Small secular colleges were off the list because they could no longer afford to compete at the highest level of intercollegiate football, but metropolitan Catholic colleges were still well represented by two new schools, Duquesne and Fordham. Particularly noteworthy was the doubling of state institutions among the leading producers. This change reflected their vigorous commitment to athletic excellence to increase their prestige and to provide entertainment for the residents of their respective states, their relatively strong financial positions, and possibly their more lenient admission standards. The Big Ten was the leading conference supplier of NFL players, with three schools among the top eleven (there was a tie for tenth place), but it was outnumbered by the four independent institutions on the list.[27]

Further changes in recruitment patterns occurred after World War II. The most obvious developments were the total absence of eastern colleges from the top producers and the extraordinary dominance of Notre Dame. The decline in eastern football was not only marked by the loss of Pittsburgh and Duquesne from the top ten, but the absence of any school east of Columbus, Ohio. The huge cost of fielding a high-quality team and academic concerns led the University of Chicago to drop football in 1940. Over the next few years several other urban institutions either deemphasized the sport or dropped it altogether for similar reasons and also in response to declining box office receipts. Administrators at schools like CCNY, NYU, and Duquesne eliminated football and instead emphasized basketball, which was cheaper to sustain and easier to build up into national prominence. Los Angeles was the only major city with a football team (USC) that was a leading producer of professional football players. USC had such advantages as a sunny climate, Hollywood glamor, and an administration committed to building a national reputation through athletics.[28]

Notre Dame was such a dominant producer of NFL players in the postwar era that its output doubled that of the next closest institution, and it alone produced 5 percent of NFL rosters between 1946 and 1959. In the first three eras of the NFL it never fared worse than third, while Ohio State was the only other school even represented in those periods. At a time when other private, Catholic, and small-town colleges were dropping the sport, Notre Dame's achievement was remarkable. It successfully built on a rich football heritage and improved on it. Between 1945 and 1978 Notre Dame was ranked in the Top Ten football polls more often (twenty-five times) than any other school.[29]

Outside of Notre Dame, USC, and Miami, the major producers were state universities whose legislatures handsomely supported intercollegiate football, which they hoped would bring prestige to their home states. The most successful conference was still the Big Ten with 40 percent of the top producers, not surprising given its football tradition and proximity to the football belt. Second was the Southeastern Conference (SEC) with 30 percent, triple its prior productivity. The productivity of the leading teams epitomized the success of their entire conferences. Among respondents to my questionnaire who were active in the 1930s and 1950s, independent schools were the most successful in the 1930s (27.1 percent) and then declined sharply for the later cohort (13.7 percent). This was the same drop suffered by non-conference leaders from the era 1933–45 (45.4 percent) to 1946–59 (30 percent). The Big Ten was the most successful conference among my respondents in the 1930s (16.7 percent), followed by the PAC Eight (10.4 percent), and continued to lead in the 1950s (15.4 percent).In the 1950s the PAC Eight (9.4 percent) was overtaken by the SEC, which doubled its representation in two decades from 6.3 percent to 12.8 percent.[30]

The NFL players active in 1982 came from a wide spectrum of institutions, including black colleges, which were all but overlooked until the 1960s. Just one-sixth (16.6 percent) came from the top ten producers compared to 22.6 percent in the postwar era. Notre Dame did not make the top ten for the first time (tied for eleventh with Alabama), which reflected the school's temporarily sagging football fortunes and relative stress on academics. There was quite a change among top producers between 1946–59 and 1982: only USC, the new leader and the only private school, and OSU were still on the list. No southern school made the list, four were from the West, and the East had regained a prominent postition with Pittsburgh and Penn State. Urban institutions made a major recovery, with four in the top ten compared to just one in 1946–59. The biggest surprises were the excellent productivity of the University of Colorado (tied for second) and the University of California, Berkeley (tenth), neither of which were football powers in the late 1970s. Their success helped their respective conferences, the PAC Ten and Big Eight, tie for productivity leaders (30 percent each), followed by the Big Ten (20 percent), which fell off the lead.[31]

The Marital Status of NFL Players

The social status of men can be measured not only by their jobs, education, or family background, but also by the social background of women they married. College football players historically came from lower socioeconomic backgrounds than athletes in more elite collegiate sports like crew, golf, or tennis, but nevertheless were still "good catches."[32] Professional football players active in the 1930s and 1950s were not merely "big men on campus" who had achieved considerable fame at an early age; they were also likely to graduate with fine prospects for the future. They typically married well-educated women of similar or superior socioeconomic backgrounds (see Table 11.5). Nearly two-thirds of players active in the 1930s (64.5 percent) had college-educated wives at a time when few people attended college, and almost half of the college-educated wives were college graduates, including those with postgraduate experience. Over three-fifths (63.6 percent) of the wives had white-collar fathers, and the rest were

Table 11.5 Education of the Wives of NFL Players Active in the 1930s and 1950s

Level of Education	1930s (n = 47) (%)	1950s (n = 113) (%)
No college	31.3	29.9
Some college	33.3	34.2
College degree	20.8	26.5
Some postgraduate education	10.4	6.8
No data	4.2	2.6
Total	100.0	100.0

Source: Author's study data.

evenly divided between blue-collar and farming fathers (see Table 11.6). Nearly half of the players (48.9 percent) married within their own social class (see Table 11.7), with the mobile players slightly more likely to marry down (21.3 percent) than up (17 percent).

NFL players active in the 1950s also married well despite their more modest origins (Table 11.5). Almost 70 percent of their spouses attended college, and half of these college women earned college degrees. One-third of the wives (32.1 percent) came from blue-collar backgrounds, significantly more than in the 1930s cohort. This change reflected the lower social backgrounds of the 1950s-era players, as well as the greater accessibility of public higher education to women from less advantaged homes. Still, over three-fifths of the wives did come from white-collar families (Table 11.6). One very big difference among these women compared to wives from the 1930s was the small proportion of farmer's daughters (4.7 percent). Postwar players were less likely to marry within their class (39.7 percent) compared to the prior cohort, mainly because they were so successful at marrying up

Table 11.6 Social Backgrounds of the Wives of NFL Players Active in the 1930s and 1950s

Father's Occupational Category	1930s*** (n = 44) (%)	1950s*** (n = 106) (%)
White-collar	63.6	63.2
Blue-collar	18.2	32.1
Farm	18.2	4.7
Total	100.0	100.0

Source: Author's study data.
***p < .001.

Table 11.7. Comparison of Occupations of Fathers of NFL Players Active
in the 1930s and 1950s to the Players' Fathers-In-Law

| Players'
Status Change | 1930s
(n = 47)
(%) | 1950s
(n = 116)
(%) |
|---|---|---|
| No change | 48.9 | 39.7 |
| Married up | 17.0 | 32.8 |
| Married down | 21.3 | 14.7 |
| No data | 12.8 | 12.9 |
| Total | 100.0 | 100.1[a] |

Source: Author's study data.
[a]Error due to rounding off.

(32.8 percent) (Table 11.7). In fact they were almost twice as likely to wed upwards than downwards (14.7 percent married down). Boys from relatively modest backgrounds were able to meet and romance girls whom they normally would never have met had they not gone to college.

The Playing Career of NFL Players

The tenure of NFL players has always been brief, especially by comparison to other college-educated men who were trained for lifelong careers. Football by its nature is a dangerous and violent sport that inflicts enormous wear and tear on its players, and occasionally even career-ending injuries. Players in the early days wore little if any padding and often no headgear; today's players are heavily armored with protective equipment, but there is still a high incidence of injuries (players even employ the equipment to injure opponents, such as spearing them with their helmets). Players in the early NFL (1920–32) lasted on the average just two years because of the danger and the low pay.[33] An athlete might put in a year or two on the gridiron after college to get the sport and the excitement of the spectacle out of his system and then get on with the business of adulthood and secure a real career. A player had little motivation to stick it out until he had to be carried off the field.

The average tenure of players active in the period 1933–45 increased by about 70 percent to a still modest 3.4 years; half (52.7 percent) lasted two years or less. In the postwar period tenure increased to 4.2 years (3.5 according to a congressional investigation of professional team sports). Estimates of tenure in the mid-1980s ranged from 3.2 (NFL Players Association) to 4.5 years (NFL League Office). The respondents to my questionnaire were considerably more successful than the norm, averaging

Table 11.8 Occupational Status of Retired Professional Football Players Active in the 1930s or 1950s

Occupational category	1930s (n = 48) (%)	1950s (n = 114) (%)
High white-collar		
Professionals	16.7	15.8
Managers, high officials, and major proprietors	35.4	29.8
Subtotal	52.1	45.6
Low white-collar		
Clerks, sales, and kindred workers	18.75	21.9
Semiprofessionals	6.25	15.8
Petty proprietors, managers, and low officials	18.75	15.8
Subtotal	43.75	53.5
Total white-collar	95.8	99.1
Blue-collar	2.1	0
Farm	2.1	0.9
Overall total	100.0	100.0

Source: Author's study data.

4.9 years for the 1930s and 6.2 for the 1950s. Four to five years was the mode for the former group, and four for the latter cohort. Tenure among both groups correlated inversely with education. Men with postgraduate degrees had the shortest tenure in both decades (4.6 and 4.8 years, respectively), while nongraduates had the longest careers (5.2 years and 7.6 years, respectively).[34] The better-educated players may have simply been inferior athletes, but given the relatively modest wages of early NFL players, it is just as likely that intelligent retirees opted to leave the sport by their own choice to pursue their chosen lifelong careers. By this reasoning, the least educated players would try to hang on longer because they had fewer career options available when they retired. In today's era, when players make six-figure incomes, everyone wants to hang on as long as physically possible. Nevertheless, the average tenure is still short because of the enormous competition for lucrative NFL spots from younger, stronger, healthier, faster and (outside of top draft choices) cheaper players.

The Retired Professional Football Player

Professional football players active in the 1930s and 1950s were extremely successful after their playing days were over. They virtually all wound up in white-collar jobs, mostly in high-level positions (see Table 11.8). Slightly more than half (52.1 percent) of the 1930s group ended up as professionals, major executives, or owners of large companies—impressive accomplishments for men who entered the work force during the Depression. Players active in the 1950s were slightly less likely to secure high white-collar jobs (45.6 percent). The single most common occupation among the low white-collar retirees of the 1950s cohort was in some aspect of sales (21.9 percent), very similar to the prior cohort (18.8 percent), but players were much more likely to have coached football after retirement (14.7 percent) compared to their predecessors (8.3 percent), with the main increase coming at the professional level. The typical coaches were better-than-average players—61.1 percent had played seven or more years in the NFL—far better than the norm.[35]

The success of the 1950s retirees is very similar to that found in other surveys of NFL alumni. For example, all but one member of the 1948 champion Philadelphia Eagles secured white-collar employment, and he became a farmer. Nearly one-third of the Eagles held high-level white-collar positions, including a judge, an attorney, an oral surgeon, and a professor. These men achieved their professional status not through athletic fame but through their education. A survey of the subsequent careers of the members of the 1963 NFL champion Chicago Bears club reported similar results in 1983. All the players secured white-collar jobs, with nearly two-fifths (38.5 percent) entering high-level careers, including corporate vice presidents, a professor, and an engineer. Nearly one-fourth of the rest (23.1 percent) had a sports-related job that was probably a product of their football achievements.[36]

Sociological studies of recent retirees indicates that NFL players active in the early 1970s continued to fare well after football. Van Roe found that about 95 percent of a sample of long-term journeymen players had white-collar jobs some time after retirement, mostly in sales (48 percent) or as entrepreneurs (45 percent), positions in which athletic fame might help someone get started. Nearly one-fourth (23 percent) found employment in football, either as coaches or scouts. One-third found positions in middle management (32 percent). Van Roe found that in the early 1980s just two out of eighty-eight retirees in his study were earning less than $20,000.[37]

Yet public awareness that NFL players may fall after retirement has increased. Two prime examples are former Green Bay Packers Lionel Aldredge, an outstanding defensive end, and Travis Williams, a kickoff return specialist—both Superbowl players who ended up destitute. Williams was the subject of a television study of the homeless. The recent sociological literature has pointed to a distinct decline in the future occupations of NFL retirees. The proportion of white-collar retirees dropped to 95 percent for the 1970s compared with a rate of 98 to 100 percent during the period from

1930 through the mid-1960s. Two studies of retirees done in the early 1980s found that 10 percent were unable to secure a white-collar job within one year of leaving the sport. These results are particularly alarming because the respondents to the questionnaires in these studies were far more likely to have graduated from college (57 percent and 78 percent, respectively) than the average player, who would presumably have a harder time in the job market than these cohorts.[38]

Former football players believe that athletic fame facilitated entrance into their initial position after retirement by certifying their athletic expertise, which was an important factor for future coaches, and by helping them make valuable connections they could not have otherwise made. Athletic fame was also useful for success in occupations like sales, which required a lot of direct contact with the public to establish a good rapport with new clients. However, most respondents to my questionnaire contended that after the initial contact they had to prove themselves by performance and could not rely on old trophies to sell a product or close a deal. They further claimed that high-level competitive athletics trained them for the future by teaching them vital interpersonal skills, accustoming them to hard work, developing their self-confidence, and reinforcing the ethic of deferred gratification. A number of the NFL alumni also benefited from professional football by saving money to go into business—though rarely into such ventures as bowling alleys, restaurants, or bars, the types of small businesses popularly identified with retired professional athletes. But in the long run, as many recognized, it was their education that prepared them for long-term success. They were far better educated than the general population, and that fact was why so many of them ended up in high white-collar occupations.[39]

Conclusion

Professional football in the early 1900s was a low-paid, low-status regional game played by a mixture of college stars and local workingmen who used the game to supplement their wages and secure a respite from labor. Soon after the NFL was organized in the 1920s, the factory workers were supplanted by more experienced and more famous collegians, for whom professional footbal was mainly a part-time job. When football became a full-time occupation in the 1930s, the players were predominantly middle-class college graduates drawn from all sections of the country, although still mainly from the football belt. They were attracted by the relatively good wages and other opportunities the sport provided during the Depression, and their presence helped raise the prestige of the game. Recruitment patterns changed during the 1940s as the sport began to draw upon a new pool of poor but well-educated second-generation eastern and southern Europeans. The complexion of rosters further changed in 1946 when blacks were readmitted after a twelve-year informal hiring ban.

Since the 1950s most of the players have come from blue-collar origins. They always earned good salaries in comparison to most citizens, but it is only very recently that they have been able to secure instant wealth in what are short and physically punishing careers. In the long run, NFL alumni active in the 1930s and 1950s did extremely well with their lifelong second careers, but that success was usually more a product of their high level of education than their athletic fame. If football played a role in the long-term social mobility of former professional football players, it was mainly as a vehicle for securing college scholarships to pay for their education, not the experience or fame derived from playing professional football. This long-term career pattern seems to be changing, though. NFL players are today paid extraordinary salaries and have no need to defer gratification for the future. At the same time many are unable to handle their money and prepare for the future, and a small minority are ending up back where they started.

NOTES

I wish to thank Rick Korch and the NFL Alumni Association for their assistance.

1. On boxing see S. Kirson Weinberg and Henry Arond, "The Occupational Culture of the Boxer," *American Journal of Sociology* 57 (March 1952): 460–61, 465, 469; Nathan Hare, "A Study of the Black Fighter," *Black Scholar* 3 (November 1971): 2–8; Steven A. Riess, *City Games: The Evolution of American Urban Society and the Rise of Sport* (Urbana: University of Illinois Press, 1989), 112–13. For baseball see Melvin L. Adelman, *A Sporting Time: New York City and the Rise of Modern Athletics, 1820–1870* (Urbana: University of Illinois Press, 1986), 172–82; Rudolph K. Haerle, Jr., "Career Patterns and Career Contingencies of Professional Baseball Players: An Occupational Analysis," in Donald W. Ball and John W. Loy, eds., *Sport and Social Order: Contributions to the Sociology of Sport* (Reading, Mass.: Addison-Wesley, 1975), 461–519; Steven A. Riess, *Touching Base: Professional Baseball and American Culture in the Progressive Era* (Westport, Conn.: Greenwood Press, 1980), chap. 7; Riess, *City Games*, 86–91. Among the sociological studies examining the professional football player are Paul Governali, "The Professional Football Player: His Vocational Status" (M.A. thesis, Teachers' College, Columbia University, 1951); Larry Van Roe, "A Descriptive Study of the Effects of Career Termination upon Journeyman Professional Football Players" (Ed.D. diss., University of Georgia, 1984); Gerard F. Middlemiss, "Occupational Attainment of Former Professional Football Players" (Ed.D. diss., Rutgers University, 1984).

2. The best survey of the origins of professional football is J. Thomas Jable, "The Birth of Professional Football: Pittsburgh Athletic Clubs Ring in Professionals in 1892," *Western Pennsylvania Historical Magazine* 62 (April 1979): 136–47. See also Tom Bennett et al., *The NFL's Official Encyclopedic History of Professional Football* (New York: Macmillan, 1979), 11–14; Emil Klosinski, *Pro Football in the Days of Rockne* (New York: Carlton Press, 1970); and Harry A. March, *Professional Football: Its Ups and Downs*, 2d. ed. (New York: J. B. Lyon, 1934), especially 65.

3. Bob Curran, *Pro Football's Rag Days* (Englewood Cliffs, N.J.: Prentice-Hall, 1969), 50, 62; Ernest L. Cuneo, "Present at the Creation: Professional Football in the Twenties," *American Scholar* 56 (Autumn 1987): 54–58; March, *Professional Football*, 99, 101, 103; Riess, *Touching Base*, 164; George Halas with Gwen Morgan and Arthur Veysey, *Halas by Halas* (New York: McGraw-Hill, 1979), chapter 7; George Vass, *George Halas and the Chicago Bears* (Chicago: Henry Regnery, 1973), chapter 7; Benjamin G. Rader, *American Sports: From the Age of Folk Games to the Age of Spectators* (Englewood Cliffs, N.J.: Prentice-Hall, 1983), 182–86.

4. Quoted in C. Robert Barnett, and Linda Terhune, "When the Tanks Were Tops," *River Cities Monthly* 1 (September 1979): 18.

5. Bennett, *The NFL's History of Football*, 25–27; Rader, *American Sports*, 253; March, *Professional Football*, 250–51; Curran, *Pro Football's Rag Days*, 107, 121, 140, 184.

6. During World War II a number of teams cut costs by merging. In 1943 the Philadelphia Eagles merged with the Pittsburgh Steelers and were known as the Steagles. The Steelers joined up with the Chicago Cardinals a year later to form the Car-Pitts, an apropos name since they lost every game. See Bennett, *The NFL's History of Football*, 55–57. On salaries, see U.S. Congress, House Judiciary Committee, *Organized Professional Team Sports Hearings before the Antitrust Subcommittee*, 85th Cong., 1st. sess. (Washington, D.C.: GPO, 1958), 2598, 2629; Rader, *American Sports*, 353; *Chicago Tribune*, December 1, 1988.

7. My inferences on recruitment patterns are drawn from biographical data in David S. Neft, Richard M. Cohen, and Jordan A. Deutsch, *Pro Football: The Early Years, 1895–1959* (Ridgefield, Conn.: Sports Products, 1978) (hereafter cited as *Pro Football*). For the 1949 sample, see Governali, "Professional Football Player," 49; and for more recent data on the recruitment patterns of Division I schools, which are the main feeders of the NFL, see John F. Rooney, Jr., *A Geography of American Sport: From Cabin Creek to Anaheim* (Reading, Mass.: Addison-Wesley, 1974), 134–45; and Rooney, *The Recruiting Game: Toward a New System of Intercollegiate Sports* (Lincoln: University of Nebraska Press, 1980), chapter 6.

8. Biographical data were drawn from a questionnaire sent in 1984 to 400 randomly chosen former NFL players active in the 1930s or 1950s in cooperation with the NFL Alumni Association. I received 164 usable responses (41 percent rate of return), of whom 48 played in the 1930s and 116 in the 1950s. It is reasonable to expect that the respondents were more successful than nonrespondents. However, given the paucity of social data on NFL players, there is no way to weight the sample or otherwise adjust for the nonrespondents. Nonetheless, the results are very consistent with impressionistic evidence, as corroborated in my discussions with

football scholar C. Robert Barnett, who has done extensive oral history work with former football players, and in the sociological study of Paul Governali. See, for example, Barnett and Terhune, "When the Tanks Were Tops," 18; Governali, "Professional Football Player," 49. On the use of weighting see Steven A. Riess, *Touching Base*, 237–38.

9. Author's questionnaire; Rooney, *Geography of American Sport*, 136–37, 140–41.

10. Computed from a random sample of 454 players drawn from the biographical data in *The Sporting News Football Register, 1982* (St. Louis: *The Sporting News*, 1982) (hereafter cited as *TSNFR*). These players (whose last names began with E, F, J, J, O, P, T, and U) did not totally reflect the entire cohort of 1,591 because 37.7 percent of the sample were black compared to 52 percent of all NFL players that year; Rooney, *Geography of American Sport*, 117.

11. Rooney, *Geography of American Sport*, 112, 117, 122.

12. Ibid., 122.

13. The ethnicity of players was computed from lists of NFL players in *Pro Football*. On ethnicity in other major sports, see Riess, *Touching Base*, 184–91; Riess, *City Games*, chapter 3.

14. Computed from data in *Pro Football*. On Italian and Slavic baseball players, see Riess, *Touching Base*, 191–92. On the social status of new immigrant groups, see Stephen Thernstrom, *The Other Bostonians: Poverty and Progress in the American Metropolis, 1880–1970* (Cambridge: Harvard University Press, 1973), 136–37, 162–63, 168–73.

15. Computed from *Pro Football*; Governali, "Professional Football Player," 52.

16. Jonathan Brower, "The Black Side of Football: The Salience of Race" (Ph.D diss., University of California, Santa Barbara, 1972), 178.

17. Computed from study data and from biographical data in David Porter, ed., *Biographical Dictionary of American Sports*, vol. 2, *Football* (Westport, Conn.: Greenwood Press, 1987). Occupational categories based on Thernstrom, *Other Bostonians*, 290–92; national male occupational distribution computed from data in Joseph A. Kahl, *The American Class Structure* (New York: Holt, Rinehart and Winston, 1967), 265. Kahl includes foremen and skilled workers in one category.

18. Governali, "Professional Football Player," 53; author's study data.

19. Computed from Porter, *Football*. Roe's sample was comprised of NFL players active between 1969 and 1980 who were "journeymen" players. They were regular players of average or above-average ability. Three groups were identified: (a) men with five to six years of participation, (b) men who had been retired for one year (they averaged over nine years in the NFL), and (c) men who had been retired at least four years (they averaged over eleven years of experience). Since an average player then lasted about 3.5 years, the members of Roe's cohort were extremely successful professional athletes. Roe, "Effects of Career Termination upon Journeyman Professional Football Players," 65.

20. Computed from *Pro Football*; Laurence R. Veysey, *The Emergence of the American University* (Chicago: University of Chicago Press, 1975), 2; Riess, *Touching Base*, 236.

21. Computed from *Pro Football*. On the attraction of pro football see, for ex-

ample, Curran, *Pro Football's Rag Days*, 90, 112–13, 140, 142; Barnett and Terhune, "When the Tanks Were Tops," 18.

22. Author's study data; Riess, *Touching Base*, 180; computed from biographical data in Ronald L. Mandell, *Who's Who in Basketball* (New Rochelle, N.Y.: Arlington House, 1973).

23. Governali, "Professional Football Player," 64; U.S. Bureau of the Census, *Statistical Abstract of the United States, 1954* (Washington, D.C.: GPO, 1954), 117.

24. Author's study data; Allen L. Sack and Robert Thiel, "College Football and Social Mobility: A Case Study of Notre Dame Football Players," *Sociology of Education* 52 (January 1979): 60–66.

25. Computed from *TSNFR*; *Los Angeles Times*, January 27, 1986, 32 (my thanks to Paul D. Staudohar for this citation).

26. Computed from *Pro Football*.

27. Ibid.

28. Ibid.

29. Ibid.; Rooney, *The Recruiting Game*, 168.

30. Computed from *Pro Football*; author's study data.

31. Computed from *TSNFR*.

32. John M. Loy, "Social Origins and Occupational Mobility of a Selected Sample of American Athletes," *International Review of Sport Sociology* 7 (1972): 5–23.

33. Computed from *Pro Football*.

34. Ibid.; author's study data; John Underwood, "Student Athletes: The Sham, the Shame," *Sports Illustrated* 52 (May 19, 1980): 60. The "official" estimates of tenure vary substantially. In 1986 the NFL estimated the average tenure at 4.5 years, but the Players Association said it was 3.2 years. See *Los Angeles Times*, January 27, 1986, 32; Jill Lieber, "Pro Football," *Sports Illustrated* 68 (December 15, 1986): 72. (I am indebted to Paul Staudohar for these citations.)

35. Author's study data.

36. Ray Didinger, "The Best Team of the Best Years," *Pro* 2 (February 1983): 69–75; Rick Korch, "The Year of the Bear," *NFL Alumni Legends Magazine*, July 29, 1983, 1E–5E. (My thanks to Rick Korch for these citations.)

37. Roe, "Effects of Career Termination," 167, 189.

38. Ibid., 167; Middlemiss, "Occupational Attainment of Former Professional Football Players," 85.

39. Author's study data; Roe, "Effects of Career Termination," 162, 165.

The Role of Sports Agents 12

Leigh Steinberg

Sports agentry has grown exponentially during the past two decades. The sheer mass of agents competing to represent professional athletes is both staggering and, to some, alarming. Yet, as with most professions, sports agents are capable of producing both good and harm. Representatives perform an important role in correcting inequities at the bargaining table, assisting athletes in the transition to adulthood, and protecting the overall health of sports. Despite its necessary function, the profession of player representation has recently been subject to a great deal of well-deserved criticism for the abuses of some agents.

The Growth of Sports Agentry

"I wouldn't get discouraged, son. Maybe your new team will talk to him."
—Coach and general manager Vince Lombardi to a player
who tried to get Lombardi to negotiate with his agent.

The first agents in professional football, baseball, and basketball were often curiosities at best and liabilities to their clients at worst. Athletes in these sports have traditionally had some of the weakest negotiating power of all professionals.[1] They could not choose among the various teams that would gladly have them. They could not refuse the offer of one team and accept a better offer from another. They had no right to renegotiate contracts and had little if any job security. Thus, bringing a representative along to assist in negotiating a player's contract rights seemed fairly absurd since, as far as anyone could tell, the player had no "rights." Agents were seen, instead, as hairy-chested, gum-chewing vulgarians who took a cut of whatever the player would probably have received anyway.

The authority and position of sports agents in professional athletics, however, has changed dramatically over the past few decades. In 1975 the

United States had only a few dozen active sports agents. Today I would estimate that they number over twenty thousand. Part of this growth is due to the fact that the four major team sports are growing in general.[2] But other factors are at work as well: (1) the players' need for representation, (2) increased opportunities for representation due to changes in the law, (3) increased economic incentives, and (4) the glamour of sports representation.

Need for Representation

Representatives would not exist if there were not a market for them. They are desired because they can help to equalize the level of negotiating experience at the bargaining table and tailor a deal to an athlete's specific needs. In addition they can help prepare athletes for second careers and protect both player and sport from various pitfalls.

Representatives as Equalizers. The standard first-time negotiation features two parties: an enthusiastic and inexperienced twenty-year-old (usually from a lower-income background) and a wealthy fifty-year-old businessman.[3] The twenty-year-old has little if any knowledge of the salary structures for various teams, the current needs of the organization that wants to sign him, the criteria the team uses for formulating salary figures, or the sincerity of the claims being made by the team. The businessman usually knows all this information and far more and will be able to dazzle the young athlete with numbers that, in the final analysis, fall far below the athlete's real value.

Even if an athlete is fairly sophisticated in business matters (some Big Eight schools do allow their players to attend classes), the athlete may nevertheless be reluctant to blow his own horn or risk making boasts that could get back to his manager or teammates. Frequently the player is so enthusiastic to play in a professional league that he will not want to think about all the hazards involved and will accept virtually any offer. Moreover, most young people in their first job desire a certain amount of approval from their employers; this desire, too, will blunt an athlete's instinct to pursue a fair contract. Thus, even when athletes have a mastery of the numbers, the nature of these negotiations is inherently oppressive and likely to make them sell short.

By introducing an agent into the negotiations, the player can more accurately express his goals as a member of the team. The agent can serve as a buffer, allowing the player to make points that he would be too embarrassed to state himself. He can also ameliorate any unfair advantage that the general manager might have in terms of information by researching salaries for other players and investigating the team's long-term needs.[4]

The benefits of equalization, moreover, do not flow to the athlete alone. Frequently an agent may aid management by disabusing an athlete of the notion that he is entitled to an unreasonably high salary. Likewise, by negotiating fair contracts or by accepting blame for shortsighted demands, an agent can prevent the kind of animosity that often develops between the player and management when a player learns that he has been shortchanged in his contract. Finally, a skilled agent makes contract negotiations operate much more smoothly and amicably since both parties start with an equal base of information and are unlikely to go off on peripheral issues. Thus, despite their public protests to the contrary, many managers appreciate working with agents. Moreover, ultimately the team/player relationship is best served by fair and equitable salary negotiations.

Preparing Athletes for Second Careers. A good sports agent can furnish a certain amount of perspective and help clients prepare for their post-career lives. The agent can do this both by structuring agreements in a manner that will assure athletes of a steady net income and by mentally preparing them for the end of their sports career. Frequently, the last thing a player wants to think about at the start of his career is its end. But professional team sports careers are all too short. For the average football player the end is only 3.5 years away.[5] Without proper financial and career planning, the athlete may find himself at mid-life with no alternative skills and very little savings or income to show for his career.

Good agents structure a contract so that the manner in which a team pays a client serves that player's best interest. Good agents will avoid long-term deferred compensation, for example, since it may never materialize or could be seriously devalued by inflation. Rather, they might demand guaranteed annuities that will assure the athlete a long income stream and avoid significant tax bites at any one time. Moreover, the agent might try to get the athlete a great deal of money up front, directing the athlete to invest it with a qualified and fairly conservative investment manager.

Agents can also force athletes to confront the future. They can help them determine what career they wish to pursue if and when they can no longer play, and they can tailor compensation agreements to assist athletes in developing their second career. Moreover, they can encourage athletes—during their playing days—to develop the skills they will need to succeed at their chosen second career. Thus, the agent can be invaluable in helping athletes integrate their present and future careers.

Improve and Protect Sports. All the services agents can provide to players serve not only the players' interests but also the interests of sports more generally. For example, by preparing athletes for a second career early on, agents may reduce the risk of athletes playing too long and risking serious or permanent injury. In addition, by making athletes more responsible, they can improve the image of sports in the public's mind—thereby encouraging attendance at professional sports events.

Thus while player representatives may not have seemed particularly valuable to Mr. Lombardi, they provide several essential services to sports in general. They protect both athletes and owners from their own excesses; they promote more equitable and just contract agreements; and they reduce the chance of strikes and unseemly conduct by athletes that lessen respect for professional sport.

The Modern Rise in Agentry

The growth of player representation cannot be explained merely by the need for representatives since that need has always existed. Other factors have combined to give it greater opportunity for expression and to induce individuals to enter the field.

Greater Opportunities to Become an Agent.   One reason why sports representation has grown has been changes in labor law over the past two decades that have expanded athletes' rights and produced greater opportunities for representation. Actions have been filed opposing the draft and restrictions on player movement in football,[6] baseball,[7] basketball,[8] and hockey.[9] In *Mackey v. National Football League*, a federal court of appeals found that NFL restrictions on player movement at the end of a contract term (the Rozelle Rule) violated the Sherman Antitrust Act—however, a substantial portion of the rights recognized had been bargained away by the players' union.[10] These cases created a qualified right to free agency under narrow circumstances.[11] More important, they gave the unions bargaining power to place a greater number of issues on the negotiating table and to remove some of the longer-term restrictions on free agency.[12]

The expansion of player's rights has provided new opportunities for negotiation. In addition, there are no limits on who can represent a player in these negotiations. Sports law is one of the few areas of law in which any person may practice without a license. Currently anyone can be a sports agent; and, regrettably, just about anyone is. The ranks of the NFL's sports agents include stockbrokers, insurance salesmen, former coaches, and could even include, if any of them so desired, mass murderers.[13] To become certified, one need only fill out some forms from the NFL Players Association and attend its one-day seminar. Thus, many of the people presently working as sports agents have no training in negotiations, business accounting, law, or finance.

Strikingly, to become an agent one does not even need to have a client.

The National Football League Players Association reports that nearly half of the agents registered to represent NFL draftees do not even represent one athlete.[14] Thus, while changes in law have created increased opportunities to practice player representation, virtually the only qualification required of representatives is a business card.

Increased Financial Rewards. Obviously, financial conditions have also contributed to the rise of sports agentry. During the 1970s the USFL and WFL competition in football, the advent of free agency in baseball, and the increase in television revenues all contributed to produce higher salaries for athletes, and with it higher fees for agents.[15] The average salary of major league baseball players rose from $34,092 in 1972 (the year before arbitration started) to $510,000 in 1989—an increase of 1,500 percent; in contrast, average earnings in the United States rose by only 162 percent.[16] With most agents taking a fixed percentage of their client's salary, salary increases have meant a concurrent increase in agent earnings. Moreover, the biggest contracts are becoming disproportionately bigger. In the first year after baseball arbitration, the highest paid baseball player, Reggie Jackson, earned $180,000—three times the paycheck of the median player in his league. Today Orel Hershiser, at $3 million, earns seven times the median player's salary.[17] Thus, a particularly great incentive exists to represent the hottest athletes each year.

Glamour. Finally, sports law has a natural allure; it offers the opportunity to socialize with celebrities. For many people, being part of professional sports is a longtime fantasy. With increases in law school and business school enrollments, it is not surprising that more and more graduates see sports agenting as a way to apply their skills while doing something more interesting than the usual work in major firms. Moreover, as agents, they may acquire a certain amount of celebrity status themselves. Agents have written best-selling books,[18] hosted television programs, appeared in ads or fashion spreads, and generally maintained profiles nearly as high as those of their clients.

The Dangers of the Increase in Sports Agentry

[Sports agent Lloyd] Bloom argues that the allegations [that he committed extortion by threatening three student-athletes with physical harm] fail to allege that the actual or threatened use of force was wrongful.

—Judge Marovich, federal judge for
the Northern District of Illinois

The increase in the number of agents has created a corresponding increase in the competition for the talented players coming out of school. It is this competition, and the fact that it goes largely unregulated, that poses the greatest danger both to sports agentry and to sports themselves. Specifically, it causes agents to lure college athletes to sign with them before they are eligible and thereby violate NCAA rules. In doing this, agents may jeopardize the athlete's career, instill unrealistic expectations that will hurt the athlete later, and create conflicts of interest that cause the agent to underrepresent his client's interests.

NCAA Eligibility Rules

Under NCAA rules, a student-athlete is ineligible to participate in a sport if he enters into a contract to be represented by an agent to market his athletic skill, takes any pay in exchange for a promise to retain an agent after he graduates,[19] or receives any other financial assistance other than from his school, family, or for work unrelated to athletics.[20] To ensure compliance with the regulations, the NCAA requires every athlete to sign and submit each year statements attesting to their eligibility.[21]

The purposes of these prohibitions are clear. The NCAA does not want its athletes distracted from their studies or subjected to divided loyalties during their college careers. More practically, the NCAA recognizes that an agent has nothing in the way of services to provide to an athlete before he becomes eligible. Rather, early signings are an open invitation to take advantage of athletes' short-term interests, which they will likely pay a steep price for later in inadequate representation.

Early Signing. Despite the NCAA's clear prohibition against early signings, I'd estimate that 25 percent of the outstanding college football and basketball seniors every year have already signed with an agent. The competition for athletes has caused some agents to stoop to unthinkable practices.[22] The most infamous recent example involved sports agents Norby Walters and Lloyd Bloom. In March 1989 a federal jury in Chicago convicted Walters and Bloom of fraud in signing college seniors before the athletes were eligible.[23] Walters and Bloom committed fraud both against the athletes (by convincing them that signing would not affect their eligibility)[24] and against the NCAA (by inducing the athletes to complete fraudulent eligibility forms).[25] Besides the usual inducements—such as money, cars, and parties—Bloom and Walters employed less common tactics, such as threatening to break the fingers of athletes who refused to sign.[26]

Although Bloom and Walters may be seen as anomalies, other less egregious violations occur, and on a much greater scale. Several college seniors have told me how agents have approached them offering money, cars, loans, and even women as inducements to sign binding representation contracts.

Athletes who sign early are invariably shortchanged for several reasons. First, the types of agents who try to sign athletes early are usually those with the least interest in the athlete's well-being (since early signing risks both the player's eligibility and ultimately his college's eligibility). Thus, even if the player does not lose his eligibility, the mere fact that he has signed early almost guarantees that the agent will be the sort who focuses exclusively on the bottom line and will not provide the various other non-remunerative services essential to good representation.

Second, because these transactions are illegal, the athletes involved are unable to investigate fully the qualifications of the agent or to seek the advice of their coaches, family, or alumni. They cannot evaluate the character, track record, and reliability of the agent. As a result, they very often place undeserved trust in their agent, thereby inviting abuse. For example, frequently an athlete entrusts the power of attorney to an agent, which gives the agent access to his bank accounts. An unscrupulous agent may either divert funds from the bank accounts or make poor investments.

Third, agents who make substantial investments in an athlete may develop strong conflicts of interest that affect their negotiating. As noted, many agents either pay athletes directly or give them "advances" beginning at the time of signing. If an agent has a lot of money invested in an athlete or runs into financial difficulties, he may be inclined to structure deals that protect his own financial position at the expense of the athlete. The agent may, for example, agree to long-term deferred compensation plans that give the athlete very little immediate money but assure the agent a hefty immediate commission. Similarly, the agent may boost the athlete's bottom-line salary by sacrificing important protections such as injury guarantees, renegotiation schedules, and option clauses.

Fourth, agents who sign athletes early must often rely upon exaggerated claims in order to lure clients. This exaggeration may cause an athlete later to hold out unreasonably because his agent has promised him an exorbitant salary prior to his rookie negotiations. In that case, when the team makes a reasonable offer, the rookie feels mistreated by the team and may refuse to train at camp, hurting his chances for a successful career.

Finally, agents who engage in early signings generally are only interested in negotiating contracts. They do not attempt to educate the athlete about what types of compensation are in his long-term interest, to brace the athlete for the possibility of injury or failure, or to counsel the athlete about how to manage his new status responsibly. Thus, even if an athlete does manage to get a good contract, he frequently will fail to manage it wisely. Instead, the agent becomes just another person who coddles the gifted athlete so that when his playing days are over, he has no independent life skills to draw upon.

Correcting Abuse: Regulation and Realism

With perhaps over 25 percent of the nation's top college athletes violating their eligibility, current enforcement methods are clearly inadequate. Punishing agents who violate these rules, of course, is appropriate, but this strategy alone will not eliminate the problem. Rather we must also eliminate the pressures and circumstances that cause athletes to sign early in order to dry up the market for early solicitation. This tactic requires that we regulate the sports industry to protect athletes from the advances of unscrupulous agents and demands that we restructure some of the rules involving scholarships, eligibility, and the draft in order to eliminate rules that create economic pressures but do not serve any beneficial purpose.

Regulation

Presently no effective body exists to regulate agents.[27] Anyone, for example, can represent a professional baseball or basketball player without restriction, although the duration of these contracts may be limited. Professional football's rules are only slightly less unobtrusive. In football, the players' union certifies agents for veteran players, and that certification may be revoked for various violations.[28] However, the union places no such restrictions upon agents for rookies or college students. As any athlete will tell you, these first contracts are the most important in their careers since they usually set the standard by which salary increases are measured and establish the schedule for renegotiation. Moreover, since most players' careers only last a couple of years, their first contract may be their only contract.

Efforts at state and self-regulation have provided little relief. Some states have tried to impose regulations. For example, California requires player representatives who are not lawyers to be bonded if more than 50 percent of their practice involves representing athletes.[29] Unfortunately, the exceptions swallow the rule. Virtually no player representative in the state admits to devoting full-time work to player representation. The penalty for failing to obtain a license or for violating bonding rules is usually minimal: loss of the fee for that transaction. Moreover, the risk is small since these penalties are rarely enforced. The bureaucrats on the state labor commission staff, which is in charge of enforcement, are not familiar with agents' tricks and thus are unable to identify instances of abuse.[30]

Other efforts to organize a voluntary self-regulating group have had only marginal success. For example, the Association of Representatives of Professional Athletes (ARPA) has developed a code of ethical standards for player representatives.[31] However, because membership is voluntary, only 150 of the 20,000 professional agents in the United States currently belong to the organization.[32] Thus, there is no nationwide group that oversees the qualifications of agents for rookies, and there is only the barest regulation imposed upon agents for veterans.

The answer lies in expanding union certification to agents for all professional athletes—rookies and veterans. The unions have the best sense of what constitutes adequate representation and have the strongest interest in upholding high standards—since their members are usually the immediate victims of shoddy representation. By entrusting certification to the unions and requiring that all agents register with a union, athletes could be assured that their interests will be protected before they sign on with an agent. At the very least, coaches and athletic directors should assemble athletes and parents once a year to explain the NCAA rules, the procedures for economic assistance, and the dangers of early signings. In addition, schools should develop advisory panels to check the qualifications of agents intending to sign senior athletes and generate some form of on-campus certification.

Realism

Regulating agents is not enough. As long as there are captive athletes anxious for money and great economic incentives to signing such players, agents will be inclined to cheat. To fully protect the interests of young athletes we need to reevaluate our current treatment of unsigned athletes and tailor reform to address those factors that have caused them to pursue hazardous paths. Specifically we need to do the following: (1) provide stipends to college athletes to reduce the financial pressures they face in college; (2) eliminate what is left of the eligibility requirements so that athletes who wish to turn professional may do so immediately; and (3) abolish the draft, thereby providing athletes with greater control over their future.

Supplementing Athletes' Scholarships. The majority of scholarship athletes who eventually receive offers from professional teams come from underprivileged backgrounds.[33] These athletes rarely have disposable income to spend on dates and evenings out like many of their peers do. Moreover, as athletes, most of them are prohibited by NCAA rules from working part time to supplement their scholarships.[34] Thus, with no way to enter the professional ranks until they graduate or wait out the graduation of their classmates, and with no money of their own, they are easy prey to persons who would give them money during their college years—regardless of the ultimate cost.

Colleges should redefine scholarship payments to include $300 to $400 per month in spending money. As it is, a scholarship provides only the bare necessities. A modest monthly stipend would allow the athlete to lead a normal social life and operate on the same economic plane as his nonscholarship friends, without being tempted to seek illegal advances from agents. In addition, if an athlete has special economic emergencies, the college he attends and the NCAA should provide for a system of student loans and aid to be repaid at a later date. In this respect, athletes should have the same opportunities as nonscholarship students on campus.

Eliminate Eligibility Requirements in Football. Although there is no way to document which student athletes sign early, my experience has been that most of them are football players. Unlike basketball and baseball, football virtually forces its athletes to remain on campus until they graduate or until their class graduates. Some improvement toward a free labor market for football players occurred in 1990, when the NFL revised its rules to allow juniors to be drafted, provided they forfeit their remaining college eligibility. However, this policy still forces young men with no academic proclivities to remain captive on a college campus. Yet it provides no service to anyone and only invites illegalities.

The ostensible reasons for having eligibility requirements are that without them (1) most athletes would not attend college and thus would be deprived of an important educational opportunity, and (2) college football would be destroyed by losing the best young athletes. Both of these claims have proved to be wrong. First, although I am an enthusiastic supporter of college education and college sports, I believe that my values should not govern others. I would encourage athletes to attend and graduate from college because I believe it is valuable to them as persons and in laying the foundation for their second careers. But the choice should be theirs, not mine. Many individuals—not just athletes—do not have any interest in higher education and are not forced to pursue it. It is easy to understand why athletes who do not wish to go to college generally perform poorly. I have yet to find a professional tackle who was convinced that a mastery of Shakespeare had improved his ability to sack a quarterback.

Rather than furthering education among athletes, forced attendance probably impairs educational advancement. College squads are corrupted by the handful of players who have no interest in studying and are able to sway the players who might have developed intellectual interests while in school. Moreover, the presence of these players merely reinforces and emphasizes the stereotype of the antiintellectual athlete, colloquially referred to as the "dumb jock." This is bad for the image of sports and may give aspiring athletes the incorrect sense that somehow there is a necessary division between intellectual curiosity and athletic skill.

The notion that eligibility rules protect college football from being pillaged by the NFL is equally unconvincing. In the first place, most NFL teams are not interested in players who have not had three or four years of seasoning. The time after high school allows the players to mature both physically and emotionally. It develops their skills and gives the NFL more of an opportunity to evaluate those skills before committing to hire new players. Thus, even without the restrictions, most professional teams would not recruit athletes until their final year of college.

Likewise, most athletes would not be so easily recruited. Student-athletes remain in college for reasons other than because they "have to." Frequently they develop strong ties to their school team and their friends. Indeed, athletes often stay in college an extra year if they think they can help their team in a future bowl performance. Moreover, contrary to public perception, many athletes do care strongly about education and believe it is important to get their diploma.

The truth of these statements has been borne out by the experiences of college basketball and baseball players. No one would contest that despite the absence of draft prohibitions, college basketball has never been better or more popular. The vast majority of NBA draftees continue to come from colleges, and more than half of those have stayed through graduation.[35] Likewise, over 70 percent of the first-round draft choices in professional baseball players in 1988 were college juniors and seniors.[36] Moreover, these percentages have been rising consistently over the past five years.[37] By contrast, even with its purported protections, only 35 percent of the National Football League's players have college diplomas.[38]

Finally, in practice the draft prohibition rules have become a sham, riddled with exemptions and exceptions. For example, the NCAA has carved out such principled exceptions as the Barry Sanders "if-your-team-is-suspended-and-prohibited-from-appearing-on-TV" exception. Many other players find themselves breaking NCAA rules just to be free of the eligibility requirements; they may sign early in order not to be eligible. By keeping athletes in school, then, the regulations serve only to keep many gifted players out of both school and the NFL. College sports has not been ruined by early departures of baseball or basketball players, nor would it be in the case of football.

Eliminate the Draft. My most radical proposal for protecting athletes and sports from the various corrupting influences in professional athletics today is to get rid of the professional draft. Some may argue that this proposal is motivated by self-interest; without a draft, players' salaries would certainly increase, and with them agents' commissions would rise as well. However, my desire to remove the causes of salary deflation is only part of it. Rather, the draft provides none of its purported benefits and stifles proper representation.

Advocates of the draft claim that it is necessary to keep professional leagues competitive. They reason that if there were no draft, then the best players would always flock to the "glamour" teams in New York and California; these teams would become the most successful; and, in turn, the best teams would be able to establish dynasties by continuing to attract players with more money and promises of league championships.

In fact this scenario is completely unrealistic. Players sign with teams for a wide variety of reasons. Phil Simms, Ken O'Brien, and Joe Montana would not want to be on the same team for any amount of money since each of them wants to be a starter and to star in his own right. Players may be motivated by geography, family, lifestyle, endorsement opportunities, coaches, organizational structure, or a team's style of play. The variety and number of these factors suggest that they will distribute randomly across the country. One need only consider professional baseball to see that this projection is true. Professional baseball players may move between clubs after six years of play. Nevertheless, a few years ago the World Series was slugged out between the glamour boys of St. Louis and the beach lovers of Kansas City.

It should strike any normal person as incomprehensible that an accounting firm in Biloxi, Mississippi, would be able to get the rights to a UCLA accounting major. That the student would have no choice but to join the Biloxi firm or abandon his or her profession. More shocking still would be the case if, after working for the Biloxi firm for four years, the accountant still could not transfer to a Los Angeles firm without first giving Biloxi Bros. an opportunity to match the Los Angeles offer or demand compensation from the Los Angeles firm in the form of its top recruits. Viewed as a whole, this system is about the closest thing we have to indentured servitude in the United States. Rather than keeping the leagues competitive, the draft serves no purpose other than to depress football players' salaries, cheat them of their ability to choose a lifestyle and team that suits them best, and force them to make concessions not required of their counterparts in other fields.

The Continuing Need for Sports Representation

As the preceding discussion suggests, many tasks remain for player representatives as a collective group. Athletes in several sports remain undervalued and thus require more effective contract representation. Furthermore, player representatives should make a commitment to protecting young athletes and to upholding the traditions of U.S. sports in order to use their role for the benefit of the entire athletic community.

The Continuing Undervaluing of Athletes

Despite frequent complaints that athletes are overpaid, athletes in most sports do not receive nearly the amount that they would command in a free market system. For example, in basketball, where there are few restrictions upon movement between teams, the average player receives approximately $600,000 per year. In baseball, where players are drafted but entitled to salary arbitration after three years and free agency after six, the average salary is $500,000. In football, the draft and rigid restrictions on negotiations have produced only a handful of free agents in its thirty-year history. Due to these market restrictions, the average football player earns only $240,000, or less than half what their basketball-playing counterparts make.

Athletes, like all other individuals, deserve to earn what a free and fair market will pay for their services. Agents, then, must continue to work to eliminate inequities in the professional leagues and enable athletes to obtain just compensation.

The Duty to Protect Athletes

Protecting athletes' pocketbooks should only be one aspect of the agent's greater duty to serve the athlete. The most important function for agents is to anticipate their clients' needs and provide athletes with personal and professional advice to help them function as mature members of society.

I tend to have a unique perspective on sports law. I entered the field of player representation largely as a favor to Steve Bartkowski. Steve, a first-round draft pick from Berkeley, was a friend of mine, and he wanted someone who understood his values to represent him rather than someone who would merely focus on the bottom line. Accordingly, my main concern was with producing a result that would not jeopardize our friendship. I knew that Steve, like many other athletes, had often been excluded from negotiations that ultimately involved his future. So I made a special effort to explore his present needs, his goals, his values, and his personal feelings in order to structure a contract that would accommodate his unique personality.

Agents are in a rare position to provide this type of personal service. Unlike coaches, agents generally have regular casual access to their clients; they travel together and spend many long days discussing their negotiating strategy. This allows agents to learn a great deal about athletes personally.

Thus agents can identify potential pitfalls in their clients' approach to their careers. They can caution athletes about the risks of injury and not succeeding in the professional leagues. They can encourage athletes to take seriously the obligation to be a role model. They can counsel athletes to pursue other fields as well as sports and to maintain a good perspective on what will inevitably be a short career.

Agents should recognize that they have a fiduciary duty to their clients. Athletes must, necessarily, place great faith in their representatives. Thus, beyond merely complying with regulations, agents should maintain the highest standards of good faith and fair dealing when transacting business with or on behalf of their athletes. In all phases of negotiations and also in offering advice, agents must place the athlete's interests ahead of their own.

All of this having been said, the agent should not coddle the client. Too often gifted athletes have had a series of "parent" figures willing to take care of their problems since the time they started in the little leagues. Coaches smoothed over eligibility problems, alumni made them gifts and managed their money, parents cut them slack on household chores, friends helped them with their homework, and teachers evaluated their work with a generous eye. As a result, many athletes entering professional leagues are not capable of managing their personal lives responsibly.

Agents should not fall into the trap of feeding on an athlete's dependence. Rather, the representative should attempt to wean athletes off of these dependent relationships. They should encourage athletes to learn how to use expert advice and direct them toward qualified lawyers, accountants, investors, and public relations personnel. The athlete must learn how to direct these various people and to take responsiblitiy for his life and career.

Duty to Protect Sports

Finally, the agent has a duty to protect sport itself—both out of respect for sport and to ensure its future as a forum for athletes to apply their skills. This means that agents have a duty to protect the financial and institutional integrity of their clients' sports.

I would never want to represent the highest paid athlete in a dying sport. Fortunately, I am not faced with that prospect, for professional sports today are at an economic peak by any measure. The NFL expected to gross over $1 billion in 1989. Franchise values are up; Seattle sold its team in 1988 for $90 million after paying only $12 million for it in 1976.[39] Television revenues are up, too; since 1979 the average television revenues per team have risen from $2 million to $30 million in 1991. Finally, average ticket prices, reflecting popular demand for sports, were up from $7 to $22 in 1989.[40]

This growth raises a ticklish issue: how high can players' salaries climb before fans rebel against increasing ticket prices? Most observers recognize that if ticket prices rise too high, attendance will slump, and with it, home viewing will slump as well. No one wants to watch a baseball game when they see that the stands are two-thirds empty. Yet people mistakenly believe that higher ticket prices are the result of passing on the costs of high salaries to fans. In fact, NFLPA studies have shown that ticket prices bear almost no relation to average team salary and are instead related primarily to how well a team performs.[41] Salaries tend to be a function of what owners can collect from fans, rather than vice versa.

Nevertheless, agents must help sports remain vital and accessible to fans in other ways. One way, of course, is by encouraging athletes to comport themselves well. By acting as role models and contributing to the community, athletes raise the overall level of respect for sports and encourage support at their events. Athletes should also be willing to make sacrifices for the fans. One of my players, for example, offered to take a pay cut if management would cut ticket prices. Furthermore, all the clients I work with agree to contribute a portion of their salary to charities and to work on behalf of those charitable organizations. In this way, we perform a service not only to the sports community but to the community at large.

Conclusion

In an industry like professional sports, the stakes are so high, the fortunes so visible, and the injustices so embarrassingly apparent, it is inevitable that someone must be blamed for the excesses. Many sports agents deserve the blame they receive because they prey upon naive young athletes and desperate owners—constructing contracts that satisfy the objectives of no one but themselves. Yet the profession of representing athletes has the potential for providing enormous good. Responsible agents can correct inequities, aid in the development and maturation of individual athletes, uphold the best standards for sports, and channel the vast energies of the sports industry toward social betterment.

NOTES

I would like to thank research assistant Jeffrey Bleich (J.D., University of California, Berkeley, 1989; M.P.P., Harvard University, 1986; B.A., Amherst College, 1983) for his work on this chapter.

1. See generally, P. Staudohar, *The Sports Industry and Collective Bargaining*, 2d ed. (Ithaca, N.Y.: ILR Press, Cornell University, 1989).

2. Franchise values in each of the major sports—football, basketball, and baseball—have more than tripled in the last decade. In the last decade alone, television

revenues have increased from $2 million per team to more than $9 million in basketball and $17 million in football. Telephone interview with M. J. Duberstein, director of research, National Football League Players Association, October 2, 1989.

3. See, for example, *Los Angeles Rams Football Club v. Cannon*, 185 F. Supp. 717, 726 (S.D. Cal. 1960), describing young athletes as frequently "untutored and unwise"; see also Fox, "Regulating the Professional Sports Agent: Is California in the Right Ballpark?" *Pacific Law Journal* 15 (1984): 1231.

4. See R. Ruxin, *An Athlete's Guide to Agents* (Bloomington: Indiana University Press, 1983), 19.

5. Data from National Football League Players Association.

6. See, for example, *Kapp v. National Football League*, 390 F. Supp. 73 (N.D. Cal. 1974), aff'd, 586 F.2d 644 (9th Cir. 1978) cert. denied, 441 U.S. 907 (1979); *Smith v. Pro Football, Inc.*, 420 F. Supp. 738 (D.D.C. 1976) aff'd in relevant part, 593 F.2d 1173 (D.C. Cir. 1978); *Mackey v. National Football League*, 407 F. Supp. 1000 (D. Minn. 1975), aff'd, 543 F.2d 606 (8th Cir. 1976), cert. dismissed, 434 U.S. 801 (1977).

7. *Flood v. Kuhn*, 407 U.S. 258 (1972).

8. *Robertson v. NBA*, 389 F. Supp. 867 (S.D.N.Y. 1975).

9. See, for example, *McCourt v. California Sports, Inc.*, 460 F. Supp. 904 (E.D. Mich. 1978), rev'd, 600 F.2d 1193 (6th Cir. 1979); *Philadelphia World Hockey Club v. Philadelphia Hockey Club*, 351 F. Supp. 462, 499 (E.D. Pa. 1972).

10. 407 F. Supp. at 614.

11. See *Mackey*, 543 F.2d at 614; *McCourt*, 600 F.2d 1193 (6th Cir. 1979); *Wood v. NBA*, 602 F. Supp. 525 (S.D.N.Y. 1984), aff'd 809 F.2d 954 (2d Cir. 1987); *Zimmerman v. NFL*, 632 F. Supp. 398 (D.D.C. 1986).

12. See, for example, Collective Bargaining Agreement between National Football League Players Association and National Football League Management Council, December 11, 1982, Art. XIII.

13. See generally, S. Gallner, *Pro Sports: The Contract Game* (New York: Scribner, 1974), 51, describing instances in which players have been represented by builders, teammates, dry cleaning managers, building contractors, athletic trainers, stockbrokers, and accountants.

14. Currently only 300 out of the 510 agents registered with the NFLPA have a client, according to data provided by the NFLPA in 1989.

15. See Gallner, *Pro Sports*, at 53–54.

16. Data provided by the Major League Baseball Players Association.

17. Ibid.

18. See, for example, D. Dell, *Minding Other People's Business* (New York: Random, 1989); and M. McCormack, *What They Don't Teach You at Harvard Business School* (New York: Bantam, 1985).

19. National Collegiate Athletic Association, *NCAA Manual 1989–90*, By-Law 12.3 (1989).

20. Ibid., By-Law 14.1.3.

21. Ibid., By-Law 3.2.4.5.

22. See Johnson and Reid, "Some Offers They Couldn't Refuse," *Sports Illus-*

trated, May 21, 1979, 28, discussing ethically questionable activities by agents in the recruitment of student athletes; see also P. Axthelm, "Marvin Barnes and the Work Ethic," *Newsweek*, December 2, 1974, 61.

23. *U.S. v. Walters*, 711 F. Supp. 1435 (N.D. Ill. 1989). Judge Marovich's statement, quoted earlier, is at p. 1449.

24. Ibid.

25. Ibid., 1444.

26. Ibid., 1438.

27. See generally, Dunn, "Regulation of Sports Agents: Since at First It Hasn't Succeeded, Try Federal Regulation, *Hastings Law Journal* 39 (1988): 1031; Fox, "Regulating the Professional Sports Agent: Is California in the Right Ballpark?"; and Comment, "The Agent-Athlete Relationship in Professional Sports: The Inherent Potential for Abuse and the Need for Regulation," *Buffalo Law Review* 30 (1981): 815, 817n. 12.

28. By-Laws of the National Football League Players Association.

29. California Labor Code, Section 1500, et. seq.

30. For an extensive discussion of the shortcomings of the California law, see Fox, "Regulating the Professional Sports Agent," 1241.

31. Association of Representatives of Professional Athletes, Code of Ethics (1988).

32. See Fox, "Regulating the Professional Sports Agent," 1238.

33. Data provided by the NCAA Office of Legislative Services.

34. National Collegiate Athletic Association, *NCAA Manual 1989–90*, By-Law 12.3 (1989).

35. Data provided by the National Basketball Association.

36. Data provided by the Major League Baseball Players Association.

37. The number of college graduates in the NBA has risen from 35 percent to 50 percent since the early 1980s, according to data provided to the author in 1989 by the National Basketball Players Association.

38. From a survey conducted by the National Football League Players Association.

39. Telephone interview with M. J. Duberstein, director of research, National Football League Players Association, October 2, 1989.

40. Ibid.

41. Data provided by the information service of the National Football League Players Association.

Are Olympic Athletes Professionals? Cultural Categories and Social Control in U.S. Sport 13

John J. MacAloon

The conventional manner of approaching the question in my title would be to produce a genus/species definition of the terms "amateur" and "professional," then to determine ways in which Olympic athletes do or do not conform to that definition. Though purely artificial, this procedure fulfills valued canons of academic rationality and assuredly can be useful for certain intellectual purposes. However, the exploration of these terms as cultural categories in practical, public use requires a different approach. The polysemous messiness of "amateur" and "professional" as lexical items in everyday discourse is precisely what is to be preserved and explored from a cultural point of view. Scrutinizing rather than suppressing historical shifts and cultural ambiguities in the content and application of these terms opens the way to monitoring changing institutional arrangements in sport itself. Wider sociocultural processes of great theoretical interest open themselves to revelation under this double representational and institutional approach.

Olympic Sport: Past Certainties and Present Ambiguities

The complex history of terms cannot be surveyed here. Suffice it to say sport historians have repeatedly shown that any claim that the categories of sports amateur and professional were ever fully fixed and consensual is mistaken, an ideological rather than a historical assertion (e.g., MacIntosh 1963, Pleket 1976, Dunning and Sheard 1979, MacAloon 1981, Young 1984). As Nietzsche taught, the certainties of the past are inevitably artifacts of the forgetfulness of the present. The French terms for "those who love" and "those who profess" were borrowed into English in the eighteenth century, quickly given a political reference—the *Oxford English Dictionary* cites Burke in 1797 on "amateurs and even professors of revolutions''—and already applied to sport by the opening of the nineteenth. From the time of their major extension through European and North and South American cultures of sport in the mid-nineteenth century, amateur and professional have represented vexatious and disputed classifications precisely because of their political and social control implications.

Rather than some unilinear and universal development, a full cultural history would reveal a most variegated picture. In different periods and locales and from different social vantage points, the terms have variously centered on social class, educational status, aesthetic style, and occupational relations. In certain instances, their persuasive force has been principally located in moral overtones; in other instances, in purely organizational and administrative criteria. At times, who is an amateur has been clearer than who is a professional; at other times, the reverse has obtained. In different contexts, transnational, national, or local usages have predominated. In some cases, actual or imagined perceptions of distant others, cultural ancestors (''Greeks'' or ''English gentlemen'') or present political rivals (''Russians''), have controlled domestic understandings.

In recent U.S. history, as shall be seen, public attributions of professional status and ''professionalism'' have variously focused on the following: economic considerations (direct payment for play in the form of a wage, indirect income in commercial endorsements or personal appearance fees); occupational characteristics (full-time activity, vocabularies of labor, worker/boss relations); legal entailments (binding contracts with commercial or public corporations and agents, unionization, collective bargaining, and the right to strike; judicial, legislative, and federal agency protections with regard to work rules, health, and safety); moral and lifestyle factors (totalizing devotion, drugs, sacrifice, and risk); and ideological implications (the ''professing'' of discrete sets of values and imageries on behalf of some class or status segment). Amateurs and amateurism are concepts dialectically constructed according to contrasts along these same criteria, from the historical-etymological (what it is that the ''amateur'' is understood to love) to the economic (the contrast, say, between expenses and wages), to the imputed status origin of games and players (rowing, say, as against boxing). Reducing this complexity to the univocality of a definition by arbitrarily selecting and privileging from among such distinctive features does not get us very far. An alternative would be to abandon the terms ''professional'' and ''amateur'' altogether, but since they have been, and remain, constitutive in American public speech, this strategy likewise ensures the impossibility of any true cultural analysis. Instead, the cultural authority of the categories and the complicated range of their features and referents must be respected, however incommensurable and contradictory they may be. Only such an approach can bring institutional arrangements, historical formations, and changing patterns of speech into proper analytical relations.

At the same time, while remaining attuned to semantic polysemy and mutability, it is possible to recognize periods of greater or lesser stability in these classification systems. In the United States, we appear to have entered a period of notable uncertainty as to how to classify Olympic athletes. Although the public worries about the persistence of an intrinsic love of the game among major league baseball, basketball, and football players, the desire to maintain this putative aspect of "amateurism" does not interfere with the unambiguous classification of these athletes as professionals. The situation is now fundamentally different with regard to Olympians, particularly the majority who are not one step away from NBA, NHL, or ice show contracts. In the Olympic situation, changes popularly labeled as "professionalization" are disorienting, even perhaps fatal to the decades-long synonymy between "amateur" and "Olympic" sport in American culture.

This is hardly to say that notable cases of disturbance have never occurred before. They range from the cases of Jim Thorpe (pay for play) and Eleanor Holm ("immoral" violations of training, professional lifestyle) to the Adidas/Puma payoffs of U.S. sprinters in 1968 (commercial endorsements), and they span the Avery Brundage era. This era was notable for Brundage's largely successful codification of an American opposition between the "amateur ideal" and the "entertainment values" of professional sport, which the era reflected back upon itself (Guttmann 1986, but compare Boorstin 1961, to see how mainstream conservative Brundage's values were). These "individual cases," however, typically were construed as exceptional. Their very scandal, regardless of public judgment for or against the particular athletes involved, reflected a broad agreement on the categorical level of cultural understanding.

The Cold War Consensus

Between 1952 and 1976 quite a different factor supplemented, and in many contexts dominated, domestic criteria for estimating the amateur status of U.S. Olympians. In the broad context of cold war ideology, the Olympic success of the Soviet Union, and later of the East bloc countries, demanded popular U.S. conventions of distinction between "our athletes" and "theirs"—political culture carrying over into sport culture and to no small extent reconstituting it. The amateur/professional dichotomy was bent to a new political purpose, with adjustments made accordingly to the features associated with the terms.

While material motivations were regularly ascribed to Soviet Olympians, such as apartments, cars, well-salaried ghost jobs, and foreign travel, purely economic criteria were insufficient for classifying them as professionals. The absence of commercial sport in the Soviet Union, the impossibility of personal service contracts between athletes and corporations, and the claim of government sports organizations on all foreign earnings (appearance fees, under-the-table prize money, etc.) were facts too well known to permit full reliance on this one Anglo-American cultural construction of the professional. The concept of "state amateur," cynical and ironic in U.S. usage, was born to accommodate this ambiguity. In a way not noticeable before, state involvement and direct investment in the organization of Olympic sport became prima facie evidence that state athletes could not be amateurs but must be professionals. The state joined, and in some contexts replaced, class, status, and occupational groups as the relevant social segment for categorizing amateurs and professionals.

Reflexively, this rhetoric demanded redoubled efforts to ignore and to deny the existence of any engagement of the U.S. federal state in U.S. Olympic sport. Ironically, or perhaps not, these efforts occurred during a period of great increases in such engagements, each legitimated in large part by "the need to compete with the Russians." These initiatives ranged from a large program of covert operations under the cover of sport initiated by the Central Intelligence Agency (MacAloon 1986a) to transfers of public property to the United States Olympic Committee (USOC). Eventually they culminated in the President's Commission on Amateur Sports and the Amateur Sports Act, which made the USOC a federally chartered agency responsible ultimately to Congress (Chalip 1987). Awareness of state-centered Olympic sport in other Western democratic capitalist countries—West Germany, for instance, but more strikingly Canada, the "Big Red Sports Machine" just to our north (Macintosh, Bedecki, Franks 1987; Kidd 1988)—was also militated against in order to preserve the structural relation of oppositions, U.S.: USSR :: Olympic amateurs: Olympic professionals.

On the motivational plane, a further entailment of this interpretive structure was a reemphasis of U.S. ideological individualism. "Theirs" win because they are creatures of the state and of large sports bureaucracies, and they are drug-filled, soulless automatons of dubious gender besides. "Ours" win (or do not) out of force of character and free individual commitment to excellence. Drug use is minimal among our "real men and women," and no social institution owns or controls them. The traditional refusal of the U.S. public to consider college scholarships for future Olympians to be a form of professionalized pay-for-play was reinforced, a stance Western and Eastern Europeans have always found quaint, to say the least.

The USOC and the National Governing Bodies (NGBs) of the Olympic sports almost entirely escaped the increased media attention and public scrutiny that was developing with respect to large organizations in other branches of sport such as the NCAA, the NFL players' union, and the baseball owners' cartel. Finally, residual leakages from this interpretive package were stopped up by blaming the International Olympic Committee (IOC) for its hypocritical inability to recognize "shamateurism" when it saw it. Attacking the IOC for its willingness to command 140-odd (now 165-odd) nations to play by U.S. rules was at least no more irrational than insisting that sport should be organized by the private sector in Soviet society, where no such sector existed (Riordan 1977).

The Institutional Revolution in International Olympism

In the late 1970s and the early 1980s, sweeping changes in the international Olympic movement provided the key context for undermining this popular consensus in the United States. Under IOC president Juan Antonio Samaranch, a new generation of IOC leaders came to power who viewed Olympic amateurism as an outdated ideology and who committed themselves to eliminating it. The Samaranch line reproduced key aspects of the traditional U.S. position, namely that it was unfair to allow the state-supported athletes from the socialist countries to compete while prohibiting or limiting commercial support for athletes in capitalist countries. Devoted to its own transnational ideology of excellence, in some ways more radical than the U.S. and Canadian versions, the Samaranch faction wanted to ensure that the world's best athletes competed in the Games regardless of their means of support.

On the one hand, the IOC leaders were obsessed by the fear that the world championships then multiplying in the different sports might offer better competition than the Olympics because of more liberal eligibility rules set by the international sports federations (IFs) in their own domains of authority. On the other hand, the IOC believed—not necessarily correctly—that the U.S. television networks and large multinational corporations would open their pocketbooks wider if Western professional athletes, especially the media stars, were eligible to compete in the Games. Important changes were permitted in the IOC's share of the television revenues, particularly its share of the burgeoning U.S. network fees, which between 1960 and 1984 grew from $400,000 to $225,000,000 for the Summer Games and from $50,000 to $91,500,000 for the Winter Games. (The 1992 figures are $401 million and $243 million respectively.) The IOC's Lausanne headquarters were modernized and expanded, and additional salaried staff were hired. For the first time IOC members' expenses were paid, which broadened potential membership beyond rich individuals or government-sponsored persons. Olympic delegations and sports development programs in the "Third World" were funded through the Olympic Solidarity Commission. These programs, in turn, were crucial in gaining Southern Hemisphere votes for Samaranch's elections; for demonstrating concern over the increasing concentration of medals in the developed countries as Olympic sport became yet more oriented to high performance; and for countering alienations from the center, especially in Africa and South Asia, which had contributed over the years to actual or threatened boycotts and breakaway movements. Keeping the television money flowing had become an organizational and political necessity, and liberalizing eligibility rules was understood to be a crucial factor to that end, despite the fact that it could only exacerbate in the short term the athletic inequality between the rich and poor countries. The relationship of these developments to the simultaneously great increase of NCAA scholarship athletes from European, Latin, and African countries is rarely recognized. In pursuit of their own athletic aggrandizement, U.S. colleges offered more scholarships to athletes from foreign countries, which encouraged the outflow as these athletes sought to gain the top-level Olympic preparation that increasingly they could not afford to provide for themselves.

A series of steps were correspondingly taken by the IOC beginning in the 1970s. The terms "amateur" and "amateurism" were banished from official Olympic publications and speech in favor of the expressions "Olympic-eligible" and "Olympism." Rule 26 of the *Olympic Charter* concerning athletic eligibility was gradually liberalized, in particular to expand trust fund arrangements by which appearance fees, commercial endorsement funds, direct grants from government and civic sports bodies, and eventually prize money could be openly earned by individual athletes. In theory at least, these funds were to be kept in escrow accounts managed by sports authorities, against which athletes could draw "training expenses" only, with the principal becoming available to them only upon retirement from competition. Such indirection in the new arrangements was required as a strategy of apparent compromise with the proponents of the old amateur order, who had by no means yet been rooted out of the IOC and IFs. The more important carrot offered to sports bodies in these arrangements, however, was the decision to leave to the national federations (NFs) and national Olympic committees (NOCs) the rights and powers to negotiate the actual terms of these contracts and to take a cut of the athletes' earnings as recompense for administrative, training, insurance, and similar expenses involved in "the opportunity to compete." Since the NOCs alone could certify and enroll athletes for Olympic competition, this policy left the competitors and their agents in the capitalist countries in a relatively weak negotiating position.

This is particularly true in the United States, with its lack of a strong government oversight agency and any tradition of collective bargaining by Olympic athletes, and given the anathema status here of wage-labor discourse in the Olympic context: key facts to which I shall return. For the moment let it be noted that in the old days of shamateurism, as I can personally testify, athletes complained that event promoters stole their earnings, giving back a pittance in under-the-table appearance fees or, in the case of equipment companies, a javelin or a pair or two of shoes in return for intensive product advertising. Today progressive (or merely self-interested) U.S. Olympic athletes charge the sports federations themselves with exploitation since the monies they "skim" from athletes' earnings go in large part to the salaries and expenses of the National Governing Body officials who have authority over the trust fund arrangements in the first place. These practices further militate against any stirrings among Olympic athletes to unionize, and the sports bodies continue to protect their own economic interests by lobbying hard against any increased federal government involvement as not being "the American way." The new modes of Olympic professionalization turned out to be precious little different from the old amateur codes as means of keeping control of the market for athletic labor out of the laborers' hands.

Commercial journalism, too, follows a similar paradigm. Print and broadcast sport reporters make their money off the doings of athletes, and few could survive in their trade without athlete interviews. Yet any suggestions that athletes should be recompensed for their time and the newspapers they sell are met by journalists with scepticism if not derision. When they are not sophisticated enough to argue that sport as news is a public good equivalent to political coverage, journalists often handle the issue with a remarkably self-promoting and sport-deprecating assertion: that if it were not for the publicity reporters generate, the general public would know little and care less about the achievements of athletes. If anything (so I have heard one or two sports journalists outrageously assert), they should have a right to a portion of the athlete's earnings. In major U.S. professional sport, television rights do contribute to the pool of funds from which athletic salaries are paid, and media celebrity can unquestionably augment the price of athletic labor in individual markets. In professional and Olympic sport, by contrast, print, academic, and non-live-coverage broadcast organs largely get a free ride. Rights-holding Olympic broadcasters, as earlier noted, contribute substantially to defraying the costs of staging the Games and the overhead of the Olympic movement as a whole. During the 1984–88 quadrennium, the USOC realized $19.4 million in television revenues from its share of the Calgary and Seoul contracts and from broadcasts of its own Olympic trials and festivals. But, as will be noted momentarily, little of this money has gone directly to athletes. (A new deal with the IOC could bring USOC television receipts to $40 million in 1989–92 period.)

In the early 1980s, the IOC executive board became convinced that the huge U.S. television contracts would not last forever and that alternative sources of funding had to be found for the future. Under the tutelage of the late Horst Dassler of the Adidas Corporation, based in West Germany, the IOC took initiatives to capture the worldwide corporate sponsorship market for the Olympics, in effect taking back from each national Olympic committee what had been its exclusive right to market the Olympic emblem in its individual country. International Sports Leisure, Inc. (ISL) was created in Switzerland as the house marketing firm of the IOC and given exclusive rights in this regard. The ISL was half-capitalized by Adidas, received a quarter of its financing from the huge Japanese advertising firm Dentsu, and obtained the rest from smaller investors. The success of the Los Angeles Olympic Organizing Committee (LAOOC) and the USOC in 1982–84 in raising corporate funds was based in part on U.S. public ignorance of, and disinterest in, the network of organizations in Olympic sport. Corporate marketing departments and advertising firms quickly discovered that the public did not know the difference between sponsorship of the LAOOC, the USOC, an NGB, or a particular team or athlete. As a consequence, huge sums of money flowed in all directions. The IOC and ISL were able to capitalize on the uniqueness of this U.S. situation and use it to convince recalcitrant NOCs to sign contracts with the ISL that would at least return to them a portion of the proceeds from centralized Olympic marketing in their countries—larger shares for rich and active countries like the United States, Britain, and West Germany and token but desired payments for smaller, poorer countries with few internal marketing opportunities. Strapped for hard currency and wooed with further private deals by Dassler, the socialist countries quietly signed up as well, though their public statements continued for some years to express horror at the "commercialization" and "sell-out" of the Olympic Movement and its sacred symbols.

During the late Brezhnev period, such considerations, along with internal research indicating that medal counts would not be greatly affected among the most powerful countries, led the Soviets to abandon serious opposition to the liberalization of the eligibility rules. Indeed, throughout the developed countries, the two processes—commercialization and liberalization of the rules—now marched hand in hand. With the IOC, IFs, NOCs, and NFs now firmly engaged in corporate licensing and marketing, it became even more difficult to argue that athletes themselves should be amateurs, reimbursed only for the expenses of training. In country after country, including those of the British Commonwealth where the volunteer system had been pioneered and remained culturally and organizationally dominant, the old forces of amateurism were crushed: by *dirigisme* from above; pressure by athletes from below; a press ever-ready to pounce on "hypocrites"; and the growing cadres of paid professional coaches, managers, marketeers, and political operatives within their own increasingly rationalized sports organizations. A new piece of language came into being to represent and encompass these changes. The commercial elites that had for so long been abhorred, the press, which had been barely tolerated in the Brundage years, and government sports bureaucrats and UNESCO officials recently perceived as threatening usurpers—all now were welcomed to join athletes, coaches, and Olympic officials as full and valued members of "The Olympic Family."

American Institutional Transformations

The massive U.S. press mobilization surrounding the Los Angeles Games slowly began to offer these international transformations to the attention of the U.S. public. While the traditional public disinterest in the international complexities of Olympic organizations persisted, related domestic developments destabilized the prior cultural consensus as to the amateur status of U.S. Olympians. For the first time in 1984, U.S. athletes were plastered across billboard, magazine, and television ads prior to the Olympics. A number, like Edwin Moses, Carl Lewis, and Mary Decker, carried six-figure incomes into the competitions with them, instead of having to wait (on the traditional basketball–figure skating–hockey model) to make their money after the Games were finished. Public chatter about new stars born in the "minor sports" in the Los Angeles Games—such as Greg Louganis and Mary Lou Retton—had them "making millions" after the Olympics.

Such facts and perceptions challenged USOC persistence in its old rhetoric that our Olympians were poor while their Soviet and East German rivals were rich in government-supplied resources. Familiar patriotic and "American way" appeals for private donations were further compromised by the publicity attending the USOC's $110 million share of the windfall profits from the Los Angeles Games, not later balanced by equal media attention to the decision to create an Olympic Foundation with this money, with the principal untouchable and only a portion of return on investment available for athletic programs. While the nationalist public relations effort proclaiming the Los Angeles Games to be the first entirely funded from private corporate sources succeeded in restricting public consciousness of the $90 to $120 million of U.S. taxpayers' funds that went into them in the form of various public services, other factors were chipping away at the USOC's assertion, packaged within the old cold war rhetoric, of disinterest in U.S. government financial involvement. Taxpayers in nine states were shortly to find check-off boxes for Olympic donations printed on their returns, and the USOC was actively lobbying Congress for a federal tax check-off bill, as it was for the Olympic Coin Act (which eventually was passed in 1987 and resulted in $25 million for the USOC by 1989).

The Soviet-led boycott of Los Angeles refocused attention on the U.S.-led boycott of Moscow, against which U.S. public opinion was widely viewed to have turned as the electorate had turned against that policy's "ineffectual" author. In 1984 Walter Mondale was running for president. His prior role as Carter administration point man in the 1980 boycott, including his reported suggestions to the USOC that federal funds might at last be forthcoming for Olympic sport in return for a vote against participating in Moscow, was unearthed and discussed in some newspapers. The Reagan campaign was able to profit from the situation (MacAloon 1987), both rhetorically and in campaign fund-raising. Several factors—the president's focus on the Olympics in his nomination acceptance speech at the Republican National Convention, *Time* Man of the Year Ueberroth's backing of Reagan, and the widespread Reaganite interpretation of the Los Angeles Olympics as a feast of reborn U.S. patriotism and entrepreneurial spirit—further threatened the popular claim that, in contrast to the USSR, the U.S. state and national politicians do not interfere in Olympic sport. Thus this crucial feature of the U.S. concept of amateurism in the 1960s and 1970s was weakened.

An increasing number of public revelations of psychopathology among U.S. Olympians and their abuse of performance-enhancing drugs added to the disruption. During the ABC coverage of Los Angeles, former champion and commentator Cathy Rigby was permitted briefly to discuss the epidemic of bulimia and related eating disorders among female gymnasts. (What remains to this day a taboo subject in the U.S. press, since they cannot be so easily passed off as "personal problems," are the physically crippling effects top-level training will have on perhaps 40 percent of the gymnasts by early middle age). Extensive doping had long been attributed to East bloc athletes and rationalized in the case of U.S. athletes caught or suspected of the same by the "need to level the playing field with communist rivals." But serious cases, hard to ignore, were multiplying in competitions where state socialist athletes were not present. A dozen U.S. athletes were either caught during testing at the Venezuelan Pan American Games or else departed precipitously prior to testing. In the aftermath of the Los Angeles Olympics, several members of the successful U.S. cycling team were revealed to have been blood-doped, not privately but by an official team physician and trainer. America's marathoners began to charge one another with the practice, and our best Nordic skier freely admitted to it after his medal-winning world championship performance. Rumors began to fly that, with regard especially to anabolic steroids, the U.S. testing program was fraudulent because athletes were tipped off in advance, protocols were purposely lax, and positives were not being reported. Perhaps the magnitude of the problem was not widely apparent to the U.S. public before the Ben Johnson affair, the Dublin and Biden inquiries, and the suspicious behaviors of U.S. track and field winners in Seoul and the flurry of accusations against them. But the groundwork for such questioning had been laid well before 1988.

Behaviors in which life, limb, and emotional balance are intentionally placed at risk in response to financial incentives and the pressures of top-class performance were in the past much more frequently associated with, and tolerated in, professional sports like football and hockey, whose players are culturally understood to be adults, the players' unions (if not the federal Occupational Safety and Health Administration) are there purportedly to protect them, and the contractual financial rewards to individual players can be great. Still today, high-school, college, and Olympic steroid testing programs are subjects of serious congressional, judicial, and popular concern, while the public continues to tolerate the bad joke of NFL practice in this area. In the mid-1980s, the evidence of physical destruction turning up in Olympic sport could not be squared so easily with the popular imagery and discourse of young athletes as role models, of unquestioned physical health and moral character, representing before the world the best things about the United States. Such was the general climate in which runner Kathy Ormsby—a "perfect young person" to all who knew her and a future Olympic star who had set a collegiate 10,000-meter record only weeks before—ran through a curve during the NCAA final, continued desperately on under the stands, over a fence, and down the highway to a bridge off which she threw herself, landing meters below in a not-quite-dead heap, a quadriplegic for life.

Public Devotion and Classificatory Confusion

It is not easy to make empirically defensible assertions about how many U.S. citizens had collected into their consciousness such events and conditions. Some similar gestalt clearly inflicted the cultural imaginations of more than the small handful of Americans who professionally follow the Olympic movement, including the four or five U.S. journalists who emerged during this period with international sport as their full-time beat, for whom the conventional U.S. categories of understanding were already dubious. Such survey data as we have seem to show clearly that broad segments of the U.S. population continued strongly to differentiate Olympic from other types of athletes and to do so largely in the terms of the earlier cultural constructions. At the same time, the logic of the total classification system was clearly becoming more confused. This situation proved at once threatening to existing sports organizations and manipulable by them.

An academic empirical study of the U.S. television audience for the 1984 games, conducted by the Annenberg School of the University of Southern California and based upon extensive telephone surveys and interviews with a carefully constructed and representative sample of adults, revealed "a relatively consensual core of ideas and sentiments in the thinking of the public about the games. These ideas essentially affirm the Olympic tradition and are distinct from the public's thinking about professional sports" (Rothenbuhler 1985, 1988, 1989). Moreover, these studies demonstrated on the demographic front, and with regard to the social stratification of attention, that the Olympic broadcast audience composed "a unique communicative gathering," not only in its size and celebratory patterns of viewing but in its attraction of attention across lines of age, gender, race, education, occupation, and income. Correlations between socioeconomic indicators and amount of Olympic viewing are smaller than those associated with general television or prime-time viewing, and the Olympic television audience is "markedly less gender divided" than that for regular professional and collegiate sports programming (Rothenbuhler 1985, 1988).

Measures of what these researchers call "Olympic cynicism"—but which, for our purposes, are better thought of as charting the contamination of Olympic/amateur with professional values—were sought through surveys preceding and following the games. While 71 percent of the respondents felt prior to the Games that "the Olympics had become mainly an arena for international political disagreements," the day after the Games concluded 52 percent favored the presented alternative—that "the Olympics and politics remained pretty much apart." Before the Games 68 percent thought them "too closely tied to commercial interests," and 53 percent continued to think so afterward. A slight plurality favoring the proposition that the Games had "become too much like show business" became a 68 percent declaration against this proposition after the Olympics concluded. Rothenbuhler is surely correct to stress the relative consistency and stability of these figures, the absence of pronounced "media effects" upon them, their suggestion of a strong core of consensus on Olympic "values and symbols," and—more contentious and challenging (MacAloon 1989)—their indication of the appropriation of the Olympics as a Durkheimian celebration of U.S. civil religion. For our purposes, we may note the differences between the final two measures. Though not very significant from a statistical point of view, it is at least suggestive that more citizens in this sample worry, and worry more consistently, about "commercial interests" in Olympic sport than they do about the "show business" feature of the category of professionalism consolidated in the Brundage years.

Unfortunately, we do not have comparable data from 1976 to 1988 to confirm the trends discursively constructed above. However, from 1987 we have another bit of survey research that further suggests increasing ambiguities in the categorical picture. A walk-up poll at the Epcot Center at Walt Disney World, conducted in association with The Roper Organization, Inc. and on behalf of the USOC, questioned 5,101 U.S. adults and 2,207 persons under eighteen on Olympic athletes and professionalism (Epcot/Roper 1987, USOC 1987). Gender, age, and region were the only socioeconomic data on respondents apparently collected. Adult responses were tabulated separately on additional questions concerning their preferred mix of Olympic funding. Typical of market research, the Epcot/Roper poll is less scientific and more distant in space and time from the actual celebration of the Olympics than the Annenberg data. Seeking indications of quotidian cultural categories and attitudes, the analysis centers on the poll's own language and question construction as much as responses to it. The USOC's rhetorical appropriation of the results likewise is useful in indicating interested institutional manipulation of the cultural system.

The wording of the first query asserted a three-category U.S. sports system rather than a simple opposition between amateurs and professionals. Respondents were asked to agree or disagree with the proposition that "U.S. Olympic athletes are held in higher esteem than other athletes, amateur or professional." Sixty-four percent agreed with this statement (24 percent strongly, 40 percent somewhat; women 6 percent more than men), 21 percent disagreed (men 6 percent more than women, few of either sex "strongly"), while 10 percent had no opinion and 5 percent did not respond. These results are, of course, ambiguous with regard to which of the two opposed categories is providing the point of distinction for respondents—the "or" should have been "and"—and contaminated by poll-sponsor identification and the absence of efforts to consistently check questions and controls against multiple responses. "Esteem" is, furthermore, highly ambiguous. Still, at least among those with marked responses, something is being suggested about the willingness of substantial numbers of U.S. citizens to recognize and operate with this categorical discrimination. Instead of loyalty to professional and school athletes, the high percentage of "somewhat" responses (taken together with the "no opinions") could be read as indicating confusion about, or a refusal to accept, the constituting categories themselves. With regard to the main thesis offered in this chapter, these two interpretations are not alternative but complementary.

Much greater polarization of opinion was discovered in response to the proposition that "Professional athletes should be allowed to compete in the Olympic Games." Overall, 40 percent agreed (27 percent strongly), while 49 percent disagreed (42 percent strongly). Men were divided equally in their opinions, but women were somewhat more opposed (52 to 33 percent among women; 52 to 46 percent as against the men). But which "professional athletes" did respondents have in mind? NBA stars, baseball players, hockey pros, or track and field athletes with six-figure incomes already Olympic-eligible? What is a "professional" to these respondents? The results are not disambiguated by an accompanying query as to whether "U.S. Olympic athletes should be able to earn funds to support themselves while training through personal appearances and commercial endorsements." Seventy-three percent agreed (48 percent strongly), while only 18 percent disagreed. But appearance fees and commercial endorsements, while surely indicators of "professionalism," are not the same as salaries and prize money. Moreover, the phrase "support themselves while training" renders the question equivocal in another way. Is it merely living expenses that are being proposed or a bankable surplus income or profit? After all, reimbursement of training expenses is a practice that has been perfectly conformable with the amateur ideal for decades; the only thing that would raise Brundage's eyebrows here is the commercial source of the money and the requirement of services rendered in return.

Additional questions about funding asked of the adults further functioned to suppress and avoid the new categorical uncertainties in a sponsor-interested way. Respondents were asked who they thought "should provide primary funding for U.S. Olympic athletes" and given a choice among "The Federal government" (15 percent), "Corporations" (9 percent), "Private citizens" (5 percent), and "Individual athletes" (4 percent). Now it is interesting that such a relatively large percentage were willing to entertain primary government funding and that so few appear to accept the USOC's own solicitory propaganda about the "American way" significance of private donations. (On another question, 66 percent revealed that they had never contributed to the USOC and would not contribute to it.) Moreover, despite the framing force of the previous question, respondents seemed quite dubious about the possibility or desirability of athletes supporting themselves, though if the "corporate" figure is added, one can divine more consistency. Taken together, these findings further suggest the breakdown of the cold war consensus, but they cannot bear too much interpretive weight since the whole question is vitiated by the option of responding "Some combination of the above" (64 percent, of course, did). Since things cannot be "primary" and "some combination" at the same time, the whole question is illogical and, indeed, nothing less than an endorsement of the status quo—that is, of the USOC's right to carry on as it chooses. This effect is additionally licensed by equivocation as to whether "funding for U.S. Olympic athletes" means direct payments to them or to the USOC for its programs.

This same equivocation appears in whether "commercial sponsors are necessary to allow U.S. athletes to compete with the rest of the world's athletes." Seventy-two percent thought so, while 10 percent did not and 12 percent were "uncertain." In the USOC press release, the prose interpreting responses to this question removes the ambiguity in a most dishonest and self-serving way by stating that "commercial sponsors who aid in supporting the Olympic Committee are definitely *not* frowned upon by the American public, according to this special Epcot poll." The respondents are just as likely to have felt they were being asked another version of the earlier question concerning direct payments to athletes by corporations. On the face of it, these data seem to conflict with the Annenberg findings that a majority of the U.S. public, though slim after three weeks of Olympics television viewing, feel the "Olympic Games have become too closely tied to commercial interests." But, here too, the question is fuzzy and fails to distinguish between commercial support for Games Organizing Committees, NOCs and NGBs and direct payments to individual athletes, or, for that matter, a superabundance of obnoxious and disruptive television commercials and signage. Of course, as previously pointed out, the U.S. public in general—in contrast to the publics of other democratic capitalist countries, where Olympic sport is more important more of the time—have not been much informed about, or interested in, these organizations and administrative distinctions.

Let me raise two final notes about the Epcot/Roper Poll. Another question asserted that "individuals should be able to make a tax-deductible contribution to the U.S. Olympic Committee, which would be deducted from their income-tax return through a voluntary check-off on the income-tax form." The report's accompanying prose stresses that 59 percent agreed, a number that might suggest that cold war antipathy to federal government involvement is breaking down, at least to the extent of willingness to permit the state to forego a small portion of its tax dollars in favor of the USOC and allow it to meet the expense of processing this mechanism. But again the message is quite mixed. Despite the question's attempt to press every prose button to reassure even the most laissez-faire, cold war, Reaganite libertarian ("individual," "tax-deductible," "contribution," "voluntary"), 23 percent still disagreed (17 percent strongly), and 13 percent declared themselves "uncertain." A 59–36 percent victory on the most benign proposal for new government involvement looks far less compelling as evidence for a substantial shift in public opinion on the general practice. Nor is it likely that the outcome would have differed greatly had a dollar amount been mentioned, which the USOC was clearly unwilling to do. To specify the standard one dollar risked offsetting new monies with decreased contributions from existing donors: the "I gave on the tax return" syndrome. To specify more than one dollar might worry the reticent and seem pretentious next to the check-off box, which assigned only the specified amount for federal funding of elections. Rothenbuhler (1988, 68) notes the same pregnant parity in another key: the percentages of Americans reporting interest in following the Los Angeles Olympics and the 1984 presidential elections were identical.

Finally, positioned directly between the "greater esteem for Olympians" and "should professionals compete" questions, came one on the desirability of mandatory drug testing. Drug use, an entailment of some conceptions of professionalism, was entering public discourse about Olympic/amateur sport. Eighty-six percent of respondents wanted mandatory testing, while only 8 percent were opposed. However, the question neither set forth which drugs were to be tested for (narcotics and "recreationals" or the performance-enhancing anabolics, beta-blockers, and emetics) nor did it specify whether the testing was to be announced versus unannounced. The question and its responses produced another tough-sounding brief that in fact left the USOC free to rest, if it wished, with the status quo.

The Historical Logic of Cultural Contradiction

I have suggested that the contradictions, ambiguities, and confusions apparent in these shards of survey data about the general state of mid-1980s U.S. opinion on whether Olympic athletes were professionals did not owe exclusively to public fickleness, proximity to successful home-country Games, unscientific and poorly designed surveys, and the self-serving manipulation of evidence by polling organizations and their clients. Rather, I assert, these data accurately reflect an underlying disordering of the cultural system of athletic classifications, in which a clinging to the received oppositions went paradoxically hand in hand with a deepening scepticism about them.

In support of this claim, anecdotal evidence—but not the less patterned and empirical—can be offered from another methodological arena, the full-time ethnography of Olympic speech. Between, say, 1983 and 1987, in casual conversation overheard or directed at me and in formal interviews that I conducted or was made the object of by journalists, I heard the repeated assertion (uttered sometimes quizzically, often smugly, occasionally in pique) that Olympic athletes "are all professionals anyway." What was new was that the reference was to U.S. Olympic athletes, not to East bloc ones. Yet if the conversation proceeded long enough or grew intense enough, such assertions were almost inevitably followed by bizarrely contradictory ones, reproducing features of the old conceptual order.

One example will have to stand as an emblem for the lot. In 1985 a radio interviewer, not a sport specialist, opened by asking, "Olympic athletes are professionals now, aren't they? With Carl Lewis making more money than most NFL players, it's pretty hypocritical to keep talking about Olympic amateurism. Those days are obviously long gone. When are the old men who run the Olympic Committee going to wake up and face reality?" I responded at some length that the IOC had not used the word "amateur" for years; the USOC retained it only for rhetorical, largely fund-raising purposes; and U.S. popular and journalistic speech preserve the old categories more than the speech of Olympic organizations does or public discourse in much of the rest of the world. I added that there was a new IOC generation of very worldly younger men and fewer but influential women, and if bankable income was the criterion of professionalism, then Carl Lewis was most untypical of American Olympians, but if the questioner meant freedom to make money where one could, then his characterization was becoming fair enough.

These responses irritated rather than satisfied the reporter; they were not what he expected or wished to hear. For a long time, I attributed such reactions largely to journalists' frustration with professors who make simple things too complicated and are unable to speak in "sound bites." I have subsequently observed, however, that the new breed of highly informed U.S. press specialists on Olympic sport, practiced in speaking in media-conventional ways, elicit exactly the same responses from their journalistic brethren when they answer this question as I did. Of course, few reporters—indeed few U.S. citizens—like to have it suggested that their queries are naive or parochial, particularly with regard to sport. In the United States, sport is the special site of democratic discourse in the sense that expert opinion is little privileged over the right all citizens feel to their own interpretations. But there is more in this example. After abruptly changing to other subjects, which occupied most of our quite friendly conversation, when the interviewer returned at the end to the language of amateurism and professionalism, it was to make rather different assertions than those with which he began. "Of course, we won a lot of medals in Los Angeles, but the East bloc nations weren't there. Our kids have to sacrifice so much and rely on their own and their families' resources. Can they really compete any more with the Russians and the East Germans, with all the special schools and coaches and rewards those governments give their athletes?"

Here, as elsewhere in U.S. discourse, Olympic athletes were now professionals, but then again they were not. The old system of classification was stretched and strained, but no one was quite prepared to abandon it or to face the implications of reordering it by reversing the terms. No longer amateurs, Olympians were not simply professionals either. What were they? Rapid institutional changes had generated a cultural gap or lag, and when confronted with it, persons and groups struggled vainly to overcome it by recourse to the outmoded language of cold war consensus. Specialists like James Riordan and Wojciech Liponski note that the sports establishments of state socialist countries have been sites of particular resistance to glasnost and perestroika. At least with regard to common speech, the same has been true of the U.S. sports establishment.

The Press Rebellion of 1988

Events in 1988 confirm that such changes had been occurring in previous years and that new and important challenges to public conception and discourse, and perhaps a real transformation of the cultural structure of sport categories, are now underway. Some of these changes are quite remarkable to the longtime observer of U.S. Olympic sport. Critical awareness of specifically institutional changes and conditions crossed over from the world of specialists into the mass circulation dailies and sports and news weeklies. It is far too soon to tell how extensively they have spread from there into popular consciousness, but there is the clear possibility that Olympic sports organizations themselves are becoming a "public problem" in the strict sense given the phrase by Joseph Gusfield (1981). If so, a methodologically "bifocal vision," in Gusfield's further characterization of the sociology of culture, is necessary to draw language and institutions into a common eye.

As in the 1972–76 period, which led to the President's Commission and the Amateur Sports Act (Chalip 1987), current developments were spurred in part by the "disappointing" medal counts that were calculated for Calgary and feared for Seoul. These were associated with marked episodes of coaching and administrative incompetence described as "rank amateurism" in the press and watched or read about by millions of Americans. Similar conditions had obtained in 1984, but a few breakthrough skiing performances in Sarajevo (Farrell 1989) and the artificially inflated medal counts in Los Angeles due to the socialist boycott had tempered attention to them. Still more in 1984, the disturbed and disturbing condition of the Soviet leadership and the height of Reaganism at home had generated a revival of cold war rhetoric and a "feast of patriotism in reborn America" atmosphere around the Los Angeles Games. The politically conservative USOC leadership served itself well in such conditions. The general intimidation of the press during this period has been widely discussed (e.g., Wills 1987).

With Peter Ueberroth as *Time Magazine*'s Man of the Year and Ronald Reagan in second place, few journalists were inclined to question U.S. Olympic institutions. Instead, as we have seen, attention to undeniable changes in the system tended to be focused upon the "professionalization" of athletes themselves, seen as a group through the lens of individual stars.

In 1988 quite different conditions obtained: the Reagan period was stuttering to a close, Gorbachevism was in full swing, the possibility of an end to the cold war was regularly discussed, and through much of the year a liberal Democratic administration seemed a real possibility. Moreover, the new IOC breed—notably vice president Richard Pound, a straight-talking Montreal lawyer, and Anita DeFrantz, a black U.S. Olympian who had sued the USOC over the Moscow boycott—became visible in the U.S. media, curtailing the old IOC-bashing habit. And the USOC itself publicly panicked amid the disappointing and even tragic athletic results of Calgary.

Out of fear that fund-raising for Seoul would be harmed and, above all, that Congress might undertake fresh hearings, the USOC explicitly admitted its difficulties by announcing a task force to investigate itself. Doing so in the middle of the Calgary Games ensured the widest media coverage and appeared to callously disregard the morale of U.S. athletes yet to compete. The impression of incompetence even in admitting incompetence was deepened by the seemingly bizarre appointment of George Steinbrenner, owner of the New York Yankees, to head the commission. Steinbrenner had no discernible prior involvement in Olympic sport, and his record in professional sport was a common object of ridicule. Further USOC cultivation of money, business connections, and status-glamour seemed the only rationales for this appointment, especially when the commission announced that it would have nothing to say for over a year.

This time when the media set to work, the USOC and the U.S. NGBs joined the more traditional targets of criticism. Olympic athletes, previously portrayed as spoiled, egotistical, and rich, now were discovered—within limits, of course—to be the victims of adult money-grubbing and incompetence. Earlier exposés by Mary Ann Hudson of the *Los Angeles Times* of tax violations, potential Justice Department investigations, and administrative chaos in the U.S. Gymnastics Federation (USGF) were picked up and expanded to other sports bodies by *Newsweek* in an August article. Its headline, "Off Balance in Amateur Sports," showed the persistence of the traditional categories; its subhead suggested the strikingly altered sense of where the bad new professionalism resided: "Extravagant bureaucracies and coaching conflicts are an Olympic trial for American athletes."

The bulk of the article—written chiefly by Pete Axthelm, a football and horseracing specialist whose previous Olympic journalism had mostly reproduced conventional U.S. ignorance about the IOC and Olympic history (Axthelm 1987)—was devoted to exposing in various ways where the money and the perks in the newly "professionalized" Olympic system were really going. "Dollars for Desk Jocks" proclaimed a prominent sidebar: "Sports federations fill tall buildings and fat committees, while athletes learn that trickle-down economics doesn't work in sports." The USGF 1987 budget was stated to be $6.9 million, of which $6,000 (0.1 percent) was directly "given to athletes." The 1987 figures listed in parallel for track and field were $9.0 million and $400,000 (4.4 percent), and for swimming, $4.5 million and $77,000 (1.7 percent). "In fairness," the article added (insufficiently for the sports functionaries set howling by it), additional funds "are funneled indirectly to athletes" in the form of "insurance, training clinics, and other benefits." The summary interpretive statement—"Anyone who happens to spy the limousines pulling away from the most luxurious hotels in Seoul next month will notice that they never contain any athletes"—contained its own hyperbole. But it exactly reversed the popular hyperbole of the 1984 period—"Olympians are all rich professionals"—and did so strongly in the direction of the truth.

To my knowledge, no formal, across-the-board studies of Olympic athletes' incomes have been done. Even partial information is difficult to come by, in part because U.S. sports bodies have shown no interest in collecting or providing it. But of the 600-odd U.S. athletes who marched into the stadium in Seoul, I would generously estimate that no more than 15 percent were making, or were about to make from their sport anything resembling a living by U.S. standards. No more than 5 percent were making or were about to make, as we say, some real money. For the rest of the competitors and their families (college scholarships aside), Olympic sport is a break-even or a losing proposition from a purely economic point of view. And if one drops the boxers and basketball and baseball players who would have made professional salaries anyway, and includes, as one must, the far greater number of aspiring athletes in the system who will never even make a national or Olympic team, the percentages professionalized in terms of income over expenses grow utterly miniscule.

The *Newsweek* article went on to attribute the drain on funds primarily to bloated and self-interested professional staff: for the gymnastics federation, 33 salaried officials, 37 executive board members, and 165 volunteer committee members all regularly receiving travel, accommodation, expenses, and other perks in connection with numerous meetings. "We're spending a heck of a lot of money on the adults in the sport," one USGF official was quoted. The dramatic leitmotif of the piece was the destructive rivalry between two national women's gymnastics coaches, but both were quoted to the same general effect. Bela Karolyi, the press's favorite sports communist-come-in-from-the-cold, stated: "I'm always hearing from those coaches and officials, when they come back from competitions, 'We had the greatest time, we went to the beach, we raised hell at the disco.' . . . We must cut off the title hunters, the position hunters, the egomaniacs. That would raise the efficiency of the whole ugly mess. . . . Behind the honest struggle of our athletes, you will find a dirty game." The *Newsweek* authors did not see fit to comment on Karolyi's own egomania or the widespread whispers about the health of his athletes, but instead let stand his claim of "professional jealousy" as the explanation why he was not initially selected the national coach. The ultimate word is left to Karolyi's rival Greg Marsden: "This is really about petty, egotistical adult bickering. I feel guilty. These are kids who have trusted us with their dreams and aspirations. And we've used them."

Three weeks later, on the eve of Seoul, *Sports Illustrated* followed with its own assault, entitled "An Olympian Quagmire," written by E. M. Swift and Robert Sullivan. Unlike the *Newsweek* piece, this article studiously avoided explicit language of exploitation of athletes, the "dirty game" of "using" kids for adult financial and professional gain. Instead it focused on the USOC's "burdensome bureaucracy," further styled as "a disorganization of organizations." However, the scant funds going directly to athletes did form a parallel main theme. The article reported that, out of a total of $149.9 million in USOC expenditures in the last quadrennium, only $2.2 million or 1.5 percent went to "direct athlete support." While no precise breakdown was given of the number of USOC employees or their salaries, benefits, and perks, expenditures for "administration" ($20.8 million/13.9 percent), "fund-raising" ($22.7 million/15.1 percent), "capital improvements" ($4.7 million/3.1 percent), and (a curious reporting category) "sports for the disabled/public information/miscellaneous" ($18.1 million/ 12.1 percent) were highlighted to obvious effect. The other $81.4 million (54.3 percent) was labeled "indirect athlete support," but only $30.0 million of that was described as going to the forty sports NGBs ("where the rubber meets the road"). A sidebar picked up the *Los Angeles Times* and *Newsweek* theme that even this left "American athletes wondering where the money went." According to the article, out of U.S. Swimming's $6.11 million 1988 budget, $160,000 (2.6 percent) went in direct grants to athletes. Expenditures for USOC committee meetings were also shown to be more than the total direct outlay of monies to athletes. Though a bias in favor of the NGBs over the USOC peeked out of the prose, when the figures provided are reaggregated and decoded, these organizations are clearly little different in their funding priorities.

Additional *Sports Illustrated* pieces in this period criticized policy-making in particular NGBs, for example, basketball. With the IOC and the

Fédération Internationale de Basketball Amateur keenly interested in the Olympic participation of the NBA "best players in the world" and the Soviet Union considering NBA contracts for members of its national team (both developments now realized), the position of the ABAUSA against eligibility for NBA players could only look self-serving. Especially after the U.S. defeat by the Soviets in Seoul and the apparent success in getting the tennis millionaires to lay down their agents and personal endorsements for the duration of the Seoul Games, it became difficult to understand the U.S. basketball NGB's policy as anything but a preference for its own authority and perks over "the national interest." In apparently not caring enough about beating the Russians, the NGB's position was only another, if more spectacular, example of the overall contradictions and breakdown of the traditional cold war line of the U.S. Olympic establishment. Pieces of this rhetoric persisted (and persist today) in USOC solicitation literature, while more Americans are realizing that we can use our professional athletes in the Games, that much of the money raised is going to pay adult workers in the sports industry, and that the majority of Olympic athletes remain, in Bruce Kidd's memorable phrase, "sweat-suited philanthropists."

More responsibly than other examples of this spate of new reporting on U.S. Olympic organizations, the September 12 *Sports Illustrated* article acknowledged some USOC efforts at reform and concluded with its own proposals. These included congressional approval of the federal tax-checkoff bill in return for the trimming of the USOC bureaucracy and the encouragement of trends that would reduce the USOC to a "central bank" and "information clearing house" in service to the NGBs, where the real power and budgetary authority would reside. This second suggestion naively ignored the potential reversal of all that the Amateur Sports Act of 1978 had sought to cure by creating an effective "central sports authority" (Chalip 1987). Above all, it failed to recognize the complicated and sensitive international mission of the USOC, which is carried out inadequately now and would decline further if the NOC were domestically weakened. The odd and occasionally destructive situation in which U.S. corporate executives and politicians frequently have more influence over international sports bodies than do U.S. Olympic officials could only be worsened by increased NGB power at the expense of the USOC. Finally, placing more power in the hands of those "closer to the gym"—that is, single-sport coaches, managers, and medical personnel, whose job security is more directly tied to the records and medals achieved by "their" athletes—could only exacerbate already dangerous conditions with regard to athletes' physical and mental health, not to speak of the efforts already expended to "keep them focused on their athletic goals" in preference to and in frequent opposition to the larger educational and cultural aims of the Olympic movement

(MacAloon 1986b, Kidd 1989). The United States is the only English-speaking capitalist democracy without a federal ministry of sport or a federally chartered and funded QUANGO (quasi-nongovernmental-organization, to use the cumbersome but precise sociological jargon). Elsewhere, these latter bodies are independent of the NOCs and are charged with special responsibilities for research, protection, and advocacy with regard to athletes' health and working conditions. Under existing U.S. arrangements, the national USOC offers the only institutional location available for such efforts.

The spring and summer of 1988 offered illustrations of this potential by the few USOC officials who were not hiding under a hedge from the unprecedented critical publicity. USOC medical director Robert Voy, in a courageous statement that received wide attention at home and around the world, acknowledged that the abuse of performance-enhancing drugs, particularly anabolics, was completely out of hand in the United States and probably more extensive here than in the Eastern European countries. This long-overdue act of truth telling—in concert with the Ben Johnson case and all that surrounded it in Seoul—helped galvanize public support and institutional will for the sort of serious testing and educational program that had proved unlikely to come from within NGBs. As Dr. Voy was quoted in a November 1988 *New York Times* article in which he estimated that at least occasional drug use by Olympians was over 50 percent: "You can't have a sport test itself and be trustworthy. It's like the fox guarding the henhouse. You can't depend on it." Voy's outspokenness won him few friends in the beleaguered USOC leadership. He had "gone off the reservation in a self-serving way," as one Olympic official put it to me. In the spring of 1989, Voy chose a particularly sensitive moment in the Dubin Inquiry and Biden Judiciary Committee hearings to resign in protest. Meanwhile a bilateral pact between the USOC and the Soviet NOC was under negotiation to produce truly random, short-warning (forty-eight hours), training season testing and site testing in each other's countries. This "we'll quit if you'll quit" agreement, finalized in the autumn of 1989, was modeled on the Intermediate Nuclear Forces Treaty and could never have come about if U.S. Olympic officials had continued to cling to the cold war lie that drugs were an East bloc and not a U.S. problem.

Ideological-moral competence, as well as fiscal, administrative, and athletic competence, is likewise an entailment of the sort of professionalism U.S. Olympic officials were being attacked for lacking. Beyond the international scope of tennis and soccer, the Canadian connection in hockey, and a few cross-cultural encounters in basketball, baseball, and football, U.S. professional and collegiate sports worry little about the intercultural education of young people and sport's service to international understanding and world peace. These are, however, essential aspects of Olympic ideology and important features of difference between Olympic and other athletic forms in the total American space of sports (Bourdieu 1988; MacAloon 1987, 1988). Never as significant in the post-World War II hegemonic and insular United States as in most other parts of the world and not, since Brundage, vociferously professed by any top U.S. Olympic leader, these higher educational and humanistic aims of Olympism tend to be pushed further aside in newly rationalized sports organizations, where youthful victory, and thereby adult job security, is everything (MacAloon 1986b).

Baaron Pittenger, whose tortured ascendency to the USOC executive directorship he merited was one of the organization's public scandals of 1987–88, is sensitive to this issue. Pittenger brought the present author before a spring 1988 meeting of the NGB executive directors to offer workshops on Korean culture, and Pittenger later arranged a briefing by Korean-Americans on Korean society at the U.S. Olympic delegation's staging assembly in Los Angeles. Though modest by comparison with a Canadian Olympic Association effort (Kidd 1989), this was a notable innovation and was recalled with profit by a number of the U.S. Olympians I spoke with later in Seoul. However, Pittenger's efforts met extreme indifference or open resistance from other U.S. Olympic officials for whom sports success is an absolute end, not an important means.

At the spring meeting, the general response of the NGB executive directors was typified by one's open statement that "if he had his way, he'd lock his kids up in their hotels and the [Olympic] Village, and they'd never see a Korean," the better, of course, to keep their minds on the competition. The only directors who expressed any interest were the directors of racquetball and rowing (sports traditionally associated with the better-educated) and the hockey director (who had served in the Korean War, but whose team would not be going to Seoul, since hockey is not a summer Olympic sport). The other NGB "professional staff" were anxious to get on with the commercial sponsorship proposals from corporations and marketing firms that formed the bulk of their agenda, while Ollan Cassell, the powerful director of the U.S. track and field NGB, made a show of falling asleep during the discussion of cultural and diplomatic preparations for Seoul. The results of such attitudes were made embarrassingly apparent in Seoul in the scandals surrounding the U.S. delegation's behavior in the opening ceremonies and in the aftermath of the hotel vandalism and racist provocations by drunken U.S. swimmers and their coach (MacAloon and Kang 1989). Rather than shouldering the blame themselves, U.S. Olympic officials closest to these episodes displaced it onto the athletes, blaming "youthful highjinks" in both instances and eventually sending the two swimmers, but no officials, home in disgrace. USOC president Robert Helmick had been on the floor of Chamsil stadium, leading the U.S. athletes during their opening ceremonies as they cavorted and disrupted the parade of nations. In his belated Seoul press conference apology, Mr. Helmick spoke *in loco parentis,* taking no personal responsibility and defensively suggesting that the American young people had not understood that their behavior was insulting to their Korean hosts and the international community (or even why). The contrast to the Korean response to the scandalous boxing incident was almost grotesque. As the Korean cultural code demanded that he should, KNOC president Kim Chong-ha took full responsibility for the attack on the referee and publicly resigned, despite the fact that he was miles away at the time, not the direct supervisor of the offending officials, and had been begged by Samaranch to maintain his position.

The Steinbrenner Commission Report

In the weeks immediately following Seoul, such incidents and their meanings were diffused in the general climate of exhaustion and celebration of U.S. victories. Public discourse seemed more preoccupied with NBC's performance than the USOC's. But the steroid issue in particular helped keep up the pressure on U.S. Olympic leaders that had been launched by the press revolt and fed by the continuing possibility of new congressional initiatives, developments that USOC officials now told reporters had cost them "hundreds of thousands of dollars in fund raising" (Harvey 1989). To all challenges, the USOC responded that it was investigating itself through the Olympic Overview Commission and that critics should await its conclusions.

The Report of the Olympic Overview Commission (USOC 1989b)—aptly renamed the "Steinbrenner Report" since the industrialist and Yankee owner not only chaired but largely bankrolled the committee's activities— finally appeared in February 1989. It appeared shortly after Steinbrenner had received a presidential pardon in the final days of the Reagan administration for his earlier felony conviction for illegal political fund-raising. (Legal solicitations for Reagan's reelection campaign were made in the context of the Los Angeles Olympics.) Whatever the connections might have been between Steinbrenner's desire for civic and legal rehabilitation (including return of his passport) and his Olympic efforts, he was by all accounts an effective commission leader, that is, within its particular framing of the problems and policy questions facing U.S. Olympism. The commission's agenda not only replicated the lines of press and athlete criticism directed at the USOC in 1987–88, its report gave a truly radical autonomy and hegemony to managerial notions of professionalism at the expense of all other conceptions and traditions in the Olympic movement.

Not only in their content but in the nakedness of their prose, the commission's statements of the purpose of the USOC and the Olympic movement would have scandalized earlier generations of U.S. and international Olympic leaders. They certainly stunned present-day Olympic specialists and journalists, who inevitably made them the lead in their news reports and commentaries (e.g., Harvey 1989). "Winning medals must always be the primary goal," the report stated. And again, "The Commission has . . . [kept] in mind always that the objective of the United States Olympic Team is to win medals." Not content to radically simplify the U.S. Olympic cultural tradition, the commissioners did not shrink from rewriting the international *Olympic Charter:* "The Olympic movement is by definition about competitions, which have only three medalists per event and which exist to find . . . those medalists." These summary caricatures, barely rationalized by comments that "America has always needed heroes" and hardly softened by the occasional note that the competitions ought to be "peaceful, healthy and friendly," are delivered without the slightest compunction or hint of irony. The commissioners clearly thought their prose tough-minded, not impolitic, much less outrageous. When, for example, they complained of the relative invisibility and powerlessness of U.S. leaders in international Olympic organizations, they failed even to suspect that the problem might lie in such narrow and parochial attitudes toward Olympism as the report instantiates. Obviously it was too much to expect that any concern be shown for the Kathy Ormsby's of U.S. sport, but the fact that steroids apparently were not a problem for the commission either is simply bizarre. Drugs are never mentioned in the report, which utterly fails to recognize that obsessive devotion to winning medals produced, for example, the Ben Johnson scandal then wracking the highly efficient and well-funded Canadian system.

The Steinbrenner Report concerned itself almost exclusively with the pursuit of similar finances and organizational efficiencies with which to pursue the clear managerial goal of winning. The commissioners could not avoid reference to the familiar cold war incitement on the very first page of the report, but its rhetorical obliqueness and reversal gave evidence of a fragmentation within the USOC itself of its former anticommunist consensus. The USSR and DDR are not referred to by name but as "our strongest competitor nations." And far from the old ideological cries against these nations' considering "sport and physical fitness a major facet of governmental and national attention" and their high levels of sports funding, the Steinbrenner Report summons the United States to match them—with one caveat, of course. Whereas "many countries have a Minister of Sport with diplomatic or cabinet rank . . . we urge all possible efforts to increase the financial and moral support of [American] amateur athletics on an ongoing annual basis so that the public can have a more legitimate stake in America's Olympic achievement." In other words, more U.S. government attention, funding, and prestige are desired without any increase in government authority, oversight, or investigative interest that might compromise the USOC's power and prerogative.

Taking its lead from public criticism and criticism in the press while putting a particular spin on it, the commission asserted that it recognized "problems and inefficiencies, though these may result more from massive growth itself than from any malfeasance or inattention. It has clearly become more important to operate the USOC as an efficient organization than as a perfectly representative form of government." As to the purported absence of malfeasance, the reader must wonder (though investigative journalists have not) why the report proceeds over and over to highlight (once four times on a single page of a 21-page report) the need to eliminate financial "conflicts of interest" among Olympic officials. And surely there is something culturally curious in viewing the American love of representative and democratic institutions as a barrier to the United States' need for heroes and medals in this purportedly most voluntaristic and civic-individualist arena of social life. The rhetoric of the report endeavors to turn popular cliché and the truisms of liberal individualist ideology to a defense of a system that conceals itself, all in support of existing power relations. This is the deepest sociological significance of this language. The upshot on culturally constitutive grounds, as well as on summary institutional grounds, is increased *dirigisme,* a fact easily missed in light of the particular reforms called for in the report.

Estimable in themselves, these reforms respond almost point by point to prior public criticisms while appealing to populist sentiments in favor of athletes and the cultural common sense of productivity and efficiency. The report comes down hard in favor of sound business practices, trimming USOC and NGB staffs and committees, eliminating junkets and limousines, reducing the use of outside consultants and lawyers, evaluating employee performance on a regular basis, and minimizing administrative costs and overhead. On the income side, pages are devoted to new "Marketing Division" proposals: Smithsonian-style associate memberships; changes in income distribution from the Olympic Endowment (Foundation) that was created from the Los Angeles profits; tax checkoffs at federal, state, and local levels; increased television revenue shares; centralizing marketing in the USOC instead of diffusing it throughout the NGBs; and the creation of marketing and public relations offices (in donated space—Steinbrenner again) in New York City and Washington, D.C., run contractually by large and well-connected firms (Burson-Marsteller was thought, with no open bidding, to have a "done deal" here). The prospect of increased income is presented both to rationalize proposed organizational changes and to salve the wounds of those disempowered by them. Changes presently being enacted render the USOC's structure more oligarchical, though more "efficient," of course, than it has ever been: an executive board reduced to forty-three voting members, with real power invested in its nine-member executive committee of six USOC officers, with only one NGB and one athlete representative, and with the executive director appointed completely at the pleasure of the executive committee, together with a "gag rule" against public statements by other USOC staff. In the absence of any federal or congressional oversight, sustained press scrutiny, and athletes' unions, the net effect of public criticism and the lure of fiscal and managerial "professionalism" appears to have been delivery of the U.S. Olympic system into the hands of the small Helmick-Steinbrenner faction. Among large Olympic sports bodies, perhaps only the IOC itself will rival the new USOC in being, as has been said of classical Athens, government by the principal men masquerading as popular democracy.

It is against the triumph of this sort of managerial professionalism that the impact of the professionalization of athletes on the athletes themselves must be understood. The public outcry over the scant percentage of funds actually getting to athletes was acknowledged directly by the commissioners. "The support given to our athletes is the most important single issue the Commission has addressed," the Steinbrenner Report stated. The NGB "professional staffs" came in for particular criticism for denying athletes proper shares of both representation and financial benefits, as against the USOC's achievement of the Amateur Sports Act goals of athlete representation in policy-making councils and, by implication, the more appropriate levels of direct support in Operation Gold. However, a closer look at the commission's prose leaves doubts about the USOC's intentions with regard to the proportion of direct versus indirect support. Besides resources for competition and training "fulfilled by NGBs," the athlete support system "should operate in three areas: tuition assistance, the Olympic Job Opportunities Program (OJOP) and direct financial assistance in the currently approved [trust fund] forms." In contrast to considerable emphasis on the first two items, the only other mention of direct payment in the report consisted of the assertion that "neither the USOC nor the NGBs will ever have enough resources to support every athlete sufficiently through direct financial payments, nor is it clear that this should be done."

The second clause is a placating gesture toward the old amateur values, a demonstration of their persistence in U.S. cultural reality. The first clause is presented as a straightforward statement of fact. Yet some equally simple calculations have interesting heuristic results. A short time after the Steinbrenner Report was released, the USOC approved a budget of $249 million for the 1989–92 quadrennium. Around 700 athletes will represent the United States in the two Games of 1992. Add another 300 as a development squad, directly pay each one of the 1,000 athletes $25,000 annually for four years, and the total cost of $100 million would still leave the USOC $149 million for its other responsibilities, a figure identical to its entire expenditure for the 1985–88 quadrennium. By contrast, the USOC has announced that it has allocated $25 million from Coin Program profits for the direct support of athletes between 1989 and 1992, though $9 million of this was already spent for Seoul (a hasty appropriation that was made partly in embarrassed reaction to press criticism and achieved through a bookkeeping practice about which the Steinbrenner Commission complained). Thus, the actual figure for the next quadrennium is $16 million. In other words, as the overall USOC budget will increase 67 percent, direct athlete support will increase roughly 0.4 percent. A small number of NGBs, including those for U.S. wrestling, cycling, and most notably gymnastics (a main target of the prior press criticism), have announced additional programs of direct support for their athletes. The top eight U.S. gymnasts in each of the three disciplines are to receive direct payments of $8,000 to $20,000 per year into their USGF trust funds. (The USGF has turned progressive in other respects as well, publishing and circulating a serious and unprecedented pamphlet against sexual abuse in the sport.)

Stressing the direct/indirect payment opposition is not meant to suggest that funds delivered in the latter fashion are inconsiderable or unwelcome by athletes. The Steinbrenner Commission was certainly not wrong in suggesting that educational benefits and job opportunities might be of greater long-term value to athletes than transient lump-sum payments (though the force of the commission's concern for athletes was mitigated by explicit remarks on how these modes of financial aid would help tie in more educational establishments and corporations to the USOC's own interests). By its own official reckoning, the USOC "is raising the percentage of funds allocated for athlete support [direct and indirect] from 71.6% to 80% in 1989–1992" (USOC 1989a, 54). Since nearly anything sports bodies do can be construed as support of athletes, these figures must be taken with a large grain of salt. However, this alternative mode of calculation is by no means exclusively self-serving. Training centers, equipment, insurance programs, fund-raising, and the like are necessities that athletes as "individual corporations" could not provide for themselves. Rather, the main point for this analysis is the rivalry and rhetorical combat involving different conceptions of amateurism and professionalism and their implications for power and control of athletic labor and occupational profit in the Olympic sport industry.

Though trust fund arrangements prevent a pure wage-labor situation (and are designed to do so), the expansion or contraction of direct payments to athletes is still the best measure of general cultural willingness to categorize Olympians as professional body-workers, bringing them closer to professional athletes in the U.S. sociocultural space of sports while nonetheless defending the barrier between them and the general "American labor force." Conversely, the relative dominance of indirect over direct remunerations and the elaboration of new and more complicated forms of the latter signal the strength of the cultural preference for the continued association of Olympic athletes with school/community and recreational athletes, the regime once more consensually labeled "amateur." Unprecedented public scrutiny and criticism of the USOC, focused on sports leaders and functionaries helping themselves to funds and opportunities meant for athletes, have turned out to produce little increase (and by some measures, even a decrease) in the ratio of direct and indirect payment of Olympians. Even granting that absolute support for athletes is now increasing, the fact remains that the modes and mechanisms by which this increase is being achieved, such as tuition assistance and job programs, leave the sports bodies fully in control and the individual athletes and their immediate representatives (agents, parents, friends) in the position of dependent petitioners and beneficiaries. In the absence of effective congressional oversight, federal agency regulation, legal and judicial remedies, collective bargaining, and a constantly probing Fourth Estate, athletes—whose labors and achievements generate the whole system—are reduced to passive dependence on the "devotion to Olympic ideals," "pride in America," and now the "professionalism" of the sports authorities.

Ironic and tragic means offer Olympians as a group their only other recourses. The USOC's public declaration that medals shall now be the measure of all things reinforces a condition made periodically plain over the last two decades. Athletes can best incite public attention to their institutional condition by losing or by still more concertedly sickening, maiming, and even killing themselves with obsessional neuroses, eating disorders, steroids and growth hormones, alcoholism and car wrecks, and jumping off bridges in the effort not to lose. But these, of course, remain powers of the weak. The attention so generated cannot be turned to social reform as long as such "behaviors" are read as purely psychological disorders and excesses, aberrant individual distortions of the perfectly noble and estimable desire to win and be a hero to America. To generate reform, they must instead be understood as possession phenomena and as protests, (anti-)heroic in a very American way, against collective experiences of system-induced and structurally maintained commands to excel and to win for the benefit of institutional and generalized Others.

The Ineradicable Amateur and American Democracy

But everything now conspires against such an interpretive transformation that would mark a break with the unconscious equation of power and victimage that haunts U.S. sport, not only institutional arrangements but also liberal individualist ideology and the persistence of the amateur/professional dichotomy simultaneously with the erosion of its cultural authority. Current USOC institutional developments and public discourse about them reveal the simultaneous presence of both trends, sometimes situationally in resistance to one another, sometimes in paradoxical alliance. The net result, from a cultural systems point of view, is the increased ambiguation and destabilization of the category "Olympic athlete" from the standpoint of the traditional amateur/professional binary code. Indeed, present trends make it possible to imagine an eventual dismemberment altogether of the category as so constructed. But such projections are premature. Representational factors constitute the conditions of possibility for particular institutional arrangements and power interests. However, as the present analysis shows, actions derived from the power interests of individual and organizational actors can prove sufficient, at least for a time, not only to maintain the cultural system in its instabilities and contradictions but to leverage the resulting public ambiguity into significant historical and political change.

Thus, it is in no way accidental or merely the product of loose and unwitting speech that the Steinbrenner Report in its very first paragraphs unself-consciously deploys both the twofold vision of U.S. sport (amateur/professional) and the fourfold vision ("amateur, professional, school, and community"). The first presents itself as a properly sociological classification since it distinguishes two social classes or groups. But, like many binary oppositions (and particularly in the U.S. context), its sociological capacities are weak since professional or amateur status is here foundationally understood to be a characteristic of individual persons. The constitutive power of social structuring leaks out in favor of a liberal model of society as a collection of abstracted individuals and their characteristics. The second, fourfold classification (especially in the more apt version of Olympic, professional, school/community, and recreational sport) is more truly sociological because its greater relational capacities are organized around more differentiated institutional criteria. But it conflates two sets of criteria—those of organization (e.g., USOC, profit-making corporations, schools, governments, and clubs) and those of the related underlying civic-territorial identities (e.g., international, national, regional, metropolitan, neighborhood, and family). This conflation compels the recognition of a compulsive social system but is emasculated by an implied pluralism of free preference, while the outcomes for living individual human beings are entirely vaporized in a featureless notion of "athlete" phantomly lurking under classifications of Sport.

We are now in a position to understand why the language of amateurism and professionalism has not and will not foreseeably disappear in favor of a more descriptively sound and consistent socioeconomic typology, much less of an arbitrarily "scientific" nomenclature. The answer lies in the domains of political ideology and practical social control. In spite of, or rather because of, their present inconsistencies and contradictions, these two languages for sport can be contextually bent into an ideological complementarity. By deploying them together, institutions are reduced to, and valorized as, aggregates of individual interests, while both individuals and unrelenting institutional constraints and purposes disappear behind a rhetorical respect for plural communities. This picture grows doubly wider and recognizable. Just as present USOC rhetoric instantiates and reproduces a broader system of popular sport discourse, so that sport discourse instantiates and reproduces a fundamental and constitutive rhetoric of American liberal democratic society as a whole.

Complex system reproductions achieved through mechanisms of cultural ambiguity are not without their own theoretical interest. More than reproduction, however, is involved, namely concrete human suffering and the possibility of structural transformations that might lessen it. Recently influential social theories like those of Victor Turner and Mikhail Bakhtin have claimed a universal affinity between the determined ambiguation of cultural categories in popular performances and the empowerment of the politically weak. From their vantage point, most versions of hegemony theory assume that the reproduction of exploitative domination proceeds most smoothly when the categorical framings of everyday cultural common sense appear clear, unambiguous, and consistent. The present example indicates that, in their general claims at least, both theories are wrong. Under the cultural and institutional structures and conditions of contemporary America, the radical disordering of the categories amateur and professional and the increasing ambiguation of the Olympian as a classificatory type has instead consolidated and augmented the power of those already in control of Olympic sport. Moreover, this consolidation has been achieved primarily at the expense of the athletes themselves. Under present conditions of "elite athletic" practice, more and more of them are becoming ritual sacrifices, in a strict anthropological sense of the term, not only of American sport but of American liberal democracy itself. Recognizing what everything in popular and academic sociological speech conspires to conceal, namely the profound differences in situation of Olympic from other kinds of athletes and the more tragic outcomes available to them in a culture in which big salaries are conceived as fair exchange for adult self-mutilation in the entertainment and moral inspiration of others, offers a means of gauging the possibilities of future transformation, not only for Olympic athletes but for other, numerically much larger if much less publicized, groups of impoverished and dependent American hero-victims.

REFERENCES

Axthelm, Pete. 1988. "Off Balance in Amateur Sport." *Newsweek* (August 15): 62–63.
———. 1987. "Deceiving Stories: International Politics and Olympic Crises." *Gannett Center Journal* 1 (2): 99–110.
Boorstin, Daniel. 1961. *The Image: A Guide to Pseudo-Events in America.* New York: Atheneum.
Bourdieu, Pierre. 1988. "Program for a Sociology of Sport." *Sociology of Sport Journal* 5 (2): 153–61.
Chalip, Laurence. 1987. "The Transformation of American Sports Policy." Ph.D. diss., Committee on Public Policy Studies, University of Chicago.
Dunning, Eric, and Kenneth Sheard. 1979. *Barbarians, Gentlemen and Players.* New York: New York University Press.
Epcot Poll. 1987. "Funding the U.S. Olympic Team" and "Athletes Heroes to Americans." Released July 27 and August 3, available from United States Olympic Committee.
Farrell, Thomas. 1989. "Media Rhetoric as Social Drama: The Winter Olympics of 1984." *Critical Studies in Mass Communication* 6 (2): 158–82.
Gusfield, Joseph. 1981. *The Culture of Public Problems: Drunk-Driving and the Symbolic Order.* Chicago: University of Chicago Press.
Guttmann, Alan. 1986. *The Games Must Go On.* New York: Columbia University Press.
Haley, Bruce. 1978. *The Healthy Body and Victorian Culture.* Cambridge: Cambridge University Press.
Harvey, Randy. 1989. "Olympics Have More to Offer than Medals." *Los Angeles Times,* February 22.
Henricks, Thomas. 1977. "Sport and Social Distance in Pre-Industrial England." Ph.D. diss., Department of Sociology, University of Chicago.
Kidd, Bruce. 1988. "The Philosophy of Excellence: Olympic Performances, Class Power, and the Canadian State." In Kang S-p., J. MacAloon, and R. DaMatta, eds., *The Olympics and Cultural Exchange.* Seoul: Hanyang University Institute for Ethnological Studies, 343–71.
———. 1989. " 'The Seoul to the World, the World to Seoul' . . . and Ben Johnson." Paper read at the Seoul Olympiad Anniversary Conference, Seoul, September 12–16.
MacAloon, John J. 1989. "Critical Data and Rhetorical Theory." *Critical Studies in Mass Communication* 6 (2): 183–94.
———. 1988. "A Prefatory Note to Pierre Bourdieu's 'Program for a Sociology of Sport.' " *Sociology of Sport Journal* 5 (2): 150–52.
———. 1987. "Missing Stories: American Politics and Olympic Discourse." *Gannett Center Journal* 1 (2): 111–43.
———. 1986a. "You Don't Say: Why There Are No Spies in American Sport." Unpublished MS., Division of Social Sciences, The University of Chicago.
———. 1986b. "Intercultural Education and Olympic Sport." Montreal: Canadian Olympic Association.

———. 1981. *This Great Symbol: Pierre de Coubertin and the Origins of the Modern Olympic Games*. Chicago: University of Chicago Press.

———, and Kang Shin-pyo. 1989. "Uri Nara: Korean Nationalism, The Seoul Olympics and Contemporary Anthropology." Paper read at the Seoul Olympiad Anniversary Conference, Seoul, September 12–16.

MacIntosh, Donald, Tom Bedecki, and C. E. S. Franks. 1987. *Sport and Politics in Canada*. Kingston, Ontario: McGill-Queens University Press.

MacIntosh, Peter. 1963. *Sport and Society*. London: C. A. Watts. Rev. ed., 1987.

Malcolmson, Robert. 1973. *Popular Recreations in English Society*. Cambridge: Cambridge University Press.

Mangan, Anthony. 1982. *Athleticism in the Victorian and Edwardian Public Schools*. Cambridge: Cambridge University Press.

Pleket, H. W. 1976. "Games, Prizes, Athletes and Ideology." *Stadion* [Arena] 1 (1): 49–89.

Riordan, James. 1977. *Sport in Soviet Society*. Cambridge: Cambridge University Press.

Rothenbuhler, Eric. 1989. "Values and Symbols in Public Orientations to the Olympic Media Event." *Critical Studies In Mass Communication* 6 (2): 138–57.

———. 1988. "The Living Room Celebration of the Olympics." *Journal of Communication* 38 (4): 61–81.

———. 1985. "Media Events, Civil Religion, and Social Solidarity: The Living Room Celebration of the Olympic Games." Ph.D. diss., Annenberg School of Communications, University of Southern California.

Swift, E. M., and Robert Sullivan. 1988. "An Olympian Quagmire." *Sports Illustrated* (September 12): 38–42.

Thompson, E. P. 1974. "Patrician Society, Plebian Culture." *Journal of Social History* 7: 382–405.

———. 1967. "Time, Work-Discipline, and Industrial Capitalism." *Past and Present* 38: 56–97.

United States Olympic Committee. 1989a. "Athlete Aid Hiked, Expenses Lowered in Record USOC Budget Proposal." *The Olympian* 15 (7): 54.

———. 1989b. "Report of the Olympic Overview Commission" (The Steinbrenner Report). Colorado Springs, Colorado.

———. 1987. "Athletes Are Heroes to Americans (The Epcot/Roper Polls)." *The Olympian* 14 (4): 37–39.

Wills, Gary. 1987. *Reagan's America: Innocents at Home*. New York: Doubleday.

Young, David. 1984. *The Olympic Myth of Greek Amateur Athletics*. Chicago: Ares.

Notes on Contributors

DENNIS A. AHLBURG is Associate Professor of Industrial Relations at the Industrial Relations Center, University of Minnesota. His Ph.D. is in economics from the University of Pennsylvania. He has published articles on labor markets, demography, and labor relations in a wide variety of academic journals. He recently published "Unions and Productivity: A Review of the Research," with James B. Dworkin, in *Advances in Industrial and Labor Relations* (1985).

ROB B. BEAMISH, Ph.D., holds a joint appointment as Associate Professor to the Department of Sociology and the School of Physical and Health Education at Queen's University, Kingston, Ontario, Canada. He was a varsity athlete in college, playing hockey and wrestling, and later became a professional box lacrosse player. As a professor, Beamish combines his interest in social theory, sociology of work, and labor relations with his research on sport. He recently completed a monograph and is working on two books.

JOAN M. CHANDLER is Professor and American Studies Program Head at the University of Texas at Dallas. Born in Great Britain, she graduated from Cambridge University with a B.A. (honors) in history. She also holds M.A. degrees from Cambridge and Bryn Mawr and the Ph.D. from the University of Texas at Austin. Professor Chandler is the author of three books on U.S. history that are used in British schools and a book titled *Television and National Sport* (1988).

JAMES B. DWORKIN is Associate Dean of the Graduate School at Purdue University and Associate Professor of Industrial Relations at the Krannert Graduate School of Management. He has published articles on a variety of labor relations topics and is the author of *Owners versus Players: Baseball and Collective Bargaining* (1981). Professor Dworkin is also active as a mediator, fact-finder, and arbitrator in a variety of labor-management disputes in the private and public sectors.

LAWRENCE M. KAHN is Professor of Economics and Labor and Industrial Relations at the University of Illinois, Urbana-Champaign. He received his B.S. degree with high honors and distinction from the University of Michigan, Ann Arbor, and his Ph.D. in economics from the University of California, Berkeley. He is the author of *Wage Indexation in the United States: Cola or Uncola?* (1985) with Wallace Hendricks. Professor Kahn is a member of the Board of Editors of *Industrial Relations* and has authored numerous articles in scholarly journals.

LEONARD KOPPETT, who wrote the Foreword to this volume, is a distinquished former sportswriter for the *New York Times* and the author of *Sports Illusion, Sports Reality: A Reporter's View of Sports, Journalism, and Society* (1981), among other books. Currently he writes for the *Peninsula Times Tribune* in Palo Alto, California, as Editor Emeritus, and he occasionally lectures at Stanford University.

CHARLES P. KORR is Professor of History and a Research Fellow of the Center for International Studies at the University of Missouri, St Louis. He is the author of *Cromwell and the New Model Foreign Policy* (1975) and *West Ham United: The Making of a Football Club* (1987), as well as many articles concerning professional sports in England and the United States. He is completing *A History of the Major League Baseball Players Association*, forthcoming from the University of Illinois Press.

JOHN J. MacALOON is Associate Professor of Social Sciences at the University of Chicago, where he received his Ph.D. His book, *This Great Symbol: Pierre de Coubertin and the Origins of the Modern Olympic Games* (1981), has been critically acclaimed and widely read around the world. He is editor of the series "The Olympic Games: International Perspectives."

JAMES A. MANGAN, coeditor of this book, is Head of Education, Jordanhill College of Education, and a member of the Education Department of the University of Glasgow. He was a founder and the Inaugural Chairman of the British Society of Sports History and the founder and editor of the *International Journal of the History of Sport*. Dr. Mangan is the author of the internationally acclaimed *Athleticism in the Victorian and Edwardian Public School* (1981) and *The Games Ethic and Imperialism* (1986); coeditor of *Manliness and Morality: Middle-Class Masculinity in Britain and America 1800–1940* (1987); and editor of *Pleasure, Profit and Proselytism: British Culture and Sport at Home and Abroad 1700–1914* (1988) and *Benefits Bestowed? Education and British Imperialism* (1988).

DAVID MILLS is Associate Professor of History at the University of Alberta. He holds the Ph.D. from Carleton University in Ottawa. His articles have appeared in the *Canadian Encyclopedia, Alberta,* and *Horizon Canada,* and he is the author of the book *The Idea of Loyalty in Upper Canada* (1988). Among his professional affiliations is membership in the Society for American Baseball Research.

ROGER G. NOLL is Professor of Economics and Director of the Public Policy Program at Stanford University. He holds a Ph.D. in economics from Harvard University and an undergraduate degree in mathematics from the California Institute of Technology. He has published extensively on the economics of public policies toward business. Among his publications is *Government and the Sports Business* (1974), a compendium on the economics of professional sports. He has consulted for the players' associations in baseball, football, and basketball on both antitrust and collective bargaining matters and for the City of Anaheim regarding lease arrangements for city-owned facilities.

STEVEN A. RIESS is Professor of History at Northeastern Illinois University, and he received his Ph.D. from the University of Chicago. Among the books that he has authored are *Touching Base: Professional Baseball and American Culture in the Progressive Era* (1980) and *City Games: The Evolution of American Urban Society and the Rise of Sports* (1989). Professor Riess is also the editor of *The American Sporting Experience: An Historical Anthology of Sport in America.*

GARY R. ROBERTS is Professor and Vice Dean of the Law School at Tulane University. He was a member of Law Review while completing his law degree at Stanford University. Prior to becoming a law professor, Roberts was in private practice in Washington, D.C., for almost a decade and represented the National Football League and National Hockey League in major antitrust cases. He currently chairs the Law and Sports Section of the American Association of Law Schools and is editor-in-chief of *The Sports Lawyer.*

STEPHEN F. ROSS is Associate Professor of Law at the University of Illinois, Urbana-Champaign. He received his B.A. and J.D. degrees from the University of California, Berkeley. Prior to becoming a law professor, Ross was an attorney for the United States Justice Department. An extensive discussion of the issues raised in his chapter appears as "Monopoly Sports Leagues," 73 *Minnesota Law Review* 643 (1989).

PETER D. SHERER is Associate Professor of Management at the Wharton School of the University of Pennsylvania. He received his Ph.D. in Industrial Relations from the University of Wisconsin, Madison, and previously taught at the University of Illinois, Urbana-Champaign. His research focuses on wage determination, job satisfaction, and other changes in industrial relations practices. Professor Sherer's articles have appeared in *Industrial Relations, Personnel Psychology,* and several other leading journals.

PAUL D. STAUDOHAR, coeditor of this book, is Professor of Business Administration at California State University, Hayward. After receiving his B.A. from the University of Minnesota in 1962, he earned an M.B.A. in finance in 1966 and a Ph.D. in economics in 1969 from the University of Southern California. Among Staudohar's many books are *Grievance Arbitration in Public Employment* (1977); *The Sports Industry and Collective Bargaining* (1986); *Industrial Relations in a New Age: Economic, Social, and Managerial Perspectives* (1986) and *Economics of Labor in Industrial Society* (1986), with Clark Kerr; and *Deindustrialization and Plant Closure* (1987), with Holly E. Brown.

LEIGH STEINBERG is an attorney engaged in the practice of sports and media law with offices in Los Angeles, Newport Beach, and Berkeley, California. He received his B.A. and J.D. degrees from the University of California, Berkeley. Besides a large group of professional athletes such as Troy Aikman, Warren Moon, Jeff George, and Will Clark, Mr. Steinberg represents numerous performers in the broadcasting industry. He works only with clients who are willing to contribute to charities, benefits, or schools.

DAVID Q. VOIGT is Professor of Sociology and Anthropology at Albright College in Reading, Pennsylvania. He holds the Ph.D. degree from Syracuse University. Among his seven books are *Little League Journal* (1974), *America through Baseball* (1976), *American Baseball* (3 vols., 1983), and *Baseball: An Illustrated History* (1987). A prolific author of scholarly articles, Voigt is past president of the Society for American Baseball Research.

Index